Where to watch birds in

Dorset, Hampshire & the Isle of Wight

THE *WHERE TO WATCH BIRDS* SERIES

Where to watch birds in Africa

Where to watch birds in Asia

Where to watch birds in Bedfordshire, Berkshire, Buckinghamshire, Hertfordshire and Oxfordshire

Where to watch birds in Cumbria, Lancashire and Cheshire

Where to watch birds in Devon and Cornwall

Where to watch birds in Dorset, Hampshire and the Isle of Wight

Where to watch birds in East Anglia

Where to watch birds in the East Midlands

Where to watch birds in France

Where to watch birds in Herefordshire, Shropshire, Staffordshire, Warwickshire, Worcestershire & the former West Midlands County

Where to watch birds in Ireland

Where to watch birds in Italy

Where to watch birds in Kent, Surrey and Sussex

Where to watch birds in the London area

Where to watch birds in Northeast England

Where to watch birds in Scotland

Where to watch birds in Somerset, Avon, Gloucestershire and Wiltshire

Where to watch birds in South America

Where to watch birds in Southern Spain

Where to watch birds in Wales

Where to watch birds in Yorkshire and North Humberside

Where to watch birds in

Dorset, Hampshire & the Isle of Wight

Second edition

George Green and Martin Cade
Illustrated by Richard Allen

Christopher Helm
A & C Black · London

Second edition 1997
First edition 1989

© 1997 George Green and Martin Cade
Line drawings by Richard Allen

Christopher Helm (Publishers) Ltd, a subsidiary of
A & C Black, 35 Bedford Row, London WC1R 4JH

0-7136-4313-7

A CIP catalogue record for this book
is available from the British Library

Typeset and designed by D & N Publishing
Membury Business Park, Lambourn Woodlands, Hungerford, Berkshire

Printed and bound by Biddles Limited, Guildford, Surrey
in Great Britain

CONTENTS

Contents

Contents

ACKNOWLEDGEMENTS

We are particularly grateful to Darren Hughes and Dave Hunnybun (Isle of Wight Ornithological Group) for their help with sites on the Isle of Wight. We would also like to record our thanks and appreciation to the following people who provided information and/or commented on earlier drafts of this 2nd edition: Dave Chown, K. Cook, J.R. Cox, B.S. Duffen, Paul Harris, Don Moxom, B.P. Pickess, Gerry Quinn, M. Slater, N. Spring, Grahame Walbridge, E.J. Wiseman. In addition, when revising Eversley and Yateley Gravel Pits, I.H. Brown's excellent paper in the 1993 *Hampshire Bird Report* was invaluable.

Special thanks also to Jon Ponting for his invaluable help in preparing my computer for wordprocessing the revised text.

Finally we would like to express our thanks to the staff at Christopher Helm for their professional guidance, and to Robert Kirk in particular for his support and patience.

INTRODUCTION

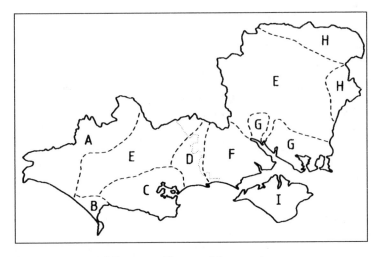

Sub-regions of Dorset, Hampshire and the Isle of Wight

A West and North Dorset
B Portland and Weymouth
C Purbeck and Poole Basin
D East Dorset and the Hampshire Avon
E The Chalk

F The New Forest and nearby Coast
G Southeast Hampshire
H Northeast Hampshire
I The Isle of Wight

There can be few other regions of Britain that can offer the birdwatcher such a wide variety of birds, in such attractive and pleasant surroundings, as the counties of Dorset, Hampshire and the Isle of Wight. This is perhaps a biased statement from one who has spent most of the last 35 years birdwatching in the former two counties. Nevertheless, this view would appear to be shared by many others, judging by the numbers of birdwatchers who visit such areas as the Dorset coast and New Forest.

Why does this region support so many different kinds of birds? Having a coastline is an obvious advantage. Prominent headlands such as Portland and St Catherine's Point are ideally situated, not only to attract many small migrants as they arrive and leave our shores, but also as vantage points to observe the movements of seabirds passing through the English Channel. The region lies closer to the European Continent than much of the rest of Britain. This means that we are usually the first to see our summer visitors arrive and the last to see them go. In addition, we can expect more than our fair share of rarities overshooting or drifting over from mainland Europe.

Our local climate of relatively mild winters and warm summers is the most favourable in Britain for a variety of scarce and rare breeding birds. These include residents such as Cetti's and Dartford Warblers and summer visitors such as the Hobby. The region is also a transitional zone between the wetter west of Britain and the drier east. Several species such as the Turtle Dove and Nightingale, which are characteristic of eastern Britain, become progressively scarcer the further west one goes in the region. Furthermore when much of northern and eastern Britain is caught in the grip of hard winter weather, many birds move south to seek the less severe conditions that usually exist in our region.

Another factor that has an obvious influence on our local birdlife is the diversity of habitat, which in turn is a reflection of the underlying geology. Reference to a geological map shows that much of the region's topography is centred around the Hampshire Basin. The mainly Tertiary clays, sands and gravels within the basin have developed a variety of soil types, some of which support the most important vegetation type found in the region – lowland heath. The counties of Hampshire and Dorset hold over 90 per cent of Britain's quota of this valuable habitat resource. At present the heathlands of the New Forest remain largely intact, but those of Dorset have been severely depleted and fragmented as a result of reclamation for farming, afforestation and more recently the increasing pressures of expanding urbanisation. The Dartford Warbler is the true bird speciality of the heathlands, which are also the haunt of such noteworthy breeding species as Nightjar, Woodlark and Stonechat, but sadly no longer the Red-backed Shrike; whilst Hen Harriers and Great Grey Shrikes are regular visitors in winter. In the New Forest the presence of extensive broadleaved woodlands further enhances the habitat, creating an environment that is unique for wildlife within the British Isles. These woodlands are rich in birdlife and typically support such birds as Redstart and Wood Warbler as well as the elusive Hawfinch. The mixture of woodland and heathland is undoubtedly responsible for healthy populations of breeding raptors which include Honey Buzzard and Hobby.

It is the chalk, however, that dominates the landscapes of all three counties. Today the downlands with their gently curving slopes and dry valleys present a predominantly agricultural scene. Compared with other habitats in the region, birds of interest are in short supply. It is regrettable to report that the numbers of Stone Curlew, the main speciality of the chalk downs, have declined in recent years. Generally the greatest variety of birds occurs in areas where chalk scrub and woodland survive.

In some respects the greatest contrasts in land-based habitats become evident around the fringes of the region. A flavour of the West Country can be found in west Dorset. Here fast-flowing streams drain clay vales comprising a patchwork of small fields which are overlooked by steep-sided, well wooded hills. These streams mark the eastern limit of the Dipper's British range; whilst the wooded hillsides are home to Buzzards, Redstarts and Wood Warblers amongst others. In north Dorset the gently rolling landscape of the Blackmore Vale is mostly given over to dairy farming. Sites of ornithological interest are scarce, but the few surviving damp woodlands and scrubby commons hold such notable species as Nightingale and Willow Tit. The London Basin with its Tertiary clays, sands and gravels intrudes into north Hampshire; whilst the western extremity of the Weald extends into the eastern corner of the county. Both sets of deposits give rise to soils that naturally support heathland. Those areas that have escaped the continuing pressures of development hold the same range of species associated with the more extensive heathlands of the Hampshire Basin. One of man's local activities, the commercial extraction of gravel, has been a benefit to a variety of birds including the Little Ringed Plover which is very much a speciality of northeast Hampshire.

The counties of Hampshire and Dorset share, in the Avon, perhaps the finest river of its type in lowland Britain. Despite this, recent years have seen a disturbing decline in the breeding populations of such wetland specialities as Snipe, Redshank and Yellow Wagtail. On a more positive note, the valley still supports large numbers of winter wildfowl including regular flocks of Bewick's Swans and White-fronted Geese. The region boasts several other excellent chalk rivers, notably the Frome and Piddle in Dorset and the Test, Itchen and Meon in Hampshire; whilst the more sluggish Stour, a much underrated river, adds further to the variety of river habitats. Hampshire seems to have the edge when it comes to water bodies. In addition to the more established lakes and ponds, which are mostly associated with large country estates, extensive gravel workings have left a multiplicity of flooded pits. These are mainly found in the Hampshire Avon Valley just north of Ringwood and along the Blackwater Valley in the northeast corner of the county. Dorset can claim the only reservoir in the region, although most of Sutton Bingham lies within the neighbouring county of Somerset. There is a distinct paucity of lakes and ponds on the Isle of Wight.

Undoubtedly it is the variety of coastal habitats that most interests and excites local and visiting birdwatchers alike. The spectacular cliffs of Portland, Purbeck and West Wight support the most easterly seabird colonies of substance along the south coast; whilst the Peregrine has become a familiar sight in these areas. The Chesil and the Fleet are unique coastal features which are important for their breeding terns and winter waterfowl. In the lee of the Purbecks lies Poole Harbour, reputed to be the second largest natural harbour in the world. The harbour and its environs, which includes such noteworthy sites as Brownsea, Studland and Arne, are an important haven for waterbirds throughout the year including breeding terns in summer and a large flock of wintering Avocets. Once of Hampshire, now of Dorset, Christchurch Harbour with its diversity of habitat is regarded by many as the best single locality for birdwatching in the region attracting a wide variety of winter, migrant and breeding birds. Much of the Hampshire coast can be regarded as one huge estuary, extending from Hurst Castle in the west to Hayling Island in the east. *Spartina* saltmarshes and intertidal mudflats fringe much of the shore of the Solent and parts of Southampton Water as well as dominate the vast harbour complexes of Portsmouth, Langstone and Chichester. Brackish and freshwater wetlands of note can be found at Keyhaven and Pennington Marshes, the mouth of the Beaulieu Estuary, Titchfield Haven and Farlington Marshes. These areas provide feeding and refuge for an abundance of waterfowl, waders and other birds, particularly during the winter and at times of passage. The Solent shore and Langstone Harbour also support important breeding colonies of terns. In addition, the Solent shore of the Isle of Wight offers some attractive estuarine and wetland habitats notably the Yar Estuary, Newtown Estuary, River Medina and the Bembridge area.

Obviously the status of the many species within the region has changed since the first edition was published. These have been dealt with in the revised text. The greatest of these changes undoubtedly concerns the Little Egret which now occurs with increasing numbers every year and presumably may start breeding before the third edition is published!

When I started to compile the first edition of the book in October 1984, my experience of birdwatching within the region varied considerably. Since Dorset had been my home for about ten years, I was familiar with many but by no means all of the birdwatching sites of interest within the county. For the most part my knowledge of Hampshire dated back to the 1960s when I was resident and actively birdwatching there; whilst the Isle of Wight was virtually unknown to me. As a result I spent many happy hours in all three counties renewing acquaintance with sites last visited some 20 years ago and exploring some excellent birdwatching places which I never realised existed. This further confirmed my belief that the counties of Dorset, Hampshire and the Isle of Wight offer some of the best birdwatching to be enjoyed in Britain. The potential of the region for turning up the unexpected was well exemplified by my discovery, while researching the book, of a Little Egret in Fareham Creek (Hampshire), three Tawny Pipits on the Needles Headland (IOW), a singing Melodious Warbler on Ludshott Common (Hampshire) and a Yellow-browed Warbler at Alum Bay (IOW).

During this period of research and consultation, I was made aware that some of those actively concerned with conservation had strong reservations about the publication of detailed information that might bring additional pressures to bear on sensitive birds and sites alike. Others, however, were of the opinion that conservation should adopt a 'high-profile' approach and that by promoting and publicising the efforts and achievements of the various bodies interested in the welfare of our countryside, one is more likely to gain public support and interest for the battles ahead. I have tried to steer the middle course by balancing both viewpoints, but inevitably there will be criticism from those who feel that the book's contents are too detailed and those who consider that not enough information has been given. Whatever their views, it must be a lasting tribute to all the conservation bodies active in the three counties that so many superb birdwatching sites are now protected. We would urge all birdwatchers, including the hordes of twitchers that often descend upon a site in search of a rarity, to remember that many years of hard work by individuals and organisations may have been spent to enable them to enjoy their hobby and add another 'lifer' to their list. Perhaps the best way to show their appreciation is by always behaving responsibly and following the Code of Conduct for Birdwatchers when visiting a site and by joining one or more of the conservation bodies such as the RSPB and the county wildlife trusts.

Although it may appear churlish to single out any particular conservation body for praise, the progressive attitude of Hampshire County Council's Countryside Service deserves special mention. There can be few other county councils in Britain that control and manage so many sites of outstanding value to wildlife and birds. The Isle of Wight County Council should also be commended, not only for the abundance of public bridlepaths/footpaths that give access to the island's countryside, but also for the clear and conspicuous way they are marked.

GG

HOW TO USE THIS BOOK

The Region

The region under discussion consists of the counties of Dorset, Hampshire and the Isle of Wight. These counties have been divided into sub-regions which generally correspond to fairly distinctive geographical and/or geological areas. It was felt that readers would find it more convenient if all sites, irrespective of their relative importance, were included within the appropriate sub-region.

Criteria for Site Inclusion

Since the region supports such a rich diversity of habitats for birds, the choice of sites for this book has not been easy. An attempt has been made to include all those places that either hold a wide variety of species and/or support certain specialised and uncommon birds. Further sites have been chosen either because they are particularly good examples of their habitat type or to ensure that the less well-known and more remote areas of the region are adequately represented in the book. The final criterion for inclusion in the book is access. Most of the places in the book are open to the public, although in the case of some of the reserves this may involve obtaining a permit in advance of a visit. Private sites of ornithological interest have been included only if they can be viewed sensibly from a public place, e.g. a footpath or road.

The final selection involved 120 sites. These are divided into MAJOR SITES, minor sites, and Other Sites Worthy Of Attention. Obviously the major sites are dealt with in more detail than the others. Some of the larger sites, for example the New Forest, have been further divided into a series of Recommended Sites.

Measurements

Throughout the text measurements are given in those units most readily understood by British readers. Distances are normally stated in miles followed by the metric equivalent in kilometres. This is particularly important when using a car's milometer to follow some of the directions for access to sites.

Habitat

This section gives a brief description of the site (or sub-region), concentrating on features that are particularly important to the birds. Details are also given of any historic notes of interest, other aspects of the flora and fauna and ownership or reserve status.

Species

This section describes the more significant and interesting aspects of a site's birdlife. The text is arranged roughly in chronological order starting with the season that is generally best for birdwatching. It has sometimes been very difficult to decide which species to include for each site. Common birds are generally excluded unless they are of particular significance, e.g. a large roost of Black-headed Gulls. The presence of certain rare and vulnerable breeding species has been either ignored or their whereabouts treated with suitable discretion. Rare migrants and vagrants have been included for interest and to demonstrate the potential of the site for attracting such birds. It has been impossible to avoid giving long lists of species, although these have been reduced as much as possible, sometimes referring to groups of birds collectively, e.g. rarer winter grebes, seaduck, landbird migrants etc. These terms are fully defined in the Glossary. Some attempt has been made to give the scale of numbers to be expected, whether single individuals, small parties, or flocks of hundreds of birds; the frequency with which the various species occur; and any circumstances that might be related to such occurrences, e.g. hard weather, gales etc.

Timing

This section gives information regarding the best season or part of the year, time of day, state of the tide, weather etc. to see the various birds mentioned for each site. Inevitably, it has been impossible to avoid repeating the same or similar details for those places that are good for the same sorts of birds and birdwatching. Warnings are also given for those sites where disturbance may be a problem.

Access

This section gives direction to the sites, which generally start from the nearest town, village, or major road, and continue with details of the minor roads, footpaths etc. Where appropriate road names and useful landmarks, for example public houses, are mentioned to further help guide visitors to a site. Wherever possible public rights of way have been recommended and details given of restrictions on access at the time of writing. Visitors are warned, however, that on private land the owner's permission should always be sought before deviating from public paths. For reserves we have given details of any special arrangements for access such as obtaining permits. It should be noted that at some reserves where permits are not required for individuals, organised visits by groups of birdwatchers must be booked in advance with the warden. Even where this is not a necessity, we strongly recommend that those arranging group visits to an 'open' reserve should contact those responsible for the site. The names and addresses of wardens are given in the Reserve Visit Arrangements section. Further information regarding reserves may also be obtained from the appropriate body – see List of Organisations. Many reserves and country parks are well signposted and have Information/ Visitor Centres. In addition, there are detailed maps showing footpaths and hides often available either in leaflets and/or on notice boards. Visitors are urged to take heed of all such relevant information that is available on site. Access to those areas which are controlled by the Forestry Commission but not crossed by public rights of way cannot be taken for granted. Visitors should contact the appropriate Forest District Office for further information and advice. Sites where a charge is made for car parking and/or entry (other than reserve permit) at any time during the year are marked with an asterisk.

For each of the main sites (and sub-sites) use this section in conjunction with the outline maps that have been carefully prepared to complement the text. For most of the minor sites and Other Sites Worthy Of Attention, we have used OS Grid References. In fact, for detailed exploration of all sites, it is difficult to improve on the 1:50,000 Ordnance Survey maps. The 1:25,000 Ordnance Survey Outdoor Leisure Maps of Purbeck, the New Forest and the Isle of Wight are also strongly recommended.

Calendar

This is a quick reference section giving the most interesting species and groups of birds that can be expected throughout the year and during each season. Species and groups of birds that may occasionally or possibly be seen have also been included. For sites that are renowned for attracting scarce and rare birds, those oddities that are most likely to turn up are mentioned. Where appropriate, more precise timings to the likely occurrence of some species are given. If no further qualifying comment is made, the bird concerned may be looked for with equal success at any time during the season or peaks may occur randomly throughout the period. At those sites that are good for seawatching, details of sea passage are dealt with in a separate sub-section at the beginning of the appropriate season. Furthermore mention is also made of extreme conditions, e.g. severe gales/storms, hard winter weather, that may also influence the occurrence of certain species. This section should be used in conjunction with the more detailed Species account.

Key to the Maps

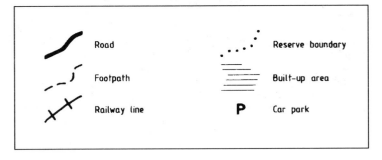

WEST AND NORTH DORSET

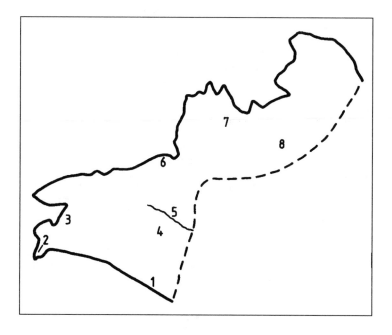

1 WEST BEXINGTON TO BURTON CLIFF	5 River Hooke and Kingcombe Reserve
2 Lyme Regis to Charmouth	6 Sutton Bingham Reservoir
3 Lambert's Castle	7 Sherborne Lake
4 Powerstock Common NR	8 Deadmoor and Lydlinch Commons

General Introduction

These areas lie principally to the west and north of the chalk downs. The complex geology of West Dorset creates a typical 'West Country' landscape of steep hillsides, often covered by broadleaved woodland and forestry, giving way to deep narrow valleys with fast-flowing streams. Some of these are tributaries of the Rivers Brit and Char, the latter draining the Marshwood Vale; whilst other streams form the headwaters of the River Axe, which flows along the country boundary with Somerset and the River Frome, which flows south and then east to Poole Harbour.

The West Dorset coast, particularly between Lyme Regis and Bridport, is dominated by high crumbling cliffs consisting mainly of fossil-rich Lias mudstones and clays capped in places by Cretaceous greensands.

Narrow beaches of shingle fringe the base of these cliffs. Scrub covers much of the cliff-top areas, which overlook the long sweep of Lyme Bay from Devon in the west to Portland in the east. Sheltered spots are at a premium along this exposed coastline, the most notable sites being the freshwater meres at West Bexington and Burton.

In North Dorset the Blackmore Vale presents a low-lying landscape of gently rolling pasture formed largely on Oxford Clay. The area is drained by the River Stour and its headwaters, which prior to recent drainage schemes, were prone to winter flooding. Although much of the land is given over to dairy farming, there are some noteworthy habitats in the form of damp broadleaved woodlands and poorly drained, scrub-covered commons.

There are two important sites of open water in these areas of Dorset: Sutton Bingham Reservoir, which lies mostly within the neighbouring county of Somerset, and Sherborne Lake.

Species

West Dorset is very much 'Buzzard and Dipper' country. The former species is a familiar sight throughout the area and it is not unusual to see anything up to half a dozen Buzzards soaring over the steep hillsides in spring. It is also worth keeping an eye open for the Raven which is now frequently reported from this part of the county. Most of the rivers west of a line between Yeovil and Weymouth have their resident Dippers and Grey Wagtails.

The broadleaved woodlands of West Dorset are good sites for such notable species as Redstart, Wood Warbler and Willow Tit; whilst areas of young forestry typically support Woodcock, Nightjar and Tree Pipit.

Raven

During the spring and summer Fulmars prospect the cliffs from Lyme Regis to Burton Bradstock, and Rock Pipits and Stonechats breed along the cliff-tops. Winter wildfowl are mostly restricted to such sites as West Bexington, Sutton Bingham and Sherborne Lake. Due to the paucity of suitable coastal habitats, waders are rather scarce. A scattering of the commoner species, however, occurs during the winter and at times of passage; whilst the Cobb at Lyme Regis appears to be a fairly reliable site for Purple Sandpipers. Inland a wide selection of waders has been recorded at Sutton Bingham, mainly in autumn when good numbers of Green and Common Sandpipers are seen. The flocks of commoner gulls that congregate in and around such coastal sites as Lyme Regis, Charmouth and Bridport, and the large roost of Black-headed and Common Gulls off West Bexington are always worth checking through for the more unusual species. Offshore, Cormorants are present for much of the year and divers, grebes, sea-duck and auks may be seen during the winter months. Seawatching from any vantage point along this coast may be rewarding, particularly in spring; whilst autumn gales have produced reports of various storm-blown oddities. At times of passage the coastal parks, gardens and scrub attract small numbers of landbird migrants including the occasional subrarity such as Wryneck and Golden Oriole.

The damp woods and poorly drained commons of the Blackmore Vale are favoured sites for Nightingale and Willow Tit. A few pairs of Tree Sparrows used to breed in this area of Dorset during the 1960s, but only sporadically since. During the winter the wet fields around the upper Stour often held large concentrations of Snipe together with smaller numbers of Teal and occasionally other wildfowl. The abundance of Snipe and wildfowl, however, have declined in recent years as winter flooding has become less frequent. The upper Stour and its tributaries support breeding Tufted Duck, Kingfisher and Grey Wagtail; whilst waders such as Green and Common Sandpipers occur in spring and autumn and there is always a good chance of seeing Goosander on the river during hard winter weather.

1 WEST BEXINGTON (DWT) TO BURTON CLIFF (NT)

OS Maps 193 & 194
SY48/58

Habitat

The village of West Bexington is situated on the Dorset coast midway between Burton Bradstock and Abbotsbury. To the west of the village and immediately behind the Chesil Beach, there is a small seasonally flooded mere which is flanked on the east side by a scrub-fringed reedbed. This area is now managed as a nature reserve by the Dorset Wildlife Trust. A little further to the west along the Chesil lies Burton Mere, a small reed-choked lagoon surrounded by rough ground and scrub. Further west still, the high sandstone cliffs at Burton Bradstock dominate the scene. The entire stretch of coast is backed by open farmland.

Species

In winter and at passage times the mere at West Bexington attracts small numbers of wildfowl and waders. There is a large gull roost off the beach and careful scrutiny in recent years has revealed the presence of several Mediterranean Gulls amongst large numbers of Black-headed and Common Gulls; whilst the Ring-billed Gull has been reported on several occasions. Lyme Bay is one of the best sites in the region for Red-throated Divers which are best looked for offshore between West Bexington and Cogden Beach. Further west off Burton Cliff, a flock of Common Scoter is usually present in winter. These birds are frequently joined by smaller numbers of Velvet Scoter; whilst the scoter flock occasionally attracts other sea-duck such as Eider and Long-tailed Duck. Dorset's most recent sighting of Surf Scoter also occurred here in January 1989. The other diver species, grebes and auks are rather scarce visitors.

West Bexington is probably the best vantage point along the West Dorset coast to observe the sea passage across Lyme Bay. Most of the commoner seabirds can be seen in spring, albeit at longer range than from the more established seawatching sites such as nearby Portland Bill; whilst scarcer species such as Pomarine Skua have appeared from time to time. Autumn and winter gales may produce storm-blown skuas and Little Gulls. These conditions have also resulted in sightings of more unusual seabirds such as Leach's Petrel, Grey Phalarope, Sabine's Gull and Little Auk. Movements of wildfowl between the Fleet and the East Devon estuaries often take place during the late autumn and winter.

At times of passage a scattering of landbird migrants occur along this entire stretch of coastline; whilst in autumn, the visible movements of hirundines, pipits and finches are sometimes pronounced.

The potential of this area for attracting rarities is shown by records of Green-winged Teal, Black-winged Stilt, Lesser Yellowlegs, Forster's Tern, Great Reed and Sardinian Warblers and Rose-coloured Starling; whilst a variety of subrarities including Hoopoe, Wryneck, Tawny Pipit, Blue-throat, Aquatic Warbler, Golden Oriole, and Red-backed and Great Grey Shrikes have also been seen here.

The reedbeds at West Bexington and Burton Meres support breeding Sedge and Reed Warblers, and Reed Bunting. Cetti's Warblers are well established in the reedswamp scrub at West Bexington where Bearded Tits have also bred in recent years. Both Peregrines and Ravens are a frequent sight along this stretch of coast throughout the year and Fulmars can be found on Burton Cliff during the spring and summer.

Timing

General visits are best made early in the day to avoid disturbance from walkers and anglers using the beach. The mere at West Bexington is usually dry between late spring and late autumn.

Check the gull roost from early afternoon onwards between November and May.

Spring seawatching is most rewarding early in the morning, between mid April and mid-May, when the winds are light to moderate and onshore (SW to SE) in direction. Observation can be difficult during gales due to excessive spray.

Access

West Bexington, Burton Mere, and Burton Cliffs can be reached from the B3157 between Abbotsbury and Burton Bradstock.

For West Bexington: take the minor road southeast from Swyre and continue to the beach car park*. From here walk northwest along the

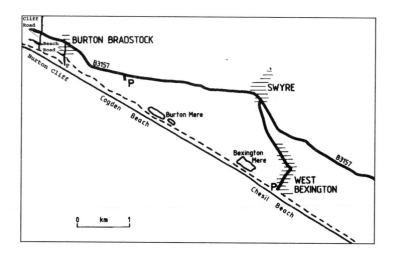

South West Coast Path to view the reedbeds and mere.

For Burton Mere: park in Cogden Beach car park (NT) to the south of the B3157 1.5 miles (2.5 km) west of Swyre. From here walk south to the beach and then southeast along the South West Coast Path to view the reedbed and lagoon.

Burton Cliffs can be reached from the B3157 at Burton Bradstock either by taking Beach Road south to the car park* or by taking Cliff Road south to the parking area by the road near the cliff-top.

Calendar

All Year: Cormorant, Peregrine, Cetti's Warbler, Raven, Reed Bunting.

Winter (November–March): Red-throated and occasional other divers; occasional grebes; wildfowl including Shelduck, Wigeon, Gadwall, Teal, Shoveler, Pochard, Tufted Duck, Common Scoter, frequent Velvet Scoter, occasional Pintail, Goldeneye and other sea-duck; common waders; gull roost including Mediterranean and possible Ring-billed Gulls; occasional auks; Rock Pipit.

Spring (April–May) and Autumn (August–October): sea passage best in spring (mid-April–mid-May) – for likely species see Site 9 The Fleet and Chesil Beach. Migrant wildfowl, waders and landbirds; offshore gull roost to May.
  Most likely oddity: landbird subrarity.

Summer (June–July): occasional terns offshore; Sedge and Reed Warblers.

2 LYME REGIS TO CHARMOUTH

Habitat and Species

Lyme Regis is a small picturesque fishing resort situated at the most westerly point along the Dorset coast. To the east, the River Char flows into the sea at Charmouth Beach. Although relatively small in extent, the low-lying beach and nearby reedbeds with their muddy edges are attractive features to birds along this otherwise cliff-dominated coastline.

In winter, the famous Cobb at Lyme Regis is a regular site for a flock of Purple Sandpipers. Otherwise a scattering of waders, mainly Oyster-catcher and Ringed Plover, feed along the beaches between Lyme Regis and Charmouth. Cormorants are usually present, particularly around Lyme Regis, but divers, grebes, sea-duck and auks are rarely seen offshore. It is worth checking through the commoner gulls that inhabit the shoreline areas for the odd Kittiwake and perhaps scarcer species. Although numbers remain small, the variety of waders frequenting the beaches increases at times of passage. Indeed the small area of shingle and mud at the mouth of the River Char held a Temminck's Stint and Jack Snipe in September 1995. In addition to the commoner seabirds, autumn gales have sometimes brought the likes of Grey Phalarope, skuas and Little Gull close inshore. In spring and autumn the local parks, gardens and coastal scrub attract small numbers of landbird migrants including the occasional Black Redstart which has also wintered in the area. Fulmars regularly prospect the cliffs around Lyme Regis, Herring Gulls nest on the town's rooftops and a few pairs of Rock Pipits inhabit the seafront and harbour areas. Both Grey Wagtail and Dipper breed on the River Lim and River Char; whilst the reedbeds at Charmouth Beach hold Reed Warbler and perhaps Reed Bunting. Like much of the west Dorset coast, Peregrines and Ravens are frequently seen overhead throughout the year.

Access

The car parks* closest to the Cobb and Lyme Regis seafront are well sign-posted from the outskirts of town; whilst Charmouth Beach car park* is well signposted from the A35 in Charmouth. There is easy access to most areas of interest including the Cobb, the beaches between Lyme Regis and Charmouth and the lower reaches of the River Char.

3 LAMBERT'S CASTLE (NT)

Habitat and Species

Lambert's Castle is a prominent hill-fort which provides stunning views over the west Dorset countryside. Habitats are diverse with some particularly fine woods comprising mostly beech and Scots pine covering the western side of the hill; whilst birch woodland and scrub cloaks the eastern slopes. The top is covered by open grass and there is some heathland at the west end of the hill-fort.

Breeding Redstart and Wood Warbler are the specialities of the beech and Scots pine woods which also hold a wide variety of other breeding birds including Green and Great Spotted Woodpeckers, Marsh Tit, Nuthatch, Treecreeper and possibly Siskin. Crossbills have occurred here in late summer and may breed locally. The birch woodlands and areas of scrub support a different selection of species including Tree Pipit, Whitethroat, Willow Warbler, Linnet and Yellowhammer amongst others. Buzzards are a familiar sight as they soar over the hill; whilst Ravens are regularly reported from this part of the county.

Access

The access track to Lambert's Castle is situated at SY364988 on the B3165 1.1 miles (1.8 km) southwest of the Bottle Inn in Marshwood. Please note that from the Marshwood direction, the turning into this access track is rather obscure and easy to miss. There is a small car park by the main entrance to Lambert's Castle.

4 POWERSTOCK COMMON NR (DWT)

OS Map 194
SY59

Habitat and Species

This attractive reserve offers a rich variety of habitats including forestry, ancient oak woodland and hazel coppice, heathy and calcareous grasslands, and several small ponds. The site is perhaps best known for its butterfly fauna.

The diversity of breeding birds has declined as the forestry plantations have matured. Nevertheless a wide range of woodland birds including Buzzard, Woodcock, Tree Pipit, Garden Warbler and Willow Tit can still be seen here. Winter may bring the occasional flock of Siskins and Redpolls and possibly the odd wandering Hen Harrier; whilst a Great Grey Shrike appeared in one recent winter.

Access

Powerstock Common can be reached from Toller Porcorum by taking the minor road southwest to the offset crossroads at SY550968 (track to Barrowland Farm opposite), then turning right and continuing down the hill to the small car park on the left just before the disused railway bridge at SY547973. Please keep to the bridlepath and well marked footpaths when crossing the reserve.

5 RIVER HOOKE AND KINGCOMBE RESERVE (DWT)

Habitat and Species

This is one of the best examples of the small fast-flowing rivers that are typical of West Dorset. The River Hooke is a tributary of the River Frome and flows through an attractive steep-sided valley where farming practices have changed little since the 1920s. As a consequence the river flows through some fine unimproved wet meadows. A substantial area of land around Lower Kingcombe is owned and managed by the Dorset Wildlife Trust. The reserve supports a rich flora and insect fauna.

Breeding birds include such riverine species as Kingfisher, Grey Wagtail, Dipper, Sedge and Reed Warblers and Reed Bunting; whilst the nearby copses hold a wealth of woodland birds including Tree Pipit and Willow Tit. Canada Geese and Tufted Duck nest by the small lakes at Toller Whelme. Buzzards are commonly seen overhead and may be joined by the elegant Hobby in the summer. In winter, the wet meadows support small numbers of Snipe.

Dipper

Access

The River Hooke can be reached by various minor roads west and south from the A356 between Maiden Newton and Rampisham Down, notably at SY587979 to Toller Fratrum and at SY577982 to Toller Porcorum. There is also a minor road along the length of the valley between Toller Porcorum and Hooke. The river can be viewed from roadbridges at Tollerford, Toller Fratrum, Toller Porcorum, Lower Kingcombe, Higher Kingcombe and Hooke; whilst the lakes at Toller Whelme can be viewed from the public footpath at ST519014.

Access to the Kingcombe Meadows Reserve (DWT) is from the car park and Visitor Centre at Round Cottage in Lower Kingcombe at SY554990.

24

The Visitor Centre provides information about the reserve and permissive paths through it.

Nearby the Kingcombe Centre offers a wide range of residential and non-residential courses, many of which will be of interest to the bird-watcher and general naturalist. In addition there are public guided walks* which in 1995 took place on Wednesday afternoons starting at 2.15 pm. For further details contact the Director of the Centre (Nigel Spring), The Kingcombe Centre, Toller Porcorum, Dorchester, Dorset, DT2 OEQ (tel: 01300 320684).

6 SUTTON BINGHAM RESERVOIR (WW)

OS Map 194
ST50/51

Habitat and Species

Since all but the southernmost tip of this large T-shaped reservoir lies within Somerset, a detailed account of this site is inappropriate. Nevertheless the Dorset part of Sutton Bingham is often the most rewarding for birds and so justifies some inclusion in this book. Although Sutton Bingham now attracts fewer wildfowl and waders than it did prior to the mid 1980s, it still remains an important site for birdlife.

During the winter a wide selection of waterfowl is normally present including Great Crested Grebe, Cormorant, Grey Heron, Canada Goose, Wigeon, Teal, Pochard and Tufted Duck; whilst the likes of Scaup, Goldeneye, Smew, Goosander and Ruddy Duck appear from time to time, usually during periods of cold weather. There is always the possibility of something unusual – divers, rarer winter grebes, American Wigeon, Green-winged and Blue-winged Teals, Red-crested Pochard, Ring-necked and Ferruginous Ducks have all been seen here. Flocks of mostly Black-headed, up to 3,000+ in recent years, and Common Gulls congregate on the reservoir during winter afternoons prior to moving to the coast to roost. Mediterranean Gulls are regularly found amongst the gull roost – November, December and March being the best months; whilst Ring-billed Gulls are occasionally reported. Lapwing and Snipe are the only waders that can be expected during the winter months. In spring and autumn attention passes to the waders and terns, both groups being most numerous during the latter season. An impressive list of waders has been noted with Little Ringed and Ringed Plovers, Little Stint, Curlew Sandpiper, Dunlin, Ruff, Spotted Redshank, Greenshank, Green and Common Sandpipers the most likely species to occur; whilst rarities such as Semipalmated, Pectoral, Broad-billed, Buff-breasted and Terek Sandpipers, Temminck's Stint, Long-billed Dowitcher, Wilson's and Grey Phalaropes have all been seen here. Small numbers of Common and Black Terns along with a few Little Gulls, pass through mainly in the autumn. There are several autumn records of White-winged Black Terns and a spring sighting of Whiskered Tern. There is also a scattering of landbird migrants which have included such noteworthy species as

25

Red-throated Pipit, Aquatic Warbler and Ortolan Bunting. Ospreys occur with increasing frequency on migration; whilst the Peregrine is a regular visitor, particularly during the winter months. The Great Crested Grebe is the most noteworthy of the breeding birds that frequent the reservoir.

Access

Sutton Bingham Reservoir is well signposted along the minor road south-west from the A37 Dorchester to Yeovil road at ST560130 (by the Obelisk). The reservoir can be viewed well from the minor road along its western side, notably from the causeway at ST547113 and near the southern tip at ST545101. There is a car park and picnic area just south of the causeway at ST548112.

7 SHERBORNE LAKE

OS Map 183
ST61

Habitat and Species

This large ornamental lake used to be a regular site for small numbers of wintering Goosander, but the species has become much scarcer since 1989 and now appears to be only a sporadic visitor. Other winter water-fowl that can be expected include Great Crested Grebe, Cormorant, Teal, Pochard and Tufted Duck; whilst Wigeon, Shoveler, Goldeneye and Ruddy Duck are occasionally present. Almost anything can turn up; Red-throated and Black-throated Divers, Pintail, Scaup and Smew have been reported from here. In addition, there is a large population of Canada Geese and the exotic Mandarin is also a resident of the lake. A few Snipe skulk along the margins in winter; whilst passage waders and terns may appear in spring and autumn. The lake holds breeding Great Crested Grebe, Canada Goose, Pochard (occasional), Tufted Duck, Sedge and Reed Warblers and Reed Bunting; whilst Kingfisher, Grey Wagtail and Dipper frequent the nearby River Yeo. The grounds of Sherborne Castle support a wide range of woodland birds including Buzzard.

Access

For much of the year Sherborne Lake can be partially viewed from Sherborne Old Castle* (English Heritage), which is signposted from the Oborne Road in Sherborne at ST645168 – opposite the Black Horse PH. The site is open* 9.30 am–6.30 pm daily (except May Day) 15 March to 15 October; 9.30 am–4.00 pm Monday to Saturday and 2.00 pm–4.00 pm on Sunday, 16 October to 14 March, closed 24 to 26 December and 1 January. The grounds of Sherborne Castle*, including the lake, are open Easter Sunday to 30 September on Thursdays, weekends and bank holi-day Mondays. The main entrance lies off the A30/A3030 (New Road) at ST645162. View the River Yeo from the roadbridge at ST645166.

8 DEADMOOR AND LYDLINCH COMMONS

Habitat and Species

These are good examples of the damp broadleaved woods (Deadmoor) and poorly drained scrubby commons (Lydlinch) that are characteristic of the Blackmore Vale. These sites are better known for their flora and butterfly fauna.

Both are amongst the best sites in Dorset for Nightingale. Otherwise these sites support a wide selection of birds typical of woodland and scrub including Buzzard, Garden Warbler and Willow Tit.

Access

Deadmoor Common can be reached from Woodrow near Fifehead Neville by taking the footpath northwest at ST760108 past Elm Tree Cottage and Hambledon and then across the field to the style into the wood. The footpath continues northwest through the wood towards Holbrook Farm.

There is general access to Lydlinch Common from the A357 between Lydlinch and the junction with the A3030 Sherborne road and from the A3030 between the above junction and Brickles Wood.

PORTLAND AND WEYMOUTH

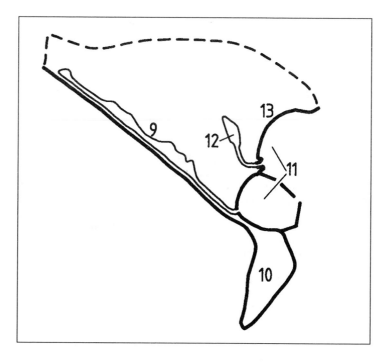

9 THE FLEET AND CHESIL BEACH
10 PORTLAND
11 PORTLAND HARBOUR,
   THE NOTHE AND
   WEYMOUTH BAY

12 RADIPOLE LAKE NR
13 LODMOOR NR

General Introduction

Dominated by the limestone massif of the Isle of Portland, this comparatively short section of the Dorset coast between Abbotsbury and Preston supports a rich diversity of coastal and wetland habitats. These include the high cliffs of Portland, the unique shingle bank and shallow lagoon of the Chesil and Fleet, the sheltered waters of Portland Harbour and Weymouth Bay, the lake and reedswamp of Radipole Lake NR and the marshy pasture and remnant saltmarsh of Lodmoor NR. This concentration of ornithologically important sites provides varied and exciting bird-watching throughout the year. Divers, grebes, wildfowl including sea-duck, waders and gulls can be seen in winter; migrants including seabirds, waders, gulls, terns and landbirds feature at times of passage; and breeding seabirds, terns and reedbed specialities are present in spring and summer. The potential for finding and seeing unusual and rare birds is greater in this area than anywhere else in the region.

9 THE FLEET AND CHESIL BEACH

OS Map 194
SY58/67/68

Habitat

The Chesil Beach dominates the coastal scenery to the west of Portland extending for 10 miles (16 km) from Chesil Cove to Abbotsbury and for 8 miles (13 km) encloses the Fleet, a shallow estuarine lagoon. To the seaward, the Chesil is exposed to the full force of the prevailing southwesterly gales and lacks any vegetation, but on the sheltered inland side mats of short turf and characteristic shingle flora cloak the more stable areas. A line of seablite marks the transition of the beach into the muddy shores of the Fleet.

The Fleet itself varies in width from a half a mile at Butterstreet Cove to less than 100 yards by the Bridging Camp. The tidal flow that enters through the narrow channel (Small Mouth) at Ferrybridge penetrates little further than the middle reaches of the lagoon beyond which seepage through the Chesil Beach and freshwater flowing in from several small streams combine to produce a brackish environment in the West Fleet. Although most of the Fleet is normally very shallow with extensive mudflats exposed between Ferrybridge and the East Fleet at low tide, water levels vary considerably. These may be quite high during periods of persistent easterly winds, which cause a build up of water particularly in the West Fleet. The aquatic flora and fauna are very rich and include extensive beds of eel grasses and tasselweed.

At the head of the Fleet lies Abbotsbury Swannery, an attractive mixture of reedbeds and damp woodland. Otherwise the landward shore of the Fleet is fringed mostly by farmland. The Fleet is one of the oldest wildlife sanctuaries in Britain. At present the entire Fleet and neighbouring Chesil Beach are maintained as a nature reserve by the Strangways Estate.

Species

The Fleet provides shelter and feeding for an abundance of wintering waterfowl including several thousand Brent Geese, Wigeon and Coot; whilst in recent years the Mute Swan has reached the 1,000+ mark. Peak counts for Canada Goose, Gadwall, Teal, Mallard, Pintail, Shoveler, Pochard, Tufted Duck, Goldeneye and Red-breasted Merganser usually reach treble figures and smaller numbers of Little and Great Crested Grebes, Cormorant and Shelduck are also present. The majority of the wildfowl, including Wigeon, Gadwall, Teal, Pintail and Shoveler, are found on the West Fleet with the greatest concentrations often at

Abbotsbury which is also the main site for Pochard and Tufted Duck. Goldeneye are more evenly distributed along the Fleet; whilst Brent Geese, Shelduck and Red-breasted Merganser tend to favour the East Fleet. A few Scaup regularly winter with the Pochard/Tufted Duck flock at Abbotsbury with numbers increasing during periods of hard weather. Such conditions invariably bring Smew and Goosander to the Fleet; whilst flocks of Bewick's and Whooper Swans, and grey geese (mostly White-fronted) are also distinct possibilities. Although only a few birds are normally involved, the Fleet is the most reliable site in the region for Long-tailed Duck which show a preference for the Abbotsbury and East Fleet/Ferrybridge areas. Other sea-duck along with the divers, rarer winter grebes and auks, including the diminutive Little Auk, are occasionally reported from the Fleet, but they are much more likely to be seen off the Chesil Beach in Lyme Bay. Indeed in recent years, Lyme Bay between Abbotsbury Beach and West Bexington has regularly attracted good numbers of Red-throated Diver in winter. With such large numbers of waterfowl frequenting the Fleet in winter, it is no surprise that rarer species/ subspecies are occasionally found. In recent years there have been reports of Bean and Greenland White-fronted Geese, Black Brant, American Wigeon, Blue-winged Teal, Red-crested Pochard and Ferruginous Duck.

Ringed and Kentish Plovers

A wide selection of waders winter on the Fleet, the best feeding areas being Langton Herring (Rodden Hive/Herbury Gore), East Fleet and Ferrybridge. The most abundant species are Dunlin, Ringed and Grey Plovers; whilst Oystercatcher, Curlew, Redshank and Turnstone also occur in moderate numbers and a few Knot, Bar-tailed Godwit and Greenshank are usually present most winters. Snipe mainly frequent the landward margins of the Fleet with large gatherings sometimes noted in the reedbeds at Abbotsbury. Ruff occasionally appear in winter, usually during cold snaps when there is also a good chance of finding the odd Jack Snipe and Woodcock. Amongst the rarer waders, there are winter reports of Avocet (near annual), Long-billed Dowitcher and Grey Phalarope; whilst up to two Kentish Plovers were present at Ferrybridge for two consecutive winters in the early 1990s.

The large numbers of gulls that inhabit the Fleet are well worth checking through for the more unusual species. In recent years Mediterranean Gulls have been regularly reported from Abbotsbury with frequent sightings from the East Fleet/Ferrybridge/Chesil Cove area; whilst Little, Iceland and Glaucous Gulls occasionally appear. A well watched Ivory Gull was present in Chesil Cove in January 1980 and there are reports of Laughing and Ring-billed Gulls from the Fleet itself.

In recent winters the Abbotsbury reedbeds have regularly held small numbers of Bearded Tit and Cetti's Warbler. A few Kingfishers and Rock Pipits can be found along the margins of the Fleet; whilst Stonechats and the odd Black Redstart, Chiffchaff and Firecrest may be located in suitable habitat along the landward shore. With such concentrations of wintering birds on the Fleet, it is not surprising that Merlin and Peregrine often patrol the Fleet in search of prey. Both Hen Harriers and Short-eared Owls are occasionally seen and may winter in some years.

The first migrants appear during March with the arrival of such species as Sandwich Tern, Wheatear and Chiffchaff. The main passage period, however, is April and May when waders are a conspicuous group, favouring the same areas as they do during the winter. Parties of Whimbrel and Bar-tailed Godwit are a familiar sight, the latter species often feeding on the mudflats at Ferrybridge where small groups of Sanderling regularly consort with larger numbers of Ringed Plover and Dunlin. Careful scrutiny of these wader flocks may reveal smart summer-plumaged Curlew Sandpipers, which occur with some frequency, and sometimes the odd Little Stint. The undoubted wader speciality of the season, however, is the Kentish Plover. Ferrybridge is the best site in the region for this species with one to three birds appearing most springs. A variety of other migrant waders can be expected including the occasional report of Avocet; whilst there are spring sightings of such rarities as Black-winged Stilt, Collared Pratincole, American Golden Plover, Sharp-tailed and Broad-billed Sandpipers, and Lesser Yellowlegs.

By mid-April the Sandwich Terns have been joined by Common and Little Terns, both of which remain to breed locally; whilst passage Little Gulls and Black Terns occasionally wander to the Fleet. Many of the wintering waterfowl remain well into the spring when migrant Garganey may also put in an appearance, most often at Abbotsbury. Spoonbills are virtually annual visitors to the Fleet, favouring the Langton Herring and Abbotsbury areas; whilst there is a recent sighting of a Great White Egret. Large migrant raptors such as Marsh Harrier and Osprey along with the smaller Hobby are also likely visitors.

The usual common landbird migrants, including Yellow Wagtail, Whinchat and Wheatear, can be found at Ferrybridge and along the landward margins of the Fleet. Scarcer birds such as Black Redstart, Ring Ouzel, Firecrest and Pied Flycatcher occasionally occur and there have been several records of the exotic Hoopoe. There are also recent spring sightings of Wryneck, Golden Oriole, Woodchat Shrike and Serin.

The upchannel (easterly) passage of seabirds through Lyme Bay can be observed from the vantage of the Chesil Beach at Ferrybridge and Abbotsbury Beach. These movements involve the same variety of birds that pass off nearby Portland Bill including divers, Manx Shearwater, Common Scoter and other sea-duck, various waders, skuas and terns. Most birds tend to follow the shore, moving east along the Chesil and then south towards Portland Bill. A significant proportion of the waders, skuas and terns, however, overfly the Chesil and pass eastwards through Portland Harbour. Flocks of passage waders often stop and linger to feed at Ferrybridge before continuing on their journey; whilst skuas, including spectacular parties of Pomarines, sometimes loaf for a few hours in Chesil Cove waiting to attack passing seabirds. Occasionally the odd Roseate or Black Tern may be located amongst the gulls and terns feeding along the exposed Chesil shore. Later in the spring and summer large movements of Manx Shearwaters are sometimes observed off the Chesil in Lyme Bay; whilst there are occasional sightings of Storm Petrels, particularly in Chesil Cove.

The Chesil Beach is sanctuary to the only colony of breeding Little Terns in Dorset. Common Terns, which once bred in good numbers on the Chesil, now nest mainly on artificial islets constructed in the Fleet at Abbotsbury. The bulk of Dorset's breeding Ringed Plovers together with the odd pair of Oystercatcher are also found along the Chesil; whilst a few pairs of Shelduck and Redshank nest along the shores of the Fleet.

The famous Swannery at Abbotsbury has probably been in existence for about 900 years, with the present breeding population of Mute Swans averaging 100 to 130 pairs. The Gadwall is now a regular breeder in small numbers; whilst Shoveler have also nested in recent years. Sedge and Reed Warblers and Reed Buntings nest in the reedbeds at Abbotsbury where a few pairs of Bearded Tit bred regularly in the early 1990s, but unfortunately not in 1995. Although the Cetti's Warbler appears to be mainly a non breeding visitor to this site, occasional birds remain to breed as in 1990 and 1995. There is also a small heronry at Abbotsbury; whilst Grey Herons can be expected almost anywhere on the Fleet throughout the year. The landward habitats fringing the Fleet support birds typical of the open country including Red-legged and Grey Partridges as well as Corn Bunting; whilst Buzzards can be seen soaring over the nearby hillsides throughout the year. A few non-breeding water-fowl, waders and gulls along with the occasional oddity such as Spoonbill remain on the Fleet throughout the summer. There is a midsummer report of Caspian Tern; whilst Britain's second ever White-tailed Plover was seen at Abbotsbury in July 1979.

The trickle of migrant waders, which is evident from late June, rapidly builds up to a full-scale passage by mid-July. Langton Herring is the most rewarding area for autumn waders, although East Fleet and Ferrybridge are well worthy of attention. In addition to the commoner waders that winter on the Fleet, more typical migrants such as Bar-tailed Godwit, Whimbrel, Greenshank and Common Sandpiper can be seen. Scarcer species such as Knot, Little Stint and Curlew Sandpiper regularly occur, sometimes in good numbers for Dorset; whilst the odd Little Ringed Plover, Ruff, Black-tailed Godwit, Spotted Redshank, Green and Wood Sandpiper appear most years. There is always the chance of finding something more unusual, such as Avocet, Kentish Plover, Temminck's Stint or Pectoral Sandpiper, amongst the wader flocks. Rarities such as Sociable Plover, Semipalmated, White-rumped and Buff-breasted Sandpipers, Long-billed Dowitcher and Terek Sandpiper have also been reported from the Fleet in autumn.

Sandwich, Common and Little Terns occur throughout the autumn and mix with the Black-headed and other gulls inhabiting the Fleet. These flocks of gulls and terns should be checked through for the less common species including Mediterranean and Little Gulls, Arctic, Black and Roseate Terns; whilst there is a recent report of two Caspian Terns involving an adult feeding a juvenile bird. Little Gulls and Black Terns are likely to be seen anywhere along the Fleet, especially after severe gales. Such conditions, particularly late in the season, often bring Grey Phalaropes to the shelter of the Fleet and Sabine's Gulls to seek brief respite at Ferrybridge; whilst skuas may overfly the Chesil to harry gulls and terns over the lagoon. Chesil Cove is a particularly good site for storm-blown seabirds with Storm and Leach's Petrels (notably during the famous wreck of December 1989), Grey Phalarope, Sabine's Gull, White-winged Black Tern and Little Auk all seen in recent years.

Passage Garganey occasionally appear at Langton Herring and Abbotsbury in autumn with many species of winter wildfowl returning by late August and early September. In common with so other many coastal sites in southern Britain, the Little Egret is a regular feature of the autumn when counts have reached the 10 to 20 mark. The species occurs less frequently at other times of the year. As in spring and summer, the Spoonbill is a likely visitor. Ospreys occur most autumns with birds sometimes spending several days, if not weeks, on the Fleet; whilst Marsh Harriers are reported annually.

Landbird migrants feature well in the autumn, notably along the landward fringes of the Fleet. All the commoner species can be expected; whilst scarcer birds like Black Redstart, Firecrest and Pied Flycatcher occur annually in small numbers along with occasional sightings of Ring Ouzel. Amongst the rarer migrants, a few Aquatic Warblers have been seen in the reedbeds at Abbotsbury in recent autumns; there are also reports of Wryneck, Richard's, Tawny and Red-throated Pipits, Bluethroat, Icterine, Melodious and Yellow-browed Warblers, Red-breasted Flycatcher, Red-backed and Woodchat Shrikes and Ortolan Bunting. The potential of the area for landbird rarities was shown by the discovery of a Red-eyed Vireo in a small wood by Littlesea Holiday Park in October 1995.

Timing

This is not too important for winter waterfowl, although at Abbotsbury the ducks often huddle in tight flocks on the furthest edge of the Fleet during strong winds, particularly easterlies. Hard weather increases the number and diversity of wildfowl.

To see waders on the East Fleet the tide must be partially out, but avoid extreme low-water when the birds may be too distant to observe satisfactorily. At Ferrybridge one to two hours before and after high-water are the best times to visit, since waders are forced to feed near the car park. At Langton Herring tidal conditions are difficult to predict, but there should be some mud exposed at most times; only after prolonged easterly winds will so much water back up the Fleet that all the mud is covered here.

Spring seawatching from the Chesil Beach is best early in the morning, between mid-April and mid-May, in light onshore (SW to SE) winds. Mist or drizzle may be helpful, but seabird passage will occur in clear weather. Lack of shelter makes seawatching difficult in strong onshore winds. Check Chesil Cove for storm-driven seabirds during/after severe gales in autumn and winter.

The landward shore of the Fleet between Ferrybridge and Rodden Hive is well used by walkers throughout the year. Ferrybridge is also subject to disturbance from bait diggers at low tide and bathers in summer.

Access

The Fleet and Chesil Beach are best approached by the A354 between Wyke Regis (Weymouth) and Portland, and various minor roads south and west from the B3157 between Wyke Regis (Weymouth) and

Abbotsbury – see below. There is also a footpath (Dorset Coast Path) along the landward shore of the Fleet between Small Mouth (Ferrybridge) and Rodden Hive near Langton Herring.

Please note there is no access to:
(i) the entire Chesil Beach between Ferrybridge and the tank traps at

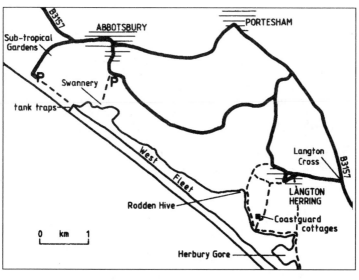

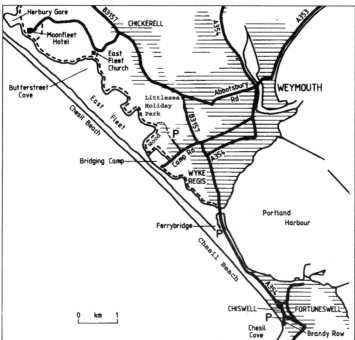

Abbotsbury Beach from 1 May to 31 August. This is to prevent disturbance to breeding birds.

(ii) the inside (Fleet shore) of the Chesil Beach between Langton Herring and the tank traps at Abbotsbury Beach throughout the year. Visitors between 1 September and 30 April must keep to the seaward shore below the crest of the beach to avoid disturbing the wildfowl.

(iii) the landward shore of the Fleet to the west of Rodden Hive near Langton Herring, except at Abbotsbury Swannery – see below.

Chesil Cove: from the A354 roundabout in Victoria Square, Portland, take the road signposted to Chiswell south as far as the small parking area and then walk up Brandy Row to view the sea from the promenade.

Ferrybridge and Chesil Beach are best approached from the Chesil Beach Car Park* that lies to the west of the A354, just after crossing Ferrybridge on the causeway to Portland. There is now an Information Centre (Chesil Beach Centre) in the car park.

The Bridging Camp can be reached from the sharp bend of the B3157 in Wyke Regis by taking Camp Road southwest to the shore. Follow the Dorset Coast path either southeast to view Ferrybridge or northwest to view East Fleet.

Littlesea Holiday Park can be reached from Camp Road (see above) by taking Mandeville Road to the supermarket car park. From the car park, there is a footpath northwest towards the holiday park. On reaching the wood, either turn southwest and follow footpath to the Fleet shore and the Dorset Coast Path or continue northwest to the holiday park. Note: this wood is good for small migrants including the Red-eyed Vireo of October 1995!

East Fleet and Herbury can be reached from the B3157 roundabout in Chickerell by taking the minor road southwest, which is signposted to Fleet. For East Fleet and Butterstreet Cove, walk from East Fleet Church to the shore and follow the Dorset Coast Path either southeast towards Ferrybridge or northwest towards the Moonfleet Hotel. For Herbury, continue on the minor road to within 200 yards of the Moonfleet Hotel and follow the Dorset Coast Path west to Herbury and on around the shore to Rodden Hive – also see below. Please note that car parking is very limited by East Fleet Church and near the Moonfleet Hotel.

Langton Herring is well signposted along the minor road west from the B3157 at Langton Cross. From the southwest corner of the village, walk along the rough road signposted to the Coastguards west and then south to the shore. Follow the Dorset Coast Path either southeast to Herbury Gore or northwest to Rodden Hive. Please note that there is no right of way for motor cars along the rough road and that there is very limited parking available in the village. As alternatives there are footpaths (i) from the village south to Herbury Gore and (ii) from the sharp bend in the rough road to the Coastguards west to the stream and south to Rodden Hive.

Abbotsbury Swannery is well signposted along the minor road south from the B3157 in Abbotsbury. The Swannery* is open from April to

October, 10.00 am–6.00 pm. For further details contact the Swanherd, the Swannery, New Barn Road, Abbotsbury, Dorset (tel: 01305 871130).

Abbotsbury Beach is reached from the B3157 just to the west of Abbotsbury by taking the minor road southwest past the Sub-Tropical Gardens to the beach. Walk southeast along the inside of the Chesil to view the West Fleet and the Abbotsbury reedbeds from the line of tank traps.

Further information on the Chesil Bank and the Fleet Nature Reserve can be obtained from the Warden, The Royal Manor of Portland Chesil Beach Centre, Portland Beach Road, Portland, Dorset, DT4 9XE (tel: 01305 760579).

Calendar

All Year. Cormorant, Little Egret, Grey Heron, Mute Swan, Shelduck, Buzzard, Red-legged and Grey Partridges, Water Rail, Oystercatcher, Ringed Plover, Redshank, Cetti's Warbler, Bearded Tit, Reed and Corn Buntings.

Winter (November–March): Red-throated and occasional other divers; Little, Great Crested and occasional rarer winter grebes; wildfowl including Canada and Brent Geese, Wigeon, Gadwall, Pintail, Shoveler, Pochard, Tufted Duck, Scaup, Long-tailed Duck, Goldeneye, Red-breasted merganser, occasional other sea-duck, in cold weather Smew, Goosander, occasional Bewick's and Whooper Swans, and grey geese (usually White-fronted); Merlin, Peregrine and occasional Hen Harrier; waders including Knot, Bar-tailed Godwit and Greenshank; gulls including regular Mediterranean, occasional Little and Kittiwake, possible Iceland and Glaucous; occasional Short-eared Owl; Kingfisher, Rock Pipit, Stonechat, occasional Black Redstart, Chiffchaff and Firecrest.
Most likely oddity: rare wildfowl.

Spring (mid-March–May): sea passage best mid-April to mid-May – including divers, Fulmar, Manx Shearwater, Gannet, Common Scoter and other sea-duck, waders, skuas, Little Gull, terns – also see Site 10 Portland.
Occasional Garganey; migrant waders including Knot, Sanderling, Bar-tailed Godwit, Whimbrel, Greenshank, Common Sandpiper, annual Kentish Plover and Curlew Sandpiper, occasional other species; gulls including occasional Mediterranean and Little; terns including occasional Black; landbird migrants including occasional Black Redstart, Ring Ouzel, Firecrest and Pied Flycatcher.
Most likely oddities: Spoonbill, Marsh Harrier, Osprey, Hoopoe.

Summer (mid-May–mid-July): non-breeding wildfowl and waders; Common, Little and occasional other species of tern; Sedge and Reed Warblers; possible Spoonbill; Manx Shearwater and occasional Storm Petrel in Lyme Bay.

Autumn (mid-July–October): during/after gales – storm-blown seabirds including Storm and Leach's Petrels, Grey Phalarope, skuas, Sabine's Gull and Little Auk.
Returning winter wildfowl and occasional passage Garganey; migrant waders including Knot, Little Stint, Curlew Sandpiper, Bar-tailed Godwit, Whimbrel, Greenshank, Common Sandpiper, occasional other species;

gulls including occasional Mediterranean and Little; terns including occasional Black; landbird migrants including Black Redstart, Firecrest, Pied Flycatcher and occasional Ring Ouzel.

Most likely oddities; Spoonbill, Osprey, Kentish Plover, Temminck's Stint, Pectoral Sandpiper and other rare American waders, landbird subrarities and rarities.

10 PORTLAND

OS Map 194
SY66/67/77

Habitat

The Isle of Portland is a long triangular limestone massif that juts out some 5 miles (8 km) from a point about midway along the Dorset coast. Joined tenuously to the mainland by the Chesil Beach, the island rises sharply to a peak of 425 ft at its northern end before gently sloping and tapering away to the southernmost point, the Bill which is only a few feet above sea level. Much of the island is flanked by cliffs, although in many places these have become partially cloaked by a combination of natural landslips and quarry waste known as Weaves. Defence installations, housing developments and active or abandoned quarry workings, cover large parts of Portland; only in the southern half does a mainly agricultural landscape of ancient field systems and common land survive. Vegetation is limited by strong winds and salt spray, but in the relative shelter of the east side, Verne Common and East Weare are covered by areas of dense scrub. A few hardy clumps of sycamores grow in all the settlements. A strong tide race occurs where the currents meet off the Bill.

Although traditionally Portland Bill and its immediate environs has been the best watched area for birds, there are several other sites on the island that provide interesting and productive birdwatching. The Bill area is predominantly open farmland, the main patches of cover being at Culverwell and around the Bird Observatory and adjacent Hut Fields. Apart from the working lighthouse at the Bill itself, there are two disused lighthouses one of which, the Old Lower Light, has housed the Portland Bird Observatory and Field Centre (PBO) since 1961. Another good area for birds is Verne Common, which lies between Portland Prison and the Naval Dockyard at the north end of the island. It consists of steep sloping ground largely overgrown with dense bramble, blackthorn and elderberry scrub. There is some rough pasture and a small Naval Cemetery surrounded by sycamore trees. The remaining sites of interest offer a variety of habitats including sycamore woods, disused quarry workings covered with areas of dense scrub, residential gardens and open farmland.

The island's flora boasts several local specialities; whilst the butterflies and moths, including many migrant species, are also well represented. Passing cetacea are regularly spotted offshore.

Species

Portland is one of the best known birdwatching sites in Britain. The island's prominent position makes it ideal for attracting a wide range of landbird migrants and observing the offshore movements of seabirds. This was recognised by the Rev. F.L. Blathwayt as long ago as 1918. The island's full potential as a site to study bird migration, however, was not established until the start of systematic coverage in the autumn of 1951. This was undertaken by an enthusiastic group of observers based at Portland Bill. These studies eventually led to the formation of the Portland Bird Observatory in 1955, since when Portland and in particular the Bill area has become a mecca for birdwatchers who visit in search of scarce and rare migrants. Spring Hoopoe, and autumn Melodious Warbler and Ortolan Bunting are more likely to be seen here than anywhere else in mainland Britain; whilst the island's list of rarities is truly impressive and includes Britain's first Calandra Lark (1961), Desert Warbler (1970), Savannah Sparrow (1982) and Lesser Short-toed Lark (1992).

Spring migration commences in early March with the arrival of Wheatears and Chiffchaffs on the land and the start of the upchannel movements of seabirds – mainly divers, Fulmar, Gannet, Common Scoter, Kittiwake and auks. The numbers and diversity of landbird migrants gradually builds up during the second half of the month when significant falls of Wheatears and Chiffchaffs along with a scattering of other early migrants may occur. These often include such scarce birds as Black Redstart, Ring Ouzel and Firecrest which continue to appear in small numbers through to early May. The first two species favour the limestone quarries, such as Tout Quarry, and landslips that dominate much of Portland's landscape. The greatest volume of passage takes place in April and May when large falls of landbirds are likely, usually involving several hundred *Phylloscopus* warblers. Other migrants that can be seen during this period include Turtle Dove, Tree Pipit, Yellow Wagtail, Redstart, Whinchat, Wheatear, the commoner warblers, Spotted and Pied Flycatchers amongst others. Certain species, such as Turtle Dove, Reed Warbler and Spotted Flycatcher, may continue to arrive well into June. A few Nightingales and Wood Warblers are seen most springs; the latter favouring areas of sycamores such as the North Woods. It is the subrarities that cause most interest. Hoopoe and Serin are regular visitors with several individuals of the latter noted annually. Both species may occur at any time between mid-March and mid-May, but the latter is notoriously a 'fly-over job'. Golden Orioles sometimes occur, usually in late May, and often feed in a shrike-like fashion on moth caterpillars in the Top Fields. Wryneck, Woodchat Shrike and Ortolan Bunting are seen most springs; whilst there are records of Richard's and Tawny Pipits, Bluethroat, Icterine and Melodious Warblers, Red-breasted Flycatcher, Red-backed Shrike and Ortolan Bunting for this season. Visual passage mainly concerns Meadow Pipits from mid-March to early April, followed by hirundines and some finch movements in April and May and finally the arrival of Swifts from late April onwards. There is a regular, but small passage of Merlins (mostly April) and Hobbies (mostly May); whilst a few Short-eared Owls regularly pass through. Larger raptors, including Honey Buzzard, Red and Black Kites, all three harriers and Osprey, have been observed on migration. Quail are almost annual visitors in late spring and summer. There is always a good chance that something rare will turn up during this period, typically species overshooting from southern and eastern Europe. These have included sightings of Red-footed Falcon, Scops Owl, Alpine Swift, Bee-eater, Short-toed Lark, Red-rumped Swallow, Black-eared Wheatear, Rock Thrush, Subalpine and Sardinian Warblers and Black-headed Bunting. There have also been representatives from

Siberia and Scandinavia in the form of Olive-backed Pipit, Pine, Rustic and Little Buntings. Despite the lack of water on Portland, there are records of Little Bittern, Night Heron, Little Egret and Spoonbill in spring.

Pomarine Skuas

By early April Manx Shearwaters, waders, skuas and terns have joined the upchannel movements of seabirds, which gradually intensify during the month to reach a peak during the first fortnight of May. The main attraction is the passage of Pomarine Skuas. This normally takes place during the comparatively short period between late April and mid-May. Numbers can vary from spring to spring but in recent years 40 to 80 birds have been recorded, the species sometimes passing in loose flocks of up to ten or more individuals. It is the Arctic Skua, however, which is the most likely member of this group to be seen; whilst Great Skuas also occur and there have been several reports of the elegant Long-tailed Skua. Terns are very much a feature of these offshore movements with Sandwich dominant in April to be replaced by Common and Arctic in May. A few Little Gulls and Black Terns together with occasional Roseate and Little Terns also move with these flocks of Common and Arctic Terns. Passing gulls are always worth checking, particularly during the early spring when the occasional Iceland and Glaucous Gull are most likely to be seen. Common Scoter is the main species of sea-duck passing upchannel, often in large flocks which may also include a scattering of Velvet Scoter. A few Eider, Long-tailed Duck and Red-breasted Merganser along with the odd flock of Brent Geese are noted most years. The most conspicuous of the waders involved in these upchannel movements are Bar-tailed Godwit and Whimbrel; whilst parties of smaller waders fly past from time to time. Unsettled weather in late May and June may bring Storm Petrels inshore, sometimes in good numbers, e.g. 78 offshore on 31 May 1993. Cory's Shearwaters have also been reported on a number of occasions. The wintering flock of Purple Sandpipers is often present well into May, usually inhabiting the rocks by the Bill and along the East Cliffs where waders such as Oystercatcher and Common Sandpiper are sometimes found. Ploughed fields occasionally attract migrant Dotterel and there is a recent spring record of a Collared Pratincole.

Portland's high vertical West Cliffs support small numbers of breeding Fulmar, Kittiwake and Guillemot along with a few pairs of Razorbill and Puffin. Herring Gulls nest in suitable areas around the island including rooftops in North Portland. Shags are present throughout the year, but do not breed on Portland. Offshore, small numbers of Gannets still occur, but the regular large summer fishing flock no longer exists. Movements of Manx and occasionally Mediterranean Shearwaters are a feature of summer evenings; whilst summer gales may also produce Storm Petrels and the occasional skua.

Both Peregrine and Raven have recently returned to Portland's cliffs and these species are likely to be encountered almost anywhere on the island throughout the year. Apart from the seabirds, Portland's cliffs also support breeding Stock Dove, Rock Pipit and Jackdaw; whilst the quarries used to provide nesting sites for the odd pair of Little Owl, a species that has declined dramatically in recent years. Although inward migration has largely ceased by early June, the midsummer period can still produce the odd overshooting rarity. In recent years there have been several sightings of Greenish Warbler and Common Rosefinch along with records of Bee-eater, Red-rumped Swallow and Thrush Nightingale. One of Portland's best rarities, an Egyptian Nightjar, was seen in June 1984.

July sees the first signs of autumn passage with the overhead movements of Swifts and a trickle of landbird migrants. Initially attention is focused on departing summer visitors, but towards late September the emphasis gradually changes to the movements of Skylarks, Meadow Pipits, thrushes, finches and buntings which continue through October into November. During the early part of the autumn one can expect to find the same variety of landbird migrants as the spring, but usually in larger numbers. Of the scarcer birds that regularly pass through, Pied Flycatchers mainly appear in August and September, but Black Redstarts, Ring Ouzels and Firecrests are generally seen later in the season. Locally dispersing Dartford Warblers have increasingly become a feature of the late autumn in recent years. Portland is renowned for the frequency with which certain landbird subrarities occur. One such speciality is the Melodious Warbler. In some autumns the numbers of individuals reported have reached double figures, although more recently the species has become rather scarce. Melodious Warblers normally appear from early August through to mid-September. The closely related Icterine Warbler is also noted most autumns and in some years has outnumbered the previous species. Ortolan Buntings regularly occur from late August onwards, favouring stubble and potato fields where they can be very elusive and difficult to see but birds sometimes drink at Culverwell or briefly 'drop-in' to the Observatory garden. Away from the Bill area, Windmill Fields at Weston is also a good area to search for Ortolan Bunting. September is the best month for Tawny Pipits which have become more frequent in recent years with at least ten, possibly as many as 18, individuals recorded in the autumn of 1983. This species shows a preference for open areas of short grass such as the Common and Admiralty Slopes. Richard's Pipits appear most years, but are more likely to be seen in October and early November. Other annual subrarities include Wryneck and Barred Warbler, mainly in late August and September followed by Yellow-browed Warbler and Red-breasted Flycatcher in late September and October and Pallas's Warbler in late October and early November. The last three species favour gardens and small sycamore copses in the centre and north of the island; Sweethill Gardens in Southwell and the environs of Easton being particularly good

Pallas's Warbler

areas. There is usually a small passage of Lapland Buntings in October and early November with the odd bird occasionally wintering. Bluethroat, Aquatic Warbler and Woodchat Shrike are also 'good bets' for the autumn, but these species do not appear every year. The visual passage of finches can be impressive during October and may include Tree Sparrow, Brambling, Siskin and Redpoll; whilst flocks of Goldfinches are worth checking through for the occasional Serin. Unlike the spring, most of the landbird rarities recorded in autumn originate from Siberia and Scandinavia ranging from Olive-backed, Pechora and Red-throated Pipits to warblers (Pallas's Grasshopper, Booted, Greenish, Arctic, Radde's and Dusky) and buntings (Rustic, Little and Yellow-breasted). More southerly 'goodies' have included the likes of Red-footed Falcon, Pallid and Alpine Swifts, Short-toed Lark, Pied and Desert Wheatears, Orphean and Bonelli's Warblers and Rose-coloured Starling. American landbirds have been few and far between, but Yellow-billed Cuckoo, Red-eyed Vireo, Northern Parula, Bobolink and Northern Waterthrush (1996) have been recorded. With Portland's track record, almost anything is likely to appear.

Migrant raptors are very much in evidence during the autumn with a few Hobbies passing through in September giving way to small numbers of Merlins in October and November, which is also a good time for Short-eared Owls and the occasional Long-eared Owl. Honey Buzzard, all three harriers and Osprey have also been seen in autumn. As a result of the now annual post-breeding influx of Little Egrets into Southern England, this species has been reported with increasing frequency from midsummer onwards as birds pass by or over Portland heading for the wetlands of the Fleet and Weymouth area. As in spring, there are also several autumn sightings of Spoonbills. Again, as in spring, Dotterel are occasional visitors, favouring ploughed fields and areas of bare ground. There are also autumn reports of Baird's, Pectoral, Buff-breasted and Upland Sandpipers.

Generally sea passage in autumn is less reliable than during the spring. Nevertheless, given the right conditions seawatching can be rewarding.

The main species to be seen include Fulmar, Manx Shearwater, Gannet, Common Scoter, Arctic and Great Skuas, Kittiwake, Sandwich, Common and Arctic Terns and auks. Early autumn is the peak time for Mediterranean Shearwaters, which have occurred offshore in modest numbers during the early 1990s; whilst tape luring at night has confirmed the presence of Storm Petrels in the English Channel at this time of year. There are also several records of Cory's Shearwater for July and August; whilst small numbers of Sooty Shearwaters pass offshore throughout the autumn. The odd Pomarine Skua and Little Gull are also likely, especially during or after gales. Other notable storm-driven seabirds such as Leach's Petrel, Grey Phalarope, Long-tailed Skua, Sabine's Gull and Little Auk, are reported most years.

Winter is rather uneventful. Offshore movements of seabirds, however, may take place, particularly during stormy and unsettled weather when the occasional Leach's Petrel, Grey Phalarope, skua (most likely Great) and Little Auk may appear. Large shoals of sprats moving upchannel often attract large numbers of divers, Gannets, sea-duck, gulls including Kittiwakes, and auks. Cold weather may induce movements and influxes of wildfowl, which have included oddities such as Barnacle and Pink-footed Geese, as well as Golden Plover, Woodcock, Skylark, winter thrushes and finches. A flock of Purple Sandpipers regularly frequents the rocks around the Bill. In mild winters a few Black Redstarts, Blackcaps, Chiffchaffs and Firecrests remain on Portland, often favouring the central and northern parts of the island. Although not a prime time for rarities, winter has produced a few surprises including a Dark-eyed Junco which overwintered in 1989/90 along with a long-staying Rose-coloured Starling; whilst there are occasional sightings of Serin.

Timing

To see landbird migrants, fall conditions are ideal, but almost any weather will produce some birds.

In spring, early mornings are best as birds rarely stop long, but diurnal migrants such as Swifts and hirundines will not begin arriving until several hours after dawn. Check the Verne and other sites later in the day for migrants that arrived at the Bill overnight and have taken a few hours to move up the island. Persistent southerlies are most likely to produce rarities.

In autumn, although mornings are again good, timing is not so important since migrants often arrive throughout the day and birds may remain in the area for several days. Persistent southerlies and easterlies are most likely to produce rarities.

In winter choose a calm fine day to look for landbirds. Hard weather may induce movements of wildfowl, waders and other birds.

Sea passage is most rewarding in spring, notably between mid-April and mid-May, and in autumn during periods of unsettled weather. Seawatching from the Bill can be attempted in any onshore (SW to SE) wind, particularly when either mist or drizzle reduces visibility. Most routine passage occurs in the first few hours after dawn. Heavier movements, however, are more likely immediately before and after weather fronts or more localised squalls pass through and could occur at any time during the day. Winds need not be strong to produce birds, in fact avoid very strong gales and heavy rain when little will be moving. Spring and summer evenings are best for observing the feeding movements of Manx Shearwaters.

Breeding seabirds, notably the auks, should be looked for during early mornings and evenings in spring and summer.

Access

Portland is reached by taking the A354 south from Wyke Regis (Weymouth) and crossing the Causeway at Ferrybridge.

Portland Bill is well signposted from Southwell which can be reached via either Weston or Easton. There is public access to the common land in the Bill area; whilst there are footpaths through the Top Fields and along the West and East Cliffs. Please note that entry to farm fields within the Bill area (and elsewhere on Portland) is strictly prohibited. Furthermore the road south from Southwell is a clearway and visitors must use the large car park at the Bill.

Portland Bird Observatory, which occupies the Old Lower Light on the left of the road between Southwell and the Bill, is normally open between March and November. Accommodation and group visits must be booked in advance with the Warden, M. Cade, Portland Bird Observatory, Old Lower Light, Portland Bill, Dorset DT5 2JT, from whom further details regarding the facilities and charges can be obtained. Members of Portland Bird Observatory are also entitled to use the facilities. Day visitors should remember that access to the Observatory's grounds is at the Warden's discretion and should not be taken for granted. Car parking is also restricted to visitors staying at the Observatory and its members.

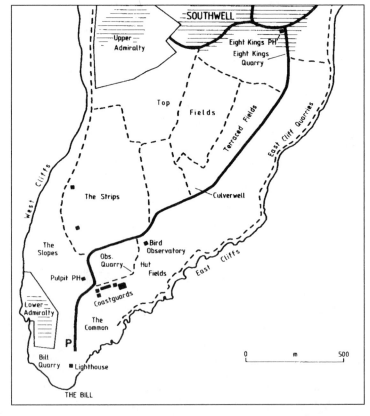

Sweet Hill Gardens can be reached from the Eight Kings PH in Southwell by following Southwell Street west, taking Sweet Hill Road left and then almost immediately left again (towards the Upper Admiralty) at the junction with Sweet Hill Lane. The gardens can be viewed from the road, but please respect the privacy of the local residents.

Weston Fields can be accessed by a circular route west along Barleycrates Lane to the West Cliffs, then south along the cliff-top footpath and returning back east past the barns and northeast along Reap Lane. Barleycrates Lane lies by the toilet block opposite the junction of Weston Road and Weston Street. The early morning passage in spring of landbird migrants along the West Cliffs can be spectacular.

Windmill Fields can be reached north along Watery Lane, which lies off Weston Street in Weston 0.2 miles (0.3 km) east of the junction with Weston Road.

Easton: the gardens, woods and disused quarry workings that lie mainly to the east and south of Easton are best accessed via numerous footpaths from Straits and Wakeham Street, the roads running east and south from Easton Square towards Pennsylvania Castle. Delhi Lane (on the right off Straits and next to Pete's Hardware shop) and Bumpers Lane (on the left off Wakeham Street) are particularly worthy of attention.

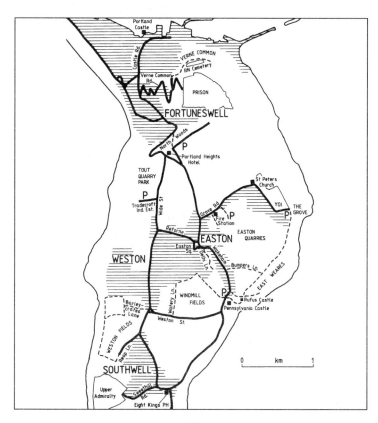

Pennsylvania Castle: from the south end of Wakeham Street follow Church Ope Road, which is signposted to Rufus Castle, East Weares and Church Ope Cove, through the arch and walk down the steps on the right past Rufus Castle. About halfway down, turn right and continue through the old churchyard into the wood. Alternatively there is a new footpath from Pennsylvania Road (almost opposite a small car park in Perryfield Quarries), past Pennsylvania Castle and down into the wood.

East Weares can be reached from Rufus Castle (see above), but by turning left halfway down the steps.

The Grove is reached from the A354 on the northern outskirts of Easton by turning east along Grove Road. The grounds of St Peter's Church and the 'ark', which is opposite the Young Offenders Institute, are both good for migrants, but the latter is private and must be viewed from the periphery. A footpath south from Grove Road by the playing fields (opposite Portland United Football Club) gives access to fields, disused quarries and the small wood behind the Fire Station.

Tout Quarry is reached from Wide Street (between Portland Heights and Reforne) by taking the road (Tradecroft) west past the industrial units and following the signs to Tout Quarry Park.

The North Woods, which comprise mainly sycamores, cloak the northern slope of Portland. These woods are the last 'stopping off' post for spring migrants moving up the island. Access is via a steep path called 'Old Hill', which lies next to the Memorial off Priory Road and opposite the back of the Portland Heights Hotel.

Verne Common is reached from the A354 (Castle Road) in Fortuneswell by taking Verne Common Road, which is signposted to H.M. Prison and R.N. Cemetery, through the housing estate to just beyond the roadbridge over the disused railway where a metalled track leads down to the entrance gate. There is general access to much of the area.

Calendar

All Year: Fulmar, Gannet, Cormorant, Shag, Peregrine, Kittiwake, Guillemot, Razorbill, Stock Dove, Little Owl, Rock Pipit, Raven.

Spring (March–May): sea passage best mid-April to mid-May – including divers; Manx and possibly Cory's Shearwaters; occasional Storm Petrel after May gales; Common Scoter and other sea-duck; waders including Bartailed Godwit and Whimbrel; skuas including Pomarine and possible Longtailed; occasional Little Gull; terns including occasional Roseate, Little and Black. Breeding seabirds from mid-March – see Summer for species.

Migrant raptors including Merlin (March–mid-April), Hobby (late April–May) and occasional larger species; Purple Sandpipers lingering to mid-May, Common Sandpiper and occasional other migrant waders; Short-eared Owl; landbird migrants including from mid-March Black Redstart, Ring Ouzel and Firecrest, from mid-April Pied Flycatcher, also annual Hoopoe and Serin anytime throughout the period, and near annual Wryneck, Golden Oriole, Woodchat Shrike and Ortolan Bunting mainly in May.

Other possible subrarities and rarities most likely in May.

Summer (mid-May–mid-July): offshore – mainly evening movements of Manx and occasional Mediterranean Shearwaters; also Gannet, terns, and during/after gales Storm Petrel and occasional skua.

Breeding seabirds including Fulmar, Kittiwake, Guillemot, Razorbill and Puffin.

Possible subrarity and rarity.

Autumn (mid-July–mid-November): sea passage best during/after gales – including Sooty, Manx and Mediterranean Shearwaters; occasional Storm and Leach's Petrels; Common Scoter and other sea-duck; occasional Grey Phalarope; skuas including Pomarine and possible Long-tailed; Little and occasional Sabine's Gulls; terns including occasional Black; auks including occasional Little Auk.

Migrant raptors including Merlin (late September–October), Hobby (late August–September) and occasional larger species; returning Purple Sandpiper flock, Common Sandpiper and occasional other migrant waders; Short-eared and possible Long-eared Owls (mainly October); landbird migrants including from early August Pied Flycatcher, from mid-September Black Redstart, Ring Ouzel, Dartford Warbler and Firecrest; also annual subrarities: from early August Icterine and Melodious Warblers, from mid-August Wryneck, Tawny Pipit, Barred Warbler and Ortolan Bunting, from mid-September Richard's Pipit, Pallas's and Yellow-browed Warblers, Red-breasted Flycatcher, Serin and Lapland Bunting.

Other possible subrarities: most likely Hoopoe, Bluethroat, Aquatic Warbler; and rarities: most likely Alpine Swift, Woodchat Shrike,.

Winter (mid-November–mid-March): during/after gales, during cold weather, following sprat shoals upchannel – occasional sea passage including divers, Common Scoter and other sea-duck/wildfowl, skuas (usually Great), Kittiwake and auks including possible Little Auk.

Fulmar from December; occasional Merlin; Purple Sandpiper; cold weather movements/influxes of Golden Plover, Woodcock, Skylark, thrushes and finches; Black Redstart, Blackcap, Chiffchaff, Firecrest, occasional Lapland Bunting.

11 PORTLAND HARBOUR, THE NOTHE AND WEYMOUTH BAY

OS Map 194
SY67

Habitat

The coastal waters to the south and east of Weymouth are sheltered from the prevailing winds by the Isle of Portland and Chesil Beach. Portland Harbour is also protected from the east by a series of large breakwaters. Shingle or sandy beaches fringe most of the coastline; whilst at

Overcombe and along the northwestern side of Portland Harbour, low crumbling cliffs back the shore. Immediately behind the southwestern shore of the harbour, a broad strip of grass sward follows the disused railway between Small Mouth, which marks the entrance to the Fleet at Ferrybridge, and the oiltanks. The Nothe, an area of public gardens behind an old fort, projects into Weymouth Bay beside the entrance to Weymouth Harbour; whilst Newton's Cove lies between the southern shore of these gardens and the most northern of the harbour breakwaters. In addition to the Nothe, further areas of cover are provided by the overgrown gardens and scrub that lie behind the northwestern shore of Portland Harbour between Sandsfoot Castle and Bincleaves.

Species

These waters are most interesting during the winter. Portland Harbour is undoubtedly the best site in the region for divers and also attracts a wide range of grebes, sea-duck and auks. Many of these birds wander to nearby Newton's Cove and Weymouth Bay.

Black-throated and Great Northern Divers are regularly present in small numbers; whilst the Red-throated Diver is somewhat scarcer, although it is recorded most winters. The grebes are also well represented and include Great Crested, the main species, along with Slavonian and Black-necked. In recent years the numbers of Slavonian Grebes have dwindled to single features, but those of Black-necked, once rare here, have increased to the extent that it is often the commoner of the two species. These waters are the most reliable in the region for the Red-necked Grebe with counts generally ranging between one to six individuals. The Red-breasted Merganser is by far the most abundant of the wildfowl, winter counts usually reaching the 300–450 mark. Small numbers of Goldeneye occur, mostly in the southwest corner of the harbour; whilst Eider, Long-tailed Duck, Common and Velvet Scoters can be expected most years. Cold snaps may bring Scaup, Smew and Goosander to Portland Harbour as well as increasing the numbers of the more regular inhabitants. Prolonged periods of easterly winds often have the same effect. A few Guillemots and Razorbills also frequent these waters; whilst Black Guillemots have wintered several times, often favouring the more distant of the harbour's breakwaters, but sometimes venturing closer inshore to Sandsfoot Castle and Newton's Cove. Little Auks occasionally appear

Red-breasted Mergansers

after late autumn and winter gales. Cormorants and Shags inhabit these waters for much of the year.

At low tide flocks of Brent Geese and waders, notably Oystercatcher and Turnstone, feed along the shores of Portland Harbour. The odd wintering Greenshank and Common Sandpiper occur, the latter species usually inhabiting Newton's Cove. Purple Sandpipers occasionally visit the harbour breakwaters and the Nothe; whilst Sanderling is a distinct possibility on the sandier shores of Weymouth Bay.

Weymouth Bay supports a massive roost of Black-headed and Common Gulls in winter with smaller gatherings at other times of the year. The roosts usually contain those Mediterranean Gulls that pass through Radipole and Lodmoor NRs earlier in the day. These birds, however, can prove difficult to locate amongst the immense numbers of commoner gulls spread across the entire width of the bay. The occasional Little Gull and Kittiwake may also appear; whilst Ring-billed Gulls have been recorded several times. The presence in recent winters of Russian trawlers and factory ships sheltering in Weymouth Bay has proved a great attraction for feeding gulls including the larger species such as Herring, Great Black-backed and Lesser Black-backed. Not surprisingly, both Iceland and Glaucous Gulls have appeared more frequently than of late with birds commuting between Weymouth Bay to feed and nearby Lodmoor NR to rest. There are also records of Franklin's, Bonaparte's and Ross's Gulls from Weymouth Bay.

Amongst the smaller birds, Rock Pipits are a familiar sight, particularly around the shores of Portland Harbour. Black Redstarts also frequent these rocky shores most winters; whilst the scrub and gardens between Sandsfoot Castle and the Nothe are favoured by Blackcaps, Chiffchaffs and Firecrests in mild winters.

Many of the divers, grebes and sea-duck remain well into the spring. Sandwich Terns appear from mid-March onwards followed by Common and Little Terns a month later. Seawatching from the Chesil has shown that a significant proportion of waders, skuas and terns pass through the harbour and Weymouth Bay, but such movements are rarely detected from the various vantage points overlooking these waters. Otherwise a scatter of landbird migrants occur, notably on the Nothe where such scarce species as Black Redstart, Wood Warbler, Firecrest and Pied Flycatcher have been seen. Wheatears are sometimes conspicuous along the disused railway by the southwest shore of the harbour which also looks a likely spot for the occasional Hoopoe.

During the spring and summer the more remote and inaccessible of the harbour breakwaters still offer refuge to a few pairs of breeding Common Terns; the remnants of a much larger colony that moved to the breakwaters after deserting their traditional breeding sites on the Chesil in the early 1980s. There is some evidence that these birds are now returning to the Fleet to breed. Oystercatcher, Great Black-backed Gull and Rock Pipit have also nested on these breakwaters.

The autumn brings a trickle of landbird migrants to such areas as the Nothe where Firecrest and Pied Flycatcher occur annually and subrarities such as Wryneck have been encountered. There are also recent sightings of Pallas's Warbler and Lesser Grey Shrike from this site. Black Redstarts regularly appear along the rocky shores and open country birds such as the Wheatear frequent the disused railway track. Seabird movements may result from autumn gales bringing the likes of skuas, Little Gull, Kittiwake and Black Tern to these waters. Grey Phalaropes often seek shelter close inshore, a flock of 28 gathered off the Nothe after one recent October storm. Other storm-driven seabirds of note recorded recently include Leach's Petrel, Sabine's Gull and Little Auk.

Timing

In winter choose a calm day for watching divers, grebes, sea-duck and auks. Overcast weather is best as glare and shadow caused by low winter sunshine can be a problem, particularly before midday. Calm days are also recommended when searching for winter landbirds.

Gulls roosting in Weymouth Bay gather from early afternoon, but the last hour of the day should be the most productive. Only in strong off-shore winds will the birds be close enough to study easily and even then a telescope is essential. From Weymouth Pavilion Pier, which is the best viewing point, the most favourable conditions are strong to gale force northwesterlies when gulls will be fairly close and side-on to the observer. Any accidental 'fish spills' from the Russian trawlers and factory ships will attract huge numbers of gulls to feed along the tideline of Weymouth Bay; Overcombe Corner being a particularly favoured site.

Seawatching is worthwhile only in autumn and winter, notably when strong easterlies with mist and rain may push birds which would otherwise be passing Portland Bill closer inshore. Severe gales from the south and west may produce the odd wrecked seabird.

Fall conditions in spring and autumn should result in a scatter of land-bird migrants. Visible passage overhead will be strongest on bright early mornings in early spring and autumn.

Disturbance is a problem at all sites throughout the year.

Access

Portland Harbour is best approached from the A354 between Wyke Regis (Weymouth) and Portland. Access to much of the shore can be attained from the Chesil Beach car park* at Ferrybridge, either along the route of the disused railway between Small Mouth (Ferrybridge) and the oiltanks or along the Dorset Coast Path from Small Mouth (Ferrybridge) to Sandsfoot Castle and then along the Underbarn footpath to Bincleaves. From Bincleaves the footpath continues north towards Newton's Cove and the Nothe. Sandsfoot Castle, which is a good vantage point to view the northern part of the harbour, can also be reached by taking Old Castle Road southwest from the sharp bend of the A354 in Rodwell (Weymouth). Bincleaves Cove in the northeast corner of Portland Harbour can be reached by taking Bincleaves Road east from the sharp bend of the A354 in Rodwell (Weymouth), parking at the end of the road and walking south across the grassy area towards the Coastguards. The southern part of the harbour is best viewed from Portland Castle. This can be reached from Cadets Corner (the hairpin bend) in Fortuneswell (Portland), by taking Castle Road towards Castletown and following the signs to the 'Aircraft viewing area' and Portland Castle.

The Nothe is well signposted from Hope Square (opposite the Brewer's Quay) east along Horsford Street and Barrack Road to the gardens and car park*. Alternatively the Nothe can be reached either (i) by parking in the car park* off Newton's Road (opposite the Brewer's Quay), walking southeast down the road to Newton's Cove and then taking the footpath northeast past the MAFF Fisheries Laboratory to the gardens; or (ii) by the Dorset Coast Path north from Bincleaves – see Portland Harbour.

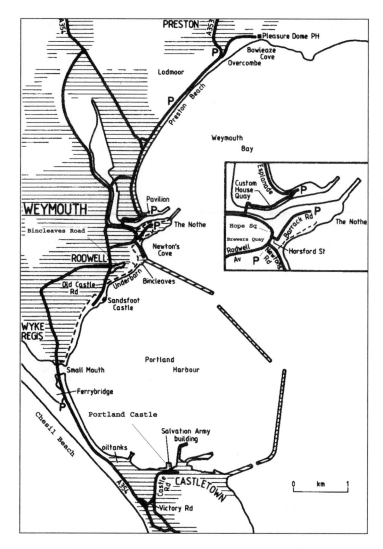

Weymouth Bay can be viewed along much of the A353 between the Pavilion Pier and Overcombe including Weymouth seafront and the sea-wall opposite Lodmoor NR. There are car parks at the Pavilion Pier (free for 20 minutes), Lodmoor NR* and Overcombe Corner*.

Calendar

All Year: Cormorant, Shag, Oystercatcher, gulls, Rock Pipit.

Winter (November–March): Red-throated (scarce), Black-throated and Great Northern Divers; Great Crested, Red-necked, Slavonian and Black-necked Grebes; wildfowl including Brent Goose, Eider, Long-tailed Duck, Common and Velvet (occasional) Scoters, Goldeneye, Red-breasted merganser, in cold weather – occasional Scaup, Smew and Goosander; waders including Common Sandpiper, occasional Sanderling, Purple

Sandpiper and Greenshank; gulls including Mediterranean, occasional Little, Iceland, Glaucous and Kittiwake; auks including occasional Black Guillemot and Little Auk; Black Redstart, Blackcap, Chiffchaff, Firecrest.

Spring (April and May): lingering divers, grebes, sea-duck and auks mainly to mid-April; possible sea passage involving waders, skuas and terns; gulls including occasional Mediterranean, Little, Iceland and Glaucous; terns; landbird migrants including occasional Black Redstart, Wood Warbler, Firecrest and Pied Flycatcher.
Most likely oddity: landbird subrarity.

Summer (mid-May–July): terns.

Autumn (August–October): during/after easterly gales – occasional sea passage including skuas, Little Gull, Kittiwake and storm-driven oddities such as Leach's Petrel, Grey Phalarope, Sabine's Gull and Little Auk.
Migrant waders including Common Sandpiper; gulls including occasional Mediterranean and Little; terns including occasional Black; landbird migrants including Black Redstart, Firecrest and Pied Flycatcher.
Most likely oddities: storm-driven seabird, landbird subrarity.

12 RADIPOLE LAKE NR (RSPB)

OS Map 194
SY66/67/68

Habitat

Situated in the heart of Weymouth and virtually surrounded by urban development, Radipole NR is the former estuary of the River Wey. The lake itself is no longer saline, the tidal influence having been eliminated by the construction of Westham Bridge at its southern end. The lower reaches of the lake consist of a shallow lagoon within which islands of reed have colonised many of the old estuarine mudbanks. Scrub-fringed footpaths run through the reedbeds and enclose the Buddleia Pool. To the north and west of the main lagoon lies the Island Sanctuary, a drier area where the reedbeds give way in places to rough meadows and invasive scrub. Further west still, beside a small tributary stream flowing into the River Wey, there is a narrow stretch of reedbed, marshy vegetation and scrub known as Chafey's Lake.

Part of Radipole Lake was designated as an official bird sanctuary by Weymouth Borough Council as far back as 1928, but it was not until 1975 that the present reserve was established under the management of the RSPB. In addition to the birds, a rich insect fauna is found on the reserve with butterflies, moths and dragonflies particularly prominent.

Species

Radipole Lake is a birdwatching site of national repute. There are several important facets to the reserve's birdlife. These are the breeding waterfowl

Mediterranean Gull

and reedbed specialities; the regularity with which unusual and rare gulls appear; the prolific winter waterfowl; and the passage of a wide range of migrants which invariably includes the odd surprise and rarity.

Although they are most numerous during the winter and early spring, gulls are present throughout the year. The main species are Black-headed and Common which during the afternoons gather in a large pre-roosting flock in front of the Visitor Centre. Smaller numbers of Herring, Great Black-backed and Lesser Black-backed Gulls can also be expected. Since the early 1970s, Radipole Lake has been one of the best sites in Britain to see Mediterranean Gulls. This species can be rather sporadic in its appearances, however, being regularly seen for several days or weeks at a time, but absent during other periods. Up to half a dozen birds sometimes pass through during a winter afternoon watch, although rarely more than two or three individuals are on view at any one time. Dorset's first Ring-billed Gulls were identified at Radipole Lake in 1976 followed by further sightings in 1978 and 1980. Subsequently this species has become somewhat of a local speciality with over 70 records to date. Birds have occurred during the winter, but there is a marked peak of reports during the spring indicating onward passage, perhaps from wintering areas in southwest Britain. Some individuals stay briefly, but others have remained for long periods and taken up temporary residence. There has been an increase in sightings of Yellow-legged Herring Gulls in recent years with most reports in winter and spring. Although Iceland and Glaucous Gulls appeared annually during the 1980s, the latter species has become much scarcer in recent years. These large white-winged gulls occur mainly during the winter and spring, but tend to be rather erratic in their visits, wandering to the lake from nearby areas such as Lodmoor NR and Weymouth Bay. Kittiwakes are seen from time to time, usually after winter storms; whilst the Little Gull is rare in winter, scarce in spring and most likely to appear in autumn. Records of Laughing, Franklin's, Sabine's and Bonaparte's Gulls complete the picture.

The lake is also an important site for wintering waterfowl. The most abundant species are Teal, Shoveler, Pochard, Tufted Duck and Coot; whilst Little and Great Crested Grebes, Cormorant, Mute Swan, Shelduck, Wigeon, Gadwall and Moorhen are also present. Scaup are rather sporadic with up to 20 or more birds mingling with the Pochard/Tufted Duck flock in some winters, but only isolated reports of one or two individuals in others. Pintail are uncommon at Radipole, being most often encountered during hard weather. Such conditions are also likely to produce such classic species as Smew and Goosander along with the occasional overflying flock of wild swans (usually Bewick's) and grey geese (usually White-fronted). There are a few reports of Goldeneye and Red-breasted Merganser most winters; whilst the odd diver, rarer winter grebe and Long-tailed Duck occur infrequently. Rarer waterfowl include records of Pied-billed Grebe, Red-crested Pochard, Ring-necked and Ferruginous Ducks.

Waders are not a major feature of the reserve during the winter. Small numbers of Snipe together with the odd Jack Snipe inhabit the wet meadows, ditches and reedbed margins; whilst influxes of Woodcock and overflying flocks of Golden Plover often occur during periods of severe cold. A variety of other waders including Greenshank are occasionally noted. Although the Radipole reedbeds used to be the best site in Dorset for the elusive Bittern, with one or perhaps two birds seen during most winters, the species has become particularly scarce in recent years with no reports in 1992, 1993 and 1994. Reedbed residents including Water Rail, Bearded Tit, Cetti's Warbler and Reed Bunting can also be seen and Blackcap, Chiffchaff and Firecrest may be present in mild winters. A few Water Pipits have also wintered in recent years. In hard weather small flocks of Bramblings sometimes appear, favouring nearby Radipole Park Gardens. There is always the chance of the odd Merlin and Peregrine passing overhead in search of prey.

Early March brings the first Chiffchaffs and Sand Martins to Radipole Lake and, in early springs, these are joined by Swallows, Sedge and Willow Warblers by the end of the month. In most years there is a pronounced passage of Swifts and hirundines which peaks during early May when daily counts of 500 to 1,000 are not unusual. In the reedbed areas there is a steady increase in the numbers of Sedge and Reed Warblers throughout the season, the latter species still arriving well into June. Grasshopper Warblers can be heard reeling in the reedbeds from mid-April onwards; whilst Savi's and Marsh Warblers are occasionally reported in spring but seldom remain longer than a few days. Large falls of *Phylloscopus* warblers together with smaller numbers of other common landbird migrants including Cuckoo, Tree Pipit, Yellow Wagtail, the chats, *Sylvia* warblers and Spotted Flycatcher, often occur in April and May. Scarcer birds such as Nightingale, Wood Warbler and Pied Flycatcher appear annually; the last two species being mostly seen in Radipole Park Gardens. Amongst the rarer landbirds, there are sightings of Hoopoe, Wryneck, Red-rumped Swallow, Bluethroat, Great Reed Warbler, Golden Oriole, and Red-backed and Woodchat Shrikes.

Large numbers of gulls including the usual selection of scarce species remain well into the spring when they are joined by a scattering of terns – mostly Common and Little but occasionally Sandwich and Black. There are also spring reports of Whiskered and White-winged Black Terns. Waders are more frequent during this season, their presence generally depending on the exposure of mud near the Visitor Centre. A wide selection of species are likely to 'drop-in' to this favoured area, including the occasional rarity – Black-winged Stilt, Temminck's Stint and Terek Sandpiper have all been seen here. Radipole Lake is one of the most reliable localities in the region for spring Garganey which occur annually from March onwards; whilst winter wildfowl frequently linger well into May. A few Hobbies pass through in late April and May and Marsh Harriers are almost annual in occurrence. Rare southern herons and their allies are a local speciality with records of Little Bittern, Night Heron, Purple Heron and Spoonbill.

The reserve supports a rich diversity of breeding birds including a number of scarce and unusual species. Bearded Tits first appeared in autumn 1964 and started breeding in 1967 with numbers reaching a peak of 34 pairs in 1978. Recent hard winters, however, have resulted in a dramatic decline with only two pairs in 1984, recovering to 15 pairs in 1990. Another speciality is the Cetti's Warbler which has become well established at Radipole Lake since its arrival in the early 1970s. This species' distinctive song is now a familiar sound on the reserve, particularly around the Buddleia Pool. Despite the cold winters of the early 1980s, the local population has seemingly survived well. There is a large colony of Reed Warblers involving several hundred pairs; whilst the reedbeds also hold good numbers of nesting Sedge Warblers and Reed Buntings, a few pairs of Water Rail and perhaps the odd pair of Grasshopper Warblers. Breeding waterfowl include Little and Great Crested Grebes and Gadwall; whilst the odd pair of Teal, Garganey, Shoveler, Pochard and Ruddy Duck have also nested or attempted to do so. Cuckoos are plentiful and a single pair of Kingfisher breeds locally. It is no surprise that recently the Little Egret has become a regular visitor, particularly during the summer and autumn. This elegant species, however, can occur at any time of the year. Its commoner relative, the Grey Heron, frequents the reserve throughout the year. A few non-breeding wildfowl remain throughout the summer and terns, mostly family groups of Common and Little, continue to visit the lake from time to time. There is always a good chance of a rarity – Squacco Heron, Purple Heron, Glossy Ibis, Spoonbill, Black-winged Stilt, Wilson's Phalarope and Caspian Tern have all appeared in summer.

Autumn is the best time for waders which, as in spring, favour the area in front of the Visitor Centre. Although numbers are small, variety is good and may include Little Ringed Plover, Little Stint, Curlew Sandpiper, Ruff, both godwits, Spotted Redshank, Greenshank, Green, Wood and Common Sandpipers amongst others; whilst oddities such as Pectoral Sandpiper, Long-billed Dowitcher, Lesser Yellowlegs, Wilson's and Red-necked Phalaropes have been reported. Little Gulls and Black Terns are seen most autumns, often after gales which may also produce the occasional Grey Phalarope. Mediterranean Gulls start to appear amongst the gull flock; whilst Sandwich, Common and Arctic Terns occur intermittently throughout. White-winged Black Terns have also been observed on several occasions in recent years. Passage Garganey are noted most years amongst the returning winter wildfowl. Radipole Lake is one of the best sites in the region for Spotted Crakes which are near annual visitors in autumn. Apart from Little Egrets, the most likely rare heron to appear in autumn is the Spoonbill; whilst there is also a recent record of a Black Stork.

Landbird migrants are again conspicuous with large numbers of Swifts and hirundines passing through, Swallows and House Martins often remaining into early November. Ringing studies in the early 1970s showed that there is a substantial passage of *Acrocephalus* warblers through the reserve's reedbeds; whilst significant arrivals of *Phylloscopus* warblers may also occur. Smaller numbers of the other common landbird migrants appear together with the occasional scarcer species such as Black Redstart, Firecrest and Pied Flycatcher. In recent years the occasional dispersing Dartford Warbler has appeared in the late autumn. Aquatic Warblers were regularly trapped during the ringing activities of the early 1970s with double figure totals in several autumns; whilst odd birds have been seen in subsequent years. There are autumn reports of such subrarities as Hoopoe, Wryneck, Bluethroat, Icterine and Melodious Warblers and Red-backed Shrike. Visual movements of Meadow Pipits and finches can be conspicuous during October when the irruptive behaviour of the Bearded Tit is at its highest.

Timing

In winter and early spring most of the local gulls feed inland by day, so a late afternoon visit as they stop to bathe and rest before going out to roost in Weymouth Bay is best; numbers and variety being greatest in windy, overcast weather. At other seasons, inland feeding is more limited, so any time of the day should suffice.

The majority of waders and gulls feed in front of the Visitor Centre, so beware of high water levels that will cover the mud normally exposed there. Levels are kept artificially high in spring/summer for the benefit of reed growth and may otherwise be high after heavy rainfall in any season.

Generally avoid very windy weather when many waterfowl and reedbed birds are likely to be skulking out of view. Very cold winter weather increases the chances of seeing such elusive reedbed specialities as Bittern and Water Rail.

At migration times, early morning are likely to be most productive, although arrivals of diurnal migrants such as Swifts and hirundines in spring will not begin until later in the day. Fine anticyclonic weather is best for southern rarities in spring.

In the breeding season reedbed birds are easiest to see early in the morning when they are singing. There may be another flurry of activity towards dusk when Grasshopper Warblers are likely to be reeling.

Access

Access to Radipole NR is best from the Swannery car park* which lies off Radipole Park Drive just to the north of Kings Roundabout. This can be reached either from the mini-roundabout opposite the clocktower on Weymouth seafront, by turning west along King Street; or from Westham Roundabout on the A354 (Weymouth Way), by turning east and crossing the new roadbridge. There is public access to the southern part of the reserve, but a permit is required for the Island area and hides – see Reserve Visit Arrangements below. The northern part of the main lake can be viewed well from Radipole Park Drive opposite the tennis courts car park, which also is a good access point to Radipole Park Gardens.

Reserve Visit Arrangements: visits by groups must be booked in advance with the Warden, M Slater, 52 Goldcroft Avenue, Weymouth, Dorset DT4 0ES (enclosing a s.a.e.). Access to the Island area and North hide is either by RSPB membership card or permit; the latter can be obtained from the Visitor Centre. Summer only concessionary car park rates for RSPB members can also be obtained from the Visitor Centre. Although the Centre is generally open daily (except Christmas Day and Boxing Day) throughout the year, times may vary. For further information contact the RSPB Visitor Centre, The Swannery Car Park, Weymouth, Dorset DT4 7TZ (tel: 01305 778313).

Calendar

All Year: Little and Great Crested Grebes, Cormorant, Little Egret, Grey Heron, Shelduck, Gadwall, Water Rail, Kingfisher, Cetti's Warbler, Bearded Tit, Reed Bunting.

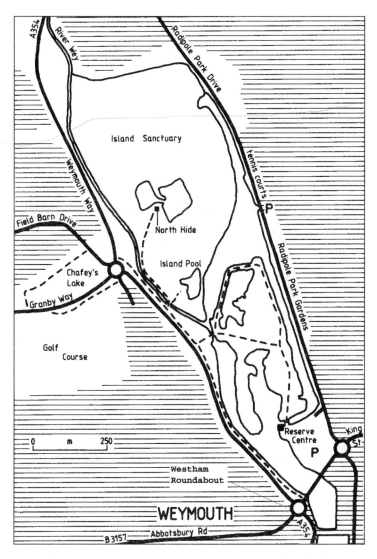

Winter (November–mid-March): possible diver and rarer winter grebe; possible Bittern; wildfowl including Wigeon, Teal, Shoveler, Pochard, Tufted Duck, occasional Pintail, Scaup, Goldeneye, Red-breasted Merganser and Ruddy Duck, in cold weather – Smew, Goosander, occasional Bewick's and Whooper Swans, and grey geese (usually White-fronted); possible Merlin and Peregrine; Snipe and occasional other waders; gulls including Mediterranean, annual Yellow-legged Herring and Iceland, occasional Little, Glaucous and Kittiwake, and possible Ring-billed; Blackcap, Chiffchaff, occasional Water Pipit, Firecrest and Brambling.

Most likely oddities: rare wildfowl and gulls.

Spring (mid-March–May): Garganey and lingering winter wildfowl; migrant raptors including Hobby and near annual Marsh Harrier; migrant waders including Common Sandpiper and occasional other species; gulls including Mediterranean, near annual Little and Iceland, occasional Glaucous, and possible Ring-billed; terns including Common, Little, occasional Sandwich and Black; landbird migrants including Swift, hirundines, Grasshopper, Sedge and Reed Warblers, annual Nightingale, Wood Warbler and Pied Flycatcher.

Most likely oddities: rare heron and allies, Temminck's Stint and other rare waders, rare gulls and terns, Savi's and Marsh Warblers.

Summer (mid-May–mid-July): occasional summering wildfowl; Common and Little Terns; Cuckoo, Grasshopper, Sedge and Reed Warblers, Lesser Whitethroat.

Most likely oddities; rare heron and allies, rare wader.

Autumn (mid-July–October): Garganey and returning winter wildfowl; migrant raptors including Hobby and occasional larger species; near annual Spotted Crake; migrant waders including Little Ringed Plover, Little Stint, Curlew Sandpiper, Ruff, both godwits, Spotted Redshank, Greenshank, Green, Wood and Common Sandpipers, possible storm-driven Grey Phalarope; gulls including Mediterranean and Little; terns including Sandwich, Common, Arctic and Black; landbird migrants including Swift, hirundines, Yellow Wagtail, Sedge and Reed Warblers, occasional Black Redstart, Dartford Warbler and Firecrest.

Most likely oddities; rare herons and allies, rare waders, White-winged Black Tern, Bluethroat, Aquatic Warbler and other landbird subrarities.

13 LODMOOR NR (RSPB)

OS Map 194
SY68

Habitat

Lodmoor Nature Reserve is situated between Weymouth to the west and the expanding village of Preston to the north and east. The southern side is bordered by the main A353 road beyond which lie the sheltered waters of Weymouth Bay. Like its near neighbour Radipole Lake, Lodmoor was once estuarine in character, but it is now an area of low-lying marshland over which there is only a little saline influence. These marshes consist of an expanse of damp pasture which is intersected by drainage ditches and several shallow lagoons and pools, some choked with rushes and sedges. Small reedbeds flank the west and east of the grazing pasture; whilst scrub fringes the drier margins of the site. The whole area is susceptible to flooding and after prolonged spells of heavy rainfall, little or none of the pasture may be visible above extensive floodwater.

The RSPB undertook to manage this area as a nature reserve in 1983. A footpath now runs around most of the reserve linking three hides overlooking Lodmoor from the south, west and north. Although the birds attract most attention, the reserve also supports an important insect fauna including hoverflies, dragonflies, bush-crickets, moths and butterflies. In addition foxes and roe deer are frequently seen.

Species

Like nearby Radipole Lake NR, Lodmoor is one of the region's best bird-watching sites; there being considerable interchange of birds between the two reserves. Since the inception of the RSPB's management plan, Lodmoor's birdlife has shown some significant changes and improvements. This is most obvious in winter with marked increases in the numbers of waterfowl, waders and gulls using the reserve notably during periods of less extensive flooding.

Wigeon is a prime example with several hundred birds now feeding and resting on the central moor when conditions are suitable; whilst good numbers of Teal, Gadwall and Shoveler along with a few Shelduck and Pintail can also be expected. Small parties of Brent Geese appear sporadically, wandering from their main wintering grounds on the nearby Fleet. Diving ducks are rather scarce, but small numbers of Pochard and Tufted Duck together with the occasional Goldeneye, Red-breasted Merganser and perhaps even Long-tailed Duck sometimes frequent the deeper pools and ditches. Smew are regularly seen during periods of hard weather, which may also produce the odd Scaup and Goosander as well as small flocks of wild swans (usually Bewick's) and grey geese (usually White-fronted). Little Grebes inhabit the pools and ditches on Lodmoor and now several pairs remain to breed; whilst divers and the other grebes occur very rarely, birds being usually oiled or storm-blown.

Large numbers of gulls loaf and rest on Lodmoor during the winter; whilst smaller gatherings are present at other times. In recent years the nearby rubbish tip has become less attractive, particularly to the larger species such as Herring, Great Black-backed and Lesser Black-backed Gulls. This has been compensated, to some extent at least, by the presence in recent winters of Russian trawlers and factory ships sheltering in Weymouth Bay. As a result of this population of larger gulls, both Iceland and Glaucous are frequent visitors, although both species have become a little scarcer than in earlier years. There have also been several sightings of the Yellow-legged Herring Gull. The numbers of Black-headed and Common Gulls increase dramatically during flood conditions when a substantial proportion of the birds that normally pass through Radipole Lake are diverted to gather in their masses on the floodwater of the open moor, prior to roosting in Weymouth Bay. This is the best time to see Mediterranean Gulls, which are otherwise rather erratic in occurrence here. Kittiwakes appear from time to time, usually oiled or storm-blown individuals; whilst Little Gulls are uncommon visitors in winter. The rare Ring-billed Gull has been reported on several occasions, mainly during the spring. There are also sightings of Laughing, Sabine's and Bonaparte's Gulls.

During the winter large flocks of Golden Plover, Lapwing and Snipe frequent Lodmoor which is also one of the best sites in Dorset for Jack Snipe. Other waders are scarce, but almost any species may turn up including the likes of Ruff and Greenshank; whilst Woodcock often feature during periods of hard weather. There are also winter records of Pacific Golden Plover and Lesser Yellowlegs. Like nearby Radipole Lake, the Bittern has become much rarer in recent winters. Cormorants, Grey Herons and resident reedbed specialities including Water Rail, Cetti's Warbler, Bearded Tit and Reed Bunting are present throughout the year. A few Water Pipits winter on the moor; whilst Kingfishers search for fish along the drainage ditches and by the pools. Finch flocks, which are often to be found around the margins of the reserve and nearby country park, may include Brambling and perhaps something more unusual such as Serin or Twite.

Bearded Tit

Of the winter raptors, the Peregrine is now a regular visitor and there is always a chance of the occasional passing Hen Harrier, Merlin or Short-eared Owl.

Waders are more obvious during the spring with the first birds, usually Oystercatcher, Curlew and Redshank, arriving in early March. These are followed later in the season by a wider range of species including Little Ringed and Ringed Plovers, Ruff, both godwits, Whimbrel, Spotted Redshank, Greenshank, Green and Common Sandpipers. Most of these occur in small numbers, but large easterly movements of Bar-tailed Godwit and Whimbrel have been witnessed on occasions. During most springs other waders such as Grey Plover, Knot and Sanderling together with the occasional Curlew Sandpiper and Wood Sandpiper are seen; whilst recent oddities include Avocet, Black-winged Stilt, Kentish Plover and Temminck's Stint. Sandwich Terns usually appear in late March followed by Common and Little Terns in April. All three species frequent Lodmoor throughout the spring and may be occasionally joined by Roseate, Arctic and Black Terns. There are also records of Whiskered and White-winged Black Terns. Large numbers of gulls are still to be seen, amongst which there is still a good chance of finding Mediterranean, Iceland, Glaucous and possibly Ring-billed Gulls. Little Gulls are more likely to pass through in spring with a few noted most years. Like Radipole Lake, Lodmoor is a good site for Garganey which occur annually in small numbers. Migrant raptors include a few Hobbies as well as the occasional larger species such as Marsh Harrier and Osprey; whilst vagrant Black Kite and Red-footed Falcons have been reported. Again, like nearby Radipole Lake, rare herons and their allies are a local speciality with records of Little Bittern, Purple Heron, White Stork and Spoonbill.

Landbird passage starts in March with the first Sand Martins, Wheatears and Chiffchaffs which may be followed before the month is out by Swallows, Yellow Wagtails, Sedge and Willow Warblers. Peak numbers of Water Pipits also occur in late March and early April. The main arrivals, however, take place during April and May. Swift and hirundine movements are not as pronounced as at nearby Radipole Lake, but three-figure counts are usually reached in early May. Throughout the spring the reedbeds attract increasing numbers of Sedge and Reed Warblers together with a few Grasshopper and the occasional Savi's Warblers. Moderate falls of *Phylloscopus* warblers sometimes occur in the scrubby areas;

whilst Yellow Wagtails, Whinchats and Wheatears favour the open moor. There is scattering of other landbird migrants which may include the odd Black Redstart and Firecrest. Hoopoes have been seen on several occasions; whilst other noteworthy landbird migrants include Wryneck, Golden Oriole and Serin.

The main breeding specialities of the reserve are Cetti's Warbler and Bearded Tit, both of which have nested regularly since the late 1970s. The reedbeds also hold good breeding populations of Sedge and Reed Warblers and Reed Buntings together with the odd pair of Grasshopper Warblers. Occasionally Gadwall and Shoveler nest on the open moor, as do the odd pair of Yellow Wagtail; whilst the scrubby drier areas fringing Lodmoor support breeding Stonechat and Lesser Whitethroat amongst others. The Cuckoo is a conspicuous bird of the reserve during the spring and early summer. Small numbers of Sandwich, Common and Little Terns, often in family groups, occasionally visit throughout the summer. Like nearby Radipole Lake NR, the Little Egret is now a regular visitor, mainly in summer and autumn although birds may appear in any month of the year. There is also a distinct chance of a summer rarity – Great White Egret, Purple Heron, Spoonbill, Bridled Tern, Bee-eater, Fan-tailed Warbler and Woodchat Shrike have all been noted during this season.

Post-breeding flocks of Lapwing are present on the moor from early June onwards; whilst the appearance of Curlew, Redshank, Green and Common Sandpipers later in the month heralds the start of the autumn wader passage. Although numbers are never high, variety is good and invariably includes Little Ringed Plover, Little Stint, Curlew Sandpiper, Ruff, both godwits, Whimbrel, Spotted Redshank, Greenshank and Wood Sandpiper amongst others. Rarer species such as Avocet, Temminck's Stint and Pectoral Sandpiper occur with some frequency; whilst Sociable Plover, White-rumped Sandpiper, Long-billed Dowitcher, Lesser Yellowlegs and Wilson's Phalarope have been seen on Lodmoor in autumn. Grey Phalaropes regularly appear during and after gales, which often bring Little Gulls, Kittiwakes and perhaps even the odd skua to seek shelter on the moor. Again Sandwich and Common Terns are noted throughout the autumn; whilst a few Black Terns pass through most years, occasionally lingering to hawk for insects over the ditches and open pools. Garganey are regular in autumn mingling with the first of the returning winter wildfowl. Migrant raptors involve annual sightings of Hobby, Merlin and Short-eared Owl, plus the occasional larger species like Marsh Harrier and Osprey.

Flocks of Swifts feed over Lodmoor during the summer and early autumn to be gradually replaced by hirundines later in the season. August and September sees a strong passage of *Acrocephalus* warblers through the reserve's reedbeds. Small numbers of the commoner landbird migrants occur along with the occasional Black Redstart, Firecrest and in recent years Dartford Warbler. Aquatic Warblers are seen most autumns; whilst Bluethroats have appeared on a number of occasions. Other landbird subrarities/rarities reported from Lodmoor include Hoopoe, Wryneck, Shorelark, Richard's, Tawny and Red-throated Pipits, Melodious and Barred Warblers. Other rarities not already mentioned for the autumn involve reports of Black Stork, Glossy Ibis, Spoonbill and American Wigeon.

Timing

In all seasons there are likely to be more birds present when Lodmoor is partially flooded after heavy rainfall. Otherwise timing is not too important for waterfowl and waders as there is little disturbance and no tidal influences to consider.

In recent years the arrival of Russian trawlers and factory ships in winter has attracted large numbers of gulls which visit Lodmoor to loaf and rest. The smaller species of gull attracted to Lodmoor during flood conditions follow the same diurnal pattern as described for Radipole Lake NR.

Although hard winter weather should increase both the abundance and variety of birds present, numbers will drop if persistently cold weather causes the water to ice over and reduce feeding opportunities.

Reedbed birds will be most active and easiest to see early on a calm morning. Similarly landbird migrants are best looked for early in the morning, although in spring there may be further arrivals later in the day as birds filter through after making earlier landfall on Portland.

There is a good deal of interchange of birds between Lodmoor and Radipole Lake NRs, so if conditions are unfavourable at one site, try a visit to the other.

Access

Lodmoor NR is best approached from the Preston Beach Road car park*, which is well signposted from the A353 between Weymouth and Preston just to the east of the Country Park. There is public access around the perimeter of the reserve and to the hides by means of footpaths. This now includes the Overcombe end of the reserve where paths eventually link into the Overcombe car park*.

Reserve Visit Arrangements: no permits are required, but visits by groups must be booked in advance with the Warden, M Slater, 52 Goldcroft Avenue, Weymouth, Dorset DT4 0ES (enclosing a s.a.e.).

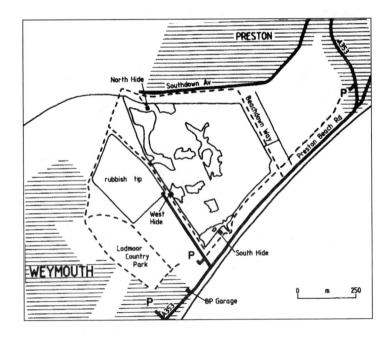

Calendar

All Year: Cormorant, Little Egret, Grey Heron, Shelduck, Water Rail, Cetti's Warbler, Bearded Tit, Reed Bunting.

Winter (November–mid-March): Little Grebe; possible Bittern; wildfowl including Wigeon, Gadwall, Teal, Pintail, Shoveler, Pochard, Tufted Duck, occasional Brent Goose, Goldeneye and Red-breasted Merganser, in cold weather Smew, occasional Bewick's Swans, grey geese (usually White-fronted), Scaup and Goosander; Peregrine, occasional Hen Harrier and Merlin; Golden Plover, Lapwing, Jack Snipe, Snipe and occasional other waders; gulls including Mediterranean, near annual Iceland and Glaucous, occasional Little and Kittiwake, and possible Ring-billed; occasional Short-eared Owl; Kingfisher, Water Pipit, occasional Chiff-chaff, occasional Brambling amongst finch flocks.

Most likely oddities: rare wildfowl and gulls.

Spring (mid-March–May): Garganey and lingering wildfowl; migrant raptors including Hobby and near annual Marsh Harrier; migrant waders including Little Ringed Plover, Ruff, both godwits, Whimbrel, Spotted Redshank, Greenshank, Green and Common Sandpipers, occasional other species; gulls including occasional Mediterranean, Little, Iceland and Glaucous, and possible Ring-billed; terns including Sandwich, Common, Little, occasional Roseate, Arctic and Black; landbird migrants including Swift, hirundines, Water Pipit, Yellow Wagtail, Whinchat, Wheatear, Grasshopper, Sedge and Reed Warblers, occasional Black Redstart and Firecrest.

Most likely oddities: rare heron and allies, Temminck's Stint and other rare waders, rare gulls and terns, Savi's Warbler.

Summer (mid-May–mid-July): Sandwich, Common and Little Terns; Cuckoo, Yellow Wagtail, Grasshopper, Sedge and Reed Warblers, Lesser Whitethroat.

Most likely oddities: rare heron and allies, rare wader.

Autumn (mid-July–October): Garganey and returning winter wildfowl; migrant raptors including Merlin, Hobby and near annual Marsh Harrier; migrant waders including Little Ringed Plover, Little Stint, Curlew Sandpiper, Ruff, both godwits, Whimbrel, Spotted Redshank, Greenshank, Green, Wood and Common Sandpipers, occasional storm-driven Grey Phalarope; possible storm driven skua; gulls including Little and occasional Kittiwake; terns including Sandwich, Common, Little and Black; occasional Short-eared Owl; landbird migrants including Swifts, hirundines, Yellow Wagtail, Sedge and Reed Warblers, occasional Black Redstart, Dartford Warbler and Firecrest.

Most likely oddities: rare herons and allies, Temminck's Stint, Pectoral Sandpiper and other rare American waders, Bluethroat, Aquatic Warbler and other landbird subrarities.

PURBECK AND POOLE BASIN

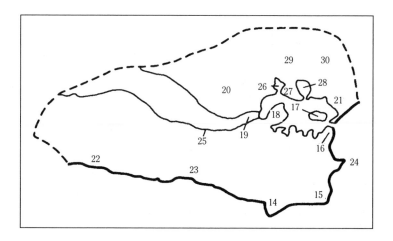

14 ST ALDHELM'S HEAD, WINSPIT
    AND DANCING LEDGE
15 DURLSTON COUNTRY PARK
16 STUDLAND NNR
17 BROWNSEA ISLAND
18 ARNE NR
19 WAREHAM WATER-MEADOWS
    AND SWINEHAM POINT
20 WAREHAM FOREST
21 POOLE PARK AND SANDBANKS

Other Sites Worthy Of Attention
22 West Purbeck Coast from
    Redcliff Point to White Nothe
23 Tyneham Valley and Gad Cliff
24 Ballard Down
25 Lower Frome Valley
26 Lytchett Bay
27 Ham Common LNR
28 Upton County Park and
    Holes Bay
29 Upton Heath
30 Canford Heath and Hatch
    Pond

General Introduction

A varied geology and striking landscape makes this the most scenically impressive area of the region. Habitats are diverse, the Jurassic limestone and Cretaceous chalk creating spectacular coastal cliffs and rolling downland including the high Purbeck Ridge; whilst the Tertiary deposits naturally give rise to heathland which surrounds, albeit fragmentally, Poole Harbour. Like elsewhere in the region, these heathlands have steadily diminished in extent due to a number of factors such as building development and reclamation for farmland and forestry – the latter being particularly extensive to the north and west of Wareham. Poole Basin is transected by the floodplains of two major rivers, the Frome and the

Piddle, which flow eastwards into what is reputed to be the world's second largest natural harbour. With its deeply indented shoreline and islands (the largest being Brownsea), Poole Harbour supports a wide selection of wetland and estuarine habitats. To the south of the harbour entrance, the low shoreline consists of long sweeping bays with sandy beaches backed by dunes. The area is of great importance for breeding birds which include colonies of seabirds on the Purbeck Cliffs, waders, gulls and terns in Poole Harbour and heathland specialities such as the Dartford Warbler. Poole Harbour also hosts an abundance of waterfowl, waders and gulls in winter and at times of passage; whilst there are several good migration sites along the Purbeck coasts, notably at Durlston Country Park and in the vicinity of St Aldhelm's Head.

14 ST ALDHELM'S HEAD, WINSPIT AND DANCING LEDGE

OS Map 195 & Purbeck
SY97

Habitat

St Aldhelm's Head with its spectacular cliffs, which are some of the highest along this coast, forms the southernmost point of Purbeck. A boulder scree colonised by scrub surrounds the undercliff; whilst at the top there is a small disused quarry. Inland from the head there are large open fields, some stone walls and comparatively little cover.

To the northwest of St Aldhelm's Head lies Chapman's Pool, a sheltered bay behind which a steep-sided valley extends inland. There is a large wood in the middle of this valley; whilst the remainder is filled with dense scrub. Much of the land between St Aldhelm's and Chapman's Pool, notably along the base of Emmetts Hill, suffers from landslips. This has resulted in slopes of irregular relief which are densely vegetated by scrub and sycamore trees.

Winspit is a sheltered valley, which runs from the village of Worth Matravers south to some disused limestone quarries on the edge of the Purbeck Cliffs. Most of the lower slopes, particularly where a stream has formed a deep gully, are cloaked by dense scrub; whilst further cover is provided by an overgrown garden and a small wood in the grounds of a disused quarry. The upper slopes of the valley consist mainly of downland pasture and fields, some of which are bordered by stone walls and scrubby hedges. From the coastal quarries, high vertical cliffs extend southwest towards St Aldhelm's Head and northeast towards Seacombe. Further east beyond Seacombe lies Dancing Ledge, yet another disused quarry set in the limestone cliffs.

The entire area is famous for its limestone flora and fauna; orchids and butterflies being particularly well represented.

Species

The cliffs between Seacombe and St Aldhelm's Head are the best and most accessible in the region for watching breeding seabirds. During the

Puffins

spring and summer months good numbers of Fulmar, Shag, Herring Gull and Guillemot along with a few Razorbills and Puffins are present. The once thriving population of Kittiwakes has declined dramatically on the Purbecks in recent years, the surviving birds favouring Blackers Hole just to the east of Dancing Ledge. The most reliable sites for seeing Puffins are from Dancing Ledge (particularly in the evening) and the cliffs about halfway between Winspit and St Aldhelm's Head. Both the Peregrine and Raven have re-established themselves on the Purbeck Cliffs in recent years; whilst Stock Dove, Rock Pipit and Jackdaw breed widely along this coastline. There is also a cliff-nesting colony of Swifts near Dancing Ledge. Amongst the other breeding birds of interest that reside in this area, Grey and Red-legged Partridges occur in rough grassland and open downland, Little Owls frequent the disused quarries and Corn Buntings can be found in the fields behind St Aldhelm's Head.

St Aldhelm's Head is a good vantage point for seawatching. In spring, seabird movements involve a similar variety of species to those recorded off nearby Durlston CP. These regularly include divers, Manx Shearwater, Gannet, Common Scoter and other sea-duck, waders including Bar-tailed Godwit and Whimbrel, skuas including a few Pomarine and Great, Little Gull and terns including Little and Black. Movements of some seabirds, particularly Manx Shearwater, may continue throughout the summer which in some recent years has also produced a small number of Storm Petrels. Otherwise a few Sandwich and Common Terns may drift along this coast in search of fish. Less is known about autumn seawatching, but observations suggest that Gannet, Common Scoter, Kittiwake and terns are all likely to be seen; whilst there are reports of Sooty, Manx and Mediterranean Shearwaters, Pomarine, Arctic and Great Skuas and Sabine's Gull. After severe gales Grey Phalaropes often seek shelter in Chapman's Pool. A scattering of waders occur along the shoreline, notably at times of passage. The most favoured area is Chapman's Pool and the small freshwater pools behind. Oystercatcher and Common Sandpiper are the most frequent species to appear, but a wide variety of waders has been recorded.

The Winspit Valley, Chapman's Pool and to a lesser extent St Aldhelm's are good areas to search for landbird migrants. Although the numbers of birds in spring can be small compared to those passing through during the autumn, a wide selection of species can be expected in both seasons.

Peregrine

These include Turtle Dove, Tree Pipit, Yellow Wagtail, Nightingale, Black Redstart, Whinchat, Wheatear, Ring Ouzel, the commoner warblers, Firecrest, Spotted and Pied Flycatchers. The disused quarries at Winspit and St Aldhelm's are favoured by Black Redstarts. Ring Ouzels also like these areas as well as the scrub-covered undercliff between St Aldhelm's Head and Chapman's Pool; whilst Nightingales, Firecrests and Pied Flycatchers prefer the scrub and woodland in the Winspit Valley and around Chapman's Pool. Visual migration includes a huge passage of House Martins in September and finch movements during October and early November. The latter may involve small numbers of Siskins and Redpolls along with the occasional flock of Bramblings. The potential of this part of the Purbeck Coast to attract unusual and rare landbird migrants is considerable. Noteworthy species seen in recent years include Great Spotted Cuckoo, Hoopoe, Wryneck, Richard's and Tawny Pipits, Bluethroat, Black-eared Wheatear, Marsh, Booted, Icterine, Melodious, Barred, Radde's, Pallas's and Yellow-browed Warblers, Red-breasted Flycatcher, Isabelline and Woodchat Shrikes, Serin, Common Rosefinch and Ortolan Bunting as well as the much admired Red-flanked Bluetail of October/November 1993.

Amongst the migrant raptors a few Hobbies together with the occasional Merlin and Short-eared Owl, occur in spring; whilst all three species regularly appear in small numbers during the autumn. Honey Buzzard, Red Kite, Marsh and Montagu's Harrier, Goshawk and Osprey have also been observed on passage. There have been several sightings of Spoonbills passing off St Aldhelm's Head and a Purple Heron was seen flying south from Chapman's Pool early one October morning.

Winter is the least rewarding time to visit the area. Nevertheless a number of interesting birds may be seen. Fulmar, Kittiwake, Guillemot and Razorbill return to the cliffs during January and February; whilst movements of divers, Gannet, various sea-duck, Kittiwake and auks occasionally take place offshore. The odd flock of Oystercatcher, Redshank and perhaps Purple Sandpiper sometimes visit Chapman's Pool and the Winspit Ledges. Hen Harriers and Merlins frequently roam this area of Purbeck in search of prey. In mild winters Chiffchaffs and Firecrests inhabit the more sheltered parts of the Winspit Valley and Chapman's Pool and there is a good chance of finding Black Redstarts in the quarries. Winter rarities include the famous Wallcreeper, which took up temporary residence in the Winspit area in 1969/70; whilst there are also records of Common Crane and Serin.

Timing

Breeding seabirds are present between March and early July. Most species are active throughout the day, but Puffins and the other auks are most likely to be seen in the early morning and evening.

Spring seawatching is most productive early in the morning, between mid-April and mid-May, when the winds are onshore (SW to SE) in direction. If conditions are particularly good, movements may continue throughout the day. Autumn sea passage is most likely to occur during unsettled weather when the winds are just below gale force and onshore.

Early morning visits are also advisable when searching for landbird migrants, notably in spring. The best arrivals of birds occur in fall conditions.

Since the area suffers from considerable disturbance during the summer and at weekends throughout the year, an early start is to be recommended.

Access

This part of the Purbeck Coast is within easy reach of Worth Matravers. There is a small car park* just north of the Square and Compass PH on the outskirts of the village.

St Aldhelm's Head can be reached from Worth Matravers by taking the minor road west to the car park by Renscombe Farm and then walking south on the unmade road to the chapel and Coastguards Station. From here, the Dorset Coast Path can be followed either east towards Winspit or north towards Chapman's Pool.

Chapman's Pool is reached by walking along the gated road from Renscombe Farm north and then west to Hill Bottom. Just after the road crosses a stream, diverging footpaths continue either side of the valley down to the shore.

Due to landslips, access is now difficult and the Dorset Coast Path between Chapman's Pool and St Aldhelm's Head has been diverted along the top of Emmetts Hill.

Winspit can be approached on footpaths either south from the centre of Worth Matravers by the village green or south from the minor road immediately to the west of the village. These footpaths merge by the sewage works and continue as a rough track south to the coastal quarries, passing a small wood in a quarry on the right and an overgrown garden on the left. From the coastal quarries, the Dorset Coast Path can be followed either southwest to St Aldhelm's Head or northeast to Seacombe. From Seacombe, which can also be reached on a footpath east and then south from Worth Matravers, the Dorset Coast Path continues east to Dancing Ledge and beyond to Durlston CP.

Alternatively there is a shorter route to Dancing Ledge from Langton Matravers by taking Durnford Drove south past Spyway House to a small car park. From here follow the footpath south to Spyway Barn and beyond to Dancing Ledge.

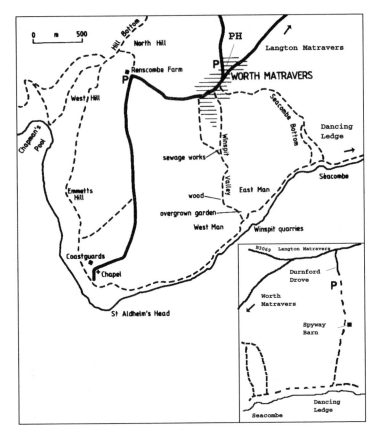

Calendar

All Year: Fulmar, Gannet, Cormorant, Shag, Peregrine, Red-legged and Grey Partridges, Kittiwake, Guillemot, Razorbill, Stock Dove, Little Owl, Rock Pipit, Stonechat, Raven, Corn Bunting.

Spring (March–May): sea passage best mid-April to mid-May – including divers; Manx Shearwater; Common Scoter and other sea-duck; waders including Bar-tailed Godwit and Whimbrel; skuas including Pomarine and Great; frequent Little Gull; terns including Little and Black. Breeding seabirds from mid-March – see Summer for species.

Migrant raptors including Hobby, occasional Merlin and possible larger species; migrant waders including Common Sandpiper and occasional other species; occasional Short-eared owl; landbird migrants including from mid-March Black Redstart, Ring Ouzel and Firecrest, from mid-April Pied Flycatcher and occasional Nightingale.

Most likely oddities: Hoopoe, Wryneck and other landbird subrarities.

Summer (mid-May–mid-July): offshore – frequent evening movements of Manx Shearwater and occasional Storm Petrel; also terns, and during/after gales occasional skua.

Breeding seabirds including Fulmar, Shag, Kittiwake, Guillemot, Razorbill and Puffin.

Autumn (mid-July–mid-November): sea passage most likely during/ after gales – including Manx, occasional Mediterranean and possible Sooty Shearwaters; Common Scoter and occasional other sea-duck; occasional Grey Phalarope; skuas including occasional Pomarine and Great; occasional Little and possible Sabine's Gulls; terns.

Migrant raptors including Merlin (October), Hobby (September), and possible larger species; migrant waders including Common Sandpiper and occasional other species; Short-eared Owl (October); landbird migrants including from early August Nightingale and Pied Flycatcher, from mid-September Black Redstart, Ring Ouzel and Firecrest.

Most likely oddities: Wryneck, Tawny and Richard's Pipits, Icterine, Melodious and Yellow-browed Warblers, Red-breasted Flycatcher and other landbird subrarities.

Winter (mid-November–mid-March): during/after gales, during cold weather, following sprat shoals upchannel – occasional sea passage including divers, Common Scoter and other sea-duck/wildfowl, skuas (usually Great), Kittiwake and auks.

Hen Harrier and Merlin; occasional waders on shore; Blackcap, Chiffchaff, Firecrest and occasional Black Redstart.

15 DURLSTON COUNTRY PARK (DCC)

OS Map 195 & Purbeck
SZ07

Habitat

Durlston Country Park is situated in the extreme southeast corner of the limestone block that forms the southern part of the Isle of Purbeck. The Country Park supports a variety of limestone habitats, the most impressive being the spectacular high cliffs along the southern coastline. The short eastern shoreline of Durlston Bay, which lies between Durlston Head and Peveril Point, is backed by steeply sloping cliffs covered with dense scrub. There are several woods and small copses in the park, notably overlooking Durlston Bay, in the vicinity of Durlston Castle and behind the Information Centre. Another major feature of the area is the deep scrub-filled gully that extends from Tilly Whim inland towards Round Down. Otherwise the south-facing slopes consist of open downland with patches of scrub; whilst further inland the park comprises a mosaic of small fields divided by stone walls and dense scrubby hedges.

Durlston Country Park was established by Dorset County Council in 1978. In addition to the birds, a diverse limestone flora and fauna can be found in the park with orchids and butterflies particularly noteworthy groups.

Species

For many years the Purbeck Cliffs between Durlston Head and St Aldhelm's Head have been famous for their breeding seabirds. Furthermore, Durlston Head's commanding position has made it a likely place to attract migrants and a good vantage point for seawatching. The full potential of this area, however, was not realised until the Country Park was established. Since then, almost daily coverage of the park has shown it to be one of the most important sites in the region for studying bird migration. An impressive variety of scarce and uncommon species has been noted here; whilst the numbers of some of the commoner landbird migrants often match or exceed those recorded at Portland Bird Observatory. When conditions are good, sea passage can be very rewarding.

March heralds the first signs of spring migration with the arrival of Chiffchaffs and Wheatears, and the visual passage of Meadow Pipits. The second half of the month is a good time to see some of the scarcer landbird migrants such as Black Redstart, Ring Ouzel and Firecrest. The bulk of the passage, however, takes place during April and May when large falls of *Phylloscopus* warblers are likely. A wide selection of other landbird migrants, including Turtle Dove, Tree Pipit, Yellow Wagtail, Redstart, Whinchat, Wheatear, the other common warblers, and Spotted Flycatcher, also pass through. Durlston CP is the best coastal site in the region for passage Wood Warblers; whilst other scarce migrants such as Nightingale and Pied Flycatcher regularly occur. Serins have been recorded annually in recent years. Other spring oddities have included sightings of Alpine Swift, Bee-eater, Hoopoe, Wryneck, Richard's and Tawny Pipits, Subalpine Warbler, Golden Oriole, Red-backed Shrike and Common Rosefinch.

Hoopoe

Migrant raptors include a few Hobbies, which have been observed chasing incoming migrants such as hirundines; whilst Merlin and Short-eared Owl are seen most springs. Large raptors such as Honey Buzzard, Black Kite, Marsh and Montagu's Harriers, Goshawk and Osprey have also been recorded here. There is a small passage of Common Sandpipers which favour Durlston Beach; whilst other migrant waders occasionally pass overhead. Spring rarities not already mentioned above involve two sightings of Bonaparte's Gulls and one of Common Crane.

Sea passage, which occurs mostly between mid-March and mid-May, is a reflection on a smaller scale of the movements that take place off

Portland Bill to the west. Birds to be expected during these spring sea-watches include divers, Manx Shearwater, Gannet, Common Scoter and other sea-duck, waders including Bar-tailed Godwit and Whimbrel, skuas including Pomarine and Great, Little Gull and terns including Little and Black. There is also a spring record of Long-tailed Skua.

During the spring and summer the cliffs are alive with nesting seabirds. The most abundant species are Herring Gull and Guillemot; whilst smaller numbers of Fulmar, Shag and Razorbill are also present. The once thriving Kittiwake colony deserted the cliffs in 1991, although a few birds can still be expected offshore. The Puffin is a rather scarce and erratic visitor to the country park and is best looked for further west along the Purbeck Coast. Cormorants can be seen throughout the year. Other breeding birds associated with the cliffs include Stock Dove, Rock Pipit and Jackdaw. Away from the cliffs, the woods and scrubby areas support a wide selection of breeding birds including Green Wood-pecker, Stonechat, Lesser Whitethroat, Garden Warbler, Treecreeper, Linnet and Yellowhammer and occasionally Nightingale. Peregrines can now be seen throughout the year; whilst Ravens are recorded with increasing frequency. There have also been midsummer sightings of such rarities as Red-footed Falcon and Woodchat Shrike.

Seabird movements can occur throughout the summer, Manx Shear-water, Gannet, Common Scoter, Sandwich and Common Terns are the most likely species to be seen. In recent years Storm Petrels have been seen with increasing frequency, particularly in June; whilst there is always the chance of something more unusual such as Cory's Shear-water. Otherwise a few Sandwich and Common Terns regularly fish in Durlston Bay, most often in the evenings.

The autumn migration of landbirds commences in July with the overhead passage of Swifts and hirundines, the latter continuing well into September when spectacular movements of Swallows and House Martins have been recorded. Nocturnal migration, involving the same variety of species as the spring but usually in larger numbers, builds up to reach its peak in August and September. This nocturnal passage diminishes during October when diurnal movements of Skylarks, Meadow Pipits and finches become prominent. Amongst the scarcer migrants that regularly appear, Nightingale, Wood Warbler and Pied Flycatcher can be expected early in the autumn; whilst Black Redstart, Ring Ouzel and Firecrest occur later in the season. The late autumn finch movements frequently include such species as Brambling, Siskin and Redpoll. The Country Park boasts a good list of autumn landbird subrarities and rarities. In recent years such species as Wryneck, Tawny Pipit, Icterine, Melodious and Yellow-browed Warblers, Red-backed Shrike, Lapland and Ortolan Buntings have almost become annual in their occurrences. There have also been autumn reports of Alpine Swift, Hoopoe, Red-rumped Swallow, Richard's Pipit, Aquatic, and Pallas's Warblers, Red-breasted Flycatcher, Isabelline and Woodchat Shrikes and Serin.

Migrant raptors are very much a feature of the autumn. A scattering of Merlins, Hobbies and Short-eared Owls pass through; whilst larger species such as Honey Buzzard, Marsh, Hen and Montagu's Harriers, and Osprey have been seen. There is a small passage of commoner waders, mainly involving birds either passing offshore or overhead although some species such as Common Sandpipers often frequent Durlston Beach.

Autumn seawatching can be very rewarding when conditions are suitable. The most likely species to be seen are Fulmar, Manx Shearwater, Gannet, Common Scoter, Arctic Skua, Kittiwake, Sandwich, Common and Arctic Terns and auks. A few Sooty and Mediterranean Shearwaters, Pomarine and Great Skuas occur each autumn; whilst Little Gull and Black Tern occasionally pass offshore. Amongst the more unusual species noted in recent years, there are reports of Storm and Leach's Petrels, Grey Phalarope, Long-tailed Skua, Sabine's Gull and Little Auk.

Winter tends to be a fairly quite season for birds. Offshore, large movements of seabirds sometimes take place, mostly involving divers, Gannet, sea-duck and other wildfowl including the occasional surprise such as Pink-footed Geese, waders, the odd skua – usually Great, Kittiwake and auks. These movements are usually associated with either gales, cold weather or the presence of sprat shoals offshore. Amongst the breeding seabirds, Fulmars return during December and Guillemots follow in January. A few Oystercatchers and Redshank feed on Durlston Beach and the odd flock of Purple Sandpipers occasionally visit the rocky ledges. Hen Harriers and Merlins appear from time to time; whilst in mild winters Blackcaps, Chiffchaffs and Firecrests may be found in the woods and areas of scrub and the occasional Black Redstart inhabits the cliffs and rocky beaches. By contrast, periods of severe cold invariably brings such classic birds as Golden Plover, Woodcock, Snipe, winter thrushes and finches to the park.

Winter has produced Durlston's two best rarities – Britain's and Europe's only Brown Thrasher, which took up temporary residence between November 1966 and February 1967; and a Black-browed Albatross, which sailed past with Gannets in February 1980.

Timing

Landbird migrants are most likely to be found when fall conditions prevail. Early morning visits are advisable, particularly in spring, as birds which have arrived overnight tend to move on quickly. Diurnal migrants, however, may not appear until later in the day.

Spring seawatching is most consistent between mid-April and mid-May when the winds are onshore (SW to SE) in direction. Most passage takes place during the early morning, but movements may continue through the day if conditions are suitable. In autumn seawatching tends to be most rewarding when the winds are strong, but just below gale force (5–7) and onshore (SW to SE) in direction.

Most of the breeding seabirds can be seen well throughout the day, but Guillemots and Razorbills are best observed early in the morning and evening.

Generally the Country Park is popular with visitors and holidaymakers, so again early mornings are recommended to avoid undue disturbance.

Access

Durlston Country Park is well signposted from Swanage and can be reached from the seafront by taking Seymer Road south by the Peveril Inn and continuing along Durlston/Lighthouse Roads to the Country Park car parks*. Well marked footpaths and nature trails give access to much of the park and cliff-tops. Guided walks are available and visitors should check for details at the Information Centre which also has excellent educational facilities and exhibits. The centre is open 10.30 am–5.30 pm, 1 April (or Easter) to 30 September and at limited times during the winter. Organised groups wishing to visit the Country Park should book in advance with the Warden, R.J.H. Murray, Durlston Country Park, Swanage, Dorset. Visitors are also urged to send their records to the Warden.

Calendar

All Year: Fulmar, Gannet, Cormorant, Shag, Peregrine, Oystercatcher, Kittiwake, Guillemot, Razorbill, Stock Dove, Rock Pipit, Stonechat, Raven, common resident woodland birds.

Spring (March-May): sea passage best mid-April to mid-May – including divers; Manx Shearwater; Common Scoter and other sea-duck; waders including Bar-tailed Godwit and Whimbrel; skuas including Pomarine and Great; Little Gull; terns including Little and Black. Breeding seabirds from mid-March – see Summer for species.

Migrant raptors including Hobby occasional other species; occasional Short-eared Owl; landbird migrants including from mid-March Black Redstart, Ring Ouzel and Firecrest, from mid-April Nightingale, Wood Warbler and Pied Flycatcher.

Most likely oddities: Hoopoe, Golden Oriole, Serin and other landbird subrarities.

Summer (mid-May–mid-July): offshore – occasional evening movements of Manx Shearwater; also Gannet, terns, occasional Storm Petrel and Puffin, and during/after gales occasional skua.

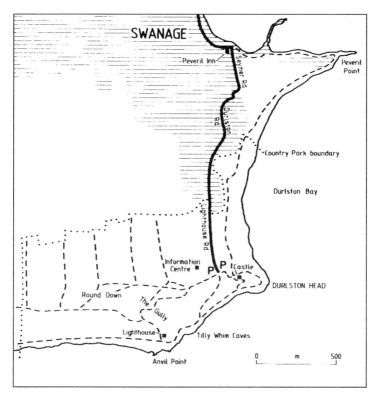

Breeding seabirds including Fulmar, Guillemot and Razorbill; occasional Nightingale.

Autumn (mid-July–mid-November): sea passage most likely during strong winds – including Manx and annual Sooty and Mediterranean Shearwaters; occasional Storm and Leach's Petrels; Common Scoter and other sea-duck/wildfowl; occasional Grey Phalarope; skuas including Pomarine and possible Long-tailed; occasional Little and Sabine's Gulls; terns including occasional Black; auks including occasional Little Auk.

Migrant raptors including Merlin, Hobby and occasional larger species; migrant waders including Common Sandpiper and occasional other species; Short-eared Owl; landbird migrants including from early August Nightingale and Pied Flycatcher, from mid-September Black Redstart, Ring Ouzel and Firecrest.

Most likely oddities: Wryneck, Tawny Pipit, Icterine, Melodious and Yellow-browed Warblers, Red-backed Shrike, Lapland and Ortolan Buntings, and other landbird subrarities.

Winter (mid-November–mid-March): during/after gales, during cold weather, following sprat shoals upchannel – occasional sea passage including divers, Common Scoter and other sea-duck/wildfowl, skuas (usually Great), Kittiwake and auks.

Fulmar from December, Guillemot from January, Kittiwake from February; occasional Hen Harrier and Merlin; Oystercatcher, Redshank and possible Purple Sandpiper; cold weather movements/influxes of Golden Plover, Woodcock, Skylark, thrushes and finches; Blackcap, Chiffchaff, Firecrest and occasional Black Redstart.

16 STUDLAND NNR (EN) OS Map 195 & Purbeck SZ08

Habitat

Studland National Nature Reserve lies in the southeast corner of Poole Harbour and supports a wide range of coastal, estuarine, freshwater, heathland and woodland habitats. The Studland Peninsula is dominated by Little Sea, which is a large freshwater lake formed during the last century by the northwards development of sand dunes along Studland Bay. The lake is fringed by reedswamp and surrounded with extensive woodlands of birch, sallow, oak and Scots pine. The remainder of the reserve, including Godlingston Heath, mostly comprises heathland with areas of gorse and sphagnum bog. The seaward coastline of the peninsular consists of long sandy beaches backed by sand dunes which overlook the sheltered waters of Studland and Shell Bays. The harbour foreshore is estuarine in character with muddy shingle and *Spartina* saltmarshes; the latter being particularly extensive in Brand's Bay where they are intersected by numerous muddy creeks and channels.

This is undoubtedly one of the finest areas for heathland natural history in the region. In 1962, 430 acres of Studland Heath were designated a National Nature Reserve under the management of the Nature Conservancy Council (now English Nature). A further 1127 acres of Studland and Godlingston Heaths were added to the reserve in 1980. The area is renowned for its dragonfly fauna with some 20 species, including several scarce specialities, occurring on the reserve; whilst butterflies are equally well represented with at least 30 species recorded. All six British reptiles are also present including those national rarities the smooth snake and sand lizard.

Species

The Studland Peninsula is ideally situated for observing the great diversity and abundance of birds using Poole Harbour and the inshore waters of Poole Bay during the winter.

Perhaps the most obvious species of wildfowl is the Red-breasted Merganser with a wintering population of several hundred birds. Small parties are commonly found scattered throughout the harbour and Studland/Shell Bay areas. Somewhere in the region of 100 to 200 Goldeneye are also present, but unlike the previous species they are mainly confined to the harbour itself and Little Sea. The Long-tailed Duck is also a local speciality, numbers varying from one or two individuals in poor winters to six or more birds in good ones. This species can be rather elusive, favouring the harbour's waters close to South Haven and Brand's Bay. A small flock of Eider usually frequents Studland and Shell Bays with birds occasionally wandering into the harbour. A few Common Scoter also winter in Studland Bay; whilst the Velvet Scoter is a scarce and erratic visitor, but odd individuals may sometimes associate with flocks of Eider and Common Scoter for several weeks at a time.

Slavonian and Black-necked Grebes

One of the main attractions of the area is the small wintering population of Slavonian and Black-necked Grebes. Studland and Shell Bays are the best sites for these species, but birds can often be seen inside the harbour. Red-necked Grebes also appear most winters, but they are rather sporadic in occurrence and prone to periodic influxes. Individuals of all three species sometimes linger well into the spring by which time they have attained full summer plumage. Great Crested Grebes can also be seen in good numbers.

Although a few divers inhabit Studland and Shell Bays in winter, they seldom occur inside the harbour. The Great Northern is the most likely species to be encountered followed by the Black-throated; whilst the

Red-throated, although noted most years, is generally the scarcest of the three divers. Cormorants and Shags along with small numbers of Guillemots and Razorbills are regularly present and Little Auks have also been seen on a number of occasions in late autumn and winter.

At high tide the sandy beaches of Studland and Shell Bays provide roosting sites for waders such as Oystercatcher, Ringed and Grey Plovers, Dunlin and Bar-tailed Godwit; whilst a few Sanderling also scuttle about these beaches.

The harbour shore, particularly the saltmarshes and muddy creeks of Brand's Bay, attract large numbers of wildfowl and waders. Since the early 1970s, the flock of Brent Geese has increased to reach recent peaks of over 1,000 birds. Good numbers of Shelduck, Wigeon, Teal and Pintail are usually present and the occasional flock of Shoveler may also appear. Most of the commoner waders including Knot and Black-tailed Godwit occur; whilst a few Greenshank winter most years. Recently small numbers of Avocets have occasionally frequented Brand's Bay at low tide. Amongst the numerous gulls frequenting the area, there is always the chance of locating one of the more unusual species such as Mediterranean, Iceland or Glaucous.

Little Sea is an important wintering site for waterfowl. Wigeon, Gadwall, Teal, Pintail, Shoveler, Pochard, Tufted Duck, Goldeneye and Coot can all be expected. Scaup used to occur in some numbers during the 1970s and, after a marked decline in the early 1980s, has shown signs of a recovery in recent winters. Smew, Goosander and the odd flock of Bewick's Swans sometimes visit Little Sea during periods of hard weather. Other waterbirds including Little Grebe, Cormorant, Grey Heron and Water Rail are also usually present.

Winter raptors are very much a feature of the area. Hen Harriers can often be seen, sometimes quartering low over Brand's Bay and Little Sea. In recent years Marsh Harriers have become fairly regular visitors to Little Sea, the surrounding reedswamp being a favoured roosting site; whilst Merlins and Peregrines are frequently observed. Flocks of Siskins and Redpolls inhabit the woods around Little Sea, where the occasional Chiffchaff and Firecrest may be found amongst the flocks of tits. A few Woodcock also winter in the damper woodlands. The beaches and sand dunes of Studland and Shell Bays are occasionally the haunt of Snow Buntings.

Little Egrets are now a feature of the winter with birds favouring Brand's Bay at low tide and roosting in the evening at nearby Little Sea. Although numbers are not so high as the late summer and autumn, peak counts at the Little Sea roost reached 54 in November 1994 and 43 in January 1995. A few birds remain into the spring and early summer.

Although the Studland Peninsula is not particularly well known for spring migrants, a number of interesting species occur. Sandwich Terns often arrive here earlier than elsewhere in the region with birds usually appearing during the first half of March. These are followed by Common and a few Little Terns from mid-April onwards. Wader passage includes a few Bar-tailed Godwit, Whimbrel, Greenshank and Common Sandpiper along with the occasional flock of Sanderling. There is a scattering of landbird migrants throughout the spring. Scarcer species such as Wood Warbler, Firecrest and Pied Flycatcher are seen most years in the Little Sea woodlands; whilst the odd Black Redstart occasionally frequents the beaches. There is always the chance of an oddity such as Spoonbill and Marsh Harrier, both of which are annual visitors to Poole

Harbour; whilst there are several sightings of Hoopoes from the sand dunes of Studland and Shell Bays.

Breeding birds include Nightjar, Stonechat and the true speciality of the heathland, the Dartford Warbler with some 80–100 pairs residing on the reserve in good seasons. The woods around Little Sea support a wide range of breeding birds including a few pairs of Redpoll. Little Sea itself attracts relatively few nesting birds – the odd pair of Little Grebe, Canada Goose and Teal; whilst the reedbeds hold Water Rail, Reed Warbler and Reed Bunting. A few pairs of Shelduck and Redshank breed on the salt-marshes of Brand's Bay. Sandwich and Common Terns from the nearby colonies on Brownsea fish the waters off the Studland Peninsula throughout the breeding season; whilst both Great Crested Grebe and Eider have summered.

The annual influx of Little Egrets is evident from late June with numbers building up during the autumn to reach a maximum in late August and early September. The roosting flock at Little Sea is the second largest in Britain and reached peak counts just in excess of 100 birds in August and September 1995. During the day and at low tide birds are best looked for in and around Brand's Bay. Passage waders include Black-tailed Godwit, Whimbrel, Greenshank, Common Sandpiper and the odd Spotted Redshank and Green Sandpiper. Sandwich, Common and a few Little Terns are present for much of the season; whilst Black Terns are occasional visitors to mainly Little Sea and Brand's Bay. Strong gales from the south-east may bring storm-driven seabirds including Gannet, Kittiwake and perhaps the odd Grey Phalarope, skua or Little Gull close inshore. There is a more pronounced passage of landbird migrants including a few Black Redstarts, Firecrests and Pied Flycatchers together with the occasional sub-rarity – Wryneck, Bluethroat, Melodious and Yellow-browed Warblers and Lapland Bunting have all been noted in autumn. Other oddities such as Spoonbill, Marsh Harrier and Osprey appear with some frequency.

A number of rarities have occurred in the Studland area; the most noteworthy being Pied-billed Grebe, Lesser Scaup, Common Nighthawk, Little Swift and American Robin. There are also sightings of White Stork, Ring-necked Duck, Red-footed Falcon, Common Crane, Alpine Swift and Great Reed Warbler.

Timing

Birds can be seen at all states of the tide, but one to two hours before and after high-water are best for viewing wildfowl and waders along the harbour shore and in Brand's Bay. At high tide waders roost on the beaches of Studland and Shell Bays.

Landbird migrants should be looked for when fall conditions prevail. In autumn, strong gales from either the south or southeast may bring storm-driven seabirds close inshore to Studland Bay and the harbour entrance.

During the summer, particularly at weekends, the Studland Peninsula is often crowded with holiday-makers. This usually results in long delays at the ferry.

Access

The Studland Peninsula can be approached either by ferry from Sand-banks to Shell Bay (see below) or along the road north from Studland Village. Numerous footpaths give access to much of the area including the woods around Little Sea. There is also an Observation Centre (including hide) overlooking Little Sea, which can be reached by foot-path from the road almost opposite the track leading to Greenland Farm. The hide can be used at all times, but the centre is only open on Sundays and bank holidays (except Christmas) 11.00 am–4.00 pm (winter), 11.00 am–5.00 pm (summer). There are car parks* at South Haven (near ferry) and at the south end of Studland Bay (Knoll car park).

Reserve Visit Arrangements: no permits are required, but groups intending to visit the reserve should book in advance with the Warden, Mr J.R. Cox, 33 Priests Road, Swanage, Dorset (tel: 01929 423453).

Sandbanks Ferry* operates at 20–30 minute intervals throughout the year, except for a fortnight usually in November – check with either the AA or local press for details.

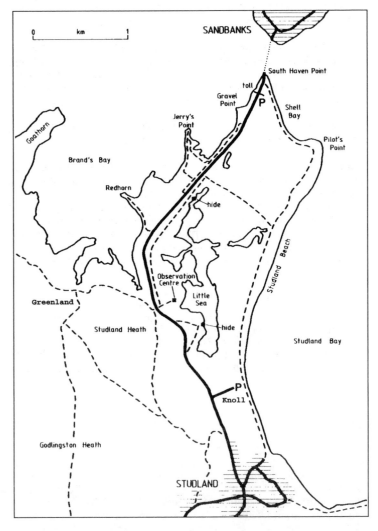

Calendar

All Year: Little Grebe, Cormorant, Little Egret, Grey Heron, Canada Goose, Shelduck, Teal, Water Rail, Redshank, Stonechat, Dartford Warbler, Redpoll, Reed Bunting, common resident woodland birds.

Winter (mid-November–mid-March): Red-throated, Black-throated and Great Northern Divers; Great Crested, Slavonian, Black-necked and occasional Red-necked Grebes; Shag; wildfowl including Brent Goose, Wigeon, Gadwall, Pintail, Pochard, Tufted Duck, Scaup, Eider, Long-tailed Duck, Common and occasional Velvet Scoters, Goldeneye, Red-breasted Merganser, in cold weather occasional Bewick's Swan, Smew and Goosander; Marsh and Hen Harriers, Peregrine and occasional Merlin; waders including Knot, Sanderling, Purple Sandpiper, Woodcock, both godwits and Greenshank; gulls including Kittiwake, occasional Mediterranean, Little, Iceland and Glaucous; Guillemot and Razorbill; Rock Pipit, Siskin, occasional Black Redstart, Chiffchaff, Firecrest and Snow Bunting.
Most likely oddity: rare waterfowl.

Spring (mid-March–mid-May): migrant waders including both godwits, Whimbrel, Greenshank, Common Sandpiper and occasional Sanderling; Sandwich, Common, Arctic and Little Terns; landbird migrants including near annual Black Redstart, Wood Warbler, Firecrest and Pied Flycatcher.
Most likely oddities: Spoonbill, Marsh Harrier, Osprey, Hoopoe.

Summer (mid-May–mid-July): occasional Great Crested Grebe and Eider; Sandwich and Common Terns; Nightjar, Reed Warbler.

Autumn (mid-July–mid-November): during/after gales – occasional storm-driven seabirds including Gannet, skua, Little Gull, Kittiwake, auks, possible Grey Phalarope and Little Auk.
Migrant waders including Black-tailed Godwit, Whimbrel, Greenshank, Common Sandpiper and occasional Green Sandpiper; Sandwich, Common, Arctic, Little and occasional Black Terns; landbird migrants including annual Black Redstart, Firecrest and Pied Flycatcher.
Most likely oddities: Spoonbill, Marsh Harrier, Osprey, landbird subrarity.

17 BROWNSEA ISLAND (NT/DWT)
OS Map 195 & Purbeck
SZ08

Habitat

Brownsea is by far the largest of the islands present in Poole Harbour and supports a wide variety of habitats. Ornithologically the most important of these is the large (70 acres) brackish non-tidal lagoon. This lies within a seawall at the eastern end of the Island and owes its existence to an attempt to reclaim an area of saltmarsh during the last century. At present the east shore of the lagoon closest to the seawall is bordered by remnant saltmarsh; whilst along the west shore fringing reedswamp extends inland and merges with damp sallow and alder carr. A number of small gravel islands have been constructed to encourage breeding terns. Near the centre of the Island, there are two freshwater lakes set amongst the predominantly coniferous woodland. In fact, most of the Island is covered by attractive coniferous (Scots and maritime pine) and mixed woodlands; whilst there are smaller areas of rhododendron thicket, heathland and open grass. Much of the present vegetation is a relic of past management. The Island coast mainly consists of a muddy foreshore with beaches of sand and shingle, backed for the most part by low crumbling cliffs.

Brownsea Island is owned by the National Trust from whom the Dorset Wildlife Trust leases 250 acres in the north of the Island including the lagoon and freshwater lakes as a nature reserve. In addition to the birds, an interesting and varied flora and fauna can be found on Brownsea. Perhaps the best known inhabitants are the red squirrels; whilst other mammals present include Sika deer, water vole and several species of bat. Insect groups, notably dragonflies (23 species recorded) and moths, are also an important feature of the Island's natural history.

Species

Brownsea Island is one of the most important sites for birds in Poole Harbour. The lagoon provides a refuge for feeding and resting wildfowl, waders and gulls, notably at high tide, as well as supporting nesting waders, gulls and terns. Other of the Island's habitats also hold a number of interesting breeding birds.

The lagoon is the favoured site in Poole Harbour for the wintering flock of Avocet which has increased dramatically in recent years to reach counts of up to 600 or so birds. A wide selection of other waders including Knot, Black-tailed and Bar-tailed Godwits, and Greenshank can also be expected.

Avocets

Good numbers of wildfowl also frequent the lagoon. The main species are Shelduck, Wigeon, Teal, Pintail and Shoveler. Although a few Pochard and Tufted Duck are sometimes present, these species are much more likely to be encountered on the freshwater lakes. Goldeneye and Red-breasted Merganser occasionally visit the lagoon from the nearby harbour. Small groups of Brent Geese often feed on the remnant salt-marsh, but much larger flocks can be seen offshore. The lagoon is also the base for a large population of Canada Geese which are joined from time to time by feral Greylag, Snow and Barnacle Geese.

Although large numbers of the commoner gulls gather on the lagoon, the site is not noted for the scarcer species. Nevertheless, there are recent records of Mediterranean, Little, Yellow-legged Herring, Iceland and Glaucous Gulls; whilst the odd Kittiwake may appear after winter storms. Little Egrets are now regular visitors to the lagoon where one or two Spoonbills have also wintered in recent years. Other waterbirds such as Cormorant, Grey Heron and Water Rail frequent the lagoon and reedswamp for much of the year.

The occasional Merlin and Peregrine may be seen hunting over the lagoon, obviously attracted by the abundance of potential prey. Of the smaller birds, Kingfishers and Rock Pipits are regular winter inhabitants of the lagoon and shore areas; whilst flocks of Siskins and Redpolls forage in the woodlands where the odd wintering Chiffchaff and Firecrest may be found amongst mixed bird parties.

Offshore in the harbour itself, Great Crested Grebe, Goldeneye and Red-breasted Merganser along with the occasional diver, rarer winter grebe, sea-duck (most likely Eider and Long-tailed Duck) and auk may also be seen.

The first Sandwich Terns appear from mid-March onwards followed by Common Terns during early April, both species remaining to breed on the lagoon. A few Little Terns occur on passage; whilst Little Gulls and Black Terns sometimes appear. The lagoon hosts a variety of migrant waders including both godwits, Whimbrel and Common Sandpiper and less frequently Knot, Sanderling and Greenshank. Amongst the scattering of landbird migrants that pass through, Wood Warblers are annual visitors, but Black Redstarts, Firecrests and Pied Flycatchers are infrequent in occurrence. The most likely oddity to be encountered is the Spoonbill; whilst spring rarities and subrarities have included American Wigeon, Terek Sandpiper and Hoopoe.

The main feature of the summer is the colony of breeding terns that inhabits the lagoon. With the encouragement of artificial islets, Common Terns first nested in the early 1960s followed by Sandwich Terns in the mid-1970s. Subsequently the numbers of both species have increased to between 100 and 150 pairs in the mid-1990s. Other breeding birds, including Canada Goose, Shelduck, Water Rail, Oystercatcher, Black-headed, Lesser Black-backed, Herring and Great Black-backed Gulls, Reed Warbler and Reed Bunting are associated with the lagoon and fringing reedswamp. Both Teal and Shoveler have occasionally nested or attempted to do so in recent years. It is always worth checking amongst the breeding terns for Roseates which occasionally visit the lagoon in summer. Late June and early July sees the start of the now regular influx of Little Egrets into Poole Harbour; the lagoon on Brownsea being a favoured feeding and daytime roost site. Numbers increase during the autumn to peak in late August and September.

Brownsea once boasted the second largest heronry in Britain with about 100 or more nests usually present, but numbers have declined to around 60 in recent years. The freshwater lakes hold breeding Little Grebe and occasionally Tufted Duck. A wide selection of birds including Golden Pheasant (a local speciality best looked for in the Wilderness area), Woodcock, Nightjar, Nuthatch and Treecreeper breed in the woodlands. The odd Hobby may be seen hawking over the Island; whilst parties of Crossbills occasionally occur from midsummer onwards.

There is always the possibility of a rarity – Great White Egret, Black-winged Stilt and White-winged Black Tern have all been seen during the summer.

During the autumn the lagoon attracts good numbers of returning winter and migrant waders. Although Brownsea was the premier site in Dorset for autumn Spotted Redshank, this is no longer the case. Indeed numbers in Poole Harbour have fallen in recent years with Arne NR and Lytchett Bay now the main sites for the species. Small numbers of Knot, Sanderling, Little Stint, Curlew Sandpiper, Ruff, Whimbrel, Greenshank and Common Sandpiper pass through. Green and Wood Sandpipers occur more infrequently; whilst there is always the chance of an oddity such as a Red-necked or Grey Phalarope – the latter usually appearing after severe gales. Large post-breeding flocks of terns, mostly Sandwich, Common and Little plus the occasional Roseate use the lagoon as a feeding and roosting site. Little Gulls and Black Terns are infrequent visitors, often after autumn gales which may also bring the odd skua to harry the local gulls and terns. As in the spring, small numbers of landbird migrants pass through. Amongst the scarcer species, a few Pied Flycatchers are seen annually but Black Redstarts and Firecrests are uncommon visitors. Landbird subrarities such as the Wryneck are reported from time to time; whilst other likely oddities include Spoonbill and Osprey.

Timing

Birds use the lagoon throughout the tidal cycle, but numbers and variety are greatest at high-water. Water levels in the lagoon can be critical, particularly for attracting waders, so avoid visits after periods of heavy rain when conditions can be unfavourable. The Avocet flock usually leaves the lagoon when the water is frozen during periods of severe cold.

When Brownsea is open to the public, an early visit is advisable to avoid disturbance in areas other than the DWT Reserve. This is important when looking for Golden Pheasants and red squirrels.

Access

Brownsea Island is open to the public 1 April to 30 September with boat services, weather permitting, operating every 30 minutes between 10.00

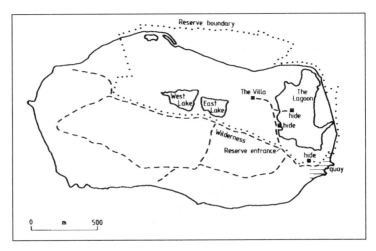

84

am and 4.30 pm (5.30 pm high season) from Sandbanks Ferry and Poole Quay. There is a landing fee (not applicable to NT members) on arrival at Brownsea. Rough tracks and footpaths give access to much of the Island. There are large car parks* at Sandbanks and near Poole Quay (Old Orchard).

Reserve Visit Arrangements: non DWT members may visit the reserve which includes access to hides overlooking the lagoon as follows:

April to June and September: self guided trails 10.30 am–1.00 pm Monday to Saturday: start at the reserve gate: entrance charge payable at the Villa.
April to June and September: guided tours* at 2.45 pm on Sundays: start at public hide.
July and August: daily guided tours* as above.

DWT members have free access to the reserve, but should inform the Warden on arrival. During the winter (1 October to 31 March) the DWT arranges monthly boat trips for its members. These must be booked in advance. For further details contact the DWT Warden, Mr K. Cook, The Villa, Brownsea Island, Poole, Dorset, BH15 1EE.

Calendar

All Year: Cormorant, Little Egret, Grey Heron, Canada and occasional feral Greylag and Barnacle Geese, Shelduck, Tufted Duck, Golden Pheasant, Water Rail, Oystercatcher, Lesser and Great Black-backed Gulls, common resident woodland birds.

Winter (mid-November–mid-March): offshore – occasional divers; Great Crested and occasional rarer winter grebes; Shag; Goldeneye, Red-breasted Merganser and occasional sea-duck; occasional auk.
Wildfowl including Brent Goose, Wigeon, Gadwall, Teal, Pintail, Shoveler, Pochard, occasional Goldeneye and Red-breasted Merganser; occasional Merlin and Peregrine; waders including Avocet (mid-August–mid-March), Knot, both Godwits, Greenshank; gulls including occasional scarce species; Kingfisher, Rock Pipit, Siskin, Redpoll, occasional Chiffchaff and Firecrest.
Most likely oddity: Spoonbill.

Spring (mid-March–mid-May): migrant waders including both godwits, Whimbrel, Common Sandpiper, occasional Knot, Sanderling, Greenshank and other species; occasional Little Gull; Sandwich, Common, Little and occasional Black Terns; landbird migrants including annual Wood Warbler, occasional Black Redstart, Firecrest and Pied Flycatcher.
Most likely oddity: Spoonbill.

Summer (mid-May–mid-July): Little Grebe, Woodcock, Sandwich, Common, Little and possible Roseate Terns, Nightjar, Reed Warbler, Reed Bunting, occasional Crossbill from mid-June.
Most likely oddity: Spoonbill.

Autumn (mid-July–mid-November): migrant waders including Knot, Sanderling, Little Stint, Curlew Sandpiper, Ruff, both godwits, Greenshank, Common Sandpiper, occasional Green and Wood Sandpipers, possible Grey Phalarope; occasional skua; occasional Little Gull; Sandwich, Common, Arctic, Little, occasional Black and possible Roseate Terns; landbird migrants including annual Pied Flycatcher, occasional Black Redstart and Firecrest.

Most likely oddities: Osprey, landbird subrarity.

18 ARNE NR (RSPB)

OS Map 195 & Purbeck
SY98

Habitat

The Arne Peninsula lies in the southwest corner of Poole Harbour and offers an attractive mixture of estuarine, heathland and woodland habitats. The west and north shores border the Wareham Channel where extensive mudflats are exposed at low tide. The east side of the peninsula overlooks the Wytch Channel and Long and Round Islands. The shore is dominated by two areas of *Spartina* saltmarsh intersected by muddy creeks, the first extending across Arne Bay between Patchins and Shipstal Points and the second lying offshore from Grip Heath to the south of Shipstal. The south shore borders the long inlet of Middlebere Lake with its extensive reedbeds. The peninsula itself consists mostly of lowland heath with substantial areas of gorse, wet heath and bog. There are also some fine coniferous and broadleaved woodlands, the latter being prominent along the edge of Arne Bay.

Arne Nature Reserve was established by the RSPB in 1965 and now covers over 1300 acres of the peninsula. Like so many of the Purbeck Heaths, the reserve supports an impressive flora and fauna. Insect groups are particularly important with 22 species of dragonfly, 33 species of butterfly and over 800 species of moth recorded. All six species of British reptile are present, the smooth snake and sand lizard being national rarities. Mammals are also well represented on the reserve.

Species

Although the speciality of Arne NR is the Dartford Warbler, the estuarine fringes of the peninsula and neighbouring waters of Poole Harbour are important sites for waterfowl, waders and gulls.

During the winter large flocks of waders roost in the Arne Bay/ Patchins Point area and, in lesser numbers, around Shipstal Point and on the saltmarshes to the south. At low tide, most of these birds disperse to feed elsewhere in Poole Harbour. The main species are Oystercatcher, Grey Plover, Dunlin, Black-tailed Godwit, Curlew and Redshank. In recent winters the Arne area and in particular Middlebere Lake has become the other main site (apart from Brownsea Island) in Poole Harbour for the Avocet flock. Snipe, Bar-tailed Godwit and Turnstone are also usually present in small numbers; whilst Knot, Spotted Redshank and Greenshank are occasionally seen. A few Woodcock frequent the damper woodland areas.

Winter wildfowl are not as abundant and varied as at some sites in Poole Harbour. Nevertheless, good numbers of Shelduck, Wigeon and Teal can

Dartford Warbler

be expected, particularly in Arne Bay. Brent Geese prefer the Middlebere area where flocks often feed on farmland. Pintail are scarce, but small parties regularly appear, mainly in January and February. Both Gadwall and Shoveler are rather sporadic visitors throughout the winter. Pochard and Tufted Duck are uncommon and usually occur during periods of severe cold, which may also bring flocks of grey geese (usually White-fronted), Scaup, Smew and Goosander to the area. Although the species is not always present, Arne is one of the more reliable sites in Poole Harbour for Scaup. Small parties of Bewick's Swans occasionally wander to the peninsula from their Frome Valley wintering grounds. The offshore waters of the harbour hold Great Crested Grebe, Goldeneye and Red-breasted Merganser, sometimes in large concentrations; whilst divers (usually Red-throated), the rarer winter grebes, sea-duck and auks are occasionally seen. The commoner gulls are present throughout the winter and the odd Little Gull and Kittiwake may appear after gales. Cormorants and Grey Herons are non-breeding residents. Like elsewhere in Poole Harbour, small numbers of Little Egrets are present in winter; whilst Spoonbills have also become an increasingly regular feature of the season.

Hen Harrier and Peregrine are the most likely raptors to be seen at this season; whilst the dashing Merlin occurs most winters. Of the smaller birds, a few Rock Pipits can be found on the saltmarshes, small flocks of Siskins and Redpolls frequent the woodlands and Firecrests occasionally overwinter.

In spring, Arne is a favoured roosting site for passage Black-tailed and Bar-tailed Godwits; both of which can occur in good numbers. Ringed Plover, Whimbrel, Spotted Redshank, Greenshank and Common Sandpiper along with the occasional Green Sandpiper and other migrant species also pass through. The small numbers of Sandwich and Common Terns, which fish offshore, may be joined by the odd Little Tern or even Little Gull. Amongst a scattering of landbird migrants, scarce species such as Ring Ouzel and Firecrest occur infrequently. There is always a chance of something more unusual turning up, the most likely candidates being Spoonbill and Marsh Harrier; whilst Hoopoe, Bluethroat and Golden Oriole have also been noted.

The most important breeding bird of the Arne Peninsula is undoubtedly the Dartford Warbler. Other heathland birds including Nightjar and Stonechat also nest on the reserve; whilst Hobbies are occasionally seen overhead. The woodland areas hold a variety of breeding birds including a few pairs of Redpoll and occasionally Wood Warbler. Reed Warblers, Reed Buntings and the odd pair of Water Rail nest in the extensive reedbeds. Other noteworthy breeding birds include Little Grebe, Canada Goose, Shelduck, Redshank and sometimes Teal. A few Sandwich and Common Terns can be seen fishing offshore in the harbour where summering Great Crested Grebes are sometimes present. In irruption years flocks of Crossbills may be encountered in the forestry areas from mid-June onwards. Little Egrets are much in evidence from late summer onwards as the annual influx of the species into Poole Harbour takes place. The species can be now be expected at Arne throughout the year.

Migrant waders are prominent during the autumn. Arne is still a favoured site for Spotted Redshank at this season, but in much lower numbers than in earlier years. Both godwits, Whimbrel, Greenshank, Green and Common Sandpipers regularly occur, but Knot, Ruff and other migrant species are infrequent visitors. Sandwich, Common and Little Terns are usually present in small numbers; whilst Little Gulls and Black Terns occasionally pass through. Hobbies appear overhead from time to time. There is a small passage of landbird migrants, which may include the occasional Black Redstart, Firecrest and Pied Flycatcher as well as a possible subrarity such as Wryneck. Spoonbill, Marsh Harrier and Osprey are also likely autumn oddities.

Although Arne NR is not noted for attracting rarities, there are reports of Cattle Egret, Black (twice) and White Storks, Long-billed Dowitcher, Woodchat Shrike and Two-barred Crossbill.

Timing
The best times for watching wildfowl and waders, particularly in Arne Bay, are one to two hours either side of high-water.

Access
The Arne Peninsula can be approached along minor roads either east from Stoborough or north from the A351 Wareham to Corfe Castle road opposite the Halfway Inn PH. Car parking is restricted to the car park* located just before Arne Village.

Shipstal Point, which is reached by taking the bridlepath from Arne Village, is the only part of the peninsula accessible to the public. This area offers a wide variety of habitats, a hide overlooking Arne Bay and a newly constructed lagoon, and a nature trail laid out throughout the year. Shipstal Beach is a good site to watch the Wytch Channel and nearest islands; whilst Shipstal Hill provides a general view of Poole Harbour and nearby heathland.

At present there is no access to other areas of the nature reserve. Further details can be obtained from the Warden, Syldata, Arne, Wareham, Dorset BH20 5BJ (enclosing a s.a.e.).

Calendar
All Year: Cormorant, Little Egret, Grey Heron, Canada Goose, Shelduck, Oystercatcher, Curlew, Redshank, Dartford Warbler, Redpoll, Reed Bunting, common resident woodland birds.

Winter (November–mid-March): possible divers; Great Crested and occasional rarer winter grebes; wildfowl including Brent Goose, Wigeon, Teal, Pintail, Goldeneye, Red-breasted Merganser, occasional Bewick's Swan, Gadwall, Shoveler, Pochard, Tufted Duck and sea-duck, in cold weather occasional grey geese (usually White-fronted) and Scaup, possible Smew and Goosander; Hen Harrier, Peregrine and occasional Merlin; waders including Avocet, Grey Plover, Snipe, Woodcock, both Godwits, Turnstone, occasional Knot, Spotted Redshank and Greenshank; gulls including occasional Little and Kittiwake; Rock Pipit, Siskin and occasional Firecrest.

Spring (mid-March–mid-May): migrant waders including Ringed Plover, both godwits, Whimbrel, Spotted Redshank, Greenshank, Common Sandpiper and occasional other species; occasional Little Gull; Sandwich,

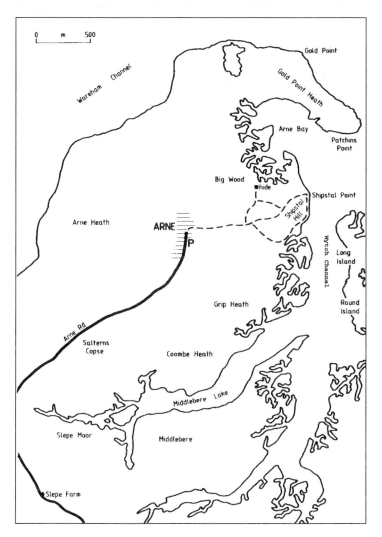

Common and occasional Little Terns; landbird migrants including occasional Firecrest and Pied Flycatcher.
Most likely oddities: Spoonbill, Marsh Harrier.

Summer (mid-May–mid-July): Little and summering Great Crested Grebes; Sandwich and Common Terns; Nightjar, Stonechat, Reed Warbler, occasional Hobby and Crossbill.
Most likely oddity: Spoonbill.

Autumn (mid-July–October): migrant waders including both godwits, Whimbrel, Spotted Redshank, Greenshank, Green and Common Sandpipers, occasional other species; occasional Little Gull; terns including Sandwich, Common, Little and occasional Black; landbird migrants including occasional Black Redstart, Firecrest and Pied Flycatcher.
Most likely oddities: Spoonbill, Marsh Harrier, Osprey, landbird subrarity.

19 WAREHAM WATER-MEADOWS AND SWINEHAM POINT

OS Map 195
& Purbeck
SY98

Habitat

The Wareham Water-meadows lie mainly to the north of the River Frome, extending from the Wareham/Stoborough Causeway eastwards towards Swineham Point. There is, however, a substantial area of wet meadows to the south of the river, between the Causeway and Redcliffe Farm. The water-meadows are prone to winter flooding when semi-permanent pools may form. The area is also intersected and drained by numerous ditches, some choked with reeds and sedges; whilst the reeds growing along the margins of the River Frome become more extensive downstream.

Situated between the mouths of the River Frome and River Piddle, Swineham Point is an area of mostly *Spartina* saltmarsh and reedbed which overlooks the Wareham Channel.

Species

When conditions are suitable during the winter, the Wareham Water-meadows are an important feeding and roosting area for waders from Poole Harbour. The meadows are a favoured haunt of Black-tailed Godwit with flocks of several hundred birds often present. Large flocks of Dunlin, Curlew and Redshank also appear at high-water; whilst good numbers of Lapwing and Snipe can be seen throughout the tidal cycle. Although many of the roosting waders fly back to the harbour as the tide ebbs, small parties remain to feed in the fields. Wintering Ruff used to be a speciality of these meadows with peak counts of 100 of more during the early 1970s. Subsequently numbers have declined to a mere handful of birds in recent years. At low tide large numbers of waders and gulls feed on the mudflats off Swineham Point. The main species are Curlew

Ruff

and Black-headed Gull, but many of the commoner waders can also be seen. The odd Jack Snipe may be found amongst the Snipe frequenting both the saltmarshes at Swineham Point and the water-meadows; whilst Spotted Redshank and Greenshank are occasionally noted. In the late afternoons and evenings vast numbers of gulls, mostly Black-headed and Common, roost in the Wareham Channel.

The water-meadows attract surprisingly few wildfowl, which are more likely to occur around Swineham Point and offshore in the harbour. Small flocks of Bewick's Swans sometimes frequent the meadows, especially when standing water is present. Grey geese occasionally appear, usually during periods of severe cold. The most likely species is White-fronted, but there have been reports of Bean, Pink-footed and Greylag Geese. Large flocks of Wigeon often seek refuge on the meadows during hard weather which may bring the likes of Smew and Goosander to the rivers. Canada Geese visit from time to time as they wander around the harbour and lower Frome Valley. Otherwise small numbers of Shelduck, Teal and sometimes Gadwall and Pintail can be seen. At high tide a scattering of Red-breasted Mergansers, Goldeneye and Great Crested Grebes inhabit the waters of the Wareham Channel. The latter two species often stray into the lower reaches of the rivers where a few Little Grebes also winter. Sightings of Red-throated Diver, rarer winter grebes and sea-duck well up the River Frome at Wareham are exceptional. Little Egrets are now likely visitors, particularly during the autumn and winter.

Hen Harriers often quarter the meadows and reedbeds in search of prey; whilst Marsh Harriers are being reported with increasingly frequency. Other winter raptors such as Merlin, Peregrine and Short-eared Owl also appear from time to time. The water-meadows host small numbers of Water Pipits; whilst Rock Pipits can be found on the saltmarshes at Swineham Point. Kingfishers regularly dart up and down the rivers, Stonechats occur in the reeds and brambles along the riverbanks from where the occasional burst of Cetti's Warbler song can be heard and Bearded Tits are sporadic visitors to the reedbeds. There is also a winter record of Penduline Tit.

During the spring the water-meadows generally become less attractive to waders, although a few Black-tailed Godwits may remain well into

91

April if wet conditions persist. Likely migrant waders include small flocks of Whimbrel, the occasional Greenshank, Green and Common Sandpipers and possibly scarcer species such as Little Ringed Plover and Wood Sandpiper. Common Terns fish in the Wareham Channel and sometimes drift up the rivers; whilst regular landbird migrants include Water Pipit, Yellow Wagtail and Wheatear, Oddities such as Savi's Warbler, Golden Oriole and Serin have been seen in spring.

The water-meadows support a good breeding population of Lapwing and Redshank; whilst Sedge and Reed Warblers and Reed Bunting nest in the reedbeds. Cetti's Warblers are resident along both the River Frome and the River Piddle.

Waders are much more prominent during the autumn. Recent reports suggest that Swineham Point is a good site for Spotted Redshank, perhaps wandering from nearby Arne NR. Small numbers of Whimbrel, Greenshank and Common Sandpiper regularly occur; whilst Ruff and Green Sandpiper occasionally appear. In wet autumns Black-tailed Godwits and other roosting waders may return to the water-meadows by September. A few terns, mostly Sandwich and Common, but sometimes including Little and Black frequent the Wareham Channel. Like the spring, there is a scattering of landbird migrants including Yellow Wagtail, Whinchat and Wheatear amongst others. There is always a chance of finding something unusual – Night Heron, Osprey, Spotted Crake, Sociable Plover and Woodchat Shrike have all been reported in autumn.

Timing
To see the Wareham Water-meadows at their best, it is important to visit when the fields are wet with standing water present and the tide is high in Poole Harbour. Low-water is required to see wildfowl and waders feeding on the mudflats off Swineham Point.

Access
Wareham Water-meadows and Swineham Point can be reached from the traffic lights in Wareham Town Centre by turning east along East

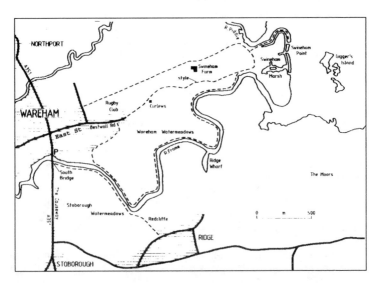

Street and Bestwall Road. The water-meadows can be viewed either by following the footpath from Bestwall Road south to the River Frome and then walking east along the riverbank; or for a more direct route, by taking the footpath from the end of Bestwall Road east along the metalled farm road to the style and then continuing east on the rough track. Both footpaths meet by the River Frome near Swineham Point. The latter can be reached by taking the footpath north to the River Piddle and then walking east along the south bank of the river to the edge of the saltmarshes.

Stoborough Water-meadows can be viewed by following the footpath from South Bridge, Wareham east along the south bank of the River Frome to Redcliffe. There is a car park* by the Old Granary on Wareham Quay.

Calendar

All Year: Cormorant, Little Egret, Grey Heron, Lapwing, Redshank, Cetti's Warbler, Reed Bunting.

Winter (November–March): Little and Great Crested Grebes; wildfowl including Canada Goose, Shelduck, Wigeon, Teal, Goldeneye, Red-breasted Merganser, occasional Bewick's Swan, Gadwall and Pintail, in cold weather occasional grey geese (usually White-fronted), Smew and Goosander; Marsh and Hen Harriers, occasional Merlin and Peregrine; Water Rail; waders including Lapwing, Dunlin, Ruff, Snipe, Black-tailed Godwit, Curlew, Redshank, occasional Jack Snipe, Spotted Redshank and Greenshank, possible Avocet; gulls; occasional Short-eared Owl; Kingfisher, Rock and Water Pipits, Stonechat, Bearded Tit.

Spring (mid-March–mid-May): migrant waders including Black-tailed Godwit, Whimbrel, occasional Greenshank, Green and Common Sandpipers, possible scarcer species; Common Tern; landbird migrants including Water Pipit, Yellow Wagtail and Wheatear.
Most likely oddity: Osprey.

Summer (mid-May–mid-July): Common Tern, Sedge and Reed Warblers.

Autumn (mid-July–mid-November): migrant waders including Black-tailed Godwit, Whimbrel, Spotted Redshank, Greenshank, Green and Common Sandpipers, occasional scarcer species; Sandwich, Common, occasional Little and Black Terns; landbird migrants including Yellow Wagtail, Whinchat and Wheatear.
Most likely oddity: Osprey.

20 WAREHAM FOREST (FC/EN)

Habitat

Wareham Forest lies to the north and west of Wareham. Much of the area is given over to forestry, which ranges from mature coniferous plantations to large open clearings replanted with conifer seedlings. Fine broadleaved woodlands mainly comprising silver birch and oak are found in places; whilst there are some important areas of bog and open heath. Other features of interest include the Sherford River, which drains east from Morden Park along the northern edge of the forest and eventually flows into Poole Harbour at Lytchett Bay; the Old Decoy Pond on Morden Heath; and the Woolsbarrow, an ancient hill-fort providing impressive views over the surrounding woodlands and forests.

Most of Wareham Forest is under the control of the Forestry Commission, who continue to develop the woodland resources with regard to the needs of wildlife. Morden Bog NNR is managed by English Nature; whilst nearby Morden park is a private estate. A wealth of plants and animals particularly associated with bog and heathland habitats are found in Wareham Forest. All six British species of reptile including those national rarities the sand lizard and smooth snake are present. There is a good population of deer in the forest; whilst insect groups such as dragonflies and butterflies are well represented.

Species

The variety of habitats present within Wareham Forest supports a wide selection of breeding birds including several species that are uncommon in Dorset. The coniferous forests are the most reliable haunt in the county for the Crossbill. Although in some years this species can be very scarce and difficult to find, in others it can be conspicuous. Since breeding was first proved in the early 1980s, the Siskin has become locally widespread in the forest areas; whilst a few pairs of Redpoll are found where silver birches predominate. The broadleaved woodlands are favoured by such scarce breeding birds as Lesser Spotted Woodpecker, Redstart, Wood Warbler and Willow Tit as well as commoner species including Green and Great Spotted Woodpeckers, Spotted Flycatcher, Marsh Tit, Nuthatch and Treecreeper.

A good population of Nightjars is present during the summer and, as night approaches, their characteristic churring can be heard from forest clearings and the heathland margins. Woodcock are widely distributed throughout the forest and, like the previous species, they are best seen during spring and summer evenings when roding males circle over the woods. Tree Pipits and the few surviving pairs of Woodlark also prefer the forest clearings and heathland margins; whilst the open heaths are home to such specialities as the Stonechat and Dartford Warbler. Although recent records are rather scarce and sporadic, there is evidence to suggest that the more extensive wet heaths and bogs still hold a few breeding pairs of Shelduck, Teal, Snipe and Curlew. Reed Buntings also nest on these wet heaths and bogs; whilst Kingfishers and Grey Wagtails breed along the Sherford River. Amongst the raptors that

Nightjar

frequent the area, Sparrowhawk, Buzzard, Kestrel and Hobby are all likely to be seen overhead during the summer months.

In winter the Wareham Forest often appears to be devoid of birdlife. Nevertheless, Siskins and Redpolls roam around the birch and alder woods with large flocks frequently reported from the vicinity of Sherford Bridge. A scattering of Teal and Snipe inhabit the wet heathland pools and bogs. Hen Harriers occasionally quarter the open heaths and bogs; whilst there is always the chance of seeing the odd wandering Merlin and Peregrine. The Great Grey Shrike is an occasional visitor which has overwintered in the area.

Migrants are not a major feature of the forest. In some springs an off-passage flock of Whimbrel, which has reached numbers in excess of 100 birds, may frequent the roadside fields by Morden Bog. Otherwise a trickle of landbird migrants, notably Wheatears, pass through in spring and autumn when the occasional wader and tern may appear on the forest pools. Rarer visitors to Wareham Forest include the odd migrant Marsh Harrier and Osprey; whilst there are single records of Roller and Lesser Grey Shrike.

Timing
Certain specialities such as Lesser Spotted Woodpecker, Woodlark and Crossbill are best looked for in late winter and early spring (February–April). Early mornings are the most productive time for finding woodland birds; whilst fine, warm, still summer evenings are recommended when searching for crepuscular species such as Woodcock and Nightjar.

Access
The main access routes through Wareham Forest are the B3075 Sandford to Morden road and the minor road between Northport, Wareham and the A35 just east of Bere Regis. There are a number of footpaths and forest trails, the most notable being (i) from Sherford Bridge east to Organford Bridge, (ii) from Sherford Bridge west to Stroud Bridge, (iii) from Sugar Hill both northeast and southwest into the forest, (iv) from North Lodge north to the A35 near Morden, (v) the Sika Forest Trail from the Forest Centre at Cold Harbour and (vi) from the B3075 at Great Ovens Hill east and south across Gore Heath.

There is strictly no entry to Morden Bog NNR (English Nature) and Morden Park (private estate). For access to other areas of the Wareham Forest, visitors should inquire for details at the Forest Centre, Cold Harbour. There are car parks at Stroud Bridge, Cold Harbour and near Gore

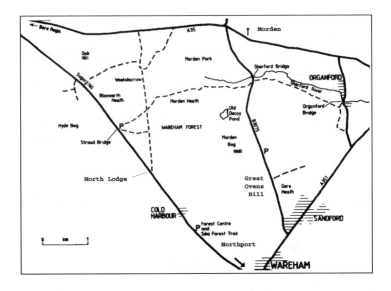

Heath; whilst limited car parking is available in the lay-by next to Sherford Bridge.

Calendar

All Year: Teal, Buzzard, Snipe, Woodcock, Kingfisher, Lesser Spotted Woodpecker, Woodlark, Grey Wagtail, Stonechat, Dartford Warbler, Willow Tit, Siskin, Redpoll, Crossbill, Reed Bunting, common resident woodland birds.

Summer (May–July): Shelduck, Curlew, Nightjar, Tree Pipit, Redstart, Wood Warbler, Spotted Flycatcher.

Winter (November–March): occasional Hen Harrier, Merlin and Peregrine, possible Great Grey Shrike.

Spring (April and May) and Autumn (August–October): possible large migrant raptor; Whimbrel flock mid-April–mid-May; possible migrant wader and tern; common landbird migrants.

21 POOLE PARK AND SANDBANKS

OS Map 195 & Purbeck
SZ08/09

Habitat

Most of this northeastern shore of Poole Harbour is highly developed and urbanised, being very much an area for winter birds. Although not so productive as the relatively unspoilt southern parts of the harbour, these sites offer some very accessible and interesting birdwatching.

Poole Park including nearby Baiter and Parkstone Bay is only a few minutes walk from Poole Town Centre. The park itself contains several artificial lakes, one (the boating lake) being much larger than the others, which are situated in a typical municipal setting of open grass and scattered trees. When the boating lake is partially drained, areas of exposed mud appear around the margins. Baiter playing fields, which overlook the sheltered waters of Poole Harbour and Parkstone Bay, lie between Poole Park and the harbour shore.

The Sandbanks Peninsula extends southwest to form with the Studland Peninsula opposite, the narrow entrance to Poole Harbour. Within the gently curving harbour shore of Whitley Bay, extensive sandy mudflats are exposed at low-water. The sandy beaches on the seaward side of Sandbanks provide views over the open waters of Poole Bay.

Species

Poole Park is the main winter haunt for the local Canada Goose population with several hundred birds often present. Both feral Snow and Barnacle Geese sometimes associate with the Canada Geese. The park is also an important wintering site for Tufted Duck with annual maxima often over 300 birds. Smaller numbers of Pochard mingle with the Tufted Duck, but the counts of both species can rise dramatically during periods of cold weather. A few Scaup usually appear amongst the Tufted Duck/ Pochard flock during these cold snaps which occasionally produce the likes of Smew, Goosander and Ruddy Duck. Due to the close proximity of Poole Harbour, small numbers of Goldeneye and Red-breasted Mergansers regularly wander to the boating lake where the odd diver, Great Crested and rarer winter grebe and sea-duck have all occurred from time to time. Cormorants can be seen for much of the year, usually perched on posts at the north end of the boating lake. Although dabbling ducks, other than Mallard, are decidedly rare visitors to the park, most of the commoner species including Shelduck, Wigeon, Teal, Pintail and Shoveler have been seen here. A male Ring-necked Duck has appeared in at least three recent winters; whilst there are records for such exotics as Ruddy Shelduck, Mandarin and Red-crested Pochard.

Winter gulls are also very much a feature of Poole Park. Large flocks of Black-headed Gulls together with lesser numbers of Common and Herring feed and rest around the lake. It is well worth checking through these commoner gulls for more unusual species such as Mediterranean and Yellow-legged Herring Gulls. Little, Iceland and Glaucous Gulls have all been reported from here and there is at least one reliable sighting of a Ring-billed Gull. The muddy margins of the lake, when exposed, attract a variety of waders from nearby Baiter and Parkstone Bay. The most likely species are Oystercatcher, Dunlin and Redshank, but oddities including Ruff, Jack Snipe, Black-tailed Godwit, Greenshank and even Curlew Sandpiper have been seen, most often during periods of cold weather.

At high tide Baiter is an important site for roosting waders, the main species being Oystercatcher and Dunlin; whilst a small flock of Brent Geese frequently grazes the playing fields. At low tide a variety of waders including Oystercatcher, Ringed Plover, Dunlin, Redshank and Turnstone can be found in Parkstone Bay. The occasional wintering Little Stint and Curlew Sandpiper have been located amongst the Dunlin flocks. A few Goldeneye and Red-breasted Mergansers are usually present offshore; whilst divers, rarer winter grebes and sea-duck are occasionally seen. Rock Pipits inhabit the shore areas.

In winter a wide selection of waders feed on the extensive sandy mud-flats of Whitley Bay at low-water. This is one of the best sites in the region for Bar-tailed Godwit, which normally occurs in flocks of 50 or 100 birds occasionally reaching peaks of 200 or more. During the 1980s one or two aberrant individuals retained their red summer plumage throughout the winter. Although only one to three birds are usually present, Whitley Bay is also one of the few reliable localities in Dorset for winter Sanderling which dash around amongst the larger flocks of Dunlin. Otherwise, Oystercatcher, Ringed and Grey Plovers, Curlew, Redshank and Turnstone can be seen here. Mediterranean and Little Gulls occasionally mingle with the larger numbers of commoner gulls, mostly Black-headed and Common, which gather in the bay during the winter afternoons. Small parties of Brent Geese frequent the harbour shore; whilst the offshore waters hold Goldeneye and Red-breasted Mergansers along with the odd diver, Great Crested and rarer winter grebe, sea-duck and auk.

Bar-tailed Godwits

The seaward side of Sandbanks is always worth a look for divers, Great Crested and rarer winter grebes, sea-duck (most likely Eider and Common Scoter) and auks. All these birds, however, can be rather sporadic in occurrence as they wander the length and breadth of Poole Bay.

The Sandbanks Ferry is an excellent spot to view Poole Harbour entrance and Shell Bay.

For much of the remainder of the year disturbance from recreational activities and holiday-makers makes the area relatively unattractive to birds. Some feral Canada Geese remain in Poole Park throughout the year and during the summer the odd Common Tern may drift over the boating lake from the nearby harbour. A few winter waders linger well into the spring to feed in Parkstone and Whitley Bays, reappearing again in the autumn. Occasionally these may be joined by such migrant species as Whimbrel and Common Sandpiper. The Sandbanks Ferry is a good vantage point to observe seabirds that are occasionally forced close inshore to the harbour entrance during or after severe gales in the autumn and winter. In recent years there have been reports of Leach's Petrel, Grey Phalarope, Pomarine Skua and Little Auk. Otherwise a few Sandwich and Common Terns fish along both shores of the Sandbanks Peninsula throughout the breeding season.

It is also worth mentioning that distant views over the Brownsea lagoon can be obtained from the top of Evening Hill. When light conditions are suitable it is possible to see, with the use of a telescope, such conspicuous species as Little Egret, Spoonbill, Shelduck, Shoveler and Avocet.

Timing

Brent Geese, waders and gulls can be seen in Whitley Bay at most states of the tide, but an hour or so before and after high-water are the best times to visit as birds are forced to feed close to the road. Low-water is required for watching waders and gulls in Parkstone Bay; whilst waders roost on the Baiter playing fields at high tide. Unusual wildfowl, and to a lesser extent waders, are most likely to appear in Poole Park during periods of severe cold weather.

Problems may be encountered when watching birds in Whitley Bay due to the increasing disturbance caused by the activities of sail boarders. This tends to be most severe at weekends.

Access

All the sites can be easily reached from Poole Town Centre and Lower Parkstone. Access to Sandbanks can be difficult at peak holiday times and summer weekends.

Poole Park: there are road entrances from Kingland Road (opposite the swimming pool), Parkstone Road (opposite the Civic Centre) and Whitecliff Road (off Sandbanks Road, Lower Parkstone); whilst there is footpath access from Baiter playing fields. There are several car parks in Poole Park.

Baiter car park is well signposted from the roundabout by Poole Pottery on Poole Quay. Alternatively the playing fields can be reached by footpath from Poole Park.

Parkstone Bay can be reached either from Baiter or by walking south-west from the recreation ground car park off Whitecliff Road.

Sandbanks is best approached from the Civic Centre, Lower Parkstone along Sandbanks, Shore and Banks Roads which eventually lead to the Sandbanks Ferry and Poole Harbour entrance. Whitley Bay can be viewed from various points along Shore and Banks Roads. Brownsea lagoon can be distantly observed from Evening Hill which is situated at the point where Sandbanks Road changes into Shore Road; whilst Poole Head, which overlooks Poole Bay, lies at the end of Shore Road. There are car parks* at Sandbanks and Poole Head.

Calendar

All Year: Cormorant, Canada Goose, occasional feral Snow and Barnacle Geese.

Winter (November–March): occasional divers; Great Crested and occasional rarer winter grebes; Shag; wildfowl including Brent Goose, Pochard, Tufted Duck, Goldeneye, Red-breasted Merganser, occasional seaduck, in cold weather Scaup, occasional Smew and Goosander; waders including Grey Plover, Sanderling, Bar-tailed Godwit; gulls including

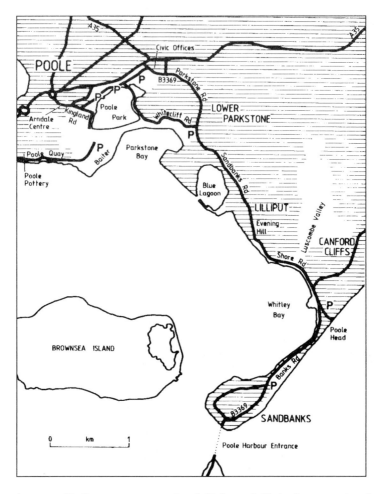

frequent Mediterranean, occasional Little and Kittiwake; occasional auks; Rock Pipit.

Most likely oddities: Little Egret, rare wildfowl and gulls.

Spring, Summer, Autumn (April–October): winter waders linger to May and return from July, occasional migrant Whimbrel, Common Sandpiper and other species; Sandwich and Common Terns; occasional seabirds during/after autumn/winter gales; occasional landbird migrant such as Wheatear.

PURBECK AND POOLE BASIN – OTHER SITES WORTHY OF ATTENTION

OS MAPS 194, 195 & Purbeck

22 WEST PURBECK COAST FROM REDCLIFF POINT TO WHITE NOTHE

SY78

A coastline of variable relief dominated in the east by the high chalk cliffs of the White Nothe. There are some patches of scrub and woodland, notably in the vicinity of Osmington Mills and Ringstead, but much of the immediate hinterland is given over to farming. This stretch of coast is rather neglected, but a number of notable sightings in recent years, including Black Stork, Honey Buzzard, Marsh Harrier, Osprey, Dotterel, Buff-breasted Sandpiper, Hoopoe, Richard's Pipit, Subalpine and Yellow-browed Warblers, shows the potential of the area for attracting good birds. There have also been records of such scarce landbird migrants as Black Redstart, Ring Ouzel, Firecrest and Pied Flycatcher. There is a breeding colony of Cormorants at White Nothe and both Peregrine and Raven are frequently seen in the area. Nightingales and Cetti's Warblers breed in the Osmington Mills/Ringstead area; whilst the coastal scrub supports Stonechat amongst other species. In winter, divers and Slavonian Grebes are occasionally present offshore. This stretch of coast is best reached from car parks at Osmington Mills at SY735818, in Ringstead Village at SY751815 and above Ringstead Bay at SY760824; but Redcliff Point is better approached by walking east from Bowleaze Cove at SY703820. Footpaths give access to much of the area.

23 TYNEHAM VALLEY AND GAD CLIFF

SY87/88

This is an attractive wooded and scrub-filled valley leading down from the deserted wartime village of Tyneham to the Purbeck coast at Worbarrow Bay. The valley is overlooked from the south by the high ridge of Gad Cliff. The latter supports a breeding colony of Cormorants along with a few pairs of Shags; whilst Fulmars are present during the spring and summer. A good population of Nightingales still resides in the area. Otherwise a wide range of breeding birds including Green and Great Spotted Woodpeckers, Stonechat, Marsh Tit and Treecreeper inhabit the scrub and woodlands. Buzzards are commonly seen overhead; whilst there are regular sightings of Peregrine and Raven throughout the year. Like much of the Purbeck coast, the area attracts landbird migrants in spring and autumn. These have included records of Hoopoe and Yellow-browed Warbler. The access road to Tyneham is situated at SY895815 on the minor road along West Creech Hill between Creech Grange and East Lulworth. There is a car park by the old village at SY882802. The MOD still controls access to the area which is generally open at weekends and during the summer. Visitors should check the

101

MOD notice boards on the access roads for the latest information regarding access.

24 BALLARD DOWN
SZ08

A high downland ridge with spectacular vertical chalk cliffs and offshore pinnacles (Old Harry Rocks). In spring and summer the cliffs support prospecting Fulmars, a large colony of Cormorants, Great Black-backed Gull, cliff-nesting House Martins and Rock Pipit; whilst Peregrine and Raven are now local residents. Sandwich and Common Terns and sometimes Kittiwake fish offshore. At times of passage the area is good for landbird migrants including the occasional Black Redstart, Ring Ouzel, Firecrest and Pied Flycatcher. Oddities including Red-footed Falcon, Hoopoe and Woodchat Shrike have been seen here. In winter the north-facing cliffs are a good vantage point for observing divers, grebes, seaduck and auks in the southern part of Studland Bay. Access along the Dorset Coast Path from Studland at SZ039824 to Swanage at SZ030802.

Also of local interest is a small colony of Ring-necked Parakeets nearby in Studland Village. The birds are best looked for from the footpath between the road at SZ038826 (opposite the National Trust car park next to the Bankes Arms Hotel) and the cliff steps overlooking Studland Bay at SZ039827.

25 LOWER FROME VALLEY
SY79/88/98

A typical lowland river with meadows prone to winter flooding. A wintering flock of Bewick's Swan regularly frequents the lower valley; the most favoured sites being at East Holme, Wool and Woodsford. Winter floods also attract wildfowl and waders; the most likely species being Wigeon, Teal, Pintail, Shoveler, Dunlin, Ruff, Snipe, Black-tailed Godwit, Curlew and Redshank. The Little Egret is now a likely visitor in winter. The cressbeds at Waddock Cross are good for wintering Green Sandpiper and Water Pipit. A scattering of migrants pass through in spring and autumn; whilst breeding birds include Kingfisher, Grey Wagtail, Sedge and Reed Warblers and Reed Bunting. Recent oddities include White Stork, Bean Goose, Green-winged Teal, Osprey, Red-footed Falcon, Golden Oriole and Yellow-browed Warbler. View East Holme from the minor road at SY894864, Wool from the A352 at SY847873, Waddock Cross cressbeds from the B3390 at SY798908 and Woodsford from the roadbridge at SY770910.

26 LYTCHETT BAY
SY99

Lytchett Bay is a large partially enclosed inlet of Poole Harbour with mudflats, *Spartina* saltmarshes and reedbeds, which is bordered by wet meadows and rough pasture along the northwest shore. In winter the area supports a good selection of wildfowl including Goldeneye and Red-breasted Merganser and waders including Spotted Redshank, Greenshank and Green Sandpiper. Marsh and Hen Harriers occasionally hunt over the reedbeds by the Holton shore. Little Egrets are now frequent visitors, particularly during the autumn and winter. In spring Lytchett Bay is a favoured site for migrant Whimbrel and Spotted Redshank; whilst a variety of other waders also occur at times of passage. Cetti's Warblers frequent the areas of reedswamp and the reedbeds sometimes attract parties of Bearded Tits. Oddities recorded here include Purple Heron, Common Crane, Pectoral Sandpiper, Aquatic Warbler and Red-backed Shrike. From Blandford Road in Upton, take Yarrells and Shore Lanes to the junction with Lytchett Way at SY979924 and continue on the footpath southwest to the shore. To view the fields behind Lytchett Bay, take Slough Lane southwest from the junction of Watery and Sandy Lanes in Upton at SY971930 to the private gate leading to the sewage works and then follow the rough track northwest towards the A35 Upton by-pass.

27 HAM COMMON LNR (POOLE BOROUGH COUNCIL)

SY99

This small reserve provides superb views over the Wareham Channel and adjacent shorelines of Poole Harbour. The area mainly consists of heathland, with scrub, thickets of willow and birch, reedbeds and a large lake adding to the habitat diversity. This is an excellent site to observe many of the birds that inhabit this part of Poole Harbour at various times during the year. In winter, waterfowl such as Great Crested Grebe, Brent Goose, Shelduck, Goldeneye and Red-breasted Merganser can be expected along with the occasional rarer grebe and sea-duck. Most of the commoner waders can also be seen during the winter with more obvious migrant species such as Whimbrel, Greenshank and Common Sandpiper appearing in spring and autumn. Sandwich and Common Terns from the nearby breeding colonies fish the offshore waters from spring through to autumn. Little Egrets are regularly recorded, notably during the autumn and winter months when Marsh and Hen Harriers occasionally quarter the nearby shorelines in search of prey. The reserve itself supports an interesting selection of breeding birds including such heathland specialities as the Stonechat and Dartford Warbler; whilst landbird migrants have included the odd surprise such as Ring Ouzel and Firecrest. The latter has also been noted in winter along with Chiffchaffs. The reserve can be reached from Hamworthy along Lake Drive and Napier Road; the latter eventually leads to Rockley Park. The best access points are from the beach car park by Hamworthy Pier at SY984905, which lies off Lake Drive; and Rockley Viewpoint car park at SY977909, which lies off Napier Road opposite the entrance to Gorse Hill Central Park.

28 UPTON COUNTRY PARK (POOLE BOROUGH COUNCIL) AND HOLES BAY

SY99/SZ09

A large area of open parkland and gardens, which overlooks an almost completely enclosed inlet of Poole Harbour comprising mudflats and *Spartina* saltmarshes. A wide range of wildfowl, mainly Shelduck and Teal, and waders including Black-tailed Godwit can be seen in Holes Bay during the winter. Cold weather often results in a marked increase in duck numbers, particularly Pochard and Tufted Duck seeking refuge from nearby frozen waters. Whimbrel, Greenshank and Common Sandpiper are the most likely of the migrant waders to be seen at times of passage. Like most sites around Poole Harbour, the Little Egret is now a regular feature of the area; whilst Kingfishers inhabit the Upton Country Park shore during the autumn and winter. The park itself supports a good selection of woodland birds including Lesser Spotted Woodpecker. Oddities recorded here include Green-winged Teal, Smew, Osprey, Collared Pratincole, Wilson's Phalarope and Ring-billed Gull. The main entrance to Upton Country Park at SY991932 is well signposted from the westbound carriageway of the A3049 (Upton by-pass). There is a hide overlooking Holes Bay at SY994927, which is maintained by the Poole RSPB Group. The east side of Holes Bay can now be accessed from various points along the new A350 Holes Bay Road between the A3049 (Upton by-pass) roundabout and Poole Town Centre.

29 UPTON HEATH

SY99

This area of heathland, bog, birch woodland and sand pits supports a variety of breeding birds including Shelduck (occasional), Nightjar, Sand Martin, Tree Pipit, Stonechat, Dartford Warbler, Redpoll and Reed Bunting. In winter the boggy areas hold Snipe and occasionally Jack Snipe; whilst Great Grey Shrike has also been recorded once. Upton Heath is best approached from various points along the Roman Road footpath between Broadstone at SY993952 and Longmeadow Lane, Creekmoor at SY991936. There is also access along a footpath from Naked Cross, Wareham Road, Corfe Mullen at SY980955.

30 CANFORD HEATH AND HATCH POND

SZ09

An extensive heathland with areas of mixed woodland adjacent to the north-west section of the heath. Despite development for housing and general disturbance, Canford Heath still supports several important breeding species including Shelduck (occasional), Woodcock, Nightjar, Lesser Spotted Woodpecker, Woodlark, Tree Pipit, Stonechat, Dartford Warbler and Redpoll. The Great Grey Shrike has occurred in winter. The main access points to Canford Heath are along footpaths from the lay-by on Gravel Hill, Broadstone at SZ015956; Wheelers Lane, Bearwood at SZ044964; and by the entrance to the golf course at the end of Francis Avenue, Alderney at SZ045953.

Hatch Pond is a small lake situated in the southwest corner of the original area of Canford Heath, but now surrounded by development. Despite this, it attracts a surprising variety of birds. Both Great Crested Grebe and Shelduck have bred in recent years; whilst in winter a few duck, mainly Teal, Pochard and Tufted Duck, are usually present. Cormorant and Grey Heron are regular visitors and the pre-roost gathering of gulls in winter occasionally attracts a Mediterranean Gull. The site's main claim to fame concerns the occurrence of a Lesser Scaup for a few days in November and December 1992.

Hatch Pond can be reached from the main junction on Waterloo Road (between Darby's Corner, Broadstone and Fleet's Corner, Poole) at SZ011939, by turning east into the Nuffield Industrial Estate along Hatch Pond Road.

EAST DORSET AND THE HAMPSHIRE AVON

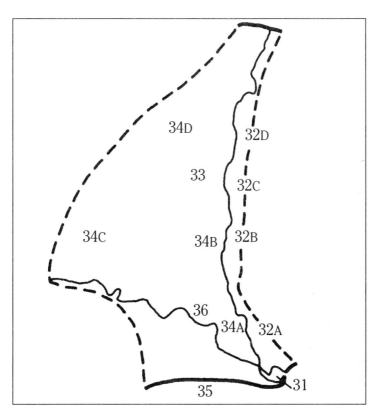

31 CHRISTCHURCH HARBOUR
32 THE HAMPSHIRE AVON AND BLASHFORD LAKES
Recommended Sites
        32A Lower Avon Meadows
        32B Bisterne and Ringwood Meadows
        32C Blashford Lakes
        32D Ibsley Meadows and Bickton Mill
33 MOORS VALLEY COUNTRY PARK AND RINGWOOD FOREST
34 EAST DORSET HEATHS
Recommended Sites
        34A St Catherine's Hill and Town Common
        34B Avon Heath Country Park
        34C Holt Heath NNR and White Sheet Plantation
        34D Cranborne Common NR
Other Sites Worthy Of Attention
35 Bournemouth Seafront
36 River Stour at Throop

General Introduction

This area mainly lies within the triangle formed by the River Stour to the southwest, the chalk downs to the northwest and the Hampshire Avon to the east. The main site of ornithological interest is undoubtedly Christchurch Harbour which forms the combined estuary of the Hampshire Avon and the River Stour. The Hampshire Avon itself is perhaps the finest river of its type in lowland Britain; whilst a series of flooded gravel pits situated just to the north of Ringwood is an additional feature of note. Otherwise the most significant of the land-based habitats is heathland, which is now greatly fragmented mainly due to urban development and afforestation. Birdwatching can be very rewarding throughout the year. Christchurch Harbour attracts a wide selection of migrant and wintering birds, the Avon Valley is an important site for winter wildfowl and breeding wetland birds and the heathlands support most of the bird specialities associated with this type of habitat.

31 CHRISTCHURCH HARBOUR

OS Map 196 & New Forest
SZ19

Habitat

Christchurch Harbour forms the combined estuary of the two largest rivers in the region, the Hampshire Avon and the River Stour. The harbour itself is the focal point for a variety of habitats. To the north lies Stanpit Marsh, an area of low-lying pasture and marsh intersected in places by deep muddy creeks, some choked with reeds and sedges. More extensive reedbeds (the Priory Reeds) border the combined channel of the two rivers just downstream of their confluence; whilst towards the back of the marsh, there is a series of semi-permanent pools (Priory Pools) near to the golf course. There are several patches of gorse scrub, notably around Crouch Hill which overlooks the East and South Marshes. The latter projects southeast into the harbour towards the shingle island of Blackberry Point and partially encloses the extensive mudflats of Stanpit Bight.

The southern side of the harbour is dominated by Hengistbury Head which rises to a height of 120 feet. To the west a broad strip of lower-lying land connects the Head to the mainland. Wick Fields are situated immediately adjacent to the main harbour channel between Wick Village and Hengistbury Head. This is an area of rough pasture and scrub with reedbeds fringing the shore. At the east end of these fields, there is a small marsh comprising muddy creeks, shallow pools and some reedbeds known as Wick Hams. The remainder of the land between Head and the mainland (Southbourne) is bisected by the main access road (The Broadway) with Solent Meads Golf Course to the north and open grass to the south.

Hengistbury Head proper starts just east of the main car park at the Double Dykes which is an Iron Age defensive earthwork. Beyond this lies an area of low-lying grassland and mainly gorse scrub known as The Common. The land rises steeply up to Warren Hill, the top of which is covered by open heathland. The slopes overlooking the harbour are densely vegetated with mainly birch and sallow thickets which merge into oak woodland along the base of the hill. The harbour shore is backed by rough grassland and low scrub with a small area of muddy creeks and saltmarsh at the eastern end. On the seaward side of the Head, high crumbling cliffs overlook a narrow shingle beach that extends as far as the Groyne and the newly constructed sea defences beyond. At the end of the headland, a low sandy spit with beach-huts projects northeast to form the narrow entrance to the harbour. Other features of note on the Head include the Old Nursery Garden (private), the Lily Pond and the Ironstone Quarry.

The close proximity of Christchurch to Bournemouth means that Christchurch Harbour is under considerable pressure from a variety of recreational activities. Fortunately most of the area forms a Local Nature Reserve under the auspices of Christchurch Borough Council. The birdlife of the area has been systematically studied since 1956 by the Christchurch Harbour Ornithological Group (CHOG), who have also manned a ringing station based in the Old Nursery Garden on Hengistbury Head. Although birds are the outstanding feature of the area's natural history, Christchurch Harbour also supports an interesting flora and insect fauna.

Species

Christchurch Harbour's geographical position and diverse habitats makes it one of the best localities in the region for studying bird migration. Hengistbury Head is the main site for landbird migrants and provides a vantage point for seawatching; whilst Stanpit Marsh and the harbour attract a wide selection of waterfowl, waders, gulls, terns and other waterbirds at times of passage.

Spring movements of landbirds start in March with the first arrivals of Wheatears and Chiffchaffs, and continues through to early June when late summer visitors such as Turtle Doves and Spotted Flycatchers are still passing through. The peak migration time, however, is from late March to mid-May. During this period suitable weather conditions can produce impressive falls of several hundred birds involving mainly Wheatears and *Phylloscopus* warblers. A wide range of other landbird migrants can also be seen. These usually include a few Black Redstarts, Ring Ouzels and Firecrests, which occur mainly in late March and April, and Wood Warblers and Pied Flycatchers, which generally appear from mid-April onwards. Some birds such as Water Pipits and Yellow Wagtails favour the wetter habitats of Stanpit Marsh. Amongst the rarer migrants, Hoopoes and Serins are reported most springs, but their visits are generally short lived with birds moving quickly inland. In fact individuals of both species have been observed to fly in off the sea without stopping. Other landbird subrarities including Wryneck, Richard's and Tawny Pipits, Savi's and Icterine Warblers, Golden Oriole, Red-backed Shrike, Common Rosefinch and Ortolan Bunting have all been seen in spring; whilst there are records of such rarities as Great Spotted Cuckoo, Alpine Swift, Red-rumped Swallow, Red-throated Pipit, Subalpine and Bonelli's Warblers, Woodchat Shrike and Little Bunting.

Seabird passage off Hengistbury is on a smaller scale to that recorded off the Purbeck coast and Portland Bill. Some movements involving divers, Fulmar, Gannet, Common Scoter, Kittiwake and the first

Sandwich Terns may take place during March. Most passage, however, occurs in April and early May when additional species including Manx Shearwater, Velvet Scoter, various waders, Pomarine, Arctic and Great Skuas, Little Gull, Common, Arctic, Little and Black Terns and auks are most likely to be seen.

A good variety of migrant waders frequent Stanpit Marsh and the harbour during the spring. Flocks of Bar-tailed Godwit and Whimbrel are particularly obvious in late April and early May; whilst there is a scattering of Common Sandpipers around the harbour's shores. Small parties of summer-plumaged Knot and Sanderling, which feed with Dunlin on the harbour's mudflats, are most prominent in May. A few Avocet, Little Ringed Plover, Little Stint, Curlew Sandpiper, Ruff, Black-tailed Godwit, Spotted Redshank, Greenshank, Green and Wood Sandpipers, appear most years. In recent years, the harbour has become one of the best sites in the region for Kentish Plovers which now occur annually; whilst there have been several reports of Temminck's Stints. Garganey are regular visitors, sometimes associating with lingering winter wildfowl such as Gadwall, Teal and Shoveler. Sandwich, Common, Arctic and Little Terns are present throughout the spring. Very small numbers of Little Gulls pass through; whilst Mediterranean Gull, Roseate and Black Terns are seen most springs. Amongst migrant raptors, Merlin and Hobby are recorded annually and larger species such as Marsh Harrier and Osprey occasionally appear. Most springs produce a few oddities and rarities. In addition to those already mentioned, there are sightings of Night and Purple Herons, Spoonbill (almost annual), American Wigeon, Black Kite, Red-footed Falcon, Little Crake, Black-winged Stilt, American Golden Plover, Broad-billed and Spotted Sandpipers and Bonaparte's Gull.

Summer can be fairly interesting for birds. Although the relatively high level of disturbance causes problems for some breeding birds, one or two pairs of Shelduck still attempt to nest. The reedbeds support Sedge and Reed Warblers, Reed Buntings and sometimes Water Rail; whilst Cetti's Warblers have recently spread to the harbour, favouring Wick Fields, and Bearded Tits have also bred in the past. In recent years a small heronry has become established in the Nursery on Hengistbury Head. The crumbling cliffs provide nesting sites for small numbers of Sand Martins and a few pairs of Rock Pipits; whilst the small patches of heathland support Stonechats and resident Dartford Warblers. Sandwich, Common and Little Terns frequent the harbour throughout the summer, no doubt wandering from the nearby breeding colonies in Poole Harbour and along the Solent; whilst Roseate Terns are virtually annual visitors in the late summer. Off Hengistbury Head seabirds such as Fulmar, Manx Shearwater, Storm Petrel, Gannet, Common Scoter and Kittiwake occasionally pass through Poole Bay, usually during and after summer gales. A summer rarity is always possible, Great White Egret, Purple Heron, Spoonbill, Red-footed Falcon, Kentish Plover, Red-necked Phalarope, Caspian Tern, Marsh and Subalpine Warblers and Common Rosefinch have all been seen in June. In common with many other coastal sites in the region, Little Egrets are regular visitors from midsummer onwards. Although most numerous during the autumn and winter, this species can now be expected throughout the year.

The first landbird migrants of the autumn appear during July. As in spring, suitable weather conditions can result in substantial falls of birds with *Phylloscopus* warblers and Wheatears predominating. Other migrants, including Turtle Dove, Tree Pipit, Yellow Wagtail, Redstart,

Little Egret

Whinchat, Wheatear, the commoner warblers and Spotted Flycatcher can also be expected. Amongst the scarcer species that regularly pass through, Wood Warblers and Pied Flycatchers may appear in the woods on Hengistbury from August through to September, Ring Ouzels may be found in the scrubbier areas from mid-September onwards; whilst October and early November is the peak time for Black Redstarts and Firecrests to occur, the latter often arriving with falls of Goldcrests. Flocks of irrupting Bearded Tits are occasionally encountered late in the season. Visual passage during the early autumn mainly involves Swifts and hirundines which are followed by Meadow Pipits and finches from late September to early November. Finch movements are very much a feature of the area and invariably includes Brambling, Siskin and Redpoll in small numbers, and in recent years a few Tree Sparrows and Twite – both very scarce birds in Dorset. Landbird subrarities including Hoopoe, Wryneck, Richard's and Tawny Pipits, Bluethroat, Aquatic, Icterine, Melodious, Barred and Yellow-browed Warblers, Red-breasted Flycatcher, Red-backed Shrike, Serin, Common Rosefinch, Lapland and Ortolan Buntings have all occurred. Some species, notably Richard's and Tawny Pipits, Aquatic and Yellow-browed Warblers, Lapland and Ortolan Buntings have been seen annually in recent autumns. There are also records of such rarities as Alpine Swift, Short-toed Lark, Red-rumped Swallow, Great Reed, Greenish, Pallas's, Dusky and Bonelli's Warblers, Woodchat Shrike, Red-eyed Vireo and Northern Parula.

Apart from movements of terns, mainly Sandwich, Common and Arctic, unsettled weather and gales are required to induce any worth-while sea passage off Hengistbury during the autumn. The main species involved in these movements are Gannet, Common Scoter and Kitti-wake together with the occasional diver, Fulmar, Manx Shearwater, sea-duck, skua, Little Gull, Black Tern and auk. Severe gales regularly bring Grey Phalaropes close inshore; whilst such conditions have produced sightings of Sooty Shearwater, Storm and Leach's Petrels, Long-tailed Skua, Sabine's Gull and Little Auk. An unprecedented total of 91 Sabine's Gulls moved past Hengistbury as a result of the Great Storm in October 1987.

Pied Flycatcher

Autumn wader passage is well under way by July. The more noteworthy of the earlier migrants include Little Ringed Plover, Whimbrel, Green and Common Sandpipers. The bulk of the waders, however, pass through in August and September when small numbers of Knot, Sanderling, Little Stint, Curlew Sandpiper, Ruff, Black-tailed and Bar-tailed Godwits, Spotted Redshank, Greenshank and Wood Sandpiper regularly occur. Grey Phalaropes frequently appear after gales which may also produce the occasional Pectoral Sandpiper. Oddities are always likely to be found; Kentish and Pacific Golden Plovers, Temminck's Stint, Baird's Sandpiper, Lesser Yellowlegs, Terek and Spotted Sandpipers and Red-necked Phalarope have all been recorded. Good numbers of Sandwich, Common, Arctic and Little Terns along with a few Little Gulls and Black Terns occur on passage; whilst Mediterranean Gull and Roseate Tern are noted from time to time. Garganey regularly appear in autumn and Spotted Crakes are virtually annual visitors, which are most often observed along the margins of Priory Bay and the Priory Pools. Migrant raptors include a few Hobbies; whilst Ospreys are occasionally seen fishing for mullet and there are several sightings of both Marsh and Montagu's Harriers at this season. As in spring, autumn is a good time to find rare and unusual birds. In addition to those already mentioned, there are records of Purple Heron, Glossy Ibis, Spoonbill, Blue-winged Teal, Red-footed Falcon, Little Crake, Common Crane, Ross's Gull, Gull-billed, Caspian and White-winged Black Terns.

During the winter Christchurch Harbour supports a wide diversity of waterfowl, waders and gulls. Amongst the wildfowl Brent Geese, Shelduck, Wigeon and Teal are usually present, sometimes in good numbers. Gadwall have become more frequent in recent years, but Pintail and Shoveler remain rather sporadic in occurrence. Small numbers of Little Grebes, Goldeneye and sometimes Great Crested Grebes and Red-breasted Mergansers, can be found inside the harbour, but divers, the rarer winter grebes and sea-duck are rarely seen here. Priory Bay often attracts a few Pochard and Tufted Duck with numbers increasing during periods of hard weather. Such conditions often result in large movements of White-fronted Geese and Wigeon along with occasional parties of Bewick's Swans, down the Avon Valley and over the harbour where Scaup, Smew and Goosander regularly seek refuge from the cold. Goosanders have also occurred increasingly in milder weather and have overwintered.

All the commoner waders winter in the harbour area. Although numbers have declined dramatically in recent winters, Stanpit Marsh and Wick Hams are still amongst the best sites in the region to see Jack Snipe; whilst up to a hundred or more Snipe can also be found in the same areas. A small flock of Purple Sandpipers often visit the groyne and rocky breakwaters off Hengistbury, although birds regularly commute between here and the breakwaters along the Southbourne and Bournemouth seafronts. Otherwise few other waders of note can be expected; Avocet, Knot, Sanderling, Ruff, Spotted Redshank, Greenshank, Green and Common Sandpipers all being infrequent in occurrence.

The large numbers of gulls that inhabit the harbour are worth checking through for Mediterranean and Little Gulls and storm-driven Kittiwakes. Iceland and Glaucous Gulls are reported annually, but most birds appear to be transients and seldom remain for long. Cormorants and Grey Herons are present throughout the year; whilst a few Shags occur, mostly off Hengistbury Head. Small numbers of Water Rails skulk in the reedbeds which may also host the occasional Bittern during periods of severe cold.

A few Eider and Common Scoter usually winter on the sea off Hengistbury Head. Occasionally Velvet Scoter mingle with the Common Scoter; whilst divers, Great Crested and rarer winter grebes, Long-tailed Duck, Red-breasted Merganser and auks also appear offshore from time to time.

Noteworthy movements of divers, wildfowl including sea-duck, Kittiwakes and auks often take place in association with either gales and/or periods of severe cold. In a recent winter, stormy weather also produced such seabird oddities as Storm and Leach's Petrels, Grey Phalarope, Sabine's Gull and Little Auk. The upchannel movements of sprat shoals may attract large numbers of divers, Gannet, sea-duck, Kittiwake and auks to feed offshore in Poole Bay.

Amongst the smaller birds of interest, Kingfishers can be seen along the harbour shores, Rock Pipits are widely scattered throughout the area, a few Water Pipits frequent Stanpit Marsh and Bearded Tits can sometimes be found in the reedbeds. In mild winters, the woods on Hengistbury are favoured by Chiffchaffs and Firecrests. Black Redstart and Snow Bunting are uncommon visitors at this season, mainly to the shore areas along Hengistbury Head.

Timing

Landbird migrants should be looked for when fall conditions prevail. Early morning visits are strongly advised, particularly in spring when overnight arrivals tend to move off quickly.

For sea passage in any season, Hengistbury Head's position requires strong onshore (SW–SE) winds to force birds into Poole Bay through the gap between Purbeck and the Isle of Wight. Spring seawatching is most rewarding early in the morning between mid-April and mid-May.

Since the harbour is comparatively small, the state of the tide is not as critical for watching wildfowl and waders as at some other coastal sites and, except for Blackberry Point, most birds feeding out on the mudflats can be seen reasonably well, even at low tide. Nevertheless, the best views of waders and other birds can be obtained an hour or so before and after high-water when they feed close inshore to Stanpit South Marsh. At high tide, many wildfowl, waders, gulls, terns and other water-birds roost on Stanpit East Marsh. Unfortunately the other roosting site on Blackberry Point is too distant to observe satisfactorily.

The entire area suffers greatly from all manner of disturbance, so early morning visits are generally to be recommended.

Access

Stanpit Marsh and the north side of the harbour are within easy reach of Christchurch; whilst Hengistbury Head, Wick Fields and the south side of the harbour should be approached from Southbourne.

Christchurch Harbour (north) can be viewed from either Mudeford Quay,* which is reached by turning south into Chichester Way from Mudeford Lane; or Fishermans Bank, which is reached along Argyle Road off Stanpit Lane. There is a pedestrian ferry across the harbour entrance between Mudeford Quay and Hengistbury Head.

Stanpit Marsh can be reached from (i) the Recreation Ground car park off Stanpit Lane, just south of the Ship in Distress PH; (ii) Christ-church Swimming Pool car park* off Stony Lane South, by following the footpath south along the east side of the golf course; and (iii) Christ-church Civic Offices car park,* by following the footpath south between the Hampshire Avon and the west side of the golf course. There is pub-lic access to much of Stanpit Marsh, although visitors should avoid dis-turbing the birds and other wildlife. Crouch Hill provides a good vantage point to observe the high tide roost on Stanpit East Marsh; whilst Blackberry Point and the mudflats of Stanpit Bight are best viewed from the end of Stanpit South Marsh. Other areas worthy of attention include Priory Bay and Priory Pools; the latter can be overlooked from the edge of the nearby golf course.

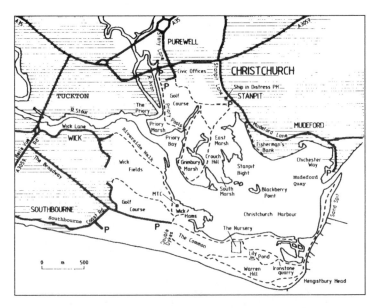

Hengistbury Head car park* is approached along the Broadway, which can be reached from either Belle Vue Road (off Tuckton round-about) or Southbourne Coast Road. Except for the Old Nursery Garden, which is maintained as a bird sanctuary, there is public access to most of Hengistbury Head. Seawatching is best undertaken from the base of the sand spit where beach-huts provide shelter from strong winds.

Wick Fields are crossed by a well signposted footpath (Riverside Walk) between the end of the Broadway at Hengistbury (by the Pitch and Putt Course) and Wick Village.

Calendar

All Year. Cormorant, Shag, Little Egret, Grey Heron, Canada Goose, Shel-duck, Water Rail, Oystercatcher, Ringed Plover, Redshank, Rock Pipit, Stonechat, Cetti's and Dartford Warblers, Reed Bunting.

Spring (mid-March–late May): sea passage best mid-April to mid-May – including divers; Fulmar; Manx Shearwater; Gannet; Common Scoter and other sea-duck; waders; skuas including annual Pomarine and Great; Little Gull and Kittiwake; terns including Black and occasional Roseate; and auks.

Garganey; migrant raptors including Hobby, occasional Merlin and possible larger species; migrant waders including Avocet, Little Ringed Plover, Knot, Sanderling, Little Stint, Curlew Sandpiper, Ruff, both god-wits, Whimbrel, Spotted Redshank, Greenshank, Green, Wood and Common Sandpipers, and near annual Kentish Plover; gulls including Little, occasional Mediterranean, possible Iceland and Glaucous; terns including occasional Black and Roseate; landbird migrants including from mid-March Water Pipit, Black Redstart, Ring Ouzel and Firecrest, from mid-April Wood Warbler and Pied Flycatcher.

Most likely oddities: Spoonbill, Temminck's Stint, Hoopoe, Serin, other landbird subrarities.

Summer (late May–mid-July); occasional sea passage – mainly involving Fulmar, Manx Shearwater, Storm Petrel, Gannet, Common Scoter, Kittiwake and terns.

Non-breeding wildfowl, waders and terns – Sandwich, Common, Little and occasional Roseate; Sand Martin, Sedge and Reed Warblers.

Autumn (mid-July–early November): sea passage most likely during/after gales – including Fulmar; Manx and occasional Sooty Shearwaters; occa-sional Storm and Leach's Petrels; Gannet; Common Scoter and other sea-duck/wildfowl; occasional Grey Phalarope; skuas including Pomarine and possible Long-tailed; Kittiwake, Little and occasional Sabine's Gulls; terns including occasional Black; auks including occasional Little Auk.

Garganey; migrant raptors including Merlin, Hobby, near annual Marsh Harrier and Osprey, and possible other larger species; near annu-al Spotted Crake; migrant waders including Little Ringed Plover, Knot, Sanderling, Little Stint, Curlew Sandpiper, Ruff, both godwits, Whimbrel, Spotted Redshank, Greenshank, Green, Wood and Common Sandpipers; Little and occasional Mediterranean Gulls; terns including Black and occasional Roseate; landbird migrants including from early August Wood Warbler and Pied Flycatcher, from mid-September Black Redstart, Ring Ouzel and Firecrest, also occasional Bearded Tit and Twite.

Most likely oddities: Spoonbill, rare waders and terns, landbird subrarities.

Winter (mid-November–mid-March): during/after gales, during cold weather, following sprat shoals upchannel – occasional sea passage including divers, Gannet, Common Scoter and other sea-duck/wildfowl, skuas (usually Great), Kittiwake and auks.

Occasional divers; Little, Great Crested and occasional rarer winter grebes; possible Bittern in cold weather; wildfowl including Brent Goose, Wigeon, Gadwall, Teal, Shoveler, Pochard, Tufted Duck, Eider, Common Scoter, Goldeneye, Red-breasted Merganser, occasional Pintail, Long-tailed Duck and Velvet Scoter, in cold weather wild swans (usually Bewick's), grey geese (usually White-fronted), Scaup, Smew and Goosander; waders including Purple Sandpiper, Jack Snipe, occasional Avocet, Knot, Sanderling, Ruff, Spotted Redshank, Greenshank, Green and Common Sandpipers; gulls including occasional Mediterranean, Little and Kittiwake, possible Iceland and Glaucous; Kingfisher, Water Pipit, Chiffchaff, Firecrest, occasional Black Redstart and Bearded Tit, possible Twite and Snow Bunting.

Most likely oddity: rare wildfowl.

32 THE HAMPSHIRE AVON AND BLASHFORD LAKES

OS Maps 195, 184
& New Forest
SZ19/SU10/11

Habitat

The valley of the Hampshire Avon supports some of the finest riverine and wetland habitats to be found in the region. Habitat diversity is further enhanced by the presence of a series of flooded gravel pits to the north of Ringwood.

The Hampshire Avon rises in the Vale of Pewsey and derives much of its water from the chalk aquifer of Salisbury Plain. The river crosses from the chalk to the Tertiaries of the Hampshire Basin near Fordingbridge and continues south to Christchurch Harbour where it forms a joint estuary with the River Stour. Downstream of the Wiltshire border the river, which is fringed in places by reedbeds and marshy thickets of willow, alder and poplar, meanders through a wide floodplain mainly comprising wet meadows prone to winter inundation.

The Blashford Lakes are a series of flooded gravel pits of various ages ranging from pre-war to those that are still being worked. As a result they offer a wide range of habitats from lakes bordered by well established scrub and woodland to more recent pits with shallows, little marginal vegetation and areas of bare gravel.

The importance of the Hampshire Avon for wildlife is recognised by the fact that much of the valley is designated as a SSSI. In addition to the birds, the area supports an outstanding flora and fauna. The wet meadows are rich in plant life; whilst several insect groups are well represented, over 20 species of dragonfly being recorded from the Blashford Lakes alone.

Species

In winter, Bewick's Swans and White-fronted Geese are the main specialities amongst the abundance of waterfowl that frequents the Hampshire Avon and Blashford Lakes.

Bewick's Swans

White-fronted Geese have regularly wintered in the valley since the early 1940s with numbers increasing to reach winter peaks of 1,500 or so birds in the late 1960s. Since then there has been a gradual decline, which has accelerated in recent years with winter maximum barely reaching the 100 mark. The goose flock can be very elusive, preferring areas out of view of most public roads and footpaths. Until the early 1980s the riverside meadows between Ibsley and Hucklesbrook were a regular haunt, but recently the geese have favoured areas near Blashford and Bisterne. When either disturbed or during periods of severe frost, the flock will temporarily leave their regular sites and may be observed flying over the lower valley, Christchurch Harbour and other neighbouring parts of Hampshire and Dorset. Bean, Pink-footed and Barnacle Geese are occasionally seen amongst the flock of White-fronted Geese, although the more recent sightings of Bean Geese have been with Bewick's Swans. There are also three records of the exotic and rare Red-breasted Goose. Although some of these birds are undoubtedly wild individuals, it should be remembered that a few feral Pink-footed, Snow and Barnacle Geese together with increasing numbers of feral Greylag Geese and a large population of Canada Geese also inhabit the valley.

The Bewick's Swan is a relative newcomer to the Hampshire Avon. A rare visitor up to 1959, an increase in sightings during the early 1960s were the prelude to regular wintering. Winter maxima built up from around 30 or so in the late 1960s to over 300 in the mid 1980s. Since then numbers have declined slightly with recent peak counts somewhere between 100 and 200 birds. In the early years the meadows to the north of Ibsley Bridge were the main locality. More recently, however, the birds have shown a tendency to frequent two main sections of the valley – Ibsley to Harbridge Green and Christchurch to Avon Village. Bewick's Swans commute between these areas and may be found almost anywhere along the entire valley from Christchurch to Breamore near the Wiltshire border. The swans often roost on the Blashford Lakes, usually Mockbeggar where they may be present during the day if disturbed from nearby Ibsley Meadows. Whooper Swans are rare visitors to the valley, most often appearing during periods of cold weather.

Of the other waterfowl that winter in the area, Wigeon is the most abundant species with recent winter maxima in the region of 1,500 to 5,000 birds. Good numbers of Little and Great Crested Grebes, Gadwall, Teal, Shoveler, Pochard and Tufted Duck are also present along with a few Shelduck, but Pintail have declined and peak counts now barely reach double figures. Since the mid 1970s, the only inland wintering flock of Goldeneye in the region has become established with birds mainly feeding on the river by day and returning to the Blashford Lakes to roost at dusk. Periods of cold weather may produce such classic species as Scaup, Smew, Goosander and Ruddy Duck. Although uncommon visitors away from the coast, there have been reports of Red-throated, Black-throated and Great Northern Divers and Red-necked and Black-necked Grebes from both the river and the lakes. Both Cormorants, which have a night roost at Avon Village and a day roost on the Blashford Lakes, and Grey Herons are present throughout the year; whilst harsh winter weather may bring the occasional Bittern to seek refuge in the riverside reedbeds. Since the mid 1990s, Little Egrets have appeared with increasing frequency along the Hampshire Avon and if the present trend continues, this species will soon become a regular feature of the valley.

Large flocks of Lapwing and Golden Plover roam the valley in winter. Snipe are also widely distributed throughout the area and gatherings of several hundred birds may occur at suitable localities. A small flock of Oystercatchers is often present in the meadows near Christchurch; whilst a few Curlew, Redshank and Green Sandpiper may be encountered almost anywhere. Extensive winter flooding usually results in an influx of waders, mainly involving Lapwing, Snipe and Redshank. Sometimes these are joined by flocks of Dunlin, mostly in the lower valley below Ringwood; whilst Ruff occasionally mingle with the Redshank. Almost anything can occur – there are winter sightings of Ringed Plover, Jack Snipe, Black-tailed Godwit, Greenshank, Wood and Common Sandpipers and even a Lesser Yellowlegs. Black-headed and Common Gulls are common and there is a daily early morning movement of Great Black-backed and a few Lesser Black-backed Gulls up the valley to feed at Somerley Rubbish Tip.

Hen Harriers frequently wander from the nearby heathlands to hunt over the river meadows; whilst there is always the chance of seeing the occasional Merlin, Peregrine and Short-eared Owl – the latter sometimes overwinters in the lower valley near Christchurch. Amongst the smaller birds of interest, a few Water Pipits inhabit the meadows near Christchurch and to the south of Ringwood and flocks of Siskin and Redpoll are widely distributed in birch and alder woodlands throughout the valley.

During the spring and summer the meadows of the Hampshire Avon support a reasonable breeding population of Lapwing and Redshank together with a few pairs of Snipe and Yellow Wagtail. Although there has been a general reduction in the numbers of these 'meadow' species in recent years, the decline of the Snipe and Yellow Wagtail has been particularly dramatic. Breeding waterfowl associated with the main river and riverside meadows include Little and Great Crested Grebes, Canada Geese, Shelduck, Tufted Duck and in recent years feral Greylag Geese. There are several small heronries scattered along the valley including one opposite the Bible College at Sopley. Sedge and Reed Warblers and Reed Buntings occur widely in riverside vegetation; whilst the Cetti's

Warbler is now well established at several sites. Due to the lack of suitable habitat, Kingfishers and Grey Wagtails are scarce breeders along the main river, showing a preference for the smaller side-streams and tributaries. The Blashford Lakes also hold a number of interesting breeding birds including a good selection of waterfowl and waders.

The valley of the Hampshire Avon is an important route for a variety of migrant birds. In spring the wet meadows, notably those in the lower valley, are particularly attractive to passage wildfowl and waders. In autumn these meadows are often dry and consequently less appealing to birds. If the river floods, however, then wildfowl and waders will take advantage of the wet conditions. The Blashford Lakes are also very good for migrant waders in both spring and autumn. A few Common and Black Terns, along with the occasional Little Gull appear on passage most years; whilst Sandwich Terns sometimes fish along the lower river in spring. Raptors are very much a feature of the migration periods. Hobbies regularly pass through and Ospreys are virtually annual visitors; whilst there are also sightings of Honey Buzzard, Red Kite, Marsh and Montagu's Harriers. There is a small passage of landbird migrants with open country species such as Whinchat and Wheatear often conspicuous. Scarcer species including Black Redstart, Ring Ouzel, Firecrest and Pied Flycatcher are occasionally seen; whilst there have been several reports of landbird subrarities.

With the wealth of bird habitats, the area has attracted a good selection of rarities in winter and at times of passage. These are mentioned under Recommended Sites.

Timing

Timing is not particularly critical. Flood conditions and periods of cold weather can be very rewarding in winter; whilst early morning and evening in spring and summer are the best times to visit the wet meadows.

General Access

The main routes to the Hampshire Avon and the Blashford Lakes are the B3347 Christchurch to Ringwood and A338 Ringwood to Salisbury roads.

Recommended Sites

The following are the best and most accessible birdwatching sites along the Hampshire Avon.

32A LOWER AVON MEADOWS

Maps p. 119 and p. 120, SZ19

Habitat and Species

This section of the valley supports some of the finest wet meadows and riverside habitats found along the Hampshire Avon. Coward's Marsh, which lies to the west of the river near St Catherine's Hill, exhibits a particularly interesting range of vegetation types including birch woodland and heath.

Lapwing and Redshank still nest in the riverside meadows, but Snipe have declined dramatically since the late 1980s with only a few pairs remaining and the Yellow Wagtail has disappeared as a breeding species. Several Cetti's Warblers reside in the riverside reedbeds and scrub along with Sedge and Reed Warblers and Reed Bunting. Both

Snipe

Kingfishers and Grey Wagtails nest in the vicinities of Winkton Weir and Knapp Mill. Great Crested Grebe, Shelduck, Tufted Duck and sometimes Pochard are present during the summer and may attempt to breed. Lesser Spotted Woodpeckers occur in the birch woods bordering Coward's March; whilst Barn Owls can often be seen hunting at dusk in the fields by the Avon Causeway.

In winter the fields between Sopley and the Avon Causeway are favoured by Bewick's Swans and Wigeon; whilst large concentrations of Snipe inhabit the meadows nearer Christchurch where a small flock of Oystercatchers is often found. Small groups Pochard and Tufted Duck regularly frequent the main river. Flooding and periods of cold weather increases the variety of wildfowl and waders that can be seen and increases the chances of finding something more unusual – Red-throated and Black-throated Divers, Bittern, Whooper Swan, Egyptian Goose, Scaup, Smew and Goosander have been reported at this season. Short-eared Owls are recorded most years and sometimes overwinter.

The lower meadows are particularly good for migrant birds, especially in spring when Garganey are virtually annual visitors and waders such as Little Ringed and Ringed Plovers, Dunlin, Ruff, Jack Snipe, Black-tailed Godwit, Whimbrel, Greenshank, Green, Wood and Common Sandpipers have been recorded. Sandwich Terns sometimes fish the lower river in spring; whilst Common and Black Terns occasionally appear in both seasons. A scattering of landbird migrants pass through and small falls of some species, such as Wheatear, have been noted. A few Water Pipits also frequent the meadows throughout the winter and early spring.

An impressive list of rarities has been recorded from this area over the years; the most famous being the Little Bustard which was present for a few days in late December 1987 and early January 1988. There are also records of Night Heron, Spoonbill, Ring-necked and Ferruginous Ducks, Honey Buzzard, Marsh Harrier, Red-footed Falcon, Common Crane, Lesser Yellowlegs, White-winged Black Tern, Hoopoe, Tawny Pipit and Serin.

Access

The meadows between Christchurch and Burton are crossed by foot-paths between the B3347 (Stony Lane) in Burton and Knapp Mill (West Hants Water Company) in Christchurch. The first footpath starts from a lay-by just north of the railway bridge and the second starts by a bridge over a small stream 0.8 miles (1.3 km) north of the A35 Purewell round-about. Coward's Marsh is reached from the B3073 (Fairmile Road) in

Christchurch by turning east into Suffolk Avenue, which lies approximately midway between Fairmile Hospital and the Jumpers/Iford round-

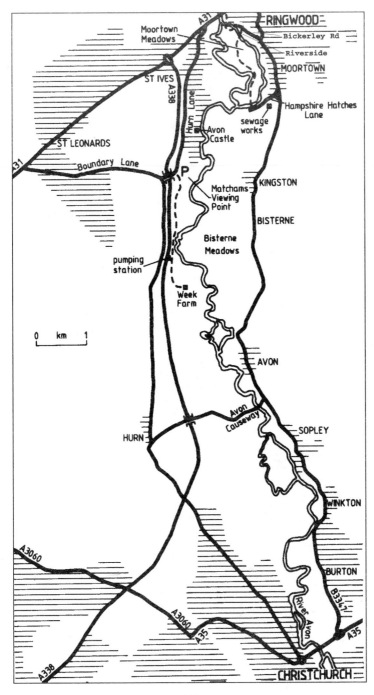

about, and continuing through the housing estate until the road turns sharply south into Marsh Lane. From here walk north along the rough

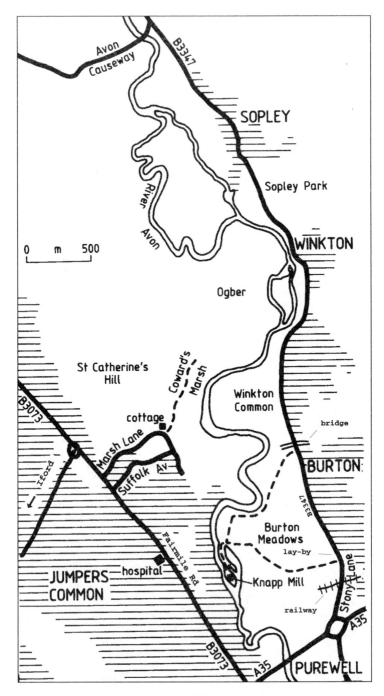

track (also Marsh Lane) to the style by Marsh Cottage. Visitors should check the notice board for access details before entering the marsh and great care should be taken not to disturb nesting waders. Ogber Field and the nearby river can be viewed well from the B3347 just south of Sopley; whilst the meadows and river between Sopley and Avon Village can be best observed from the Avon Causeway road between Hurn Village and the B3347 just north of Sopley.

32B BISTERNE AND RINGWOOD MEADOWS

Map p. 119, SZ19 & SU10

Habitat and Species

In winter the meadows between Avon Village and Bisterne and between Ringwood and Blashford are favoured by the White-fronted Goose flock and large numbers of Wigeon; whilst wandering parties of Bewick's Swans are occasionally seen. There have also been sightings of such rarities as Red-breasted Goose and American Wigeon in this area. In cold weather Goldeneye, Smew and Goosander have appeared on the river. The Bisterne Meadows are also a favoured site for Golden Plover; whilst Hen Harriers are frequently seen in this section of the valley. The riverside alders and birches often host large flocks of Siskin and Redpoll. In spring and summer the meadows hold breeding Redshank and perhaps the odd pair of Snipe and Yellow Wagtail. Great Crested Grebe and Tufted Duck can be seen on the river; whilst Cetti's Warblers reside in the riverside thickets. This is also a good area to see flocks of Canada and feral Greylag Geese. Migrant Ospreys have been noted on several occasions. A Black Stork was seen on the meadows opposite Avon Castle in April 1990.

Access

The Bisterne Meadows can be viewed for White-fronted Geese and other birds from Matchams Viewing Point, which lies off the southern end of Hurn Lane south of Avon Castle and just north of where the road crosses the A338 dual carriageway. The meadows to the north of Ringwood are overlooked from a small access road leading to an electricity sub-station, which lies to the west of the A338 immediately north of the A31 roundabout at Ringwood. The Avon Valley Path crosses Bickerley Common and the Moortown Meadows from Riverside (off Bickerley Road) in Ringwood south to the ford southwest of Ringwood Sewage Works. The latter is reached from the B3347 in Moortown, southwest along Hampshire Hatches Lane.

32C BLASHFORD LAKES (WW/HWT/NEW FOREST DISTRICT COUNCIL)

Maps p. 123 and p. 124, SU10

Habitat and Species

These flooded gravel pits and their environs offer a wide range of habitats which, in addition to the birds, support a rich insect fauna with dragonflies and butterflies well represented.

The Blashford Lakes are an important site for winter waterfowl. The main species are Wigeon, Gadwall, Teal, Shoveler, Pochard and Tufted

Duck. Smaller numbers of Little and Great Crested Grebes, Shelduck and Goldeneye are usually present, but Pintail have become very scarce in recent years. Bewick's Swans sometimes visit Mockbeggar Lake, particularly if they are disturbed from their favoured haunt just north of Ibsley. Smew and Goosander often appear during periods of cold weather. There are also reports of rarer wildfowl such as American Wigeon, Red-crested Pochard, Ring-necked and Ferruginous Ducks. Winter waders may include large flocks of Golden Plover; whilst a few Snipe and Green Sandpipers are regularly present. Waders also feature well at times of passage, showing a preference for the more recent pits such as Mockbeggar and Ellingham. Little Ringed Plover, Green and Common Sandpipers regularly occur in spring and autumn with good numbers often present in the latter season. In fact the lakes boast an impressive list of migrant waders including, in addition to the above, Oystercatcher, Ringed Plover, Knot, Sanderling, Little Stint, Curlew Sandpiper, Dunlin, Ruff, Black-tailed and Bar-tailed Godwits, Whimbrel, Spotted Redshank, Greenshank, Wood Sandpiper and Turnstone together with such rarities as Avocet, Collared Pratincole, Temminck's Stint and Pectoral Sandpiper. Little Gull, Common and Black Terns are noted most years, mainly in autumn. There is a spring report of two Whiskered Terns and an autumn sighting of a White-winged Black Tern. A Cattle Egret was also noted in July 1994. The bushes and scrub around the lakes attract a scattering of landbird migrants such as Redstart, the commoner warblers and Spotted Flycatcher; whilst Yellow Wagtails and Wheatears favour the more open areas.

A wide variety of breeding birds can be found on and around the lakes. These include such waterfowl as Little and Great Crested Grebes, Canada Goose, Shelduck, Gadwall, Tufted Duck and Ruddy Duck; whilst Pochard has bred and Shoveler sometimes summer and may attempt to nest. The younger pits provide suitable nesting sites for Little Ringed and Ringed Plovers; whilst the lakeside vegetation and nearby woodland supports a wide variety of breeding birds. A pair of Kingfishers often nest in the steep banks of one lake.

Access

Although there is no public access to any of the Blashford Lakes at the time of writing (March 1996), this may change in the future – see Blashford Lakes Reserve. At present most of the lakes can be viewed from nearby footpaths and roads. It should be noted that some of the lakes are given over to recreational activities which can cause disturbance to birds.

The main access points to the Blashford Lakes are from the A338 between Ringwood and Ibsley.

Kingfisher, Linbrook and North Poulner Lakes: from the A338 0.3 miles (0.5 km) north of the A31 roundabout at Ringwood, take Hurst Road east through the housing estate to the end of the road, then walk northeast and then east along the Avon Valley Path to view the lakes.

Snails, Linbrook and Blashford (Spinnaker) Lakes: from the A338 at Blashford, take Snails Lane east and view the lakes from various points along the road.

Ivy, Snails, Blashford (Spinnaker) and Rockford Lakes: from the A338 at Blashford, take Ivy Lane (signposted Rockford) east and view the lakes from various points along the road.

Blashford (Spinnaker), Snails and Linbrook Lakes can also be viewed from the footpath which starts just south of the junction of Ivy Lane and Gorley Road and follows the north shore of Blashford (Spinnaker) Lake southwest to Spinnaker Sailing Club. From here continue

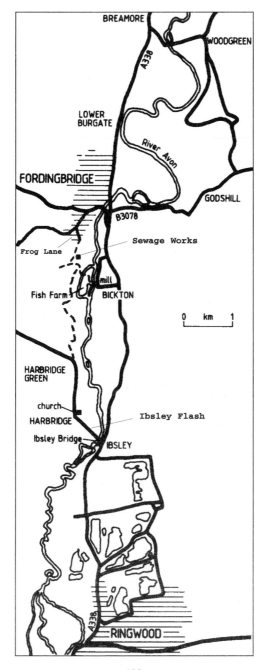

south between Blashford (Spinnaker) and Snails Lake to Snails Lane and then south along the west shore of Linbrook Lake to the Avon Valley Path from Kingfisher Lake.

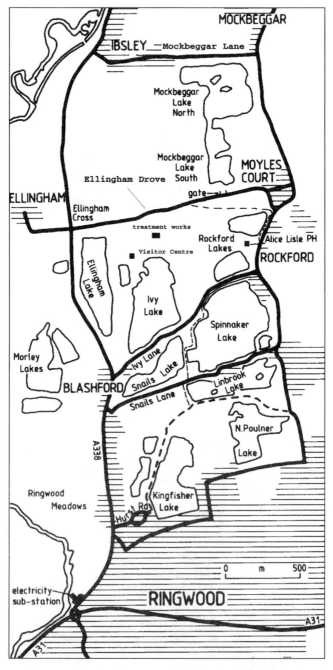

Rockford Lake can also be viewed from the footpath which starts from Ellingham Drove 0.5 miles (0. 8 km) east of Ellingham Cross and follows the Dockens Water east to the Gorley Road and then south along the east shore of the lake to the Alice Lisle PH.

Mockbeggar Lake South: from the A338 at Ellingham Cross take Ellingham Drove east towards Moyles Court. After 0.6 miles (1 km) view the lake from the gate entrance along the embankment to north (left) of the road.

Mockbeggar Lake North: from the A338 at Ibsley take Mockbeggar Lane east to Mockbeggar and then the minor road south to Moyles Court. The lake can be viewed from various points along both roads.

Blashford Lakes Reserve

This reserve, which comprises Ellingham, Ivy and Blashford (Spinnaker) Lakes and their environs, is managed by the Hampshire Wildlife Trust working on contract to and in partnership with Wessex Water PLC and the New Forest District Council. At present access to the recently constructed hide and study centre is by prior arrangement with the Warden. Access to the reserve will develop over the next few years. For further information or group bookings please write to the Warden at the Hampshire Wildlife Trust office – see List of Useful Organisations.

32D IBSLEY MEADOWS AND BICKTON MILL

Map p. 124, SU10/11

Habitat and Species

Like so much of the valley, the landscape is dominated by wet meadows, which are frequently flooded during the winter. There are also some fine riverside reedswamps and thickets in the vicinity of Bickton Mill. In winter the meadows to the north of Ibsley Bridge are the best site in the valley to see Bewick's Swans. When flooded, the meadows attract good numbers of Teal and Snipe together with other wildfowl and waders. The river upstream from Ibsley Bridge regularly holds diving duck, including a small flock of Goldeneye, which may be joined by Smew and Goosander during periods of cold weather.

Lapwing, Redshank and perhaps a few pairs of Snipe nest in the meadows; whilst further upstream near Bickton Mill, Little and Great Crested Grebes, Tufted Duck and Grey Wagtail breed by the river and Cetti's Warblers are well established in the riverside thickets and reedswamp. Odd winter and passage Green Sandpipers sometimes occur beside the fish farm ponds at Bickton Mill.

In spring the semi-permanent pools (Ibsley Flash), which lie close to minor road between Ibsley Bridge and Harbridge Church, sometimes attract Yellow Wagtails as well as such noteworthy migrants as Garganey and Little Ringed Plover. Unusual sightings from this area of the Avon Valley include Black Stork, Bean Goose, Osprey, Red-footed Falcon, Collared Pratincole and Golden Oriole.

Access

The river and meadows (including 'the Flash') at Ibsley are best viewed from the minor road between the A338 at Ibsley Bridge and Harbridge

Church. Further views of the valley can be obtained by taking the minor road north from Harbridge Church towards Harbridge Green. The river near Bickton can be reached by following footpaths from Fordingbridge south along Frog Lane (signposted to Drysdale Garden Exotics) past Fordingbridge Sewage Treatment Works, east towards Bickton Fish Farm and then south along the west side of the valley towards North End Farm.

Calendar

All Year: Little and Great Crested Grebes, Cormorant, Little Egret, Grey Heron, feral Greylag, Snow, Canada and Barnacle Geese, Shelduck, Gadwall, Pochard, Tufted Duck, Ruddy Duck, Buzzard, Snipe, Redshank, Kingfisher, Grey Wagtail, Cetti's Warbler, Reed Bunting.

Winter (November–mid-March): possible divers and rarer winter grebes; possible Bittern in cold weather; wildfowl including Bewick's Swan (from mid-November), White-fronted Geese (from mid-December to late February), Wigeon, Teal, Pintail, Shoveler, Goldeneye, in cold weather Smew, Goosander, occasional Scaup, possible Whooper Swan and other geese; Hen Harrier, occasional Merlin and Peregrine; Water Rail; waders including Oystercatcher, Golden Plover, Curlew, Green Sandpiper and occasional other species; occasional Short-eared Owl; Water Pipit, Siskin, Redpoll.
  Most likely oddity: rare wildfowl.

Spring (mid-March–mid-May): near annual Garganey; migrant raptors including Hobby and possible Osprey; migrant waders including Little Ringed Plover, Green and Common Sandpipers and occasional other species; Sandwich and occasional Common and Black Terns; landbird migrants including Water Pipit, Yellow Wagtail, Wheatear and occasional scarcer species.
  Most likely oddities: rare heron and allies, rare waders.

Summer (mid-May–mid-July): Little Ringed and Ringed Plovers, Yellow Wagtail, Sedge and Reed Warblers, Lesser Whitethroat, Garden Warbler.

Autumn (mid-July–mid-November): migrant raptors including Hobby and occasional Osprey; migrant waders including Little Ringed Plover, Green and Common Sandpipers and occasional other species; occasional Little Gull; Common and Black Terns; landbird migrants including Yellow Wagtail, Whinchat, Wheatear and occasional scarcer species.
  Most likely oddities: rare waders and terns.

33 MOORS VALLEY COUNTRY PARK (EAST DORSET DISTRICT COUNCIL) AND RINGWOOD FOREST (FC)

OS Map 195
& New Forest
SU00/10

Habitat

This area has been developed as a joint venture between East Dorset District Council and the Forestry Commission. As such the Country Park divides into two sections of very different character. First, there is the land immediately adjacent to the Moors River. Although dominated by an 18-hole golf course, there are a number of features that provide important habitats for birds and wildlife. Apart from the river itself, there are two large lakes as well as areas of wet meadow, scrub and broad-leaved woodland.

To the east lies the second and largest section of the Country Park which comprises the southern part of Ringwood Forest. This mainly consists of coniferous forest at different stages of maturity which includes several large clearings replanted with conifer seedlings.

In addition to the birds, the Country Park supports a rich flora and insect fauna with dragonflies particularly prominent.

Species

With such a diversity of habitats, it is not surprising that a wide range of breeding birds can be found in the Country Park. The lakes attract various waterfowl including Great Crested Grebe, Canada Goose, Shelduck and Tufted Duck; whilst Gadwall, Teal and Ruddy Duck have all been present during the summer in recent years. Sedge and Reed Warblers and Reed Bunting inhabit the vegetation along the margins of the lakes and river where the odd pair of Grey Wagtails also reside. Sand Martins from nearby colonies in Ringwood Forest regularly feed over the upper lake. The Grey Heron is a non-breeding resident and may be seen throughout the year; whilst Cormorants sometimes fly over the Country Park.

The forest area boasts an impressive list of scarce breeding species. The large clearings are favoured by Nightjar, Woodlark and Tree Pipit. These are joined by Stonechat and Dartford Warbler where remnant patches of heather and gorse are found. Until recently, flocks of Crossbills could be regularly seen in the mature coniferous forest. Although this species is much scarcer now, small numbers are still thought to be present. The Siskin is another speciality which is now quite common in the areas of mature forest; whilst a few pairs of Redpoll inhabit the birch thickets. Woodcock can be seen roding over the forest during spring and summer evenings.

Other breeding birds of interest that can be encountered in the Country Park include Turtle Dove, Cuckoo, Green and Great Spotted Woodpeckers, Garden Warbler and Yellowhammer. In addition the Little Owl is often seen in the fields immediately to the west of the lower lake. Buzzards may be seen overhead at any time during the year; whilst Hobbies are likely visitors during the summer.

Crossbill

An off-passage flock of Whimbrel used to be a regular feature of the Country Park in spring. The flock favoured the golf course and fields to the west, including Lower Common, with counts reaching a peak of 150 in May 1991. In recent years, however, the species has become more erratic in its appearances. A few Common Sandpipers pass through in spring and autumn with birds usually frequenting the shores of the upper lake where other migrant waders may appear from time to time. Otherwise a scattering of landbird migrants including Whinchat and Wheatear occur on passage. The Country Park does appear to have the potential to attract the occasional subrarity and rarity.

The number, albeit small, of waterfowl frequenting the lakes increases during the autumn and winter. Teal, Pochard and Tufted Duck are the only species that can be expected, but Gadwall and Shoveler are occasionally present. Obviously almost anything might turn up, a flock of Bewick's Swans roosted in the country park in January and December 1992. At present most of the waterfowl prefer the upper lake where a few Snipe can also be found skulking in the small marsh at the north end. Flocks of Siskin and Redpoll wander around the woodland and forest areas where Brambling are occasionally recorded. Balmy days in late winter can be a good time to find some of the resident breeding specialities such as Woodlark, Dartford Warbler and Crossbill.

Timing

Late winter and early spring (February–April) is the best time to search for certain specialities such as Woodlark, Dartford Warbler and Crossbill. Woodland birds are best looked for during early mornings in spring and summer; whilst crepuscular species such as Woodcock and Nightjar are most likely to be seen on warm summer evenings.

The Country Park is very popular for its various leisure activities. As

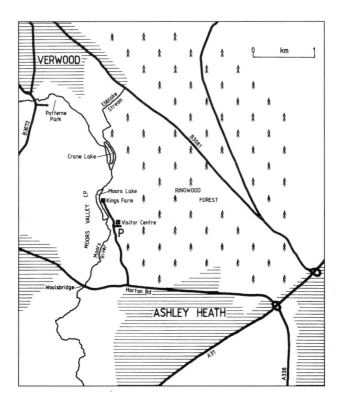

such it is best to avoid weekends, particularly during the summer, and school holidays. Early mornings and evenings are recommended for those wishing to make the best of their visit.

Access

Moors Valley Country Park is well signposted from the Horton Road between Ashley Heath and Woolsbridge. The Country Park is open every day (except Christmas Day) from 7.00 am to dusk. There are car parks* near the Visitor Centre which is open from 9.30 am–4.30 pm. Alternatively the Country Park can be reached on footpaths south from Potterne Park, Verwood and west from various points along the B3081 between Ashley and Verwood. Numerous trails and footpaths give access to much of the Country Park including the forest area. For access to other areas of Ringwood Forest visitors should inquire for details from the Forestry Commission (Dorset Forest District Office) – see List of Organisations.

Calendar

All Year: Great Crested Grebe, Cormorant, Grey Heron; wildfowl including Canada Goose, Tufted Duck, occasional Gadwall and Ruddy Duck; Buzzard, Woodcock, Little Owl, Woodlark, Grey Wagtail, Stonechat, Dartford Warbler, Siskin, Redpoll, Crossbill, Reed Bunting, common resident woodland birds.

Summer (May–July): Shelduck, Hobby, Turtle Dove, Nightjar, Sand Martin, Tree Pipit, Sedge, Reed and Garden Warblers.

Winter (November–March): Teal, Pochard, occasional Shoveler and other wildfowl; Snipe; occasional Brambling.

Spring (April and May) *and Autumn* (August–October): possible Whimbrel flock mid-April–mid-May; Common Sandpiper and occasional other migrant waders; common landbird migrants.

**OS Maps 195
& New Forest
SZ19/SU00/
01/10/11**

34 EAST DORSET HEATHS

Habitat

Like elsewhere in the county, the East Dorset Heaths have suffered from depletion and fragmentation caused by building development and re-clamation for farmland and afforestation. Nevertheless, some fine heathlands still exist within an area that extends from Christchurch and the Stour Valley in the south to Cranborne in the north, and from the Hampshire Avon in the east to the River Allen and the Dorset chalk in the west. These remnants offer a wide range of habitats including bog, open heathland with gorse scrub and scattered self-sown pines, broadleaved woodland and forestry. Fires, notably those that swept over much of the area during the summer of 1976, have added further to habitat diversity by creating open clearings comprising a short ground vegetation of grasses and mosses. Some of these have now been colonised by invasive birch scrub.

Many of these heaths are designated SSSIs; whilst others such as Avon Heath Country Park, Holt Heath and Cranborne Common enjoy further protection under the auspices of various conservation bodies. Ringwood Forest and White Sheet Plantation are managed by the Forestry Commission and the MOD controls other important sites near Matchams Park and at West Moors. These heathlands and forests sustain a rich and interesting flora and fauna. Amongst the insect groups, dragonflies and butterflies are prominent; whilst all six species of British reptile, including the two rare specialities the smooth snake and sand lizard, are also present.

Species

The East Dorset Heaths still support many noteworthy breeding birds. There is a small but thriving population of Woodlarks, which has taken advantage of the habitats found within MOD land as well as those created by the fires. Dartford Warblers and Stonechats are found on most of the drier heaths, usually where there is a good cover of gorse. Nightjars are widely distributed throughout the area showing a preference for heathlands with scattered trees and forest clearings. These habitats are also favoured by Tree Pipits. The Nightingale may still occur in some of its traditional haunts in the Hurn area. The broadleaved woodlands and birch thickets hold such scarce breeding birds as Lesser Spotted Woodpecker, Wood Warbler, Willow Tit and Redpoll; whilst Siskins are now well established in the forestry areas where Crossbills may be encountered, particularly during and immediately after invasion years.

Roding Woodcock are a familiar sight over the woodland and forest borders. The wetter heaths and bogs are the haunt of breeding Reed Buntings; whilst a few pairs of Snipe and Curlew still nest in the bogs of the northern heaths. Buzzards and Hobbies are likely to be seen almost anywhere during the summer months and the Goshawk has been observed over the southern woodlands.

During the winter these heaths appear to be rather desolate areas for birds, although some of the resident specialities, such as Woodlark and Dartford Warbler, can be conspicuous on mild calm days towards the end of the season. The numbers of Siskins and Redpolls increase significantly with large flocks often noted in the vicinity of Avon Castle and Matchams. The wetter heaths and bogs attract small numbers of Teal, Snipe and perhaps the odd Jack Snipe. Hen Harriers and Merlins are seen most winters; whilst Short-eared Owl and Great Grey Shrike occasionally occur.

A trickle of the commoner landbird migrants, including Whinchat and Wheatear, pass through in spring and autumn; whilst scarcer species such as Ring Ouzel, Firecrest and Pied Flycatcher are occasional visitors. In spring off-passage flocks of Whimbrel regularly feed in fields adjacent to some of the northern heaths flying south towards Poole Harbour in the late evening. Rare raptors and a variety of other oddities have been reported at times of passage.

Timing

Certain specialities such as Lesser Spotted Woodpecker, Woodlark and Crossbill are often easier to find on fine days in late winter and early spring (February–April) rather than later in the summer. Early morning is best when searching for most woodland and forest birds, but Woodcock and Nightjars should be looked for on warm calm summer evenings.

Access

The most interesting sites are within easy reach of the following towns: Christchurch for St Catherine's Hill and Town Common, Ringwood for Avon Heath Country Park/Avon Forest Park, Wimborne for Holt Heath and White Sheet Plantation and Fordingbridge for Cranborne Common. More specific details of access are given under Recommended Sites.

Recommended Sites

34A ST CATHERINE'S HILL AND TOWN COMMON

Map p. 132, SZ19

Habitat and Species

Close to the northern outskirts of Christchurch lies St Catherine's Hill, a prominent ridge that offers unparalleled views over Town Common and the valley of the Hampshire Avon. Apart from the open heathy eastern slopes, most of St Catherine's Hill is covered by coniferous trees; whilst Town Common consists of low-lying heathland and boggy pools. There is some gorse scrub at the southeast base of the hill and birch woodland extends along the nearby disused railway line.

St Catherine's Hill is an excellent vantage point for watching migrant and other raptors; Honey Buzzard, Red Kite, Montagu's Harrier, Goshawk and Red-footed Falcon have all been observed from here. Breeding birds, which are typical of heathland and forest include Woodcock,

Nightjar, Tree Pipit, Stonechat, Dartford Warbler and Siskin; whilst the birch woods hold the odd pair of Lesser Spotted Woodpeckers and Redpolls. Hen Harriers are occasionally seen in winter when flocks of Siskins and Redpolls inhabit the birch woodlands.

Access

St Catherine's Hill and Town Common can be reached from the junction of the B3073 (Fairmile Road) and Marsh Lane (signposted to Dudmoor Leisure Centre) in Christchurch, by following the main track (St Catherine's Lane) north up the hill. Alternatively, access can be gained from

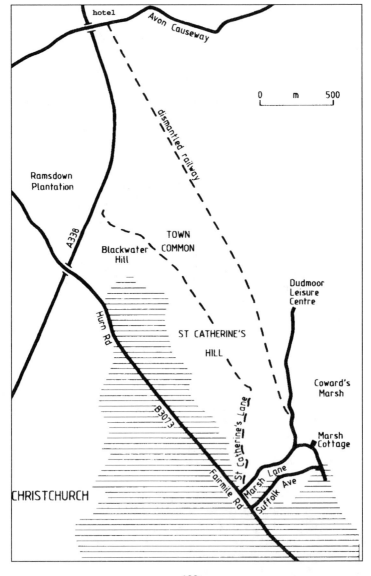

Marsh Lane near Coward's Marsh (see map 132) by following the footpath north along the disused railway. There are several small tracks and footpaths crossing St Catherine's Hill and Town Common. From the north, Town Common can be reached south along the track opposite the Avon Causeway Hotel, which is situated on Avon Causeway between Hurn Village and the B3347 just north of Sopley.

34B AVON HEATH COUNTRY PARK (DCC/DWT)

Map p. 134, SU10

Habitat and Species

Avon Heath Country Park (also known as Avon Forest Park) consists of two disjunct areas of heathland, woodland and forestry, which are separated by land controlled by the MOD. The southern section lies close to Matchams Park and offers a mixture of heath, gorse scrub, mainly birch woodland and coniferous forest; whilst the northern part of the park is centred on Barnsfield Wood and consists mainly of coniferous forest together with smaller areas of bog, heath, birch thicket and broadleaved woodland. Large clearings of short grass sward and birch scrub, resulting from fires dating back to 1976, are still a major feature of the habitat. The site is managed by Dorset County Council; whilst the Dorset Wildlife Trust also have some land within the park.

Woodlark

Several pairs of Woodlark reside in the area favouring the grassy clearings and patches of disturbed ground. Other breeding birds of interest include Woodcock, Nightjar, Tree Pipit, Stonechat, Dartford Warbler, Siskin and Reed Bunting. The Crossbill occasionally breeds in the forest areas; whilst the odd pair of Lesser Spotted Woodpeckers, Wood Warblers and Redpolls can sometimes be found in the birch woods. In winter flocks of Siskins and Redpolls roam the park; whilst Hen Harriers occasionally appear. Honey Buzzard, Montagu's Harrier and Osprey have been seen overhead on passage.

Access

Avon Heath Country Park North can be reached either from the westbound carriageway of the A31 0.5 miles (0.8 km) west of the A31/A338 junction at Ashley, by taking Birch Road and following the signs to the

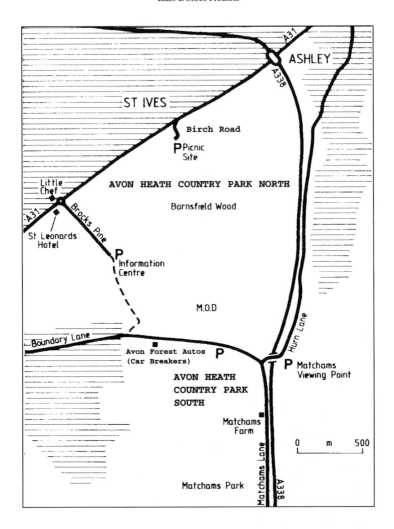

picnic site; or from the A31 at the St Ives roundabout (near Little Chef and St Leonard's Hotel), by following the signs southeast along Brocks Pine to the Information Centre car park. The car park to Avon Heath Country Park South is situated at the Matchams Park end of Boundary Lane, immediately east of Avon Forest Autos and 1.5 miles (2.4 km) east of the A31 roundabout near St Leonard's Hospital. Well marked footpaths give access to both sections of the park.

34C HOLT HEATH NNR (EN) AND WHITE SHEET PLANTATION (FC)

Map p. 135, SU00

Habitat and Species

Holt Heath is the finest example of heathland and bog remaining in East Dorset. Adjacent to the southwest corner of the heath lies White Sheet

Plantation which was mostly destroyed by fire in 1979. As a result of a replanting programme, this area now offers an interesting transitional habitat of heath, gorse, birch scrub and young forestry. The southern edge of White Sheet Plantation is overlooked by the mature mixed woodlands of Stable and Park Copses. Fortunately Holt Heath enjoys protection as a National Nature Reserve (EN).

It is not surprising that these sites support most of the breeding birds characteristic of bog, heathland and forest. Stonechats and Dartford Warblers are found throughout the area, usually where gorse is present; whilst Nightjars are particularly common in White Sheet Plantation. Although the Woodlark does not appear to be a regular breeding bird, this species has occasionally held territory, most often in the eastern part of the heath. Reed Buntings frequent the wetter heathlands and bogs where Curlew and perhaps Snipe still nest. Tree Pipits are sparsely distributed in those areas with scattered trees, notably in the vicinity of White Sheet Hill. Woodcock can be regularly seen roding over White Sheet Plantation as well as Stable and Park Copses, which also support a wide range of other woodland birds including Lesser Spotted Woodpecker and perhaps Willow Tit. Thickets of birch scrub are

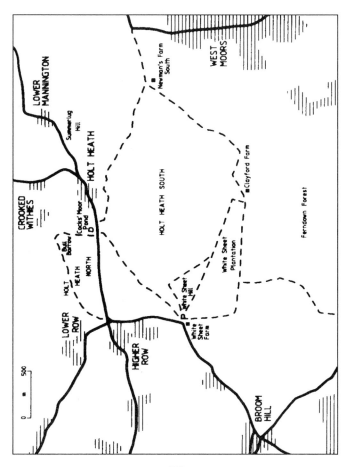

favoured by a few pairs of breeding Redpolls; whilst Crossbills occasionally visit the mature stands of conifers. The odd pair of Little Grebes nest on the small ponds close to Stable Copse. Hen Harrier and Merlin are frequent visitors in winter; whilst Great Grey Shrikes have overwintered several times in recent years. In spring off-passage flocks of Whimbrel often feed in fields adjacent to the heath, notably around Lower Row and near White Sheet Farm. These Whimbrel flocks can sometimes be seen flying south over the heath in the late evening. A trickle of landbird migrants including Whinchat and Wheatear pass through in spring and autumn. There are also reports of such oddities as Wryneck, Icterine Warbler and Red-backed Shrike.

Access
These sites are best approached from White Sheet Hill car park, which lies off a minor road at White Sheet Farm 1 mile (1.6 km) northeast of the crossroads in Broom Hill and 0.5 miles (0.8 km) south of Higher Row. There are many well-marked tracks and footpaths crossing both White Sheet Plantation and Holt Heath.

34D CRANBORNE COMMON NR (DWT)

Map p. 137, SU01/11

Habitat and Species
Cranborne Common, which is a nature reserve managed by the Dorset Wildlife Trust, is the most northern of the East Dorset Heaths. Habitats include bog and wet heath, drier heathland with gorse and scattered self-sown pines and birch woodland. The common is virtually surrounded by forestry.

A number of breeding birds including Nightjar, Tree Pipit, Stonechat, Dartford Warbler and Reed Bunting can be found on Cranborne Common. Woodcock display over the surrounding forest which is favoured by breeding Siskins and occasionally Crossbills. Buzzards are frequently seen overhead throughout the year; whilst there is always a good chance of a visiting Hobby during the summer months. Hen Harrier, Merlin and Great Grey Shrike have all occurred in winter when flocks of Siskins and Redpolls frequent birches and alders along the nearby Sleep Brook. Noteworthy sightings include Red-footed Falcon and Hoopoe.

Access
From the end of Blackwater Grove in Alderholt follow the bridlepath (signposted to Verwood) along a rough track through some pines and then fields to a T junction near some farm buildings. From here continue left past the farm buildings to reach Cranborne Common. From the notice board follow the bridlepath (marked by blue posts) southwest across the reserve towards a distant radio mast.

Calendar
All Year: Buzzard, Woodcock, Lesser Spotted Woodpecker, Woodlark, Stonechat, Dartford Warbler, Willow Tit, Siskin, Redpoll, Crossbill, Reed Bunting, common resident woodland birds.

Summer (May–July): Hobby, Curlew, Nightjar, Tree Pipit, Nightingale, Wood Warbler.

Winter (November–March): Teal, Hen Harrier, Merlin, Snipe and occasional Jack Snipe, possible Short-eared Owl and Great Grey Shrike.

Spring (April and May) *and Autumn* (August and September): Whimbrel mainly in spring; landbird migrants including Whinchat, Wheatear and occasional scarce species such as Ring Ouzel, Firecrest and Pied Flycatcher.
  Most likely oddity: scarce/rare migrant raptor.

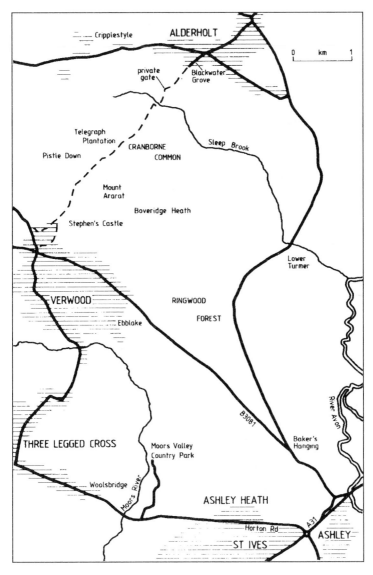

EAST DORSET AND THE HAMPSHIRE AVON – OTHER SITES WORTHY OF ATTENTION

OS Maps 195
& New Forest

35 BOURNEMOUTH SEAFRONT

SZ08/09/19

The offshore waters of Poole Bay are worth checking for divers, grebes, sea-duck and auks in winter. Autumn and winter gales sometimes bring seabirds close inshore. These storm-blown movements may occasionally involve a few skuas and, in exceptional circumstances, rarer species such as Leach's Petrel. Sandwich and Common Terns regularly fish offshore during the summer; whilst the cliffs towards the Southbourne end of the bay support breeding Kestrel, Skylark, Sand Martin and Stonechat. The coastal scrub and wooded valleys, notably at Branksome and Alum Chines, attract a few landbird migrants including the occasional Firecrest and Pied Flycatcher. There must always be a chance of finding something more unusual like a Hoopoe; whilst an Alpine Swift was seen at Branksome Chine in April 1992. There is general access to the entire seafront overlooking Poole Bay from Sandbanks in the west to Hengistbury Head in the east. Sites of particular interest include Branksome Chine at SZ065896, Alum Chine at SZ075902, Bournemouth Pier at SZ089906, Boscombe Pier at SZ112911 and Southbourne Overcliff at SZ135913.

36 RIVER STOUR AT THROOP

SZ19

This area supports fine riverine habitats typical of the lower reaches of the River Stour with damp meadows and mature woodland to the north and east. Perhaps the best site to find many of the River Stour's more characteristic breeding birds such as Kingfisher, Grey Wagtail, Sedge and Reed Warblers and Reed Bunting. One or two pairs of Great Crested Grebes are also present in summer and have nested successfully; whilst Common Terns are frequent non-breeding visitors. Cormorants and Grey Herons can be seen throughout the year. The nearby fields and scattered trees are particularly good for Barn and Little Owls; whilst a few pairs of Lapwing still nest in some of the wetter meadows. Generally the area supports a wide range of hedgerow and woodland breeding birds including Cuckoo, Green and Great Spotted Woodpeckers, Skylark, Whitethroat, Spotted Flycatcher, Treecreeper, Linnet and Yellowhammer. Relatively few wildfowl, mainly Tufted Duck, are present in winter, but flocks of Bewick's Swans occasionally feed in the riverside meadows and there are recent records of Egyptian Goose and Goosander. Common Sandpipers occur regularly in spring and autumn. The potential for inland sites such as this attracting unusual birds is shown by sightings of Common Crane and Black-throated Thrush in

January 1994 and a Serin in June 1989. Access is best from Throop Mill car park at SZ112958. The river and fields to the north and east can be reached by a circular walk. From Throop Mill take the footpath north to the metal bridge across the weir at SZ113960, northwest along the river-bank to SZ111967 and north to Merritown at SZ112971. From here follow the metalled road southeast to West Hurn and then south to SZ118959, finally returning west on the footpath along the riverbank to the metal bridge at SZ113960.

THE CHALK

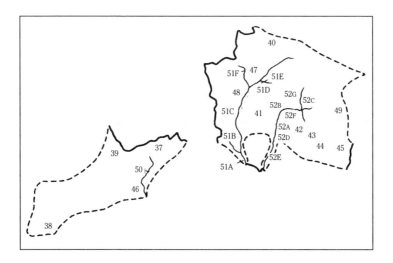

PART 1 – THE DOWNS

General Introduction

The chalk downs of Wessex are a dominant feature of the region's landscape, extending in a broad band across central, northwest and west Hampshire into northeast and central Dorset. In the south the chalk forms a very narrow but prominent ridge through Purbeck and the Isle of Wight, creating such notable landmarks as Ballard Down, Old Harry Rocks, the Needles and Culver Cliff. Portsdown Hill, the high ridge overlooking Portsmouth, is an outlier of the chalk.

From the time Neolithic farmers arrived in 3,500 BC, man has had a profound influence on the subsequent development of the chalk downs. During the Mediaeval period the downlands were mostly given over to sheep rearing, which reached a peak just prior to the Industrial Revolution. The pressure of grazing by sheep, combined with that by the rabbit population, maintained the characteristic downland sward which provides such an important habitat for plants and insects. As the wool industry became concentrated around the industrial towns, so the numbers of sheep on the chalk declined to be replaced by an increase in arable farming. The ploughing of the downs for cereal crops and grass ley accelerated dramatically during the Second World War. As a result, the original downland habitat only survived in areas unsuitable for agriculture such as steep hillsides, but even these have been threatened by the recent increase in afforestation.

Today it is remnant downland that most interests the birdwatcher and general naturalist. Where grazing by sheep and rabbits remains intense, then the short downland sward survives. If the grazing pressures diminish, as they did when the rabbit population was decimated by myxomatosis during the 1950s, the short sward will revert to coarse grassland and eventually to chalk scrub. This consists of such shrubs as hawthorn, juniper, yew and gorse amongst others. The broadleaved woodlands, which grace certain areas of the chalk downs, typically comprise either oak with hazel coppice or beech. The latter is particularly characteristic of eastern Hampshire where they form the famous Beech Hangers of Gilbert White's Selborne. As mentioned earlier, forestry plantations have become an increasing feature of the contemporary downland scene. It is farmland, however, that dominates the present habitat of the chalk downs. Modern farm practices, notably the removal of hedgerows, have tended to create an increasingly sterile environment for wildlife.

The surviving areas of remnant downland support a rich diversity of plants and insects including many rare and restricted species. It is not surprising and indeed fortunate that many of the finer examples of this habitat have been protected as nature reserves.

Species

Although the chalk downs may present a bleak prospect to the visiting birdwatcher, there are interesting birds to be found by the persistent observer. The speciality many associate with the Wessex downlands is the Stone Curlew. The population changes of this and another indicator species, the Wheatear, reflect the fluctuating balance between downland

Stone Curlew

pasture and arable land over the past two centuries. The Wheatear has long ceased to breed regularly on the chalk. Initially the Stone Curlew faired better, despite a drastic decline in breeding numbers after the ploughing campaign of the Second World War. The remnant population seemed to adapt well to the new arable habitat. Indeed the species was still widely distributed on the Hampshire Downs up to the early 1970s. More recent changes in farming methods, however, has resulted in a further serious decline due to the loss of nesting sites. Recent surveys suggest that the present status of the Stone Curlew is parlous indeed.

The secretive Quail is more likely to be encountered on the chalk downs than anywhere else in the region. Never common, this species is subject to periodic good years when its distinctive call can be heard from large fields of cereals and grass. The typical breeding birds of the open downs and farmland are Lapwing and Skylark; whilst the Meadow Pipit is present where rough grassland exists. Both Red-legged and Grey Partridges are widely distributed. There is strong evidence, however, to show that the native bird has declined in recent years; whilst the population of the former species has been adulterated by the introduction of Chukar hybrids. The Corn Bunting is another characteristic bird of the chalk downs, but like the Grey Partridge, this species has also declined recently.

The hedgerows typically host such breeding birds as Whitethroat, Linnet and Yellowhammer. The more extensive areas of scrub support a greater diversity of species including Turtle Dove, Nightingale, Lesser Whitethroat, Garden Warbler and Willow Tit; whilst the odd pair of Stonechats may occur where gorse predominates. Some of these species, notably the Nightingale and Willow Tit, also frequent the oak with hazel coppice woods where they can be found alongside a wide selection of other woodland birds. The young forestry plantations hold breeding Woodcock, Nightjar and Tree Pipit; whilst the more mature stands of conifers are the most likely sites in the region to find Long-eared Owls.

Amongst the more interesting raptors, the Hobby is sparsely distributed throughout the Wessex downlands; whilst the Buzzard is mainly confined to the chalk of Dorset and northwest Hampshire. Barn and

Little Owls were once widespread on the downs, but both species have sadly declined in recent years.

During the winter, flocks of Lapwing roam the open countryside in search of suitable feeding areas. At a few chosen sites, they may be joined by Golden Plover which occurs more widely in Hampshire than in Dorset. Large numbers of Black-headed and Common Gulls commute daily to and from their coastal roosts to feed in the open fields. Such flocks are worth checking through for the odd Mediterranean Gull, a species reported several times from the downs to the north and west of Dorchester. Fields of kale and stubble often attract mixed flocks of finches and buntings which usually comprise Chaffinch, Greenfinch, Goldfinch, Linnet and Yellowhammer. Scarcer birds including Tree Sparrow Brambling and Corn Bunting are sometimes found amongst these flocks. Winter raptors such as Hen Harrier and Merlin are frequently seen hunting over the open downs. Peregrines appear from time to time; whilst the high downs in the extreme northwest corner of Hampshire are the best area in the region for Rough-legged Buzzards which have overwintered on several occasions during the late 1970s and early 1980s. Short-eared Owls may be encountered, most often in young forestry plantations and sheltered downland valleys of rough grass and scrub where small roosts sometime gather. The smart Great Grey Shrike is an occasional visitor to areas of downland scrub.

Although the chalk downs may not be generally considered as good sites for bird migration, visible passage involving such birds as Lapwings, Swifts, hirundines, Skylarks, Meadow Pipits and finches have been observed along prominent downland escarpments well inland from the coast. Small arrivals of landbird migrants including Whinchats and Wheatears are a regular feature of the spring and autumn; whilst scarcer species such as Black Redstart, Ring Ouzel and Pied Flycatcher appear with some frequency at certain localities. Passing raptors, including Marsh and Montagu's Harriers and Osprey have been reported from several downland sites. Small parties of Dotterel are worth looking out for in spring with a number of recent sightings from the Hampshire Downs. If the records from Old Winchester and Beacon Hills are anything to go by, then any prominent downland hilltop may prove rewarding given enough observer coverage.

37 MARTIN DOWN NNR (EN/HCC), PENTRIDGE AND GARSTON WOOD NR (RSPB)

OS Map 184 & 195
SU01/02

Habitat

Martin Down is a rare example of relatively flat and gently sloping down-land comprising natural chalk grassland and scrub, mostly hawthorn and gorse, which is overlooked by a prominent ridge extending from Tidpit Common Down west to Pentridge Hill. Much of the surrounding land consists of arable farmland with scattered forestry plantations and more extensive areas of mixed and broadleaved woodland. The reserve, which is jointly managed by English Nature and Hampshire County Council, supports an outstanding chalk downland flora and fauna including several noteworthy species of orchid and butterfly.

Situated two miles (3.2 km) to the west, the newly created RSPB Reserve of Garston Wood offers some fine woodland habitats which includes hazel coppice with mature stands of oak and ash.

Species

At present Martin Down is the only site in the region where the Stone Curlew can be seen with any certainty. In recent years an artificial scrape designed to attract nesting birds has been created on the open down. In order to avoid disturbance visitors must observe this scrape from some distance, the footpath to the west and old shooting ranges to the northwest being the best vantage points. Occasionally birds may be encountered feeding on other parts of the reserve.

The other main attraction of Martin Down is the population of Nightin-gales which share the dense downland scrub with breeding Turtle Dove, Lesser Whitethroat and Garden Warbler; whilst the odd pair of Stonechats may be found in the nearby gorse. In good Quail years, this species is more likely to be heard in this area than anywhere else on the region's chalk. Characteristic breeding birds of the open downland and fields include Red-legged and Grey Partridges, Lapwing and Corn Bunting. Amongst the rap-tors, Buzzard, Hobby, Barn and Little Owls are frequently seen; whilst both Montagu's Harrier and Long-eared Owl have bred in the general vicinity.

This is also a good area for the more interesting winter raptors such as Hen Harrier, Merlin and Short-eared Owl. Flocks of Golden Plover sometimes appear in the early spring, perhaps involving birds departing from the nearby Allen Valley. Landbird migrants regularly include Whinchat and Wheatear; whilst scarcer species such as Black Redstart and Ring Ouzel are occasional-ly noted. There have also been sightings of such noteworthy species as Marsh Harrier, Osprey, Hoopoe, Golden Oriole and Great Grey Shrike.

Wyke Down to the southeast of Sixpenny Handley is a particularly reli-able area for Quail and Corn Bunting; whilst Garston Wood supports a wide range of woodland birds.

Timing

Evening visits are recommended for observing Stone Curlew and listen-ing for Quail (when present) and Nightingale.

145

Access

The main access routes to this large area are the A354 between the
Handley roundabout and Martin Drove End; minor roads from Martin
Drove End (by the Coote Arms PH) through Martin Village to Tidpit and
from Tidpit through Martin Wood to Cranborne; and the B3081 between
the B3078 just south of Cranborne and the Handley roundabout.

Martin Down NNR can be reached either from the small triangular green
(with the old waterpump) in Martin Village, by taking Sillen Lane west to
the parking area at the base of the down; or direct from the A354 at a point
0.8 miles (1.3 km) east of Woodyates and 1.1 miles (1.9 km) west of Martin
Drove End. There are footpaths giving access to much of the reserve.

Reserve Visit Arrangements: no permits are required, but visits by
organised groups should be booked in advance with the Warden, The
Limes, Damerham, Fordingbridge, Hampshire.

Pentridge area: from Pentridge Village there are footpaths (i) north
and east to Bokerley Down, southeast to Blagdon Hill and then southwest to Pentridge Hill; (ii) southeast to Pentridge Hill; and (iii) southeast
to Blackbush Down and on to Cranborne.

Bottlebush Down is best viewed from the B3081 road between Nine
Yews and the Handley roundabout. Great care is needed when parking
off the road. There is no access to the surrounding land, other than along
Ackling Dyke.

Wyke Down is best viewed from the pumping station near the junction

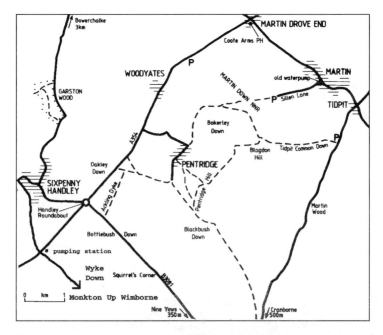

of the A354 and the minor road to Monkton Up Wimborne which lies 0.9 miles (1.4 km) southwest of the Handley roundabout.

Garston Wood lies 1 mile (1.6 km) north of Sixpenny Handley on the minor road to Bowerchalke. There are several footpaths giving access to the reserve.

Calendar

All Year. Buzzard, Red-legged and Grey Partridges, Lapwing, Barn, Little and possible Long-eared Owls, Corn Bunting, common resident scrub and woodland birds.

Summer (mid-May–mid-July): Hobby and possible Montagu's Harrier; occasional Quail; Stone Curlew, Turtle Dove, Nightingale, Stonechat, Lesser Whitethroat, Garden Warbler.

Winter (November–mid-March): Hen Harrier and occasional Merlin; Golden Plover; occasional Short-eared Owl; winter finches including occasional Brambling.

Spring (mid-March–mid-May) *and Autumn* (August–October): spring Golden Plover; landbird migrants including Whinchat, Wheatear, occasional Black Redstart and Ring Ouzel.

38 MAIDEN CASTLE (ENGLISH HERITAGE)

OS Map 194
SY68

Habitat and Species

Maiden Castle is a prominent downland hill-fort lying immediately to the southwest of Dorchester. Although numbers have declined recently, this is still one of the more reliable sites in Dorset to see Golden Plover in winter. Birds are best looked for from the main access road southwest from Dorchester and the minor roads from the A35 just west of Dorchester south to Martinstown. It is also worth checking through any finch flocks for Brambling in winter when raptors such as Hen Harrier, Merlin and Short-eared Owl occasionally appear. Breeding birds include such typical downland species as Red-legged and Grey Partridges and Corn Bunting; the latter species can often be seen perched on fences bordering the west end of the Dorchester by-pass. Maiden Castle and the downs around nearby Compton Valence are noted as good areas for Quail during influx years.

Golden Plovers

Access

Maiden Castle is well signposted along Maiden Castle Road from the A354 just south of Dorchester at SY688897. There is a car park and public access to the hill-fort.

39 FONTMELL DOWN NR (NT/DWT)

OS Map 183
ST81

Habitat and Species

This is a superb area of steep-sided chalk downland and scrub which is renowned for its plants and butterflies. Birdlife is varied with over 35 species including Turtle Dove, Garden Warbler and possibly still Nightingale breeding on the reserve. It is a good area for raptors with Buzzards regularly seen soaring overhead.

Access

A footpath crosses Fontmell Down southwest from the Blandford to Melbury Abbas road at ST887185. There is a small car park just north along the road at ST886187. Permissive footpaths give access to the DWT reserve.

40 BEACON HILL (HCC) AND GREAT LITCHFIELD DOWN

OS Map 174
SU45

Habitat and Species

These hills, which support large areas of downland grass and scrub, are amongst the highest to be found in this particular part of the Hampshire Downs.

Raptors are a feature of these high downs. The Sparrowhawk, Buzzard and Kestrel are breeding residents; whilst Hen Harrier, Merlin, Peregrine and Short-eared Owl have been seen in winter and may occur more often than records suggest. Although there are no recent sightings, wintering Rough-legged Buzzards have been reported from this area more often than anywhere else in the region. Bramblings sometimes mingle with large winter flocks of commoner finches; whilst there is at least one winter sighting of a Great Grey Shrike from the slopes of Beacon Hill. Breeding birds include such typical species of the open downland as Red-legged and Grey Partridges and perhaps still Corn Bunting; whilst Turtle Dove and the commoner warblers inhabit the areas of scrub.

Access

The area is bisected by the A34 Winchester to Newbury road. From the lay-by on the northbound carriageway of the A34 at SU463551, there is a footpath (Wayfarer's Walk) west and north across Lower and Upper Woodcott Downs to Ashmansworth. On the opposite side of the dual carriageway, there is a footpath east and then north across Great Litchfield Down to Ladle Hill. Please note that pedestrians attempting to cross the A34 at this point are invited to use the permissive route via an underpass at SU462551. For Beacon Hill follow the signs from the A34 at the Highclere/Kingsclere exit to the car park at SU463576.

41 FARLEY MOUNT COUNTRY PARK (HCC/HWT/FC)

OS Map 185
SU32/42/43

Habitat and Species

Farley Mount Country Park and its environs offer a wide range of attractive downland and woodland habitats. The latter includes Crab Wood, a particularly fine example of oak with hazel coppice which is managed as a Local Nature Reserve mainly for its rich butterfly fauna. There is also some beech woodland and several extensive forestry plantations such as West Wood.

A wide selection of woodland birds breed in the country park. These include Woodcock, Turtle Dove, Lesser Spotted Woodpecker, Nightingale, Garden Warbler and Willow Tit. Unfortunately the forestry plantations are no longer suitable for Nightjar and Tree Pipit. Breeding residents of the open downland include Red-legged and Grey Partridges; whilst Quail are occasionally heard calling from the cereal crops in summer. Raptors such as Hen Harrier, Merlin and Short-eared Owl are all possible visitors in autumn and winter when small flocks of Bramblings sometimes frequent the beech woods.

Access

Farley Mount Country Park can be reached by minor roads west from the B3041 and B3040 in Winchester, west from the A3090 at Pitt, north from the A3090 at Standon near Hursley, east from the minor road between King's Somborne and Little Somborne, and south from Sparsholt. Footpaths give access to most areas of interest notably Crab Wood (north from the car park at SU433293), West Wood (north from various car parks between SU419292 and SU409293) and Farley Mount (west from Monument car park at SU408293).

42 CHEESEFOOT HEAD (HCC)

OS Map 185
SU52

Habitat and Species

Cheesefoot Head is the highest point on the downs immediately to the east of Winchester. Much of the area is given over to farmland with remnant downland habitats restricted to the steeper slopes.

Corn Bunting

This used to be a reliable site for Stone Curlew which may still occur locally; whilst Quail are likely to be heard here in good years for the species. Amongst the commoner breeding birds of the open downs, Red-legged and Grey Partridges and Corn Bunting are all present. Short-eared Owls sometimes winter in the area; whilst Hen Harrier, Merlin and Peregrine are occasional visitors. There are also several reports of Rough-legged Buzzards from the late 1960s and early 1970s. Winter finch flocks should be scrutinised for Bramblings. In spring and autumn, land-bird migrants such as Whinchat and Wheatear can be expected; whilst Ring Ouzels have been noted in both seasons. There is also a spring record of Dotterel.

Access
Cheesefoot Head car park lies directly off the A272 Winchester to Petersfield road at SU529278. From here a footpath gives access north-east along Temple Valley to the A31. On the opposite side of the road, there are footpaths from SU530276 south along Longwood Warren and from SU528278 southwest along Fawley Down.

43 BEACON HILL NNR, WARNFORD (EN)

OS Map 185
SU52/62

Habitat and Species
Beacon Hill represents the most westerly outcrop of the South Downs and provides magnificent views over the Meon Valley. The steep slopes offer fine examples of chalk downland and mixed scrub; whilst the top of the hill is covered by woodland.

Although situated well inland, this prominent hill regularly attracts impressive numbers of landbird migrants at times of passage. These regularly include Turtle Dove, Tree Pipit, Redstart, Whinchat, Wheatear, the commoner warblers and Spotted Flycatcher. A few Ring Ouzels pass through in spring and autumn; whilst Pied Flycatchers are recorded annually during the latter season. There are also several sightings of Firecrests. The visual passage of landbird migrants, particularly during the autumn, is also a feature of the site. These movements mainly involve Swifts, Skylarks, hirundines, Meadow Pipits, winter thrushes and finches. Occasionally waders and terns are also noted on passage. Other rare and unusual migrants seen at this site include Little Egret, Pomarine Skua, Mediterranean Gull and Wryneck. The area supports a good selection of breeding birds typical of chalk downland and woodland. These include Red-legged and Grey Partridges, Turtle Dove, Garden Warbler, Willow Tit and Corn Bunting; whilst calling Quail are always possible in summer. Hen Harrier, Merlin and Peregrine are occasional visitors, mainly in autumn and winter.

Access

The site is best approached from the small car park (under the trees) at SU599228 on the minor road between Exton and Rooksgrove Farm. From the car park follow the track southeast to the trig point and reserve. Although there are no public footpaths across the reserve, a permissive pathway gives access to the steep downland slopes overlooking the Meon Valley. In addition, there is a public footpath from the car park northeast through the wood and across the fields to Wheely Down at SU613233.

44 OLD WINCHESTER HILL NNR (EN)

OS Map 185
SU62

Habitat and Species

Old Winchester Hill is an area of high steep-sided downland, dominated by the Iron Age hill-fort at the southern end. The reserve, which boasts a rich flora and butterfly fauna, supports some fine examples of the succession of chalk vegetation from short grass sward and coarse grassland through hawthorn scrub to yew woodland. There is also a beech wood at the base of the hill.

Like nearby Beacon Hill NNR, this is another surprisingly good site for landbird migrants which regularly include Turtle Dove, Tree Pipit, Redstart, Whinchat, Wheatear, the commoner warblers and Spotted Flycatcher. Ring Ouzels are virtually annual on passage; whilst there are occasional sightings of Black Redstarts, Firecrests and Pied Flycatchers. Visual movements of Swifts, Skylarks, hirundines, Meadow Pipits, winter thrushes and finches are noted at the appropriate times between late summer and late autumn. Unlikely migrants including flocks of waders and terns have sometimes been observed; whilst there are records of such oddities as Honey Buzzard, Marsh and Montagu's Harriers, Roughlegged Buzzard, Osprey, Dotterel, Mediterranean Gull, Wryneck, Great Grey Shrike and Serin.

Over 40 species of bird typical of downland scrub and woodland breed on the reserve; the most interesting being Red-legged and Grey Partridges,

Turtle Dove, Garden Warbler, Willow Tit and Corn Bunting. Quail are sometimes heard in summer from fields around the hill. Hen Harrier, Merlin, Peregrine and Short-eared Owl are all possible visitors in winter.

Access

The entrance of Old Winchester Hill at SU648208 lies on the minor road between the A32 at Warnford and Clanfield. Visitors should keep to the picnic area (by the road) and well marked footpaths as well as taking regard of the notices warning of unexploded bombs. The Information Centre is open 2.00 pm–5.00 pm, weekends April to September but every day in August. Organised groups wishing to visit the reserve should book in advance with the Warden, 8 Big Tree Cottage, Soberton, Southampton, Hampshire SO3 1PG.

45 BUTSER HILL AND QUEEN ELIZABETH COUNTRY PARK (HCC/FC)

OS Map 197
SU71/72

Habitat and Species

The spectacular steep slopes of Butser Hill comprise mainly open downland with dense thickets of mostly hawthorn and yew scrub. The remainder of the Country Park lies to the east of the A3 road where extensive broadleaved woodlands (mainly beech) and forestry plantations cloak the more gently sloping Holt, War and Head Downs.

The area supports a good cross-section of chalk and woodland wildlife. Amongst the birds, the Golden Pheasant is a local speciality with a few pairs inhabiting Head Down Plantation. A wide selection of open country, scrub and woodland birds including Woodcock, Turtle Dove, Garden Warbler, Willow Tit and perhaps still Corn Bunting, breed in the Country Park. In spring and autumn, Butser Hill is well worth a visit to search for landbird migrants which may include something unusual like Black Redstart and Ring Ouzel; whilst visual passage is also likely to be good feature of this site. Hen Harriers and Short-eared Owls are occasionally seen in winter. There is a 1955 record of a Roller from Butser Hill.

Access

The area is best approached on the A3 Portsmouth to Petersfield road. From the northbound carriageway near Clanfield follow the signs to Butser Hill picnic area and car park* at SU711200. The car park* and Information Centre for Queen Elizabeth Country Park can be reached from both carriageways of the A3 at SU717187. There is access to both parts of the Country Park along well marked footpaths and tracks. The excellent Information Centre is open 10.00 am–5.30 pm daily April to October, and 10.00 am–5.30 pm (or dusk) at weekends November to March. Access to War Down and Head Down Plantation can also be obtained from Halls Hill car park at SU733198 which lies on the minor road southwest from Buriton.

THE CHALK DOWNS – OTHER SITES WORTHY OF ATTENTION

46 BADBURY RINGS (NT)

OS Map 195, ST90

A downland hill-fort with scrub and woodland. This is a good site for Bramblings in winter; whilst Buzzards are present throughout year and Hobbies are occasionally seen during the summer. Otherwise the area supports a variety of breeding birds typical of downland, scrub and woodland. Access at ST958029 on the B3082 Wimborne to Blandford road.

47 HAREWOOD FOREST

OS Map 185, SU34/44

This extensive area of woodland and forest supports a wide selection of breeding birds including Woodcock, Tree Pipit, Nightingale and possibly Redstart. Main access points are along footpaths south from the westbound carriageway of the A303 at SU404441 and north at SU405450 on the minor road between the B3400 at Andover Down and the B3048 at Longparish.

48 DANEBURY HILL (HCC)

OS Map 185, SU33

Danebury Hill is an ancient wooded hill-fort set in a predominantly arable farming landscape. The area supports breeding birds typical of the chalk downlands including Corn Bunting. It is a good site for Quail and Stone Curlew may still occur locally. In winter large flocks of Golden Plover frequent nearby Middle Wallop Airfield; whilst raptors such as Hen Harrier, Merlin and Short-eared Owl are always possible. There is also a spring record of Dotterel. Access at SU332378 on the minor road between the A343 by Middle Wallop Airfield and the A30 just west of Stockbridge.

49 SELBORNE (NT)

OS Map 186, SU73

Famous for Gilbert White's Beech Hangers, this area supports an excellent downland and woodland natural history including birds. Selborne lies at SU742336 on the B3006 south of Alton.

PART 2 – THE RIVERS

General Introduction

Many of the region's finest rivers originate from downland springs. Since they derive much of their water from the chalk aquifer, these rivers share a number of special characteristics. The water from the springs is relatively rich in nutrients and remains at 10°C throughout the year. Consequently the rivers are very productive, supporting a prolific growth of water-weed, notably water-crowfoot, and good populations of fish including brown trout and salmon. During periods of heavy rain, the chalk aquifer acts as a buffer and prevents sudden rises in river levels. Once the rivers are in flood, however, the levels recede very slowly. This usually means that the river meadows remain inundated for long periods, particularly during the winter and early spring.

Historically these attributes were used in the widespread development of water-meadow systems. This involved the deliberate flooding of the meadows through series of carriers or channels to encourage an early growth of grass. Unfortunately most of these water-meadow systems have now fallen into disuse. More recently, however, these productive waters have been used for commercial cressbed and fish farming.

Species

The chalk rivers and their associated habitats are rich in birdlife. Typical breeding birds include Little Grebe and various other waterfowl, Snipe, Redshank, Kingfisher, Grey Wagtail, Sedge and Reed Warblers and Reed Bunting. Unfortunately the populations of Snipe and Redshank have declined dramatically in recent years. In winter the rivers and flooded fields can prove very attractive to wildfowl and waders. The rivers are also important migration routes for many birds in spring and autumn.

Sites

The best chalk river in the region, the Hampshire Avon (Site 32), has already been dealt with in the section on East Dorset. The Allen (Site 50), Test and Itchen (Sites 51 & 52) are typical of the other chalk rivers found within Dorset and Hampshire.

50 RIVER ALLEN AND CRICHEL LAKE

OS Map 195
ST90/SU00/01

Habitat

The River Allen is one of Dorset's most attractive chalk rivers. It rises from springs in the vicinity of Wimborne St Giles and flows through open downland comprising mainly large arable fields to join the River Stour at Wimborne. Wet meadows are a feature of the valley, notably upstream from Wimborne St Giles and at the confluence of the Gussage Stream and River Allen near Bowerswain; whilst riverside habitats include reedbeds and damp thickets of willow scrub.

Within the grounds of Crichel Park, which is situated just to the north of the village of Witchampton, lies a large ornamental lake. Woodland borders much of the eastern and short southern shores of this lake, which otherwise enjoys an open aspect with gently sloping parkland extending down to the water's edge. During the summer much of the lake becomes choked with weed; whilst reedbeds fringe the southern end where a stream emerges and flows into the nearby River Allen. The remainder of Crichel Park consists mostly of woodland, open parkland and farm fields.

Species

A wide selection of wildfowl and other waterbirds frequent Crichel Lake during the winter. Good numbers of Gadwall, Pochard, Tufted Duck and Coot can be expected along with a few Teal and Shoveler. A small flock of Wigeon is regularly present, grazing the lakeside fields together with Coot and the local Canada Geese. The latter are occasionally joined by feral Greylag and Barnacle Geese. Goldeneye and Goosander are occasional visitors, usually during periods of cold weather when Bewick's Swan, Scaup and Smew have also been noted. Cormorants regularly occur, often roosting in trees overlooking the lake. Grey Herons stand like sentinels around the shore; whilst the rare Bittern has been reported here in the past. Black-headed and Common Gulls gather on the lake during winter afternoons, prior to moving off to their roost sites on the coast. Parties of Redwings and Fieldfares roam the parkland; whilst flocks of finches and buntings are worth checking through for Bramblings.

Gadwall

The Allen Valley is a fairly reliable site for Golden Plover in winter. The fields between the Horton Inn and Knowlton are the favoured area, but birds sometimes wander as far away as the Stour Valley and Cranborne Chase. Small numbers of Teal and Snipe can be found in suitable habitat throughout the valley; whilst a few Tufted Duck frequent the slower, deeper stretches of the river. The disused cressbeds near Wimborne St

Giles are occasionally visited by Green Sandpipers. Amongst the winter raptors, Hen Harriers are seen from time to time hunting over open ground; whilst the Peregrine has been observed creating panic amongst the waterfowl on Crichel Lake.

Typical riverine breeding birds such as Little Grebe, Kingfisher, Grey Wagtail, Sedge and Reed Warblers and Reed Buntings are widely distributed along the River Allen; whilst the odd pair of Canada Geese, Gadwall and Tufted Duck also nest by the river. Although the wet meadows still support breeding Lapwing; Snipe and Redshank have declined to the point of extinction. Otherwise the Allen Valley is a good area for resident Buzzards, Red-legged and Grey Partridges, and Barn and Little Owls,; whilst the Hobby is frequently seen overhead during the summer. Breeding waterfowl, including Canada Geese and Tufted Duck, can be found on Crichel Lake where both Gadwall and Pochard often remain throughout the summer and may also attempt to nest. Sedge and Reed Warblers and Reed Buntings inhabit the lakeside reedbeds. The parkland surrounding the lake supports a wide selection of open country and woodland birds.

Spring and autumn bring a scattering of migrants to the Allen Valley and Crichel Lake. The most frequent of the passage waders are Green and Common Sandpipers, but there have been reports of more unusual species including Little Ringed Plover, Ruff and Wood Sandpiper. Common and Black Terns occasionally visit Crichel Lake; whilst Whinchat and Wheatear regularly feature amongst the landbird migrants. The area's rarer sightings include Dorset's first Sociable Plover which appeared near Clapgate in April 1961; whilst the author was fortunate enough to find a Little Bittern by the river at Hinton Parva in May 1990. There are also records of Red-crested Pochard, Osprey. Corncrake, Hoopoe and Black-bellied Dipper.

Timing

In winter Crichel Lake can be very rewarding during periods of cold weather, unless conditions are so severe that the lake freezes over.

Access

The main access route to the Allen Valley and Crichel lake is the B3078 between Wimborne and Cranborne.

The River Allen can be seen from roadbridges at High Hall, Witchampton, Stanbridge Mill, Brockington Farm and Wimborne St Giles; whilst the upper river meadows can be viewed from the minor road between Wimborne St Giles and Monkton Up Wimborne. There are also a number of footpaths that overlook the river and riverside meadows, notably (i) between the B3078 just north of Walford Mill in Wimborne and Stanbridge; (ii) between the main entrance to Crichel Park and Stanbridge Mill; and (iii) between Bowerswain and Brockington Farms.

Crichel Lake is best approached from Witchampton, by taking the minor road signposted to 'Moor Crichel and the Gussages' northeast past the Post Office and Lawrence Lane (both on the left) to the main gated entrance to Crichel Park. From here continue on the public footpath through the park to view the lake. A telescope is useful at this site. Please note that Crichel Park is private and visitors must keep to the footpath at all times.

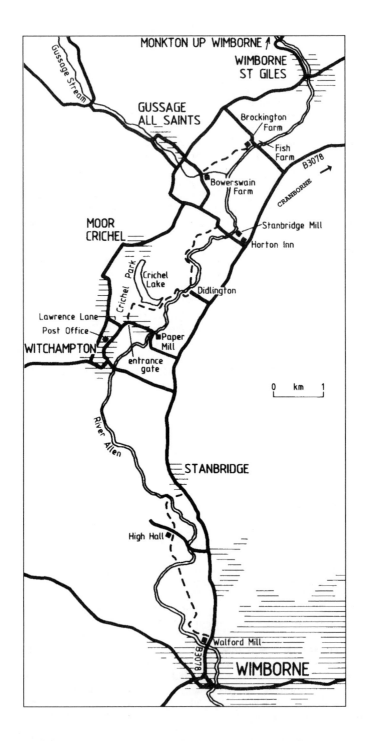

Calendar

All Year. Little Grebe, Grey Heron, Canada and occasional feral Greylag and Barnacle Geese, Tufted Duck, Buzzard, Red-legged and Grey Partridges, Snipe, Barn Owl, Kingfisher, Grey Wagtail, Reed Bunting, common resident woodland birds.

Winter (November–mid-March): Cormorant; wildfowl including Wigeon, Gadwall, Teal, Shoveler, Pochard, in cold weather occasional Goldeneye and Goosander, possible Bewick's Swan, Scaup and Smew; occasional Hen Harrier; Water Rail; Golden Plover, occasional Green Sandpiper and possible other wader species; gulls; winter thrushes; winter finches and buntings including occasional Brambling.

Summer (mid-May-mid-June): Redshank, Sedge and Reed Warblers.

Spring (mid-March–mid-May) *and Autumn* (August–November): migrant waders including Green and Common Sandpipers and occasional other species; occasional Common and Black Terns; common landbird migrants.

51 AND 52 RIVER TEST AND RIVER ITCHEN

OS Maps 185, 196
& New Forest
SU31–34/41–44/
53–55/63

Habitat

The Rivers Test and Itchen rise from springs on the chalk downland of central Hampshire before flowing west and then south into Southampton Water. The rivers themselves present a complex pattern of side channels and carriers, which partially reflects the use of their productive waters in the operation of water-meadow systems in the past and more recently in the development of fish farms and cressbeds. The latter are particularly prominent in the upper reaches of the Itchen Valley.

A rich diversity of riverine habitats including damp thickets of alder and willow, reedbeds and wet unimproved meadows can be found in these valleys. Further variety to the habitat is provided by the presence of several large lakes and flooded gravel pits notably at Nursling, Timsbury, Marsh Court, Andover, Laverstoke and Overton in the Test Valley; and at Allington, Winchester Sewage Works, Avington, Alresford and Northington Park in the Itchen Valley.

Both rivers and their associated habitats are important for wildlife in general and salmonid fisheries in particular.

Species

During the breeding season, typical riverine birds such as Little Grebe, Kingfisher, Grey Wagtail, Sedge and Reed Warblers and Reed Bunting are widely distributed along both rivers and their major tributaries. The Cetti's Warbler has recently become established at sites in both valleys,

Kingfisher

but on the debit side the Grasshopper Warbler has virtually disappeared from its old haunts. Despite a marked decline in recent years, both Snipe and Redshank still survive as breeding species. The lakes and flooded gravel pits provide suitable nesting sites for Great Crested Grebe, Canada Goose, Gadwall, Pochard, Tufted Duck and occasionally Teal and Shoveler. Mandarins are regularly seen along the River Test around Mottisfont and Leckford where they may breed. Shelduck are regular visitors, particularly during the spring and summer and have nested on occasions. The flooded gravel pits are also favoured by a few pairs of breeding Little Ringed Plovers. The Grey Heron is a familiar sight throughout the year with large gatherings often present in the vicinity of fish farms. Cormorants are regular non-breeding visitors to both the rivers and larger lakes. Turtle Dove, Nightingale, Lesser Whitethroat and Garden Warbler inhabit areas of scrub, notably along the sides of the Test Valley and Red-legged and Grey Partridges often wander to the drier meadows from nearby downland. The Test Valley remains a good area for Barn Owls; whilst Hobbies regularly hawk over both valleys during the summer.

Although the Test and Itchen Valleys do not support the same abundance of wintering waterfowl as the Hampshire Avon, a wide variety of species including Little Grebe, feral Greylag and Canada Geese, Wigeon, Gadwall, Teal, Shoveler, Pochard and Tufted Duck can be expected. Other wildfowl such as Pintail, Goldeneye and Goosander are infrequent visitors; the last two species occurring most often in cold weather which may also produce the likes of Bewick's Swan, White-fronted Goose, Scaup, Smew and Ruddy Duck. Divers, the rarer winter grebes and Long-tailed Duck have also appeared very occasionally in recent years, usually on the lakes and flooded gravel pits in the lower valleys.

In winter, Snipe are commonly found throughout both valleys and a few Redshank and Green Sandpiper regularly inhabit the cressbeds. A flock of Golden Plover is usually present around Eastleigh Airport; whilst small numbers of Curlew feed in fields at Broadlands near Romsey. One or two Common Sandpipers sometimes winter in the lowest reaches of both rivers. Other waders, including Dunlin and Ruff, occasionally appear, usually during periods of flooding.

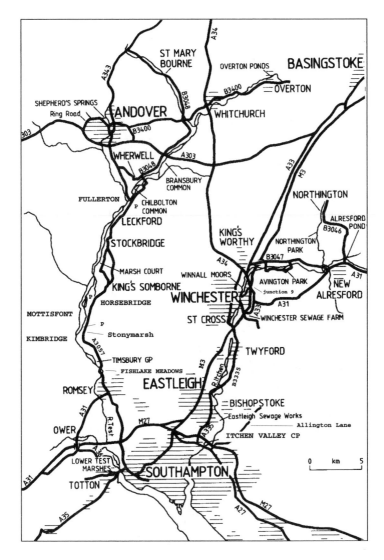

Wandering Hen Harriers and Merlins may occur from time to time. Amongst the smaller birds of note, Water Pipits are very much a winter and spring speciality of the Lower Test Marshes with a few birds also present on cressbeds. Although wintering Chiffchaffs may be found widely along both valleys, they show a preference for certain sites such as Eastleigh Sewage Farm. Thickets of alder host foraging parties of Siskins and Redpolls; whilst small flocks of Bearded Tits occasionally visit the larger reedbeds such as those on the Lower Test Marshes and around Alresford Pond. The Little Egret has been reported with increasing frequency along both valleys and seems destined to become a regular visitor, particularly in winter.

In spring and autumn there is a small but steady passage of migrants; the lakes, flooded gravel pits and sewage farms proving particularly attractive.

161

Migrant waders regularly include Green and Common Sandpipers in both seasons; whilst a wide selection of other species including Oystercatcher, Little Ringed and Ringed Plovers, Little Stint, Curlew Sandpiper, Dunlin, Ruff, Black-tailed Godwit, Whimbrel, Curlew, Spotted Redshank, Greenshank and Wood Sandpiper have also been noted. Common Terns often appear, mainly over the lakes and flooded gravel pits where Black Terns may occasionally occur. Landbird migrants typically include Yellow Wagtail, Whinchat and Wheatear amongst the commoner species, but scarcer species such as Black Redstart, Ring Ouzel, Firecrest and Pied Flycatcher are infrequent visitors, mainly in the autumn. There is always a chance of finding something unusual and rare at times of passage.

Timing
Periods of cold weather can prove very productive for birds in winter. In spring and summer, the riversides and meadows are best visited in the early morning and evening.

General Access
River Test: the main routes along the valley are the A36 between Totton and Ower, the A31 between Ower and Romsey, the A3057 between Romsey and Andover, the B3048 between Wherwell and St Mary Bourne and the B3400 between Andover and Overton.

River Itchen: the main routes along the valley are the A335 between Southampton and Eastleigh, the B3335 between Allbrook (Eastleigh) and the M3 near Winchester and the B3047 between King's Worthy and New Alresford.

Recommended Sites
The following are the best and most accessible birdwatching sites along the Test Valley.

51A LOWER TEST MARSHES NR (HWT)
Map p. 163, SU31
Habitat and Species
The Lower Test Marshes are situated at the point where the River Test flows into the estuary of Southampton Water. The northern section of the reserve, which is drained by two main channels of the river, consists mainly of rough pasture and meadows with some damp thickets of willow and alder. Extensive reedbeds dominate the southern section of the reserve where the river is tidal in character. Two artificial freshwater scrapes, which are overlooked by hides, add to the habitat diversity of the southern section. The area is managed as a nature reserve by the Hampshire Wildlife Trust.

In winter these marshes support a wide range of common waterfowl and waders. These regularly include good numbers of Little Grebe, Cormorant, Grey Heron, Canada Goose, Wigeon, Dunlin, Teal, Snipe, Curlew and Redshank. A few Jack Snipe and Green Sandpiper are also present; the latter species favouring the freshwater scrapes. Common Sandpipers have also overwintered in past years. Other species of wildfowl and wader occur from time to time. The numbers and variety of birds increases dramatically during periods of severe cold when such classic species as Scaup, Smew and Goosander often appear. Water Rails inhabit the extensive reedbeds which attract parties of Bearded Tits most years. Bitterns have also been reported several times, usually in hard weather; whilst recently the Little Egret has become a regular visitor in autumn and winter. Hen Harriers, Merlins and Peregrines also occasionally appear during these seasons. The Lower Test Marshes are now the premier site in the region for wintering Water Pipits with counts often in excess of 25 and reaching a peak of 44 in December 1993. Kingfishers can be observed along the main river channels and at close range from the hides overlooking the scrapes. Small flocks of Siskins and Redpolls sometimes feed in the riverside alder thickets.

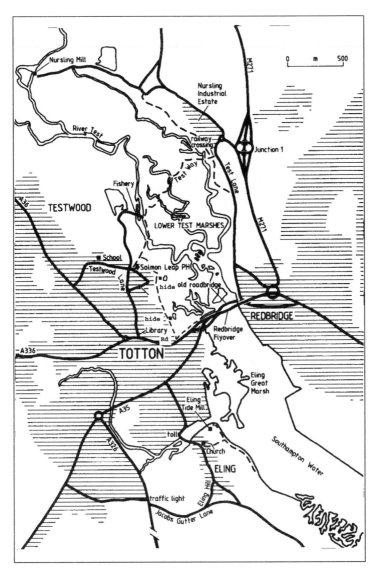

The breeding speciality of the marshes is undoubtedly the Cetti's Warbler with 23 singing males located in 1994. The riverside vegetation and reedbeds also hold Sedge and Reed Warblers and Reed Bunting; whilst Little Grebes, Kingfishers and Grey Wagtails nest along the river channels. A few pairs of Snipe and Redshank breed in the wet meadows. Tufted Duck have also nested in the area; whilst Shelduck, Gadwall and Teal have been recorded during the breeding season.

Migrant birds, particularly waders and landbirds, are a feature of these marshes in spring and autumn. Green and Common Sandpipers pass through in both seasons with good numbers often recorded in the autumn. Other passage waders that are regularly encountered include Little Ringed Plover and Whimbrel in spring and Greenshank in autumn. There have also been several reports of Ruff and Wood Sandpiper. Garganey have been noted several times in spring and autumn. Landbird migrants usually include Yellow Wagtail, Redstart, Whinchat, Wheatear and the commoner warblers; whilst scarcer species such as Black Redstart, Ring Ouzel, Firecrest and Pied Flycatcher are occasionally recorded. Both Marsh Harrier and Osprey have been seen annually on passage in recent years. There are also reports of such rare and unusual birds as Purple Heron, American Wigeon, Red-footed Falcon, Spotted Crake, Corncrake, Avocet, Temminck's Stint, White-winged Black Tern, Hoopoe, Wryneck, Bluethroat, Aquatic and Icterine Warblers.

Access

The Lower Test Marshes NR are best approached from the Salmon Leap PH in Testwood Lane, Totton. The southern part of the reserve can be reached by taking the Test Way footpath northeast a short distance to the entrance gate on the right, crossing the field and following the boardwalk to the two hides. Alternatively this part of the reserve can be reached by taking the footpath next to Salterns School, which is situated on the A336 approaching Totton Town Centre, north to the southern hide and boardwalk beyond. It is also possible to walk east from Salterns School and view the lower meadows and river from the old roadbridge at Redbridge where there is limited parking.

The northern part of the marshes can be viewed by following the Test Way footpath from the Salmon Leap PH to the style just before the second river bridge and then continuing northeast across the reserve itself to Test Lane, Redbridge. This entrance to the reserve can be reached from the M271, by turning northwest at junction 1, continuing to the roundabout by Nursling Industrial Estate and then taking Test Lane south for 100 yards (100 m) to the pedestrian railway crossing.

51B TIMSBURY GRAVEL PIT AND FISHLAKE MEADOWS

Map p. 161, SU32

This large flooded gravel pit and the nearby wet meadows are very attractive to winter waterfowl. Little Grebe, Canada Goose, Wigeon, Gadwall, Teal, Shoveler, Pochard and Tufted Duck can be expected; whilst Shelduck, Mandarin, Pintail, Scaup, Goldeneye, Smew, Goosander and Ruddy Duck are occasional visitors. There are also records of more unusual species such as Red-necked Grebe, Red-crested Pochard and Long-tailed Duck. A well watched Ring-necked Duck regularly wintered at this site between 1987 and 1995. Small numbers of Snipe also winter in the area. The gravel pit supports such breeding waterfowl as Little Grebe, Canada Goose, Pochard and Tufted Duck. Both Great Crested Grebe and Shelduck have also bred here; whilst Ruddy Duck nest on nearby Timsbury Lakes. One or two pairs of Redshank also breed on the gravel pit. A few waders occur on passage, the most likely species being Little Ringed Plover (has bred), Redshank, Greenshank, Green and Common Sandpipers. The gravel pit is private, but can be viewed through the hedge by the A3057 north of Romsey at SU351240. Fishlake Meadows lie a little to the south and can be viewed from the footpath off the A3057 at SU352236.

51C THE TEST WAY BETWEEN KIMBRIDGE AND FULLERTON (HCC)

Map p. 161, SU32/33

The Test Way footpath provides limited views over the middle section of the Test Valley and its rich riverside and wetland habitats. These include such sites as Mottisfont, Horsebridge, Marsh Court (a reed-fringed lake) and Leckford. In addition to the standard riverine breeding birds – Little Grebe, Kingfisher, Grey Wagtail, Sedge and Reed Warblers and Reed Bunting, a number of more noteworthy species may be encountered. There is a small but expanding feral population of Greylag Geese which often favour the Bossington and Horsebridge area. Counts are highest during the winter, but a few pairs are thought to remain and breed. Small numbers of Mandarins frequent the Longstock to Fullerton section where the species has nested; whilst both Pochard and Tufted Duck also breed at various sites. Despite the dramatic decline in recent years, Redshank and perhaps Snipe may still nest in some riverside meadows. Areas of reedswamp between Marsh Court and Fullerton support a good population of Cetti's Warblers with ten singing males located in 1994. In addition, Nightingales inhabit the scrub bordering the Test Way, particularly between Yew Hill and Stockbridge Common. In winter a good selection of waterfowl are present along this section of the Test Valley; the most likely species being Little Grebe, feral Greylag and Canada Geese, Mandarin, Wigeon, Gadwall, Teal, Pochard and Tufted Duck. Snipe are widely distributed; whilst a few Green and Common Sandpipers pass through on migration. Occasional oddities may occur from time to time. For example there are recent sightings of Marsh Harrier and Osprey on passage; whilst three different Red-footed Falcons were seen in the Houghton/King's Somborne area in May/June 1992 and a Purple Heron was recorded at Marsh Court in 1977. The best access points to this section of the Test Way footpath are Stonymarsh car park off the A3057 at SU336270, Horsebridge car park opposite the John of Gaunt PH at SU345304, the end of Trafalgar Way in Stockbridge at SU359350 and West Down car park at SU386392. Marsh Court is a private lake just visible from the Test Way footpath at SU354334.

51D CHILBOLTON COMMON

Map p. 161, SU34

The River Test flows through this attractive area of riverside meadow. During the spring and summer such typical riverine birds as Little Grebe,

Kingfisher, Sedge and Reed Warblers and Reed Bunting can be found here. From Chilbolton Village take Joy's Lane to SU391400; there is public access to much of the Common.

51E BRANSBURY COMMON

Map p. 161, SU44

This is an extensive area of unimproved wet meadows lying between the Rivers Test and Dever. The main attraction used to be the large wintering flock of feral Greylag Geese. Although in recent years the population has become more widely dispersed throughout the Test Valley, this site still attracts small numbers of birds. The species has also bred here. In winter small numbers of wildfowl, including Gadwall and Teal, and Snipe are usually present; whilst Short-eared Owls are occasionally recorded. The meadows look favourable for nesting Snipe, four drumming males were still present in 1993, and Redshank. Otherwise a variety of breeding birds including the standard riverside species can be expected. From the minor road between Newton Stacey and Barton Stacey at SU417406 (sharp bend), follow the footpath northwest to the river meadow and then northeast along the edge of the meadow and woodland to Bransbury at SU421422. Please note there is very limited parking on the minor road and in Bransbury Village.

51F SHEPHERD'S SPRINGS AND ANTON LAKES NR (HWT & TEST VALLEY BOROUGH COUNCIL)

Map p. 161, SU34

This area consists of a mature flooded gravel pit surrounded by reedswamp and damp thickets of alder and willow which is situated near the spring source of the River Anton. At present the site is being developed as a nature reserve by the Hampshire Wildlife Trust and Test Valley Borough Council. Breeding birds include Little Grebe, Canada Goose, Tufted Duck, Grey Wagtail, Reed Warbler and Reed Bunting; whilst a pair of Great Crested Grebes nested for the first time in 1994. Non-breeding visitors may include Grey Heron, Kingfisher and the occasional Cormorant. In winter the lake supports small numbers of wildfowl, mainly Pochard and Tufted Duck, but sometimes other species such as Teal and Shoveler. A few Green and Common Sandpipers occur on passage when other wader species and terns are occasionally reported. Several noteworthy birds such as Osprey, Wryneck, Tawny Pipit and Aquatic Warbler have also been seen here. The area is best approached by taking the rough track at SU357466 which lies off the Charlton roundabout on the A343 Andover ring-road. There is a small car park and public access to much of the area.

Recommended Sites

The following are the best and most accessible birdwatching sites along the Itchen Valley.

52A WINCHESTER SEWAGE FARM (SW)

Map p. 161, SU42

Habitat and Species

This large sewage lagoon provides an important wetland habitat for birds, notably waterfowl and waders. During the winter, good numbers of Gadwall, Teal, Tufted Duck, Lapwing and Snipe are present along with a few Little Grebe, Wigeon, Shoveler and Pochard. Large flocks of Golden Plover sometimes occur; whilst Jack Snipe and Green Sandpiper are occasionally reported. With such large concentrations of birds, there is always a chance of a visiting Merlin and Peregrine. The lagoon also attracts migrant waders, particularly during the autumn when small numbers of Green and Common Sandpipers regularly pass through. Otherwise Little Ringed and Ringed Plovers, Dunlin, Ruff and Greenshank are the most likely species to be seen; whilst there are recent sightings of Little Stint, Curlew Sandpiper, Black-tailed Godwit, Spotted Redshank and Wood Sandpiper. Passage Common and Black Terns may appear from time to time. A scattering of landbird migrants, including Whinchat, occur in spring and autumn. Breeding waterfowl include Little Grebe, Gadwall and sometimes Tufted Duck; whilst recently Shelduck have become regular visitors in spring and summer. The most notable rarities that have been found at this site are Black-winged Stilt and White-winged Black Tern.

Access

From junction 9 of the M3 at Winchester, take the (A31/A272) road south to the A31 roundabout, continue south following the signs to Winchester and Southampton and just past the minor road to Chilcomb park in the lay-by on the left with the yellow 'Winchester Park and Ride' sign. From here walk along the roadside verge and view the lagoon from the grey crash barrier just before the turning to Morestead and Corhampton. Alternatively the lagoon can be viewed more distantly from various points along the minor road to Morestead.

52B WINNALL MOORS (HWT)

Map p. 161, SU42/43

The River Itchen and its various carriers flow through Winnall Moors which were formerly managed as floated water-meadows. Today the site comprises extensive herb-rich grasslands together with smaller areas of open mixed fen and reedbeds. Breeding birds include Little Grebe, Canada Goose, Gadwall, Tufted Duck, Grey Wagtail, Cetti's, Sedge and Reed Warblers and Reed Bunting; whilst Kingfishers are regular visitors. A few pairs of Snipe and Redshank were still holding territory in 1994. In winter the area supports small numbers of wildfowl, mainly Tufted Duck, but also Wigeon, Gadwall, Teal and Pochard together with a few Snipe. A scattering of migrants occur at times of passage when such oddities as Marsh Harrier, Osprey, Red-footed Falcon and Little Bunting have been recorded.

Access

The two access points to the southern public part of the reserve are rather obscure. The first lies off Wales Street at SU486297 (by the five-bar gate between two bridges with the Ship Inn just to the east and The Willow Tree PH almost opposite); whilst the second is situated on the east side of the River Park Leisure Centre playing fields at SU487301. Views over the northern part of the reserve can be obtained from the Itchen Way between Easton Lane at SU490299 (opposite Wessex Motors Components) and the A34 at SU494314.

52C ALRESFORD POND

Map p. 169, SU53/63

Habitat and Species

Alresford Pond is a large lake surrounded on three sides by reedswamp with trees and alder carr bordering the remaining shore. The lake is drained by the River Alre which is one of the main headwaters of the River Itchen. Extensive cressbeds are a feature of the area, notably between New and Old Alresford, along the Bighton Road and at Bishop's Sutton.

A wide selection of wildfowl including Canada Goose, Gadwall, Teal, Shoveler, Pochard, Tufted Duck and sometimes Wigeon can be found here in winter. Although Shelduck may occur throughout the year, most birds are seen from late winter (Jan/Feb) through to mid summer (June/July). Pintail are near annual visitors with most sightings in spring and autumn. Reports of Goldeneye, Smew and Goosander are rare and usually associated with hard winter weather. Cormorants are present for much of the year with the highest counts during the winter months. Snipe and perhaps Water Rail, which frequent the reedbeds in small numbers, can be seen along the lake margins; whilst the reedbeds have also attracted Bearded Tits on a number of occasions during the winter and at times of passage. The nearby cressbeds hold a few Snipe and Green Sandpiper along with the occasional Redshank and Water Pipit.

Alresford Pond is a good site for breeding waterfowl including Little Grebe, Canada Goose, Gadwall, Pochard and Tufted Duck; whilst Shelduck and Ruddy Duck have also summered here. Water Rail, Sedge and Reed Warblers and Reed Buntings all nest in the lakeside reedbeds

Grey Wagtail

where the Cetti's Warbler is now well-established with ten singing males in 1994. The River Alre supports breeding Little Grebe, Kingfisher, Grey Wagtail and Cetti's Warbler; whilst there is a heronry in Arlebury Park.

Both the lake and nearby cressbeds attract small numbers of Green and Common Sandpipers on passage. Other migrant waders sometimes occur, particularly when the water level of the Alresford Pond is low and mud is exposed around its margins. In recent years there have been sightings of Little Ringed, Ringed and Grey Plovers, Little Stint, Curlew Sandpiper, Dunlin, Ruff, Black-tailed and Bar-tailed Godwits, Spotted Redshank, Greenshank and Wood Sandpiper. During the early 1990s Mediterranean Gulls have become annual visitors with the majority of sightings in spring and autumn. Common and Black Terns are seen most years on passage along with the occasional Little Gull. Although infrequent visitors, it is worth keeping a look out for migrant Garganey. A good selection of unusual and rare birds have occurred, mainly at times

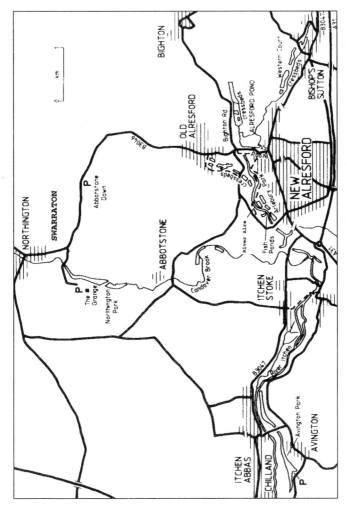

of passage; the most notable being Night Heron (Arlebury Park), Red-crested Pochard, Ring-necked Duck, Marsh and Montagu's Harriers, Osprey, Spotted Crake, Grey Phalarope, Arctic Skua, Ring-billed Gull, White-winged Black Tern and Yellow-browed Warbler.

Access

Alresford Pond is private and can be viewed only from the B3046 (Broad Street) between New and Old Alresford. Pedestrians should take care as this is a busy road. Furthermore, parking is limited and it may be best to park in New Alresford and walk the short distance to view the lake. The cressbeds at Alresford, Bighton Road and Bishop's Sutton can all be viewed from minor roads. Footpaths give access to the nearby stretch of the River Alre and Arlebury Park.

52D THE ITCHEN WAY BETWEEN SOUTHAMPTON AND WINCHESTER (HCC)

Map p. 161, SU41/42

The mosaic of riverside and wetland habitats present in the lower Itchen Valley can be viewed from the Itchen Way footpath between the angler's car park by Mans Bridge, Swaythling at SU447156 and St Cross, Winchester at SU480265. These habitats support most typical riverine breeding birds including Little Grebe, Kingfisher, Grey Wagtail, Sedge and Reed Warblers and Reed Bunting. In winter a variety of wildfowl, most likely Teal and Tufted Duck, and Snipe can be expected; whilst common migrants occur in spring and autumn. A wide range of more unusual birds has been recorded, particularly during cold winter weather and at migration times.

52E ITCHEN VALLEY COUNTRY PARK (EASTLEIGH BOROUGH COUNCIL)

Map p. 161, SU41

The Country Park comprises 440 acres of water-meadows, grazing pasture, ancient woodland and conifer plantations located either side of the River Itchen between Southampton and Eastleigh. The area supports a good variety of breeding birds, including such riverside specialities as Grey Wagtail, Sedge and Reed Warblers and Reed Bunting, as well as many of the commoner woodland species. In winter the wet meadows attract wildfowl, notably Teal, and Snipe along with the occasional Jack Snipe. Flocks of Golden Plover are also present in the general vicinity and sometimes visit nearby Eastleigh Airport. The commoner migrants that pass through in spring and autumn regularly include Redstart and Whinchat as well as occasionally something more unusual such as a Ring Ouzel or Pied Flycatcher. An immature Night Heron was present in January and early February 1993; whilst other recent oddities include sightings of Little Egret, Marsh Harrier and Osprey. The entrance to the Country Park is well signposted off Allington Lane, West End at SU461157. Further information can be obtained from High Wood Barn Visitor Centre, Itchen Valley Country Park, Allington Lane, West End, Southampton SO30 3HQ (tel: 01703 466091).

52F AVINGTON PARK (HCC)

Map p. 161, SU53

A large shallow weedy lake set in parkland. In winter the lake attracts small numbers of wildfowl, mainly Gadwall, Teal and Tufted Duck, but occasionally Shelduck, Wigeon, Shoveler and Pochard. Snipe are also likely to be present in winter; whilst Green Sandpipers are sometimes seen in autumn. Both Gadwall and Tufted Duck have bred here. Access is from the HCC Recreation Area car park at SU528321, which lies on the minor road between Avington and Easton.

52G NORTHINGTON PARK (ENGLISH HERITAGE)

Map p. 161, SU53

A large ornamental lake set in parkland. In winter the lake supports a similar variety of wildfowl to nearby Alresford Pond including Gadwall, Teal, Shoveler, Pochard and Tufted Duck. Little Grebe, Gadwall, Pochard and Tufted Duck have all bred here. Distant views of lake can be obtained from the Grange at SU562362, which lies in Northington Park (open to the public). The entrance road is situated just off the B3046 between Abbotstone Down and Swarraton.

Calendar

All Year: Little Grebe, Cormorant, Little Egret, Grey Heron, feral Greylag and Canada Geese, Mandarin (Test), Gadwall, Pochard, Tufted Duck, Red-legged and Grey Partridges, Water Rail, Snipe, Redshank, Barn Owl, Kingfisher, Grey Wagtail, Cetti's Warbler, Reed Bunting.

Winter (mid-November–mid-March): possible rarer winter grebes; possible Bittern; wildfowl including Wigeon, Teal, Shoveler and occasional Pintail, in cold weather – frequent Scaup, Goldeneye, Smew and Goosander, also occasional Bewick's Swan and grey geese (usually White-fronted); occasional Hen Harrier, Merlin and Peregrine; waders including Golden Plover, Curlew, Green and Common Sandpipers, occasional other species; occasional Short-eared Owl; Water Pipit, Chiffchaff, Siskin, Redpoll, occasional Bearded Tit.
Most likely oddity: rare wildfowl.

Summer (mid-May–mid-July): Great Crested Grebe, Shelduck, Hobby, Little Ringed and Ringed Plovers, Common Tern, Turtle Dove, Nightingale, Sedge and Reed Warblers, Lesser Whitethroat, Garden Warbler.

Spring (mid-March–mid-May) *and Autumn* (mid-July–mid-November): migrant waders including Greenshank regular in autumn, Green and Common Sandpipers, occasional other species; Common and occasional Black Terns; landbird migrants including Yellow Wagtail, Whinchat, Wheatear, occasional Black Redstart, Ring Ouzel, Firecrest and Pied Flycatcher.
Most likely oddities: rare heron, Garganey, Marsh Harrier, Osprey, rare wader, landbird subrarity.

THE NEW FOREST AND NEARBY COAST

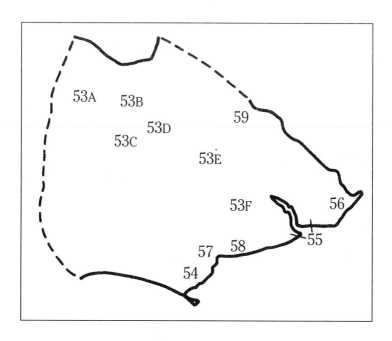

53 THE NEW FOREST
Recommended Sites
- 53A Ashley Walk and Hampton Ridge
- 53B Fritham
- 53C Bolderwood Grounds and Rhinefield Ornamental Drive
- 53D Acres Down
- 53E Beaulieu Road Station and Bishop's Dyke
- 53F Hatchet Pond and Beaulieu West Heath

54 HURST CASTLE, AND KEYHAVEN & PENNINGTON MARSHES NR
55 BEAULIEU ESTUARY, LEPE SHORE COUNTRY PARK & SOWLEY POND
56 CALSHOT SPIT AND ASHLETT CREEK

Other Sites Worthy Of Attention
57 Lymington Reedbeds NR
58 Tanners Lane
59 Eling Great Marsh

General Introduction

The southwest corner of Hampshire is dominated by the bogs, heaths and woodlands of the New Forest. To the south lies the relatively un-spoilt Solent coast where woods and fields extend down to a shore bordered by inter-tidal mudflats and *Spartina* saltmarshes. By contrast, little such habitat now exists along the highly developed west shore of Southampton Water. The Solent and Southampton Water are sheltered from the worst of the elements by the Isle of Wight.

The New Forest is undoubtedly the most important area within the region for breeding birds which include many specialities associated with its unique mixture of habitats. Winter also brings its attractions in the form of Hen Harrier and Great Grey Shrike. The marshes and waters of the nearby coast support an abundance of waterfowl, waders and gulls during the winter and at times of passage; whilst in summer the Solent is renowned for its nesting colonies of gulls and terns.

53 THE NEW FOREST (FC)

**OS Maps 195, 184
& New Forest
SU10/11/20/21/30/
31/40 & SZ29/39**

Habitat

This is an area of outstanding natural beauty consisting mostly of bog, lowland heath and woodland which covers some 144 square miles of southwest Hampshire. The New Forest owes much of its present unique character to a combination of geographical and historic factors. Geologically the area is part of the Hampshire Basin and comprises Tertiary sands, gravels and clays, extensively overlain by the more recent Plateau Gravels. A variety of soils have developed on these deposits which in turn support different vegetation types. Broadleaved woodland of mainly pedunculate oak and beech is found on the heavier clay soils. The sands and gravels, notably the Plateau Gravels, give rise to poor infertile soils supporting heathland which is dominated by ling and sometimes gorse. Where drainage is impeded, often between ridges of Plateau Gravels underlain by impervious clay, acid bogs form. These are characterised by a luxuriant growth of purple moor grass, sphagnum moss and other acid-loving plants such as bog myrtle, cotton-grass and sundews.

First appropriated as a Royal Hunting Reserve by William I in the 11th century, the early stewardship of the New Forest was closely associated with deer conservation. As deer hunting declined, the subsequent development of the area became increasingly influenced by timber production with the earliest inclosures dating back to the late 15th century. Owing to the modern demand for softwoods, rather more than half of this enclosed woodland now consists of coniferous trees. The dominant natural tree of the broadleaved woodlands is the pedunculate oak, but beeches were extensively planted in the past and the descendants of these now cover large areas. An important feature of the broadleaved woodlands is the lack of intensive management which has allowed trees to mature, become senile, die and decay. Consequently trees of all ages are present including a significant proportion that are dead and rotting. This increases the diversity of the woodland environment, creating habitats for many forms of wildlife.

The grazing of commoner's animals, notably cattle, pigs and ponies, has also had a profound effect on the forest's landscape. Periodic controlled burning of the heathland is necessary for the regeneration of the vegetation, but indiscriminate fires can cause considerable damage to the wildlife. Livestock grazing has resulted in the closely cropped forest lawns that are often found along the edges of the forest streams and woodlands. The woodland borders are also typified by areas of invasive bracken with scattered self-sown Scots pines and silver birches.

At present the crown lands of the New Forest are vested in the Minister of Agriculture and managed on his behalf by the Forestry Commission under the guidance of various Acts of Parliament. The natural history of the New Forest is one of the finest and most interesting in Britain. It includes an almost never-ending list of specialities and rarities belonging to a wide diversity of plants and animals. These range from mosses, fungi and flowers to various insect groups, reptiles, mammals and, of course, birds. Many of these species are either restricted to or only commonly found in the New Forest. Amongst the insects, dragonflies, moths and butterflies are particularly well represented. Five of the six British reptiles occur here including the rare smooth snake; whilst deer are the most conspicuous of the mammals inhabiting the area with roe, fallow, red and Sika all present. Obviously the New Forest has much to offer the general naturalist as well as the birdwatcher.

Species

One of the main attractions of the New Forest's birdlife is the population of breeding raptors. The dashing Hobby is the species many people associate with this area. Despite the continuing activities of egg collectors and other problems, the Forest still supports good numbers of this attractive falcon. Hobbies may be encountered almost anywhere with birds frequently seen hawking for insects over the more extensive bogs and surrounding heathlands. The Honey Buzzard is perhaps the most sought after of the local raptors, but as a result of a recent decline this species is not so easy to see as it used to be. There have also been sporadic sightings of Goshawks from at least one area of the New Forest. In addition to the rarer raptors, the Forest's woodlands hold reasonable numbers of Sparrowhawk, Buzzard and Kestrel.

The more extensive bogs are important habitats for a variety of wetland breeding birds including Shelduck, Teal, Lapwing, Snipe, Redshank and

Hobby

175

Curlew. Another characteristic bird of these areas is the Reed Bunting which also nests on the wetter heaths. Grey Herons often flight from breeding sites outside the New Forest to stalk prey around the bogs and Forest ponds. A few pairs of Ringed Plover breed on various disused airfields and gravel pits.

Although the Skylark and Meadow Pipit are the common breeding birds of the dry heathlands, the true speciality of these areas is the Dartford Warbler. This resident warbler thrives best on heaths where there is an extensive cover of gorse, but the species suffers greatly from hard winters and loss of habitat through fires. For example, fewer than ten pairs were located in the New Forest after the severe cold of the 1962/3 winter. Since then the population has recovered well and in 1992 it was thought to be in excess of 500 pairs. The Stonechat is another characteristic bird of the gorse-clad heaths where Red-backed Shrikes could also be found until their disappearance in the early 1980s. There are still good numbers of Woodlarks in the New Forest which remains one of the last strongholds for this species in Britain. Woodlarks inhabit both the open heaths, particularly those that have been recently burnt, and the woodland borders where birds like to feed on the forest lawns. A few pairs of Whinchats and Wheatears also breed most years. The former species favours sites with extensive areas of bracken; whilst the latter prefers disused airfields and forest lawns where they often nest in old rabbit burrows. The Tree Pipit replaces its commoner relative towards the edges of the heaths and along the woodland borders where scattered trees are present. This is also the ideal habitat for the Nightjar which is widely distributed throughout the area.

Perhaps the most evocative sound of the broadleaved woodlands in summer is the shivering song of the Wood Warbler. Another characteristic bird of these woodlands is the attractive Redstart, which together with such species as Stock Dove, Tawny Owl, all three woodpeckers, Marsh Tit, Nuthatch and very occasionally Pied Flycatcher find suitable nest holes in the many dead and decaying trees. Roding Woodcock are a familiar sight as they patrol the woodland glades and borders during spring and summer evenings. The elusive Hawfinch occurs sparingly throughout the Forest's woodlands; whilst Redpolls breed in areas dominated by silver birches, but numbers vary from year to year according to the success or failure of the seed crop. Although the mature coniferous forests support less variety of birds compared to the broadleaved woodlands, they do hold a number of interesting species. Since the early 1950s, Siskins have become well established as a breeding bird in many areas of forestry and mixed woodland. Like the Redpoll, however, their numbers can vary depending on the success of the seed crop. The Crossbill is another species closely associated with coniferous forest, notably where Scots pine and larch are present. The resident population is periodically bolstered by late summer irruptions of birds from Scandinavia and the Continent when wandering flocks occur widely in areas of forestry. The tiny Firecrest was discovered breeding in the New Forest during the early 1960s and has continued to do so in small numbers. Since this species is very unobtrusive and difficult to locate during the breeding season, its true status remains uncertain. Firecrests seem to like woods where there are some broadleaved trees inter-mixed with conifers. Young forestry plantations offer suitable breeding habitat to birds such as Nightjar and Tree Pipit which are associated with more open areas.

Since the early 1980s the Mandarin has become established as a breeding bird in the New Forest. This species favours the woodland streams and ponds which also support small numbers of nesting Kingfishers and Grey Wagtails.

During the winter the New Forest's heathlands and bogs can appear rather desolate and birdless. Careful searching, however, can reveal some noteworthy species. One of the season's specialities is the Great Grey Shrike. Although the number of individuals wintering has declined in recent years, a few birds still appear with some frequency at traditional sites such as Beaulieu Road Station and Ashley Walk. Small numbers of Hen Harriers regularly winter in the Forest; whilst Merlins and Peregrines are present most years. The more extensive bogs attract a few Teal and Snipe along with the occasional flock of Wigeon and Shoveler. Parties of Siskins and Redpolls occur widely in the woodlands, particularly where birch, alder and larch are present; whilst Bramblings often inhabit the beech woods. There is also a better chance of locating some of the more interesting resident species during the winter. Small flocks of Hawfinches gather in certain favoured localities; whilst Woodlarks and Crossbills are often conspicuous towards the end of the season.

The New Forest is not well known for bird migration. Nevertheless a scattering of the commoner landbird migrants, including Whinchat and Wheatear, pass through in spring and autumn; whilst scarcer birds such as Black Redstart, Ring Ouzel and Pied Flycatcher are occasionally recorded. Passage waders such as Whimbrel may be seen from time to time. The rarity speciality of the area is undoubtedly the Red-footed Falcon which has occurred in the New Forest more frequently than anywhere else in Britain. It is obviously well worth scrutinising any unusual or odd-looking Hobby. Other scarce and vagrant raptors such as Black and Red Kites, Marsh Harrier, Rough-legged Buzzard and Osprey have also been reported together with a variety of other rarities. These include three recent reports of Black Storks, one of which summered in the New Forest and nearby Avon Valley in 1990.

Timing

Some of the breeding specialities such as Lesser Spotted Woodpecker, Woodlark and Crossbill, are often easier to locate on fine days in late winter and early spring (February–April) rather than later in the summer. Most woodland birds should be looked for early in the morning when they are most active, but late evening is the best time to see Woodcock and Nightjars. Raptors are most in evidence during the middle (heat) of the day (10.00 am–4.00 pm) when the weather is warm and sunny. Amongst the rarer species, Honey Buzzards are most likely to be observed when they are displaying (mid-May–mid-June) and when the young are on the wing (late July–early September); whilst Goshawks, when they are present, are most obvious during their display period in late winter and early spring (February–April).

Access

The main access routes to and through the New Forest are the A35 Southampton to Christchurch, A31 Cadnam to Ringwood, B3078 Cadnam to Fordingbridge and A337 Cadnam to Lymington roads. More specific details of access are given under Recommended Sites.

Some mention should be made of the present day pressures on the New Forest and its environment. With the recent increase in leisure time, the recreational use of the New Forest has grown considerably over the last 25 years. This has resulted in a greater degree of disturbance which is almost certainly responsible for the disappearance of the Montagu's Harrier as a regular breeding species. More specific disturbance may be caused by the increasing number of birdwatchers visiting the area in search of its local specialities. Fortunately most of these, including the rarer birds of prey, can still be seen by those willing to exercise care and patience. Birdwatchers are asked to abide at all times by the Code of Conduct published by the RSPB.

Recommended Sites

53A ASHLEY WALK AND HAMPTON RIDGE

Map p. 179, SU11/21

Habitat and Species

Situated in the northwest of the New Forest, this is an area of gorse-clad ridges of heathland interspersed by boggy valleys. Pitts Wood, which is a small inclosure of mixed woodland, lies in the valley between Cockley Plain and Hampton Ridge; whilst the eastern side of the area is bordered by the extensive woodlands of Islands Thorns, Amberwood and Alderhill Inclosures.

Most birds typical of open heathland including Dartford Warbler Stonechat and perhaps Whinchat can be found here. Tree Pipits are widespread along the woodland borders which may still support the odd pair of Woodlark; whilst Curlew inhabit some of the boggy valleys. The broadleaved woodlands hold Redstart, Wood Warbler and Hawfinch. The latter species is most likely to be seen during the winter when a small flock regularly frequents the trees and bushes around the forest lawn between Lodge Hill and Pitts Wood. Raptors are very much a feature of this area. Hobbies are a familiar sight overhead during the summer; whilst several Hen Harriers reside on Ashley Walk in winter when the occasional Merlin, Peregrine and Short-eared Owl may be encountered. This is also one of the traditional wintering haunts for the Great Grey Shrike which in recent years has favoured Black Gutter Bottom. There are reports of such oddities as

Hawfinch

Purple Heron, Spoonbill, Red Kite, Marsh Harrier, Osprey and Shorelark from this area; whilst Ring Ouzels occasionally appear on passage.

Access

Ashley Walk and Hampton Ridge are best approached from car parks at Ashley Walk, Black Gutter (sometimes closed) and Telegraph Hill, which all lie on the B3078 between Godshill and Bramshaw Telegraph. There are several well marked tracks crossing this area; the most notable being (i) from Ashley Walk car park southeast to Hampton Ridge via Cockley Plain and Pitts Wood, (ii) from Cockley Plain northeast across Ashley Walk to Picket Corner, (iii) from Telegraph Hill car park and Picket Corner south-west along the woodland border to Ashley Cross and Hampton Ridge, and (iv) from Abbots Well car park east along Hampton Ridge.

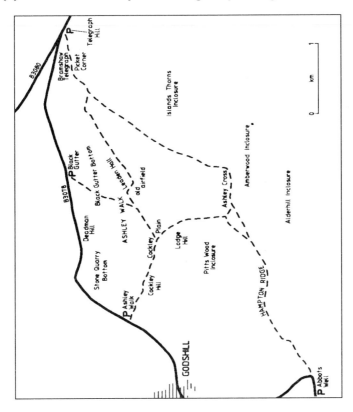

53B FRITHAM

Map p. 180, SU21

Habitat and Species

The land lying to the west of Fritham Village offers an attractive mixture of New Forest habitats including the magnificent woodlands of Eyeworth Wood, Islands Thorns, Amberwood and Sloden Inclosures as well as the open heathland of Fritham Plain. Eyeworth Pond (Irons

Well), which is situated at a site where gunpowder was manufactured, adds further interest to the area.

The prime attraction is the woodland birds. These include such elusive residents as Lesser Spotted Woodpecker and Hawfinch with several pairs of both species present in Eyeworth Wood and Islands Thorns Inclosure. In spring and summer these are joined by good numbers of Redstarts and Wood Warblers. Mandarins also nest in these woods and regularly appear along with Canada Geese and various feral wildfowl on Eyeworth Pond; whilst Grey Wagtails frequent the outlet stream. The open heath and woodland borders hold Curlew, Nightjar, Tree Pipit, Stonechat, Dartford Warbler and still perhaps Woodlark. Fritham Plain is a good vantage point to observe raptors over the nearby woodlands.

Access

Fritham is reached from the minor road between the B3078 at Longcross Plain and the eastbound carriageway of the A31 at Stoney Cross, by taking the road signposted to 'Fritham and Eyeworth only' west through the village to the Royal Oak PH. From here continue either northwest on

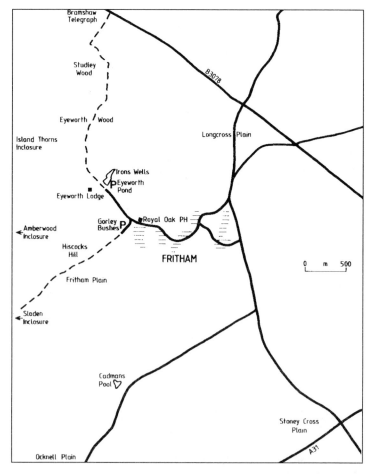

the metalled road to Eyeworth Pond car park or southwest on the gravel track to Fritham car park. There are numerous footpaths and forest walks through the woodlands and across Fritham Plain.

53C BOLDERWOOD GROUNDS AND RHINEFIELD ORNAMENTAL DRIVE

Map below, SU20

Habitat and Species

Bolderwood Grounds are situated in the north of the woodland mass that extends from Lyndhurst and Beaulieu in the east to Burley in the west. This area supports some of the best mixed woodlands to be found in the New Forest including an impressive variety of ornamental and coniferous trees that form part of the Forestry Commission's Arboretum.

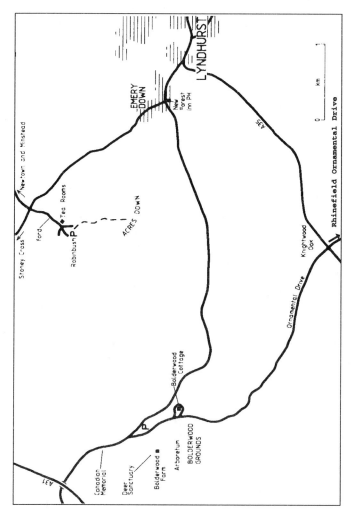

There is also a deer sanctuary nearby at Bolderwood Farm.

This area holds a number of woodland specialities. Bolderwood provided the first British breeding record of the tiny Firecrest in 1962. Subsequently this species has been found during the breeding season at a number of widely scattered localities throughout the New Forest. Firecrests can be very difficult to locate, often singing high up in tall conifers, but birds are occasionally seen at lower elevations. Traditionally the woods between the car park and Bolderwood Cottage have been the most reliable area to look for this species, but Firecrests are likely to be encountered almost anywhere in these woodlands. Crossbills and Hawfinches are frequently seen, the latter species favouring the holly bushes near the Canadian Memorial. Other interesting inhabitants of these woodlands include Woodcock, Tree Pipit, Redstart, Wood Warbler and Siskin; whilst the open heath to the north of Bolderwood Grounds supports Stonechat and Dartford Warbler.

Similar woodland habitat lies to the south along Rhinefield Ornamental Drive. One of the main attractions of this area is a winter roost of Hawfinches, which gather in the trees near the entrance to the large forest clearing on the opposite side of the road from Black Water car park. The birds are best looked for from mid-afternoon onwards. Otherwise the area holds a wide variety of woodland birds including Crossbill.

Access
Bolderwood car park can be reached either along the Bolderwood Ornamental Drive northwest from the A35 approximately 2 miles (3 km) southwest of Swan Green, Lyndhurst; or along the minor road west from the New Forest Inn in Emery Down. There are several well marked forest walks through the woodlands. The Canadian Memorial lies about 0.5 miles (0.8 km) north of Bolderwood car park.

Black Water car park can be reached along the Rhinefield Ornamental Drive either south from the A35 approximately 2 miles (3 km) southwest of Swan Green, Lyndhurst; or along Rhinefield Road west from Brockenhurst.

53D ACRES DOWN
Map p. 181, SU20
Habitat and Species
To the northwest of Lyndhurst lies Acres Down, a ridge of open heathland overlooking the mass of woodland that extends southwest across the New Forest towards Burley.

This is a good vantage point for watching raptors. For many years it has been a well known site for watching Honey Buzzards, although in recent years this species has appeared less reliably than it used to do. Nevertheless, during the spring and summer there is a good chance of seeing Sparrowhawk, Buzzard, Kestrel and Hobby; whilst Goshawks have occasionally been observed here. There are also reports of Black Kite, Marsh Harrier and Osprey passing over the ridge. A variety of heathland and woodland birds including Woodlark, Tree Pipit, Redstart, Stonechat and Siskin can be found on Acres Down; whilst the nearby woodlands hold a similar range of birds as Bolderwood Grounds.

Access
Acres Down is reached from the minor road between Emery Down and the westbound carriageway of the A31 at Stoney Cross, by taking the 'no

through road', which is opposite the turning to Newtown and Minstead, southwest to the Tea Rooms in the village and continuing on the right of three gravel tracks to Robinbush car park. There is a footpath south from the car park up and along the length of Acres Down.

53E BEAULIEU ROAD STATION AND BISHOP'S DYKE

Map p. 184, SU30

Habitat and Species

Beaulieu Road Station is situated on the B3056 road about midway between Lyndhurst and Beaulieu. To the south and west of the road, majestic woodlands form the backcloth to the extensive bogs and heathlands of Bishop's Dyke. The area supports the widest possible variety of New Forest habitats including fine examples of wet bog with willow carr, dry heath, woodland borders with forest lawn and broadleaved woodland. Other noteworthy features are the railway line, which bisects the area, and a series of tumuli across the western half of the heath which provide ideal vantage points to watch over the nearby bog and more distant woodlands.

This is perhaps the best known area in the New Forest to look for many of the local specialities. Amongst the raptors, Buzzard and Hobby are regularly seen, the latter often hawking for insects over the larger bogs. Both Honey Buzzard and Goshawk have been occasionally reported from the area; whilst there are several records of vagrant Red-footed Falcons including a party of five birds that appeared in the summer of 1959. Characteristic birds of the open heath and woodland borders include Nightjar, Tree Pipit and Stonechat along with a few pairs of Woodlark and Dartford Warbler. Wheatears sometimes nest in old rabbit burrows on areas of recently burnt heath. The extensive bogs hold breeding Shelduck, Teal, Snipe, Curlew, Redshank and Reed Bunting. The woodlands are rich in birdlife including such notable species as Woodcock, Lesser Spotted Woodpecker, Redstart, Wood Warbler, Siskin, Redpoll and Hawfinch; whilst the pines around Shatterford car park and in the vicinity of Beaulieu Road Station are amongst the most reliable in the New Forest to find Crossbills.

In winter Hen Harriers regularly quarter the bogs and open heath in search of prey; whilst Merlins and Peregrines occasionally appear.

Great Grey Shrike

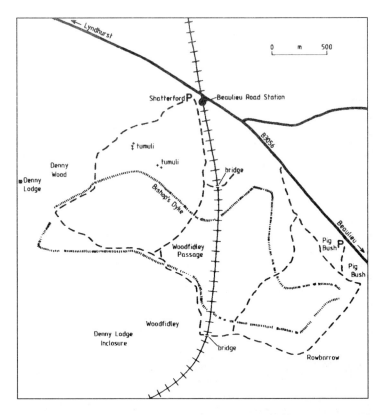

Although this area is one of the traditional wintering localities of Great Grey Shrikes, this species has appeared less frequently in recent years. Even when they are present, these striking birds can be surprisingly elusive ranging widely over the entire area. Flocks of Siskins and Redpolls are also a feature of the season. A few landbird migrants are noted at times of passage when oddities such as Purple Heron, Black Kite, Marsh Harrier, Osprey, Common Crane, Roller, Hoopoe and Wryneck have occurred.

Access

Beaulieu Road Station and its environs are best approached from car parks along the B3056 Lyndhurst to Beaulieu road at Shatterford (by Beaulieu Road Station) and Pig Bush. There are several tracks and footpaths crossing the area, notably from Shatterford car park either southwest to Denny Wood or south to Woodfidley. It is also possible to walk along the edge of the woodlands from Denny Wood to Woodfidley, then across the railway bridge to Rowbarrow and on to Pig Bush.

53F HATCHET POND AND BEAULIEU WEST HEATH

Map p. 186, SU30

Habitat and Species

This extensive area of relatively low-lying gorse-clad heathland is situated in the south of the New Forest just to the southwest of Beaulieu. In the

184

northeast corner of the heath lies Hatchet Pond, a 200-year-old lake formed as a result of gravel workings and marl pits. The remains of a disused airfield can be found in the centre of the heath; whilst the northern edge of the area is bordered by extensive woodlands and forestry.

In spring and summer Hatchet Pond and the associated bog attract most of the wader species that breed in the New Forest including Ringed Plover, Lapwing, Snipe, Curlew and Redshank. Cormorant and Grey Heron can be expected throughout the year along with the occasional fishing Common Tern in summer. Waterfowl other than Mute Swan, Mallard, Moorhen and Coot are very scarce. Nevertheless one or two individuals, perhaps more, of the less common species such as Teal, Shoveler, Pochard and Tufted Duck are sometimes present in winter; whilst there is always the chance of something more unusual – Red-throated Diver, Red-necked Grebe and Goosander have been seen here.

The surrounding heathland supports such characteristic breeding birds as Stonechat and Dartford Warbler. The area is particularly good for Hobby with birds regularly seen hawking for insects, notably during the late afternoons and evenings. As dusk approaches Woodcock display over the woodland borders; whilst a little later Nightjars emerge from areas of heath with scattered self-sown pines including the immediate environs of Hatchet Pond. In winter the occasional Hen Harrier and Merlin pass over the heath in search of prey.

Hen Harrier

Access

Hatchet Pond lies close to the junction of the B3055 road east from Brockenhurst and the B3054 Lymington to Beaulieu road approximately 2 miles (3.2 km) west of Beaulieu itself. There are car parks at Hatchet Pond off the B3055 just before the junction with the B3054 and at Hatchet Moor off the B3054 just south of Hatchet Pond. There are footpaths around Hatchet Pond with others giving access to the surrounding areas of heathland.

Calendar

All Year: Grey Heron, Canada Goose, Mandarin, Teal, Goshawk (rare), Buzzard, Snipe, Woodcock, Kingfisher, Lesser Spotted Woodpecker, Woodlark, Grey Wagtail, Stonechat, Dartford Warbler, Siskin, Redpoll, Crossbill, Hawfinch, Reed Bunting, common resident woodland birds.

Summer (May–July): Shelduck, Honey Buzzard, Hobby, Curlew, Redshank, Turtle Dove, Nightjar, Tree Pipit, Redstart, Whinchat, Wheatear,
Wood Warbler, Firecrest.

Most likely oddity: Red-footed Falcon.

Winter (November–March): wildfowl; Hen Harrier, Merlin, Peregrine;
occasional Jack Snipe; occasional Short-eared Owl; Great Grey Shrike,
Brambling.

Spring (April and May) *and Autumn* (August–October): occasional
migrant waders; landbird migrants including occasional Black Redstart,
Ring Ouzel and Pied Flycatcher.

Most likely oddities: scarce/rare migrant raptors including Red-footed
Falcon, landbird subrarity.

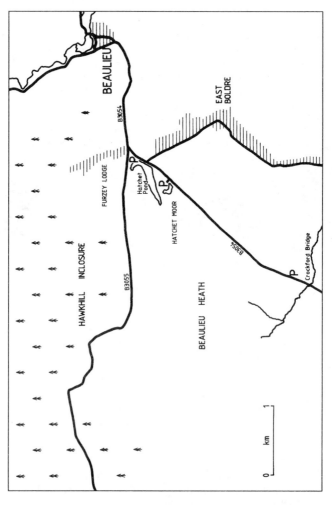

54 HURST CASTLE (ENGLISH HERITAGE), AND KEYHAVEN AND PENNINGTON MARSHES NR (HCC)

OS Maps 196
& New Forest
SZ29/38/39

Habitat

The western entrance to the Solent is marked by a long shingle bank which links Hurst Castle to the mainland. The castle together with other buildings occupy an area of rough grassland and open shingle. Cover is sparse, but there are some tamarisk bushes and isolated patches of scrub.

From the shingle bank of Hurst Beach extensive *Spartina* saltmarshes stretch eastwards along the Solent shore. These marshes are intersected by numerous muddy creeks and channels; the most notable being Oxey Lake which forms the large inlet between Oxey Marsh (Pennington) and the Lymington saltmarshes. Along the seaward edge of these saltmarshes, storms and gales have thrown up banks of shingle.

Between Keyhaven and Lymington, there is a large area of marshy rough pasture and mainly gorse scrub which is protected by a recently renovated seawall. The main feature of these marshes is a series of shallow pools and lagoons. These are mostly situated close to the seawall at various points between Keyhaven Marsh and Eight Acre Pond at Woodside. A rough track and various minor roads run along the back of the marshes which extend a little further inland before they merge into farmland. Recently this area of farmland has been extensively developed for gravel extraction producing several freshwater lakes and pools. At present these gravel workings are being used as landfill sites.

Immediately behind Keyhaven Harbour extensive reedbeds fringe the small estuary of Avon Water. In winter the fields to the west of Avon Water often flood. Further to the west at the base of Hurst Beach near Milford on Sea, the shingle bank encloses another area of open water known as Sturt Pond.

Since 1962 the Hampshire Wildlife Trust have wardened the terns that nest on Hurst Beach and the saltmarshes. More recently Hampshire County Council have purchased much of Keyhaven and Pennington Marshes to establish a nature reserve. The area supports a rich and diverse saltmarsh flora and fauna including several interesting species of plant and insect.

Species

The area was well known to the famous 19th-century wildfowler Colonel Hawker whose diaries testify to the wealth of waterfowl that occurred here in winter. Wildfowl together with waders and other winter birds can still be seen in abundance today. The most conspicuous of the wildfowl is undoubtedly the Brent Goose. Since they first started to winter here in the mid 1960s, counts have increased to reach peaks of 4,000 or more birds in the early 1990s. Shelduck, Wigeon and Teal can also be expected along with increasing numbers of Canada Geese, Gadwall, Pintail,

Shoveler and perhaps feral Greylag Geese. The offshore waters of the Solent hold small numbers of Great Crested and Slavonian Grebes, Goldeneye and Red-breasted Mergansers. Small groups of Eider are sometimes present, but divers, Red-necked and Black-necked Grebes, other sea-duck and auks are infrequent visitors. Periods of severe cold may bring flocks of grey geese to the marshes, the most likely species being White-fronted although there are recent sightings of Bean Geese. Bewick's Swan, Scaup, Smew and Goosander have also been noted during hard weather. In recent years the recently developed Iley Lane Lakes attracted good numbers of wildfowl including Gadwall, Pochard and Tufted Duck amongst others. Now that these lakes are being used as landfill sites, they will become less attractive to birdlife with the possible exception of gulls.

During the winter the area supports all of the commoner waders including Black-tailed Godwit and usually a few Bar-tailed Godwits. Wintering Ruff used to be a local speciality, but their numbers have declined from peaks of 100 to 150 birds in the late 1960s and early 1970s to fewer than 20 in the mid-1980s. The species is now an erratic visitor in winter with counts invariably in single figures. A few Greenshank are usually present, but the Spotted Redshank is less frequent in winter than it used to be in the 1980s. Flocks of Golden Plover occur, often associating with Lapwings in fields inland from Hurst Beach and the marshes. Knot are occasionally seen; whilst Avocets and Purple Sandpipers are uncommon visitors, the latter species usually being reported from Hurst Castle.

The area, in particular the landfill sites along Iley Lane, attracts large numbers of the commoner gulls throughout the winter. Kittiwakes and occasionally Little Gulls may appear after gales when birds sometimes seek shelter in the Solent; whilst Mediterranean Gulls are seen from time to time. Both Iceland and Glaucous Gulls have become very rare visitors in recent years. Grey Herons and Cormorants are present for much of the year and Shags are becoming more frequently recorded off Hurst Beach and in the Solent, particularly during the winter and spring months.

Although Keyhaven and Pennington Marshes are a favoured haunt for Short-eared Owls, the species cannot be expected every winter. Merlins and Peregrines also regularly occur, but Hen Harriers are rather uncommon appearing most often during spells of hard weather. Kingfishers are a familiar sight as they dart along the seawall and saltmarsh creeks in search of fish. Good numbers of Rock Pipits are present, notably along Hurst Beach and the seawall; whilst a few Stonechats and locally dispersing Dartford Warblers inhabit the coastal and marshland scrub. Small flocks of Reed Buntings and common finches forage along the tideline and around the marshy pools. This is one of the best sites in the region for Snow Buntings, although the species is still an infrequent visitor; whilst there are several winter reports of Lapland Buntings. The reedbeds at Avon Water occasionally host wandering parties of Bearded Tits which have sometimes overwintered here.

Hurst Beach is one of the prime sites in Hampshire for seawatching. Spring passage consists mainly of Common Scoter, waders including Bar-tailed Godwit and Whimbrel and terns – mostly Sandwich, Common and Arctic. Smaller numbers of divers, Fulmars, Gannets, other sea-duck and wildfowl, Arctic Skuas, Little Gulls, Kittiwakes and Black Terns also occur. Pomarine and Great Skuas are seen most springs, but Manx Shearwaters are uncommon and rarely observed. There is always a possibility that something more unusual will appear during these spring seawatches which in the past have produced such rarities as Cory's Shearwater, Surf Scoter and Whiskered Tern. The pattern of these offshore movements is often complicated with a substantial proportion of the waders, skuas, Little Gulls and terns passing east up the Solent either through Hurst Narrows or directly over Hurst Beach. Other birds, including most of the seabirds and sea-duck pass offshore and return out to sea to move around the Isle of Wight.

A wide selection of waders can be seen on spring migration. Large flocks of both godwit species and Whimbrel regularly occur along with small numbers of Knot, Sanderling, Ruff, Spotted Redshank, Greenshank, Green and Common Sandpipers. Scarcer species such as Avocet, Little Ringed Plover, Curlew Sandpiper, Little Stint and Wood Sandpiper occasionally appear; whilst there are several reports of Temminck's Stints as well as sightings of Kentish Plover, Red-necked Phalarope and perhaps more surprisingly Pectoral Sandpiper (twice). Rarer waders such as Black-winged Stilt, Broad-billed Sandpiper, Long-billed Dowitcher and Terek Sandpiper have also been recorded in spring.

Little Terns

The first Sandwich Terns arrive during the latter part of March followed in early April by Common and Little Terns. The Little Gulls and Black Terns that move through Solent later in the spring may occasionally linger to hawk for insects over the seawall pools. Garganey are sometimes seen in spring; whilst migrant raptors may include the occasional Marsh Harrier and Osprey.

Amongst a scattering of landbird migrants that appear in spring, Yellow Wagtails favour the damp pasture and marshy pools of Keyhaven and Pennington Marshes where the marshland scrub attracts a variety of other species including the very occasional Ring Ouzel, Firecrest and Pied Flycatcher. Wheatears prefer the drier grassland along the seawall and around Hurst Castle, the latter being a likely haunt for the odd Black Redstart.

A number of spring oddities and rarities have been recorded from this area over the years. Spoonbills have occurred on several occasions; whilst in addition to the rarities already mentioned, Purple Heron, Blue-winged Teal, Black Kite, Red-footed Falcon, Baillon's Crake, Gull-billed and White-winged Black Terns, Savi's Warbler, Golden Oriole and Serin have also been noted.

During the summer the saltmarshes between Hurst Castle and the Lymington Estuary echo to the cries of several thousand breeding pairs of Black-headed Gulls. Until some measure of protection was introduced in 1962, the indiscriminate commercial collection of gulls eggs used to cause considerable disturbance to these and other nesting birds. At present the commercial collecting of gulls eggs is under licence from the Department of the Environment. This control, together with the wardening of the saltmarshes, has been a benefit to such noteworthy breeding birds as Oystercatcher, Ringed Plover, Sandwich, Common and Little Terns. Shelduck sometimes nest on Keyhaven and Pennington Marshes; whilst the reedbed habitats, notably those by Avon Water, hold Cetti's, Sedge and Reed Warblers, Reed Bunting and occasionally Bearded Tit. A few pairs of Rock Pipit nest around Hurst Castle, the only regular breeding site for this species in Hampshire. The marshland scrub supports a variety of nesting species including Stonechat and perhaps Dartford Warbler.

Late summer heralds the now annual influx of Little Egrets. Numbers have increased considerably since the late 1980s with a recent peak of 63 in autumn 1995. The species is virtually resident in the area and can be expected throughout much of the year. Mid summer has also produced the occasional rarity, the most noteworthy being a Sooty Tern in June 1961.

Autumn wader passage is evident from late June and gradually builds up to reach its peak during August and September. Although some occur in very small numbers, a wide range of species regularly pass through including Little Ringed Plover, Knot, Little Stint, Curlew Sandpiper, Ruff, Black-tailed and Bar-tailed Godwits, Whimbrel, Spotted Redshank, Greenshank, Green, Wood and Common Sandpipers. Grey Phalaropes often take refuge on the pools behind the seawall after severe gales. Such weather is also likely to produce the occasional American wader, usually Pectoral Sandpiper which has appeared on a number of occasions. There are also several records of Buff-breasted Sandpiper, Long-billed Dowitcher and Lesser Yellowlegs as well as single sightings of Killdeer, American Golden Plover, Semipalmated, White-rumped and Baird's Sandpipers. From the opposite direction Kentish Plover, Temminck's Stint and Red-necked Phalarope have been reported on a number of occasions and there are single records of a pratincole and Marsh Sandpiper.

Sandwich, Common and Little Terns are usually present throughout much of the autumn; whilst a few Little Gulls and Black Terns appear most years. There are also several autumn sightings of White-winged Black Terns and two of Gull-billed Terns. Migrant raptors are also a feature of the autumn. Merlins and Hobbies are regularly seen on passage and Marsh Harriers and Ospreys are occasional visitors, the latter sometimes lingering for several days or even weeks.

There is a small passage of landbird migrants. Most of the commoner species occur with Yellow Wagtail and Wheatear particularly conspicuous at times. Scarcer migrants such as Black Redstart, Ring Ouzel, Firecrest and Pied Flycatcher occasionally appear; whilst subrarities including Wryneck, Richard's and Tawny Pipits, Bluethroat, Aquatic, Melodious and Barred Warblers, Red-backed Shrike, Lapland and Ortolan Buntings have all been noted. There is also a late autumn record of a Yellow-billed Cuckoo in November 1976.

Generally seawatching off Hurst Beach in autumn is rather unrewarding. Passage mainly consists of a westerly trickle of Sandwich and Common Terns along with the odd Arctic Skua and occasional flock of Common Scoter. Severe westerly gales, however, often bring storm-blown seabirds close inshore. If the weather is severe enough, as during the Great Storm of October 1987, birds may be forced to seek relief from the elements in the calmer waters of the Solent. The more noteworthy species reported during/after such conditions include Manx Shearwater, Storm and Leach's Petrels, Pomarine Skua, Sabine's Gull and Little Auk.

Timing

An hour or so before and after high-water are the best times to watch wildfowl and waders on the saltmarshes, since birds are forced to feed close inshore. At high tide waders roost on Keyhaven and Pennington Marshes, in fields inland from these marshes particularly along Iley Lane, and in fields behind the base of Hurst Beach along New Lane. Those waders that roost out on the saltmarshes are rather distant and often hidden amongst the *Spartina*. Wildfowl and waders frequent the pools on Keyhaven and Pennington Marshes at all states of the tide, but the number and diversity of birds tends to increase at high-water. In winter, if the fields to the west of Avon Water are flooded, these attract good numbers of wildfowl and waders.

Spring seawatching is most reliable between mid-April and mid-May when winds are onshore (SW to SE) in direction. Most passage takes place during the early part of the morning but if conditions are particularly good, movements may persist all day.

Landbird migrants should be looked for early in the morning when fall conditions exist.

Access

The area is best approached from Keyhaven which lies just to the east of Milford on Sea.

Hurst Castle is reached by walking along the shingle bank from either Sturt Pond car park* or from the junction of New Lane (south from Keyhaven Road in Milford on Sea) and Saltgrass Lane (west from Keyhaven).

Keyhaven/Pennington Marshes: the main access to this area is provided by the Solent Way footpath from Keyhaven Harbour along the seawall to Creek Cottage, Lower Pennington. The rear of the marshes and the fields immediately inland can be viewed from the rough track between Keyhaven Harbour and Lower Pennington Lane. There is a footpath along Ridgeway Lane between Lower Pennington Lane and Creek Cottage. Footpaths also cross the marshes to the seawall from the old rubbish tip and from Ridgeway Lane. Avon Water is private and must be viewed from either the road to the south or Iley Lane footpath to the east. The area of farmland and gravel workings inland from the main marshes can be reached north along Iley Lane footpath to the entrance of the landfill site and then along the footpath east to Lower Pennington Lane. Car parking is difficult and visitors should use the car park* by Keyhaven Harbour.

The Salterns and Normandy Marsh including Eight Acre Pond can be viewed from the Solent Way footpath between Creek Cottage, Lower Pennington and the car park by the Royal Lymington Yacht Club in Lymington.

Reserve Visit Arrangements: organised groups intending to visit Keyhaven/Pennington Marshes NR should book in advance with the Warden, Mr E.J. Wiseman, Normandy Farmhouse, Normandy Lane, Lymington, Hampshire SO41 8AE.

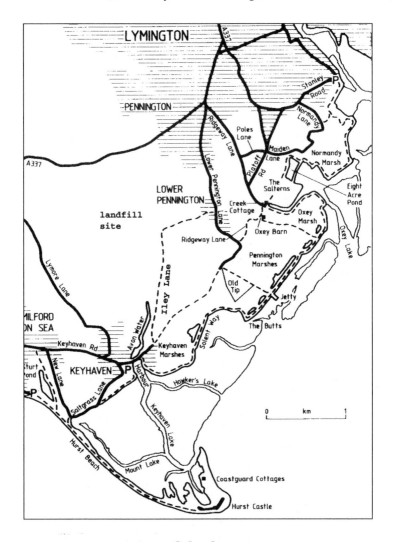

Calendar

All Year: Cormorant, Little Egret, Grey Heron, feral Greylag and Canada Geese, Shelduck, Oystercatcher, Ringed Plover, Redshank, Rock Pipit, Stonechat, Cetti's and Dartford Warblers, Reed Bunting.

Winter (mid-November–mid-March): occasional divers; Little, Great Crested, Slavonian, occasional Red-necked and Black-necked Grebes; Shag; wildfowl including Brent Goose, Wigeon, Gadwall, Teal, Pintail, Shoveler, Pochard, Tufted Duck, Goldeneye, Red-breasted Merganser, occasional sea-duck, in cold weather – occasional Bewick's Swan, grey geese (usually White-fronted), Scaup, Smew and Goosander; Merlin, Peregrine and occasional Hen Harrier; Water Rail; waders including Golden Plover, both godwits, Greenshank, occasional Knot, Ruff and Spotted Redshank, possible Avocet and Purple Sandpiper; gulls including occasional Little and Kittiwake, possible Mediterranean, Iceland and

Glaucous; occasional auks; occasional Short-eared Owl; Kingfisher; occasional Bearded Tit; possible Lapland and Snow Buntings.

Spring (mid-March–mid-May): sea passage best mid-April to mid-May – including divers; Fulmar; Gannet; Common Scoter and other sea-duck; waders including Bar-tailed Godwit and Whimbrel; skuas including annual Pomarine and Great; Little Gull and Kittiwake; terns including Black; occasional auks.

Occasional Garganey; migrants raptors including occasional Marsh Harrier and Osprey; migrant waders including Knot, Sanderling, Ruff, both godwits, Whimbrel, Spotted Redshank, Greenshank, Green and Common Sandpipers, occasional Avocet, Little Ringed Plover, Little Stint, Curlew and Wood Sandpipers; landbird migrants including Yellow Wagtail, Wheatear, occasional Black Redstart, Ring Ouzel, Firecrest and Pied Flycatcher.

Most likely oddities: Spoonbill, Temminck's Stint and rare waders.

Summer (mid-May–mid-July): non-breeding wildfowl and waders; Sandwich, Common and Little Terns; Sedge and Reed Warblers.

Autumn (mid-July–mid-November): slight sea passage involving Common Scoter, Arctic Skua and terns; during/after severe gales – occasional storm-blown seabirds such as Manx Shearwater, Storm and Leach's Petrels, Grey Phalarope, Pomarine Skua, Sabine's Gull and Little Auk.

Occasional Garganey; migrant raptors including Merlin, Hobby, occasional Marsh Harrier and Osprey; migrant waders including Little Ringed Plover, Knot, Little Stint, Curlew Sandpiper, Ruff, both godwits, Whimbrel, Spotted Redshank, Greenshank, Green, Wood and Common Sandpipers, near annual Grey Phalarope and occasional Pectoral Sandpiper; Little Gull; terns including Black; landbird migrants including Yellow Wagtail, Whinchat, Wheatear, occasional Black Redstart, Ring Ouzel, Firecrest and Pied Flycatcher.

Most likely oddities: Spoonbill, Temminck's Stint and rare American waders, landbird subrarity.

55 BEAULIEU ESTUARY (EN), LEPE COUNTRY PARK (HCC/EN) AND SOWLEY POND

OS Maps 196
& New Forest
SZ39/49 &
SU30/40

Habitat

The Beaulieu River is perhaps the most picturesque estuary in the region. The river itself rises just north of Lyndhurst and flows east and then south through the New Forest to Beaulieu Millpond which marks the upper limit of tidal influence. Below Beaulieu, the estuary proper meanders southwards to meet the Solent between Needs Ore Point and Lepe Shore. In the upper and middle reaches of the estuary, much of shoreline is bordered by attractive woodlands which include the ornamental gardens of Exbury House on the east bank. The *Spartina* saltmarshes along the margins of the main river channel become more extensive downstream, notably in the vicinity of Lower Exbury and Inchmery. In the southwest corner of the Beaulieu Estuary lie Needs Ore and The Gins, an area of low-lying marshy pasture with shallow pools (Black Water), reedbeds and a shingle shore with gorse scrub. To the east of Needs Ore Point, an island of shingle, grass and saltmarsh (Gull Island) stretches partially across the mouth of the estuary.

Lepe Country Park is situated by the Solent shore just to the east of the Beaulieu Estuary. The low crumbling cliffs behind Stone Point overlook a shingle beach, which extends east to Stansore Point and then northeast along Stanswood Bay. Low tide exposes an extensive foreshore of muddy shingle. Behind Stansore Point there is a small but interesting area of shallow pools, marsh and gorse scrub, drained by a small stream. To the east the gorse scrub merges into the woodland behind the shore of Stanswood Bay. To the west of Lepe Country Park, the Dark Water flows through marshy fields to the Solent.

Sowley Pond is a large reed-fringed lake, which is surrounded by woodland, lying to the west of Beaulieu Estuary and close to the Solent shore at Pitts Deep.

Much of the Beaulieu Estuary including Needs Ore and the Gins, along with Stansore Marsh at Lepe form the North Solent NNR. Lepe Country Park is managed by Hampshire County Council. The entire area is of interest to the general naturalist with seashore and saltmarsh plants and various insect groups particularly prominent.

Species

During the winter the lower Beaulieu Estuary supports large numbers of wildfowl, waders, gulls and other waterbirds. Like elsewhere in the Solent area, flocks of Brent Geese are conspicuous; whilst Shelduck, Wigeon, Gadwall, Teal, Pintail, Shoveler and Tufted Duck can also be expected. Little Grebes and Red-breasted Mergansers frequent the lower river where they are occasionally joined by Great Crested and Slavonian Grebes, Goldeneye and perhaps even a diver or sea-duck wandering in from the Solent. There are large populations of feral Greylag and Canada Geese, which sometimes attract feral Barnacle Geese and other exotics. All of the common waders are present in and around the lower estuary. These include large flocks of Golden Plover along with smaller numbers of Black-tailed and Bar-tailed Godwits and a few Spotted Redshank and Greenshank. The commoner gulls are worth checking through for more unusual species such as Mediterranean Gull and Kittiwake. Peregrines regularly occur throughout the year; whilst during the autumn and winter Hen Harriers and Merlins are frequent visitors along with the occasional Short-eared Owl. All three species have overwintered in the area.

Fewer birds inhabit the middle and upper reaches of the estuary, although a scattering of Little Grebes, Shelduck, Teal and waders can be found as far upstream as Beaulieu Millpond. Cormorants and Grey Herons are a familiar sight along the entire length of the estuary throughout the year; whilst the Kingfisher adds a flash of colour, particularly during the autumn and winter.

At low tide, Brent Geese and many of the commoner waders feed on the foreshore off Lepe. Stansore Marsh supports a few wildfowl – usually Shelduck and Teal and waders – mainly Ringed Plover, Dunlin, Snipe and Redshank. Shelduck, Teal and Curlew sometimes frequent the marshy fields to the west of Dark Water. The offshore waters of the Solent from Lepe westwards to Needs Ore and beyond hold small numbers of Great Crested and Slavonian Grebes and Red-breasted Mergansers; whilst divers, Red-necked and Black-necked Grebes, sea-duck – most likely Eider and auks are occasionally reported.

Sowley Pond appears to be much less attractive for wintering waterfowl than it used to be. At present Great Crested Grebe, Cormorant, Teal, Pochard and Tufted Duck are the most likely species to be encountered. There is still some interchange of birds with the nearby Solent and Beaulieu Estuary and consequently most of the other commoner species of wildfowl including Wigeon, Gadwall, Pintail and Shoveler may occur from time to time. Goosander sometimes appear during periods of cold weather, which may also bring Scaup, Smew and Ruddy Duck to seek respite on the lake. Goldeneye appear infrequently and, although they are very rare visitors, all the divers and rarer winter grebes have been recorded. Wandering flocks of Siskins and Redpolls sometimes feed in the alder woodland. The fields around Sowley Pond are worth checking for flocks of waders, notably Golden Plover and Curlew. Sowley Marsh, which lies between Sowley Pond and the Solent shore, supports small numbers of wildfowl – usually Brent Geese, Shelduck, Wigeon and Teal and waders including the occasional Spotted Redshank.

Little Egrets are now very much a feature of the area favouring both the estuary and saltmarshes as well as the freshwater pools such as Black Water (The Gins) and Dark Water (Lepe). Although highest numbers occur in the autumn, the species can be seen throughout the year. During the autumn of 1994 a large roost of Little Egrets was established at Sowley Pond; whilst odd birds sometimes appear on nearby Sowley Marsh.

March and April brings the departure of many of the winter birds from the Beaulieu Estuary. In some years, however, small numbers of Brent Geese and other winter wildfowl remain well into May. Lingering winter waders mingle with passage birds which regularly include Bar-tailed Godwit, Whimbrel, Spotted Redshank, Greenshank and Common Sandpiper; whilst scarcer migrant species such as Little Ringed Plover and Ruff are occasional visitors. There are also spring and summer sightings of Temminck's Stint and Red-necked Phalarope. On the Lepe side of the estuary, Dark Water and Stansore Marsh sometimes holds a few passage waders such as Greenshank and Common Sandpiper. The first Sandwich Terns appear during the second half of March with Common and Little Terns arriving a few weeks later. Lepe Shore and Needs Ore provide good vantage points for observing any easterly passage of seabirds through the Solent. Such movements mainly involve waders and terns, but in some years moderate numbers of Arctic Skuas along with a few divers, sea-duck, Little Gulls and Black Terns have occurred; whilst Pomarine and Great Skuas have also been noted on occasions. The scrub and woodland behind both Needs Ore and Lepe attract a scattering of landbird migrants, which may include the occasional scarcer species or perhaps something more unusual – Hoopoe, Red-backed Shrike and Serin have all appeared in recent years.

Osprey

Although the majority of noteworthy birds are recorded from Needs Ore and The Gins, the entire area is worth checking for rare and scarce migrants. Apart from the species already mentioned, the most likely oddities are Spoonbill or a passing raptor, notably Marsh Harrier and Osprey. There are also spring and summer records of such rarities as Squacco and Purple Herons, Blue-winged Teal, Black-winged Stilt and most notably White-throated Sparrow.

In spring and summer Gull Island and the saltmarshes of the lower estuary are the haunt of several thousand breeding pairs of Black-headed Gulls. This gullery is famous for being the site where Mediterranean Gulls first nested successfully in Britain in 1967. Although subsequent breeding has been rather sporadic, it is well worth looking out for this species in spring and summer. Varying numbers of Sandwich, Common and Little Terns also nest here most years. Feral Greylag Geese, Shelduck, Gadwall, Shoveler, Oystercatcher, Ringed Plover and Redshank also breed in the lower estuary; whilst Mandarins are regularly seen in the middle reaches of the estuary around Buckler's Hard and Exbury where they may nest. Sedge and Reed Warblers and Reed Bunting frequent reedbed habitats throughout the length of the Beaulieu Estuary and Lepe Country Park. Shelduck and Redshank breed by Dark Water with Oystercatcher and Ringed Plover nesting along the nearby beaches of Stanswood Bay. Terns from the nearby breeding colonies can be seen flying and fishing offshore from Lepe throughout the summer. There is a heronry in the woods overlooking Sowley Pond where Great Crested Grebes and Canada Geese also breed.

A wealth of birds reside in the local woodlands. Those around Exbury Gardens are noted for Golden Pheasant and Hawfinch, but both species are very secretive and can be very difficult to see. Amongst the summer visitors, Nightingales may still occur in Keeping Copse and the woods behind Stanswood Bay. Red-legged and Grey Partridges are widespread on farmland throughout the area which also supports a good population of Barn Owls.

Most of the commoner waders return to the Beaulieu Estuary during July and August. The Gins is a favoured site for autumn Spotted

Redshank which often wander to the main estuary and Inchmery Marshes. Other regular migrants include Black-tailed Godwit, Whimbrel, Greenshank, Green and Common Sandpipers; whilst a few Little Ringed Plover, Knot, Little Stint, Curlew Sandpiper, Ruff, Bar-tailed Godwit and Wood Sandpiper pass through most autumns. There are also records of scarcer waders such as Kentish Plover, Dotterel, Temminck's Stint and Pectoral Sandpiper. Sandwich, Common and Little Terns, which are present for much of the autumn, may be joined by passing Little Gulls and Black Terns. Although not recorded every autumn, the Beaulieu Estuary is attractive to passage Ospreys which often remain in the area for several weeks; whilst migrant Marsh Harriers are being recorded with increasing frequency.

Both Needs Ore and Lepe Shore Country Park are good sites for landbird migrants including Redstart, Whinchat, Wheatear, the commoner warblers and Spotted Flycatcher. Scarcer birds such as Black Redstart, Firecrest and Pied Flycatcher are occasionally seen; whilst subrarities such as Wryneck, Shorelark, Richard's (several) and Tawny Pipits, Melodious Warbler, Red-backed Shrike, Lapland and Ortolan Buntings have also been reported. Offshore sea passage consists mainly of a westerly trickle of terns, although severe gales may produce storm-blown seabirds such as Grey Phalarope, skuas, Little and in exceptional circumstances even Sabine's Gulls. Such conditions may bring Little Gulls and Black Terns to Sowley Pond.

Like the spring and summer, most rare and unusual migrants are most likely to be found at Needs Ore and The Gins. Apart from Osprey, Spoonbill is the most likely oddity to occur; whilst notable rarities such as Great White Egret, Purple Heron, Pacific Golden Plover and dowitcher species have been seen here.

Timing

Tidal conditions are critical when viewing birds from the north shore of the lower estuary. The Lower Exbury and Inchmery Marshes are best visited a couple of hours before and after high-water when wildfowl and waders tend to be closest to the shore. Avoid extreme low-water when birds feed distantly towards the edge of the main river channel and high spring tides when the saltmarshes are deserted with wildfowl and waders roosting on the opposite side of the estuary at Needs Ore and The Gins.

Timing is less important when visiting Needs Ore and The Gins. At low tide wildfowl and waders can be seen feeding along the estuary and Solent foreshore; whilst at high tide many of these birds roost on Black Water and the nearby fields.

Low-water is required to watch Brent Geese and waders on the foreshore off Lepe; whilst nearby Dark Water and Stansore Marsh attract most birds at high-water.

Spring seawatching is likely to be most rewarding early in the morning, between mid-April and mid-May, when winds are moderate to strong and SE in direction. Landbird migrants should be searched for in the early morning when fall conditions prevail.

Sowley Pond is well worth checking during cold winter weather as long as conditions are not so severe as to freeze the water.

Early mornings and quiet winter afternoons are recommended when looking for Hawfinches at Exbury.

Access

All sites are within easy reach of Beaulieu.

Beaulieu Estuary: the coastal footpath from Inchmery Quay to Lepe (by white house) provides good views over the lower estuary. Please note: this footpath is closed during the breeding season and is also subject to flooding at high tide. Inchmery Quay can be reached along minor roads either south from Exbury or west from Lepe. Elsewhere on the east side of the estuary, a minor road west from the road just south of Exbury Gardens Plant Centre passes through woodland to the shore at Gilbury Hard. Beaulieu Millpond can be seen from the B3056 and B3054 roads into Beaulieu. The Solent Way footpath between Bucklers Hard* and the Montagu's Arms Hotel in Beaulieu (free parking nearby in village) gives access to Keeping Copse and offers excellent views over parts of the middle and upper reaches of the estuary. Bucklers Hard is open throughout the year (except Christmas), 10.00 am–6.00 pm Easter to spring bank holiday, 10.00 am–9.00 pm spring bank holiday to September, 10.00 am–4.30 pm in winter. It is possible to gain entry to Needs Ore and The Gins by applying for a permit from the Beaulieu Settled Estate, John Montagu Building, Beaulieu, Brockenhurst, Hampshire SO42 7ZN. Access is from St Leonards Grange along Warren Lane to the car parking area behind the Yacht Club.

Lepe Country Park can be approached along minor roads either southeast from Exbury or south from Langley near Blackfield. From the car parks* there is access east along the shore to the boundary of the Cadland Estate at the far end of Stanswood Bay.

Sowley Pond can be reached by following the signs to Sowley along minor roads either south from the B3054 at Bunkers Hill just outside Beaulieu or from the Lymington Ferry Terminal east along South Baddesley Road. Please note: Sowley Pond is private and must be viewed from the road.

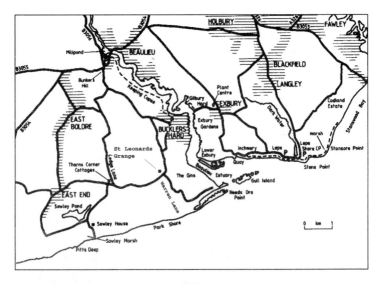

Calendar

All Year: Great Crested Grebe, Cormorant, Little Egret, Grey Heron, feral Greylag, Canada and occasional feral Barnacle Geese, Shelduck, Mandarin, Gadwall, Shoveler, Peregrine, Red-legged and Grey Partridges, Golden Pheasant, Oystercatcher, Ringed Plover, Redshank, Barn Owl, Kingfisher, Reed Bunting, resident woodland birds including Hawfinch.

Winter (mid-November–mid-March): occasional divers; Little, Slavonian and occasional Red-necked and Black-necked Grebes; wildfowl including Brent Goose, Wigeon, Teal, Pintail, Pochard, Tufted Duck, Red-breasted Merganser, occasional sea-duck and Goldeneye, in cold weather occasional Scaup, Smew, Goosander and Ruddy Duck; frequent Hen Harrier and Merlin; waders including Golden Plover, both godwits, Spotted Redshank, Greenshank; gulls including occasional Mediterranean; occasional auks; occasional Short-eared Owl; Rock Pipit, Stonechat, Siskin, Redpoll.

Spring (mid-March–mid-May): sea passage best mid-April to mid-May involving mostly waders and terns, also occasional divers, sea-duck, skuas (mainly Arctic), Little Gull and Black Tern.

Lingering winter wildfowl; migrant waders including both godwits, Whimbrel, Spotted Redshank, Greenshank, Common Sandpiper, occasional other species; occasional Mediterranean and Little Gulls; Sandwich, Common, Little and occasional Black Terns; common landbird migrants.

Most likely oddities: Spoonbill, scarce/rare migrant raptor, landbird subrarity.

Summer (mid-May–mid-July): occasional Mediterranean Gull; Sandwich, Common and Little Terns; Nightingale, Sedge and Reed Warblers.

Autumn (mid-July–mid-November): slight sea passage mostly involving terns; during/after severe gales possible storm-blown seabirds such as Grey Phalarope, skuas, Little and Sabine's Gulls.

Migrant waders including Black-tailed Godwit, Whimbrel, Spotted Redshank, Greenshank, Green and Common Sandpipers, near annual Little Ringed Plover, Knot, Little Stint, Curlew Sandpiper, Ruff, Bar-tailed Godwit and Wood Sandpiper; occasional Little Gull; Sandwich, Common, Little and occasional Black Terns; landbird migrants including occasional Black Redstart, Firecrest and Pied Flycatcher.

Most likely oddities: Spoonbill, Osprey, wader, landbird subrarity.

56 CALSHOT SPIT (HCC/ ENGLISH HERITAGE) AND ASHLETT CREEK

Habitat

Calshot Spit overlooks the approaches to Southampton Water and the western Solent. *Spartina* saltmarshes and mudflats extend from the inner shore of the spit northwest along Southampton Water to Fawley Oil Refinery. These saltmarshes are intersected by numerous muddy creeks, notably the deep-water channels at Ower and Ashlett. The shoreline between these two inlets is dominated by Fawley Power Station, whose grounds mainly consist of bare shingle. Between the spit road and the power station, there is a large reclaimed area of rough grassland, scrub and reeds which is known as Tom Tiddler's Field; whilst a smaller plot of rough ground and willow scrub lies between the power station and Ashlett Village. At low tide, an extensive beach of muddy shingle is exposed along the Solent shore of Calshot Spit. The whole coastal stretch is set against a backcloth of farmland, hedgerow and small woods.

Once the base for seaplanes operating out of Southampton Water, Calshot Spit is today managed by Hampshire County Council which has converted the hangers and buildings to form part of an Activities Centre. Recently, English Heritage has acquired responsibility for the 15th-century castle at the Spithead. The saltmarshes closest to the spit enjoy protection as a nature reserve.

Species

A wide variety of waterfowl, waders and gulls can be found in the area during the winter. Like so many places along the Hampshire coast, the Brent Goose is the most obvious of the waterfowl, particularly at high tide when their numbers are augmented by birds from the east shore of Southampton Water. Flocks of Shelduck, Wigeon and Teal can also be expected; whilst a few Gadwall, Pintail and Shoveler are usually present. Small numbers of Great Crested Grebes together with the occasional diver, rarer winter grebe, Goldeneye, sea-duck (most likely Red-breasted Merganser) and auk occur offshore in Southampton Water and the Solent. Little Grebes winter on Ashlett Millpond and often wander to Ower Creek.

All of the common waders including Black-tailed Godwit and Turnstone can be found here in good numbers. One or two Greenshank regularly winter; whilst Knot and Bar-tailed Godwit occasionally appear. There are also a few winter sightings of the attractive Avocet. It is well worth checking through the large gatherings of commoner gulls for the more unusual species; Mediterranean, Iceland and Glaucous have all been seen here. Little Gulls and Kittiwakes sometimes occur during stormy weather. Cormorants and Grey Herons reside in the area throughout the year; whilst Little Egrets are occasionally reported.

The Peregrine regularly hunts over the area in winter; whilst the Merlin is an occasional visitor. Although Short-eared Owls wintered with some

Short-eared Owl

regularity on Tom Tiddler's Field during the 1980s, the species has become very rare in the 1990s. Flocks of Skylarks, finches and buntings feed on rough ground and along the tideline. Kingfishers and Rock Pipits are also regular winter inhabitants; the latter species favouring the buildings and beach-huts on Calshot Spit where the occasional Black Redstart may be located.

In spring, departing winter and passage waders include most of the common species together with more obvious migrants such as Whimbrel, Greenshank and Common Sandpiper. Calshot Spit is a good vantage point to observe any easterly movements of seabirds through the Solent. These mainly involve waders and the commoner terns along with the occasional diver, sea-duck, Arctic Skua, Little Gull and Black Tern. A scattering of landbird migrants including Yellow Wagtails and Wheatears occur along the shore and in the areas of rough ground.

A few pairs of Shelduck, Oystercatcher, Ringed Plover and Redshank breed or attempt to do so most years. Otherwise little else of interest can be expected during the summer except perhaps for a few non-breeding waders such as Grey Plover and Curlew and Sandwich, Common and Little Terns wandering from the Solent breeding colonies.

The first of the autumn waders arrive during the second half of June. In addition to those species that commonly winter in the area, a variety of migrant birds pass through, notably during the peak passage in August and September. A few Whimbrel, Greenshank and Common Sandpipers are regularly seen, but scarcer species such as Little Stint, Curlew Sandpiper, Ruff and Spotted Redshank are infrequent visitors. The large autumn roost of mainly Common Terns, which was once a feature of the area in August and September, has declined since the mid 1980s and relocated across the Solent to Hill Head. Nevertheless this species along with Sandwich and Little Terns can be expected at this season; whilst Black Terns are occasionally present. Generally sea passage is minimal, mainly involving a trickle of terns which may be harassed by the odd passing Arctic Skua. Severe gales, however, may bring the occasional storm-blown oddity such as Grey Phalarope close inshore. Merlins and Hobbies are sometimes observed on passage; whilst Ospreys have been noted here. Landbird migrants can be found in small numbers with Yellow Wagtails, Whinchats and Wheatears often prominent. Scarcer species such as Black Redstart, Ring Ouzel and Firecrest occur from time to time; whilst the potential of the area for unusual and rare migrants is shown by sightings of Wryneck, Short-toed Lark and Richard's Pipit.

Timing

The state of the tide is not particularly important for observing wildfowl and waders, but the best views are usually obtained an hour or so before and after high-water when birds are restricted to feeding areas immediately adjacent to the shore. At low tide, many wildfowl and waders remain to feed close inshore in the deep-water creeks at Calshot, Ower and Ashlett and on the extensive foreshore off Calshot Spit. At high tide, large roosts of waders gather on the saltmarshes north of Ower Creek and in the grounds of Fawley Power Station.

For seawatching choose early mornings in spring, between mid-April and mid-May, when the winds are from the SE.

Landbird migrants should be looked for early in the morning when fall conditions exist.

Access

Calshot Spit is reached by taking the B3053 southeast from Fawley to Calshot, then turning northeast along the spit road and continuing to the various car parking areas*. There is a footpath along the shore of Southampton Water from the base of Calshot Spit northwest to Ashlett Creek. This coastal path can also be reached from the B3053 opposite the Arndale Garage in Calshot Village, northeast along the footpath that passes the northern flank of Tom Tiddler's Field. There is no public access to the Spithead beyond the entrance gates to the Activities Centre other than to Calshot Castle (English Heritage).

Ashlett Creek can also be approached along Ashlett Road east from Fawley Village.

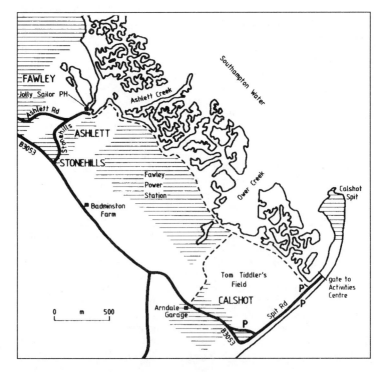

Calendar

All Year: Cormorant, Grey Heron, Shelduck, Oystercatcher, Ringed Plover, Curlew, Redshank, Reed Bunting.

Winter (mid-November–mid-March): occasional divers; Little, Great Crested and occasional rarer winter grebes; wildfowl including Brent Goose, Wigeon, Gadwall, Teal, Pintail, Shoveler, occasional Goldeneye, Red-breasted Merganser and other sea-duck; Peregrine and occasional Merlin; waders including Black-tailed Godwit, Greenshank, occasional Knot and Bar-tailed Godwit, possible Avocet; gulls including occasional Mediterranean, Little and Kittiwake, possible Iceland and Glaucous; occasional auks; occasional Short-eared Owl; Kingfisher, Rock Pipit, possible Black Redstart and Snow Bunting.

Spring (mid-March–mid-May): sea passage best mid-April to mid-May involving mostly waders and terns, also occasional divers, sea-duck, skuas (mainly Arctic), Little Gull and Black Tern.
   Migrant waders including Whimbrel, Greenshank, Common Sandpiper, occasional Bar-tailed Godwit and other species; Sandwich, Common and Little Terns; landbird migrants.

Summer (mid-May–mid-July): non-breeding waders; Sandwich, Common and Little Terns; Sedge and Reed Warblers.

Autumn (mid-July–mid-November): slight sea passage mostly involving terns; during/after severe gales possible storm-blown seabirds such as Grey Phalarope and skuas.
   Migrant raptors including occasional Merlin and Hobby; migrant waders including Whimbrel, Greenshank, Common Sandpiper, occasional Knot, Little Stint, Curlew Sandpiper, Ruff, Bar-tailed Godwit, Spotted Redshank and Green Sandpiper; occasional Little Gull; Sandwich, Common, Little and occasional Black Terns; landbird migrants including Yellow Wagtail, Whinchat, Wheatear, occasional Black Redstart, Ring Ouzel and Firecrest.
   Most likely oddities: Osprey, landbird subrarity.

THE NEW FOREST AND NEARBY COAST – OTHER SITES WORTHY OF ATTENTION

OS Map 195 & New Forest

57 LYMINGTON REEDBEDS NR (HWT)

SZ39

The lower reaches of Lymington River are bordered by one of the largest (80 acres) reedbeds in southern England. Along the sides of the valley, the reedbeds merge into damp woodland. This nationally important site is managed as a nature reserve by the Hampshire Wildlife Trust. The reedbeds support such breeding specialities as Water Rail, Cetti's Warbler and Bearded Tit as well as the commoner Sedge and Reed Warblers and Reed Bunting. Grey Herons can be seen throughout the year and may be joined by the occasional Little Egret. In winter the numbers of Water Rails frequenting the reedbeds increase; whilst small numbers of waterfowl, notably Teal, and Snipe can also be expected. Flocks of Siskins can be found feeding in the riverside alders. Access is best from the small lay-by at SZ325970 on the minor road between the B3054 and Warborne. From here there is a footpath north to Pilley. Alternatively walk south back along the minor road to the B3054, continue southeast and then southwest to the roadbridge at SZ328961 to view the lower river and reedbeds.

58 TANNERS LANE

SZ39

The shore at the end of Tanners Lane overlooks the extensive *Spartina* saltmarshes that lie to the east of the Lymington River. In winter it is an ideal site to observe the large numbers of waterfowl and waders inhabiting this part of the Solent. Typical birds include Brent Goose, Wigeon, Teal, Red-breasted Merganser, Grey Plover and Black-tailed Godwit. Not surprisingly Little Egrets are regularly seen, particularly during the autumn and winter. Migrant waders including Whimbrel, Greenshank and Common Sandpiper pass through in spring and autumn; whilst Sandwich, Common and Little Terns can be expected throughout the breeding season. From the Lymington Ferry Terminal take the minor road northeast to Pylewell, turn south along Sowley Lane and after a short distance, at a point where the road bends sharp left, follow Tanners Lane south towards the Solent shore at SZ365952.

59 ELING GREAT MARSH

Map p. 163, SU31

This is an area of estuarine mudflats and *Spartina* saltmarshes situated at the head of Southampton Water. In winter good numbers of waterfowl, waders and gulls can be expected; whilst the site often hosts hard weather species during periods of severe cold. Migrant waders and terns occur in spring and autumn. There is some interchange of birds between here and the nearby Lower Test Marshes – see Site 51A. Oddities recorded include Osprey, Avocet, Temminck's Stint, White-rumped and Pectoral Sandpipers, Ring-billed Gull and White-winged Black Tern. From Eling Church at SU367124 follow the footpath east to the foreshore.

SOUTHEAST HAMPSHIRE

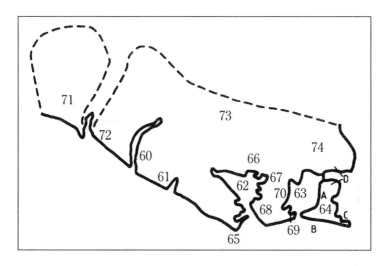

60 RIVER HAMBLE AND HOOK-
    WITH-WARSASH NR
61 HILL HEAD AND TITCHFIELD
    HAVEN NR
62 PORTSMOUTH HARBOUR
63 FARLINGTON MARSHES NR
    AND LANGSTONE HARBOUR
64 HAYLING ISLAND AND
    CHICHESTER HARBOUR
Recommended Sites
    64A West Hayling Shore and
         the Oysterbeds
    64B Sinah Common and
         Hayling Bay
    64C Black and Sandy Points
    64D North Hayling and
         Chichester Harbour

Other Sites Worthy Of Attention
Part 1 – Portsmouth Area
Including Portsea Island
65 Gilkicker Point
66 Portsdown Hill
67 Hilsea Lines Ramparts
68 Southsea Castle
69 Eastney Point
70 Milton Common and Great
    Salterns Lake
Part 2 – Elsewhere In Southeast
Hampshire
71 Southampton Common
72 Weston Shore and Westwood
    Woodland Park
73 West Walk
74 Havant Thicket

General Introduction

This area of Hampshire extends from the eastern shore of Southampton
Water and the Solent north to the chalk downs and east to the county
boundary with West Sussex. The dominant features of the coastline are
the three large estuarine harbours of Portsmouth, Langstone and

Chichester, which separate the islands of Portsea (Portsmouth) and Hayling. Immediately to the north the high chalk ridge of Portsdown Hill overlooks these harbours and islands. The predominantly rural hinterland is drained by the Rivers Hamble and Meon which form noteworthy estuarine and wetland habitats where they meet the sea. The area also supports some fine woodlands and forests, remnants of the once extensive Royal Forest of Bere.

During the winter and at times of passage, vast numbers of waterfowl, waders and gulls inhabit the coast and harbours. The latter are also important areas of nesting waders and terns; whilst the woodlands support a rich diversity of breeding birds. Hayling Island and Portsdown Hill are the best sites in Hampshire for observing landbird migration.

60 RIVER HAMBLE (HCC/ NT/HWT) AND HOOK-WITH-WARSASH NR (HCC)

OS Map 196
& New Forest
SU40/41/50/51

Habitat

The River Hamble is estuarine in character from its mouth on the eastern shore of Southampton Water upstream to Curbridge and Botley. *Spartina* saltmarshes intersected by muddy creeks border the estuary for much of its length.

Despite considerable development, the lower estuary still retains a number of noteworthy habitats. These are mainly centred around Warsash on the east side of the river. To the north lies Bunny Meadows, a large area of open mudflats and *Spartina* saltmarsh separated from the main estuary by an embankment. Just up river, the broadleaved woodlands of Holly Hill Woodland Park stretch down to the shore at Wendleholme. Low tide exposes extensive mudflats along the shore south from Warsash to the shingle bank of Hook Spit. Behind Hook Spit, a narrow reed-fringed freshwater known as Hook Lake extends inland and merges into reedswamp by Newtown Woods. Between Hook Spit and Solent Breezes, the shingle shore of Southampton Water is backed by the rough pasture and gorse scrub of Hook Links where a shallow pool has been constructed. All these sites now form part of the Hook-with-Warsash Nature Reserve managed by Hampshire County Council.

On the west side of the lower estuary, the most interesting habitat is found on Hamble Common. This is an area of rough grass, bracken, scrub and woodland which overlooks the muddy foreshore of Southampton Water immediately to the north of the river mouth.

The upper estuary is particularly attractive and relatively undisturbed. Broadleaved woodlands fringe much of the shore, notably at Upper Hamble Country Park (HCC) and Curbridge NR (NT/HWT).

The entire area supports an interesting and varied flora and fauna, the woodlands being particularly good for butterflies.

Species

The area supports moderate numbers of winter wildfowl including Brent Goose, Shelduck, Wigeon and Teal; whilst the recently constructed pool on Hook Links has attracted additional species such as Gadwall, Pintail and Shoveler. Offshore, a few Great Crested Grebes and Red-breasted Mergansers along with the occasional diver, rare winter grebe, sea-duck (Eider being the most likely species), Goldeneye and auk can be seen in Southampton Water. From time to time, these birds may wander and join the Little Grebes that frequent the lower river.

Waders are better represented with all the commoner species including Golden Plover and Black-tailed Godwit wintering in the area. In addition, a few Greenshank are usually present. The flocks of Black-headed and Common Gulls are worth checking through for the occasional Mediterranean Gull. Cormorants and Grey Herons inhabit the estuary throughout the year; whilst a few Little Egrets are usually present during the autumn and winter. Amongst the smaller birds of interest, Kingfishers and Rock Pipits can be seen along the shore and Stonechats and sometimes Dartford Warblers are found in the gorse scrub along Hook Links. Chiffchaff and Firecrest occasionally winter in the woodlands.

The upper estuary also attracts small numbers of wildfowl and waders in winter; the species most likely to be encountered being Shelduck, Teal, Dunlin, Snipe, Curlew and Redshank along with the occasional Black-tailed Godwit and Greenshank. Hamble Country Park is a good site for Kingfishers during the autumn and winter.

Many of the commoner waders can still be found in the lower estuary during the spring when they are joined by more obvious migrant species such as Whimbrel, Greenshank and Common Sandpiper. In some springs the fields around Curbridge and Botley Wood support flocks of feeding Whimbrel that fly down the estuary at dusk to roosting sites in Southampton Water. Little Ringed Plover, Knot, Sanderling, Black-tailed and Bar-tailed Godwits, Spotted Redshank and Green Sandpiper are occasionally seen on passage. There are also spring sightings of Little Stint and Curlew Sandpiper as well as rarer species such as Avocet, Temminck's Stint and Pectoral Sandpiper; whilst there are two records of Long-billed Dowitcher from the upper estuary. The first terns usually arrive in April with Common and Little generally on view throughout the spring and summer. Sandwich Terns occur less frequently; whilst the odd Little Gull and Black Tern sometimes pass through. Otherwise there is a scattering of landbird migrants which are most in evidence on Hook Links and Hamble Common.

The area supports a variety of interesting breeding birds. A few pairs of Oystercatcher, Ringed Plover and Redshank regularly nest; whilst the reedbeds, notably those around Hook Lake, hold Water Rail, Cetti's, Sedge and Reed Warblers and Reed Bunting. Shelduck are erratic breeders and both Common and Little Terns have nested or attempted to do so in the recent past. The woodlands, including Hamble Country Park and Curbridge NR, are rich in resident birds including all three species of woodpecker, Nuthatch and Treecreeper. Recent sightings of Mandarin in the upper estuary suggests that the species may soon be resident in the area.

Autumn waders are prominent from July onwards. These regularly include those species that commonly winter in the estuary together with more typical migrants such as Whimbrel, Greenshank and Green and Common Sandpipers. Little Stints and Curlew Sandpipers are seen most

Reed Bunting

years, usually mingling with the flocks of Dunlin; whilst Knot, Ruff, Bar-tailed Godwit and Spotted Redshank are occasional visitors. It is well worth looking out for something more unusual such as Little Ringed Plover, Wood Sandpiper or even a rarity – there have been sightings of Temminck's Stint, White-rumped, Baird's and Pectoral Sandpipers and Grey Phalarope. Common and Little Terns can be expected through into September. As in spring, Sandwich Terns are rather scarce; whilst Little Gulls and Black Terns may appear from time to time. The estuary looks ideal for migrant Ospreys which have been noted here on several occa-sions. Other migrant raptors may include the odd passing Merlin and Hobby. Small numbers of landbird migrants occur with Yellow Wagtails, Whinchats and Wheatears preferring the open areas such as Hook Links and the nearby shore where locally dispersing Dartford Warblers can often be found in the gorse scrub. Occasionally in late autumn, irruptive parties of Bearded Tits frequent the reedbeds by Hook Lake where the species has overwintered. Scarcer migrants like Black Redstart, Ring Ouzel, Firecrest and Pied Flycatcher are occasional visitors; whilst there are also records of such subrarities as Wryneck, Icterine Warbler and Ortolan Bunting.

In addition to the rare waders already mentioned, a number of other rarities have been seen in the area. These include Purple Heron, Black Kite, Gull-billed Tern (twice) and Whiskered Tern in spring and Whiskered Tern, Bee-eater and Olive-backed Pipit in autumn.

Timing

At low tide wildfowl and waders can be seen well throughout most of the estuary including the mudflats between Hook Spit and Warsash. Bunny Meadows are best visited just before high-water, since wildfowl and waders become concentrated on this area of mud and saltmarsh which is the last to be covered by the rising tide. At high tide there are wader roosts on Hook Spit and Hook Links.

Landbird migrants should be looked for early in the morning when fall conditions prevail.

The lower estuary is a major boating and yachting centre. As a consequence the area suffers from disturbance, notably at weekends between April and September.

Access

All the sites within the Hook-with-Warsash Nature Reserve are best approached from the shore car parks at Warsash. These are reached by taking Shore Road west from the mini-roundabout in Warsash Town Centre.

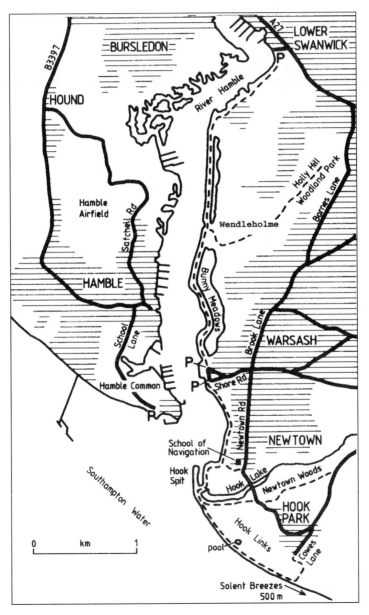

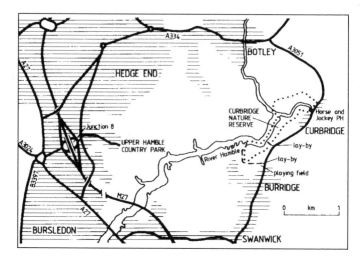

Hook-with-Warsash NR (north): from the northern of the shore car parks follow the footpath north along the embankment across Bunny Meadows to Wendleholme. The main footpath continues north along the east shore of the estuary to Lower Swanwick; whilst there is another footpath northeast through Holly Hill Woodland Park to Barnes Lane in Sarisbury.

Hook-with-Warsash NR (south): from the southern of the shore car parks (opposite Rising Sun PH), the Solent Way footpath follows the east shore of the estuary south to Hook Spit and continues southeast along Hook Links beach towards Solent Breezes. There is also a footpath from Hook Spit east along the south side of Hook Lake to the minor road just south of the bridge. From here another footpath runs northeast through Newtown Woods and along the Hook Valley.

The west side of the lower estuary is within easy reach of Hamble.

Hamble Common is reached by taking School Lane from the B3397 (Hamble Lane) in Hamble south to the shore car park. There is general access to much of the area.

The main access points to the upper estuary are restricted to Upper Hamble Country Park and Curbridge Nature Reserve.

Upper Hamble CP (HCC)* is signposted from the M27 at junction 8. Well marked footpaths and trails give access to the woods, including Catland and Foster's Copses, as well as providing views over the upper estuary.

Curbridge NR (NT/HWT) is best approached from the A3051 between Curbridge and Burridge. Access to the reserve is by means of footpaths (i) from immediately behind the Horse and Jockey PH in Curbridge; (ii) northwest from the lay-by 0.6 miles (1 km) south of Curbridge; and (iii) northwest from the lay-by next to the 'Burridge' sign and playing fields 0.8 miles (1.3 km) south of Curbridge.

Calendar

All Year: Cormorant, Grey Heron, Canada Goose, Shelduck, Water Rail, Oystercatcher, Ringed Plover, Redshank, Cetti's Warbler, Reed Bunting, resident woodland birds including Lesser Spotted Woodpecker.

Winter (mid-November–mid-March): occasional divers; Little, Great Crested and occasional rarer winter grebes; Little Egret; wildfowl including Brent Goose, Wigeon, Gadwall, Teal, Pintail, Shoveler, Red-breasted Merganser, occasional sea-duck and Goldeneye; waders including Golden Plover, Black-tailed Godwit, Greenshank; gulls including occasional Mediterranean; occasional auks; Kingfisher, Rock Pipit, Stonechat, frequent Dartford Warbler, occasional Chiffchaff and Firecrest, possible Bearded Tit.

Spring (mid-March–mid-May): migrant waders including Whimbrel, Greenshank, Common Sandpiper and occasional other species; occasional Little Gull; terns including occasional Black; landbird migrants.
Most likely oddity: rare wader.

Summer (mid-May–mid-July): Common and Little Terns, Sedge and Reed Warblers.

Autumn (mid-July–mid-November): occasional migrant Merlin and Hobby; migrant waders including Little Stint, Curlew Sandpiper, Whimbrel, Greenshank, Green and Common Sandpipers, occasional Knot, Ruff, Bar-tailed Godwit and Spotted Redshank; occasional Little Gull; terns including occasional Black; landbird migrants including Yellow Wagtail, Whinchat, Wheatear, frequent Dartford Warbler, occasional Black Redstart, Firecrest, Pied Flycatcher and Bearded Tit.
Most likely oddities: Osprey, rare wader, landbird subrarity.

61 HILL HEAD AND TITCHFIELD HAVEN NR (HCC/HWT)

OS Map 196
SU50

Habitat

Situated about midway between the River Hamble and Gilkicker Point, Hill Head is a low promontory overlooking the eastern Solent and the approaches to Southampton Water. At low tide there is an extensive foreshore of muddy shingle. Behind the shore lies Titchfield Haven Nature Reserve, which supports a variety of wetland habitats centred around the lower reaches of the River Meon. These include large reedbeds intermixed in places with willow scrub, unimproved meadows and rough grassland, remnant saltmarsh and some recently constructed freshwater scrapes and meres. There are also some patches of gorse and bramble scrub in the drier areas. The Old Canal, which is a carrier of the River Meon, drains the west side of the valley between Titchfield Village and the Lower Haven.

The Brownwich and Chilling Estates lie to the west of Titchfield Haven. Although much of the area is open farmland, there are isolated patches of woodland such as Thatchers Copse. Brownwich Bay, which extends from Hill Head northwest along the shore of Southampton Water, is backed by a shingle beach and low crumbling cliffs.

Titchfield Haven was originally created in 1611 when the Third Earl of Southampton built a seawall across the mouth of the River Meon to reclaim land. The river, which at the time was navigable as far upstream as Titchfield Village, started to silt up and subsequently create the area of wetland that is present today. The site's importance to birds and wildlife was well known by the turn of the last century. From 1945 to 1972 much of Titchfield Haven was maintained as a private sanctuary by the Alston family and copious notes and observations of the birds were kept by the late Dr Canning Suffern. Most of the present reserve was purchased in 1972 by Hampshire County Council, adding some 240 acres to the 31 already owned by the Hampshire Wildlife Trust.

In addition to the birds, the reserve supports a rich flora and fauna. Several interesting and scarce species of saltmarsh plants occur. Insects are also well represented; dragonflies, moths (which have been studied since the 1930s) and butterflies being prominent groups.

Species

Titchfield Haven is an important refuge for winter wildfowl and, as such, it rates as one of the most valuable in the region. The area also supports a wide range of waders, gulls and other waterbirds during the winter. Good numbers of migrants, notably waders and terns, pass through in spring and autumn; whilst Hill Head is a good vantage point for seawatching. A number of interesting breeding birds are also found on the reserve.

Large numbers of wildfowl inhabit the area during the winter. The most abundant species is the Wigeon, whose numbers have increased steadily since the drastic decline in the late 1960s and now regularly reach peak counts of 1,200–1,300 birds. Shelduck, Teal, Gadwall, Shoveler and Pochard are also present in good numbers, but Pintail and Tufted Duck are rather sporadic in occurrence. Large flocks of Brent Geese feed in fields on the Brownwich Estate and flight to the foreshore off Hill Head at low tide; whilst the local population of Canada Geese is boosted by the arrival of birds in the autumn when the largest flocks are recorded. Grey geese occasionally appear, most often overflying the area during periods of severe cold, but small parties have remained for short periods in the Haven's meadows and sometimes on nearby farmland at Brownwich. White-fronted are the most likely species to be seen, but there are several sightings of Bean and Pink-footed Geese. Cold weather may also bring the likes of Bewick's and Whooper Swans, Scaup, Smew, Goosander and Ruddy Duck to the Haven. A few Little Grebes also winter along the main river.

The offshore waters of the Solent hold substantial numbers of Great Crested Grebes along with a few Red-breasted Mergansers and, in some winters, Eider; whilst divers, the rarer winter grebes, other sea-duck, Goldeneye and auks occur infrequently. Most of these species may exceptionally wander to the sheltered waters of the Haven.

Black-tailed Godwits

In winter the main habitats for waders are the wet meadows, freshwater scrapes and the foreshore off Hill Head. The meadows typically support good numbers of Lapwing, Snipe, Black-tailed Godwit, Curlew and Redshank along with a few Ruff. At low tide most of the commoner waders including Oystercatcher, Grey and Ringed Plovers, Dunlin and Turnstone feed on the foreshore off Hill Head. When water levels are suitable the freshwater scrapes can also be very attractive to waders with birds moving in from the nearby foreshore at high tide to join those species that are more characteristic of the meadows. A few waders sometimes frequent any mud exposed at the southernmost tip of the Haven; whilst Snipe skulk along the reedy margins of the main river and drainage ditches. Small flocks of Golden Plover winter on nearby farmland and, during cold weather, these birds often move to the Haven's meadows.

Large numbers of gulls – mainly Black-headed, Common, Herring and Great Black-backed – use the area throughout the winter. Many birds, notably the larger gulls, feed on Hook Tip during the morning and drift back in the afternoon either to wash and rest on the Haven or, when the tide is low, to forage along the foreshore off Hill Head. Increased gull watching in recent years has shown the Mediterranean Gull to be a regular visitor; whilst there have been several sightings of Ring-billed, Iceland and Glaucous Gulls. The occasional Little Gull and Kittiwake may pass offshore as the result of winter gales.

Titchfield Haven is one of the best sites in the region for Bitterns with records in every winter but three since 1978/79. Usually only one or two birds are involved, but up to five were present in December 1983. Other waterbirds such as Cormorant, Grey Heron and the skulking Water Rail occur throughout the year. Of the winter raptors Hen Harrier, Merlin, Peregrine and Short-eared Owl are noted most years.

Small flocks of Bearded Tits, involving both local birds and immigrants from further afield, inhabit the Haven's reedbeds in the late autumn and winter. Kingfishers are a regular sight along the main river throughout the autumn and winter, often perching on posts close to the hides. Rock Pipits are scarce winter visitors to the shore areas; whilst a few Stonechats frequent the gorse and bramble scrub on the reserve. In mild winters Chiffchaffs and perhaps Firecrests may be found foraging with tits in the willow scrub, notably on the east side of the reserve where a Yellow-browed Warbler once wintered. Parties of Siskins and Redpolls feed in the alder copses; whilst finch and bunting flocks on the Brownwich Estate are worth checking through for Brambling. Although winter is not a prime time for rarities, there are several sightings of Green-winged Teal and one of a Common Crane; whilst in February 1992 a Little Bunting was trapped with Reed Buntings and remained until early April.

In spring, any passage of seabirds through the Solent can be observed from Hill Head. These movements mainly involve waders, notably Bar-tailed Godwit and Whimbrel, and terns along with much smaller numbers of Common Scoter, Arctic Skua, Little Gull, Kittiwake and Black Tern. A few divers, Fulmars and other sea-duck as well as the odd Pomarine and Great Skua are also seen most years. Some of the passing waders and terns fly over the Haven and may 'drop in' to rest and feed on the reserve.

A wide selection of waders can be found in the area on spring passage. Black-tailed and Bar-tailed Godwits, Whimbrel, Greenshank and Common Sandpiper regularly occur; whilst Little Ringed Plover, Knot, Sanderling, Ruff, Spotted Redshank, Green and Wood Sandpipers are occasionally seen. There are also spring sightings of Avocet, Kentish Plover, Temminck's Stint, Pectoral Sandpiper and Red-necked Phalarope. The first Sandwich Terns usually appear by late March, with Common and Little Terns arriving by mid-April. All three species may be seen around the area throughout the remainder of the spring and into the summer. Little Gulls and Black Terns are infrequent visitors to the reserve. The Haven is one of the more reliable sites in the region to see Garganey with birds reported most years. Amongst the migrant raptors, Marsh Harriers and Ospreys are almost annual in occurrence; whilst a few Hobbies regularly pass through. There is a scattering of landbird migrants, which normally includes Water Pipits, Yellow Wagtails and Wheatears as well as the occasional scarcer species such as Firecrest. Spring and the early summer may also produce oddities and vagrants from the Continent. There are records of Little Bittern, Night Heron, Purple Heron, White Stork, Glossy Ibis, American Wigeon, Common Crane, White-winged Black Tern, Alpine Swift, Hoopoe, Wryneck, Richard's Pipit, Savi's and Great Reed Warblers.

The most notable breeding inhabitants of the Haven's reedbeds are the Cetti's Warbler and Bearded Tit. Titchfield Haven became famous as the site where Britain's first Cetti's Warbler was identified back in March 1961, long before this recent colonist established itself in southern England. The species was next recorded at the Haven in 1975 followed by regular sightings from 1977 and breeding in 1981. Numbers steadily increased during the 1980s and by 1990 no fewer than 40 singing males were holding territory on the reserve. Despite a setback due to the severe weather of February 1991, 28 singing males were present in 1994. Bearded Tits have been regular visitors to Titchfield Haven since 1965 and breeding has occurred almost annually since 1966, reaching peaks of five or six pairs in the late 1970s/early 1980s and again in the early 1990s. Good numbers of Sedge and Reed Warblers and Reed Bunting along with a few pairs of Water Rail also nest in the reedbeds. Unfortunately the Grasshopper Warbler no longer appears to be a regular breeding species.

Lapwing and Redshank nest in the meadows; whilst a few pairs of breeding Oystercatcher and Ringed Plover are also present in the area.

The reserve also supports breeding Little Grebes and Canada Geese as well as the occasional pair of Shelduck, Gadwall and Teal. Other breeding birds of note include Turtle Dove and Lesser Whitethroat.

The first passage waders of the autumn appear during the second half of June with numbers and species diversity steadily increasing to peak in August and September. At this time of year the freshwater scrapes are particularly attractive to migrant waders, notably Green Sandpipers which regularly reach peaks of ten or more birds. Small numbers of Little Ringed Plover, Knot, Little Stint, Curlew Sandpiper, Ruff, Spotted Redshank, Greenshank and Wood Sandpiper also occur most years. Grey Phalaropes are occasional visitors, usually as a result of autumn gales. There also are reports of such rarities as Sociable Plover, Temminck's Stint, White-rumped, Pectoral and Spotted Sandpipers, Long-billed Dowitcher, Wilson's and Red-necked Phalaropes. From late July through to mid-September large flocks of Common Terns fish offshore and roost both on the beach and the reserve. In recent years up to eight Roseate Terns have regularly appeared with these Common Terns. Small numbers of Sandwich and Little Terns are also present; whilst a few Black Terns and the occasional Little Gull may also pass through. There are also several autumn records of White-winged Black Tern. Hobbies are frequently seen during August and September with birds remaining several days to chase roosting Swallows over the reedbeds; whilst Merlins occur most years. Of the larger migrant raptors, Marsh Harriers are reported annually and there are several reports of Ospreys. Short-eared Owls occasionally appear, usually in October and November. In recent years small parties of Spoonbills have appeared with some regularity during the late summer and autumn, sometimes remaining in the area for several weeks. This is the most likely time for Little Egrets to visit the reserve, although the species may occur at any time during the year. The Spotted Crake is also becoming a local speciality in the autumn with several recent records during this season.

Autumn seawatching is rather poor and generally involves a small westerly movement of the commoner terns and perhaps the odd Arctic Skua. Severe gales, however, may exceptionally produce such storm-driven oddities as Storm and Leach's Petrels, Grey Phalarope, Pomarine Skua, Sabine's Gull and Little Auk.

Landbird migrants are much more obvious during the autumn than in the spring. A reedbed roost of Yellow Wagtails is present from mid-August through to mid-September; whilst Whinchats, Wheatears and *Acrocephalus* warblers also occur in reasonable numbers. Scarcer species such as Black Redstart, Ring Ouzel, Dartford Warbler, Firecrest and Pied Flycatcher are occasionally seen; whilst subrarities including Hoopoe, Wryneck, Tawny Pipit, Bluethroat, Aquatic and Melodious Warblers and Lapland Bunting have all been reported here. There are also autumn records of Red-throated Pipit, Pallas's Warbler and Penduline Tits (several).

Other autumn rarities not already mentioned include Little Bittern, Squacco Heron, Cattle Egret, Purple Heron and American Wigeon.

Timing

Low-water off Hill Head is required for feeding Brent Geese and waders in winter, gull watching during late autumn and winter afternoons and roosting terns (including Roseates) in late summer and early autumn. The greatest variety and numbers of waders occur on the freshwater scrapes around high-water, although some birds are present at all states of the tide. In late summer and early autumn, the roosting terns also use the freshwater scrapes at high tide. Winter visits to the Haven during periods of hard weather can be very rewarding.

Spring seawatching is most reliable early in the morning, between mid-April and mid-May, when the winds are onshore (SE) in direction.

Landbird migrants are most likely to occur when fall conditions exist.

Access
Hill Head and Titchfield Haven Nature Reserve can be approached either south from Titchfield Village along Posbrook Lane (signposted to Meon) and Triangle Lane; or from Stubbington either south along

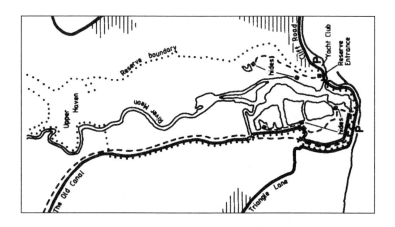

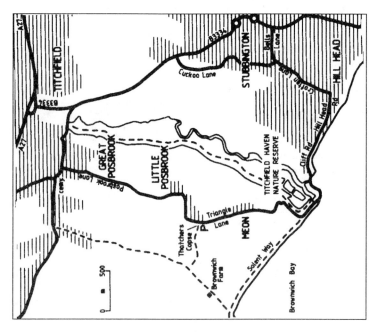

Cuckoo Lane or west along Bells Lane, then southwest along Croften Lane and finally northwest along Hill Head and Cliff Roads. There are car parks by the Yacht Club off Cliff Road and overlooking the beach at Hill Head.

Titchfield Haven NR: the main entrance to the reserve and Information Centre lies off Cliff Road opposite the car park by the Yacht Club. Much of the south and west of Titchfield Haven can be seen from the road along the shore and from the footpath (by the Old Canal) between the southwest corner of the reserve and Titchfield Village.

Reserve Visit Arrangements: the reserve is open from 9.30 am–5.00 pm on Fridays, Saturdays and Sundays throughout the year. Entry is by permit only, which can be obtained from the Information Centre. Groups wishing to visit the reserve must book in advance with the Naturalist Ranger, Haven Cottage, Cliff Road, Hill Head, Fareham, Hampshire PO4 3JT.

Brownwich: the Solent Way footpath follows the shore of Brownwich Bay from Hill Head northwest to Warsash. There is another footpath from Thatchers Copse (off Triangle Lane) west and then south by Brown-wich Farm to the shore.

Calendar

All Year: Little Grebe, Cormorant, Little Egret, Grey Heron, Canada Goose, Shelduck, Water Rail, Oystercatcher, Ringed Plover, Redshank, Cetti's Warbler, Bearded Tit, Reed Bunting.

Winter (mid-November–mid-March): occasional divers; Great Crested and occasional rarer winter grebes; Bittern; wildfowl including Brent Goose, Wigeon, Gadwall, Teal, Shoveler, Pochard, Tufted Duck, Eider, Red-breasted Merganser, occasional Pintail, other sea-duck and Golden-eye, in cold weather occasional wild swans, grey geese (usually White-fronted), Scaup, Smew, Goosander and Ruddy Duck; occasional Hen Harrier, Merlin and Peregrine; waders including Golden Plover, Ruff, Black-tailed Godwit, occasional Greenshank and Green Sandpiper; gulls including Mediterranean, occasional Little and Kittiwake, possible Iceland and Glaucous; occasional auks; occasional Short-eared Owl; Kingfisher, Rock Pipit, Stonechat, Siskin, Redpoll, occasional Chiffchaff, Firecrest and Brambling.
Most likely oddities: rare wildfowl and gulls.

Spring (mid-March–mid-May): sea passage best mid-April to mid-May – including divers; Fulmar; Common Scoter and other sea-duck; waders including Bar-tailed Godwit and Whimbrel; Arctic and near annual Pomarine and Great Skuas; Little Gull, Kittiwake; terns including Black.
Garganey; migrant raptors including Hobby, near annual Marsh Harrier and Osprey; migrant waders including Ruff, both godwits, Whimbrel, Greenshank, Common Sandpiper, occasional Little Ringed Plover, Knot, Sanderling, Spotted Redshank and Wood Sandpiper; occa-sional Little Gull; terns including occasional Black; landbird migrants including Water Pipit, Yellow Wagtail, Wheatear and occasional scarcer species like Firecrest.
Most likely oddities: rare heron and allies, rare wader, landbird sub-rarity.

Summer (mid-May–mid-July): non-breeding waders including Black-tailed Godwit; Sandwich, Common and Little Terns; Turtle Dove, Sedge and Reed Warblers, Lesser Whitethroat.

Autumn (mid-July–mid-November): slight sea passage mainly involving terns and occasional Arctic Skua; during/after severe gales – possible storm-blown seabirds such as Grey Phalarope, skuas, Sabine's Gull and Little Auk.

Near annual Spoonbill; occasional Garganey; migrant raptors including Merlin, Hobby, near annual Marsh Harrier and Osprey; near annual Spotted Crake; migrant waders including Little Ringed Plover, Knot, Little Stint, Curlew Sandpiper, Ruff, both godwits, Whimbrel, Spotted Redshank, Greenshank, Green, Wood and Common Sandpipers, occasional Grey Phalarope; occasional Little Gull; terns including Roseate and Black; occasional Short-eared Owl; landbird migrants including Yellow Wagtail, Whinchat, Wheatear, occasional Black Redstart, Ring Ouzel, Dartford Warbler, Firecrest and Pied Flycatcher.

Most likely oddities: rare heron and allies, rare wader, landbird sub-rarity.

OS Map 196

62 PORTSMOUTH HARBOUR

SZ69 &
SU50/60

Habitat

Portsmouth Harbour is a large estuary consisting of extensive mudflats and saltmarshes intersected by various channels, the most notable being Fareham Creek. This is formed by the Wallington River which flows into the northwest corner of the estuary. Much of the harbour is surrounded by dockyards and intensive urban development with Gosport to the west, Porchester to the north and Portsmouth to the east; whilst the narrow entrance to the Solent lies in the south. Unlike Langstone and Chichester Harbours, there is little open land immediately adjacent to the estuary, the main areas being situated to the north of Gosport between Fort Brockhurst and Foxbury Point and along the north shore of Fareham Creek at Wicor Fields. The IBM Lake, which is situated close to the northeast corner of the harbour, is a site of ornithological interest. Unfortunately the lake and surrounding grounds are private. During the 1980s nearby Paulsgrove Reclamation proved very attractive for birds, particularly waterfowl, waders and gulls. Sadly the area has now been developed as Port Solent.

Species

Although Portsmouth Harbour is the least important of the three eastern estuaries for birds, it still supports an abundance of winter wildfowl, waders, gulls and other waterbirds.

The Brent Goose is by far the most conspicuous of the wintering wildfowl with peak counts of between 2,500 and 3,500 birds; whilst Shelduck, Wigeon and Teal are also present in moderate numbers. Shoveler counts have declined since the demise of Paulsgrove Reclamation in the late 1980s and the Pintail has become an infrequent visitor. The sheltered waters of the harbour hold good numbers of Little Grebes, Goldeneye and Red-breasted Mergansers together with a few Great Crested Grebes and the occasional diver, rarer winter grebe and sea-duck – most likely Long-tailed Duck. The IBM Lake is the main site for Pochard and Tufted Duck in the area. If the lake becomes frozen during periods of severe cold, these freshwater diving ducks move to the nearby harbour where they may be joined by a few Scaup.

Most of the common waders can be seen in the harbour during the winter. Knot, Black-tailed and Bar-tailed Godwits and Greenshank are occasionally present; whilst a Common Sandpiper has also wintered in Fareham Creek on a number of occasions.

Knot

Large numbers of gulls, mainly Black-headed, Common and Herring, frequent the harbour. During the 1980s and early 1990s one or two Mediterranean Gulls occurred in the vicinity of Fareham Creek. More recently Paulsgrove Tip and the IBM Lake appear to be the favoured sites for this species. Between 1984/85 and 1992/93 a Glaucous Gull regularly wintered in the Hardway area. Cormorants and Grey Herons remain around the harbour area for much of the year; whilst Little Egrets are regular visitors, particularly during the autumn and winter. Amongst the smaller birds of note, a few Kingfishers and Rock Pipits can be found along the harbour shores.

Although many of the common waders can be seen well into the spring, migrant species are rather scarce involving mostly Whimbrel together with the occasional Greenshank and Common Sandpiper. A few Sandwich, Common and Little Terns are usually present; whilst a scattering of landbird migrants include both Yellow Wagtail and Wheatear.

Little of interest can be expected during midsummer apart from a few non-breeding waders and terns – the latter wandering from their breeding sites in neighbouring Langstone Harbour.

Most of the waders that commonly winter in the harbour have returned by July. Obvious migrants such as Whimbrel, Greenshank and Common Sandpiper regularly appear; whilst Little Stint, Curlew Sandpiper, Ruff and

Spotted Redshank are occasionally noted. Sandwich, Common and Little Terns, which occur throughout much of the autumn, may sometimes be joined by the odd migrant Little Gull and Black Tern. There is also a small passage of landbird migrants including Yellow Wagtail, Whinchat and Wheatear amongst others.

Other than Paulsgrove Reclamation in the early 1980s, very few rare or unusual birds have been recorded in the Portsmouth Harbour area; the most noteworthy sightings being a White Stork in spring and two Common Cranes in winter.

It is perhaps worth mentioning that during the early 1980s Paulsgrove Reclamation regularly attracted a wide selection of scarce migrants including Garganey, Little Ringed Plover, Little Stint, Curlew Sandpiper, Spotted Redshank, Wood Sandpiper, Little Gull and Black Tern. The potential of the site for rarities was shown by the occurrence of Spotted Crake, Temminck's Stint, Pectoral and Broad-billed Sandpipers and Aquatic Warbler. In addition, the nearby IBM Lake regularly held one or two Smew for six consecutive winters prior to 1986/7 and in January 1995 hosted a storm-blown Little Auk.

Timing

Due the vast size of Portsmouth Harbour, good views of wildfowl and waders are best obtained one to two hours before and after high-water when birds are restricted to feeding areas closest to the shore.

Access

Generally Portsmouth Harbour is best approached from Porchester.

Fareham Creek can be reached from the A27 roundabout at the west end of the Porchester by taking Cornaway Lane south past the Seagull PH to where the road bends sharp left into White Hart Lane. Here turn right into Cranleigh Road and continue west to Wicor Fields car park. There is a footpath west along the shore towards Fareham. Alternatively Fareham Creek can be reached from the A32 on leaving Fareham south towards Gosport, by taking Salterns Lane east past the sewage works and viewing the creek from the Eastern Parade playing fields.

Portsmouth Harbour: the main access points to the northern part of the harbour are (i) Porchester Castle, which is reached by taking Castle Street and Waterside Lane south from the A27 at the east end of Porchester (by National Westminster Bank); (ii) various minor roads south from White Hart Lane, which lies between Castle Street and Cornaway

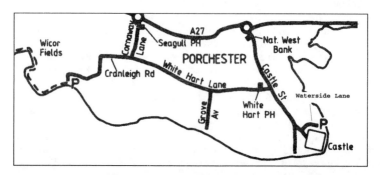

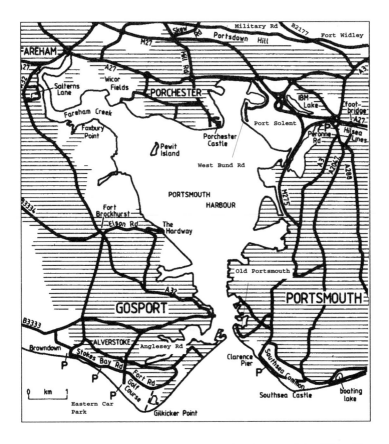

Lane, notably Grove Avenue 0.3 miles (0.5 km) west of the White Hart PH; (iii) along the A27 between Porchester and Paulsgrove – car parking can be difficult here; and (iv) from West Bund Road at the southwest end of Port Solent – park at the Boardwalk Shopping Centre.

Please note: there is no public access to the IBM Lake.

Calendar

All Year: Cormorant, Little Egret, Grey Heron, Shelduck, Oystercatcher, Redshank, Reed Bunting.

Winter (mid-November–mid-March): occasional divers; Little, Great Crested and occasional rarer winter grebes; wildfowl including Brent Goose, Wigeon, Teal, Shoveler, Goldeneye, Red-breasted Merganser, occasional Pintail and sea-duck, in cold weather Pochard, Tufted Duck and occasional Scaup; waders including occasional Knot, both godwits and Greenshank, possible Common Sandpiper; gulls including frequent Mediterranean; Kingfisher, Rock Pipit.

Spring (mid-March–mid-May): migrant waders including Whimbrel, occasional Greenshank and Common Sandpiper; Sandwich, Common and Little Terns; landbird migrants including Yellow Wagtail and Wheatear.

221

Summer (mid-May–mid-July): non-breeding waders; Common and Little Terns.

Autumn (mid-July–mid-November): migrant waders including Whimbrel, Greenshank, Common Sandpiper and occasional scarce species; occasional Little Gull; Sandwich, Common, Little and occasional Black Terns; landbird migrants including Yellow Wagtail and Wheatear.

63 FARLINGTON MARSHES NR (HWT) AND LANGSTONE HARBOUR (RSPB)

OS Maps
196 & 197
SZ69, SU60/70

Habitat

Langstone Harbour is a large estuary lying between Portsea Island (Portsmouth) to the west and Hayling Island to the east. Farlington Marshes form a low peninsula that projects south into the northwest corner of the harbour.

Although some reclamation work took place earlier, the present shape of Farlington Marshes was determined in about 1770 when the Lord of the Manor of Farlington joined his holdings of marsh, mudflats and islands within a wall to exclude the sea. At present most of the land within this seawall consists of rough pasture intersected by numerous drainage ditches. There is also a substantial cover of hawthorn bushes along the northern edge of the marshes. The main features of the area, however, are the shallow mud-fringed lagoon and large reedbed. These are fed by a freshwater stream which rises from springs at the base of Portsdown Hill. In addition, there are several smaller pools scattered about the marshes, notably close to the east side of the seawall at 'The Deeps'.

The seawall around Farlington Marshes overlooks Langstone Harbour. At low tide, this becomes a vast expanse of mudflats and *Spartina* saltmarshes drained by large creeks such as the Langstone Channel. The islands in the upper harbour are low areas of rough grass, saltmarsh and shingle; the higher remnants of surrounding land which long ago was reduced to mudflats by erosion.

Farlington Marshes have been leased and managed by the Hampshire Wildlife Trust since 1962. The marshes were purchased by Portsmouth City Council in 1970 and granted Statutory Local Nature Reserve Status in 1974. The Langstone Harbour islands, which are important nesting and roosting sites for birds, are wardened by the RSPB. The area supports a noteworthy flora and fauna. Insects including a wide selection of the commoner dragonflies and butterflies are particularly well represented.

Species

Langstone Harbour is undoubtedly the most important estuary for wildfowl, waders and other waterbirds that lies entirely within the region.

Brent Geese

Together the harbours of Langstone and Chichester support the main population of Brent Geese wintering along the south coast of England. Since systematic counts started, their numbers in Langstone Harbour have increased from a peak of 70 in 1952/53 to around 7–8,000 in the early 1990s when the combined maximum for both estuaries was in the region of 18–20,000 birds. Flocks of Brent Geese are conspicuous throughout the harbour and adjacent areas. Since the early 1970s birds have fed increasingly on pasture, including Farlington Marshes, playing fields and autumn-sown cereals.

Large numbers of Shelduck, Wigeon, Teal, Pintail and Shoveler can also be expected in winter, but Gadwall are rather scarce and sporadic in occurrence. All these species frequent Farlington Marshes where they often congregate around the lagoon area. The harbour's waters hold good numbers of Little Grebes (mainly in Bedhampton Creek), Great Crested Grebes, Goldeneye and Red-breasted Mergansers. The Black-necked Grebe is a local speciality with up to 20 to 30 birds favouring the Langstone Channel area. Slavonian Grebes are less common, but a few birds are usually present. The harbour is the most reliable site in Hampshire for Long-tailed Duck with one to three birds, sometimes more, appearing most winters. Small flocks of Eider sometimes visit the harbour; whilst divers, Red-necked Grebe, Common and Velvet Scoters and auks occur infrequently. Periods of severe cold occasionally bring flocks of Bewick's Swans and grey geese, usually White-fronted, to the marshes. Such conditions often force the local Pochard and Tufted Duck to move to the ice-free waters of the harbour where they may be joined by a few Scaup and perhaps even Smew and Goosander.

At low tide the harbour's mudflats attract many thousands of feeding waders, which roost on Farlington Marshes and the harbour islands at high-water. All of the commoner waders including Knot, Black-tailed and Bar-tailed Godwits occur in large numbers. The most abundant species, however, is the Dunlin with winter maxima of up to 35,000+ birds. In addition to the roosting waders, Farlington Marshes are favoured by Snipe together with a few Jack Snipe; whilst Ruff, Spotted Redshank, Greenshank and Green Sandpiper occasionally appear here.

Budds Farm Sewage Works near the north shore of Langstone Harbour is a good site for wildfowl, notably Teal and Tufted Duck, and waders including Snipe and occasionally Jack Snipe. In addition, one or two Common Sandpipers sometimes winter along the north shore of the harbour, favouring the Bedhampton Creek area.

During the winter an abundance of gulls inhabit the harbour and its environs; the main species being Black-headed, Common, Herring and Great Black-backed with Lesser Black-backed also present in small numbers. In recent years a few Mediterranean Gulls have regularly been seen at various sites within the harbour. These include Eastney Outfall by the harbour entrance where many Black-headed and Common Gulls gather to feed. Although most reports of Mediterranean Gulls are for the winter, birds have been observed in all months of the year. Little Gulls and Kittiwakes sometimes occur after winter gales. There have been several reports of Ring-billed, Iceland and Glaucous Gulls; whilst Britain's first Franklin's Gull was discovered at Farlington Marshes in February 1970. Cormorants and Grey Herons are present in and around the harbour throughout the year. The same now applies to the Little Egret with numbers peaking in the autumn. The birds that feed in and around Langstone Harbour are thought to roost with birds from neighboring Chichester Harbour on Thorney Island in West Sussex.

Farlington Marshes and the harbour islands are the best sites in the region for Short-eared Owls with up to three birds, sometimes more, present in winter. The owls usually roost on North Binness Island and hunt over the nearby marshes in search of prey. Occasionally Long-eared Owls also overwinter on Farlington Marshes. Both Merlin and Peregrine are frequently present in winter, but reports usually involve only one or two individuals of each species. The Hen Harrier is an occasional visitor, which seldom remains for long except during periods of cold weather.

Kingfishers can be seen around the lagoon and along the seawall ditches; whilst good numbers of Rock Pipits frequent the shore and saltmarsh areas. Although the reedbed on Farlington Marshes is a favoured site for Bearded Tits, birds are not present every winter. A few Chiffchaffs are usually present at this season, notably around Budds Farm Sewage Works where a Yellow-browed Warbler has also resided in two recent winters. There is always the possibility of finding the odd Black Redstart along the harbour shore and a Firecrest flitting amongst the hawthorn scrub on Farlington Marshes. Snow Buntings are recorded almost annually; whilst there are several winter sightings of Lapland Buntings.

All the species of wader that commonly winter in the harbour can be seen throughout the spring. The lagoon and marshy pools are particularly attractive to the scarcer migrants. These include Little Ringed Plover, Ruff, Spotted Redshank, Greenshank, Green and Common Sandpipers in small numbers; whilst Avocet, Little Stint, Curlew Sandpiper and Wood Sandpiper are occasionally seen. There are also several spring records of Temminck's Stint as well as sightings of such rarities as Black-winged Stilt, Least and Terek Sandpipers and Long-billed Dowitcher. Visual movements of waders inland, north over Portsdown Hill, is a feature of fine calm evenings in April and May.

The first Sandwich Terns usually appear in late March with Common and Little Terns arriving by mid-April. Small numbers of Little Gulls and Black Terns pass through most springs; whilst there are reports of Gull-billed and White-winged Black Terns. The lagoon is a good site for Garganey which occur most years in ones and twos. Marsh Harriers are sometimes seen on spring passage; whilst other migrant raptors are likely to include a few Hobbies and perhaps even an Osprey. The wintering

Short-eared Owls often linger well into May. There is a steady passage of landbird migrants including Yellow Wagtail, Wheatear and the occasional scarcer species like Black Redstart, Ring Ouzel, Firecrest and Pied Flycatcher. Landbird subrarities such as Hoopoe, Wryneck and Red-backed Shrike have also been noted in spring.

Being such an important area for bird migration, it is hardly surprising that Farlington Marshes and Langstone Harbour often attract rarities, notably the southern herons and their allies. Spoonbills are occasionally seen; whilst there are records of Little Bittern, Cattle Egret and Purple Heron. Other rarities not already mentioned include Blue-winged Teal, Red-footed Falcon, Common Crane and Pallid Swift.

Since 1979 the islands in Langstone Harbour have provided seclusion for breeding colonies of Common, Little and very occasionally Sandwich Terns as well as nesting Oystercatchers and Ringed Plovers. Several pairs of Yellow Wagtails still breed on Farlington Marshes; whilst Sedge and Reed Warblers and Reed Buntings inhabit the reedbeds. Other breeding birds of interest include Shelduck and Redshank. Substantial numbers of waders involving late spring migrants, non-breeding individuals and early autumn passage birds can be found in the harbour throughout June. There is always a possibility of a rarity turning up at this time of year; Red-footed Falcon, Black-winged Stilt, Broad-billed, Buff-breasted, Marsh and Terek Sandpipers, Lesser Yellowlegs, Ring-billed Gull, Citrine Wagtail, Black-eared Wheatear and Woodchat Shrike have all occurred during the summer.

The passage of autumn waders is under way by late June and builds up to a peak during August and September. In addition to those waders that commonly winter in the harbour, a wide selection of more obvious migrants can be expected. There is a heavy passage of Greenshank with up to 70–80 or so birds usually present in August; whilst Whimbrel, Spotted Redshank, Green and Common Sandpipers also appear in good numbers. As in spring, the lagoon is favoured by the scarcer waders which regularly include a few Little Ringed Plover, Little Stint, Curlew Sandpiper, Ruff and Wood Sandpiper. Grey Phalaropes often appear after gales; whilst Temminck's Stints and Pectoral Sandpipers have been seen on a number of occasions. There are also records of such rarities as White-rumped, Baird's, Broad-billed and Marsh Sandpipers and Lesser Yellowlegs.

During the autumn large post-breeding flocks of Common Terns gather in the harbour. Smaller numbers of Sandwich and Little Terns are also present; whilst a few Little Gulls and Black Terns usually pass through. The lagoon and reedbed is the best locality in Hampshire for Spotted Crakes, although this species is by no means annual in its visits. Garganey are seen most autumns, again showing a preference for the lagoon area. A scattering of Merlins and Hobbies pass through; whilst Marsh Harriers and Ospreys are reported most autumns. Arctic Skuas sometimes appear after gales to harry the gulls and terns inside the harbour. As mentioned earlier, Little Egret numbers peak in the autumn.

Landbird migrants are fairly prominent during the autumn. There are usually roosts of hirundines and Yellow Wagtails in the reedbed on Farlington Marshes where ringing activities have revealed a strong passage of *Acrocephalus* warblers. Scarcer species like Black Redstart, Ring Ouzel, Firecrest and Pied Flycatcher occasionally occur; whilst there are reports of such subrarities as Wryneck, Tawny Pipit, Bluethroat, Aquatic (mostly trapped), Melodious, Barred and Yellow-browed Warblers.

Autumn is also a good time to see rarities. In addition to those already mentioned, there are records of Black Stork, Little Crake, Common Crane, Bonaparte's Gull, White-winged Black Tern, Citrine Wagtail, Black-eared and Desert Wheatears.

Timing

One to two hours before and after high-water are the best times to see wildfowl and waders in the harbour, since birds are limited to feeding areas closest to the seawall. At high tide many of these birds roost on Farlington Marshes. The lagoon attracts wildfowl and waders throughout the tidal cycle, but this site is most rewarding just after high-water when birds briefly 'drop-in' as they leave the marshes to feed on the ebbing tide in the harbour. High tide tends to bring divers, grebes and sea-duck close inshore.

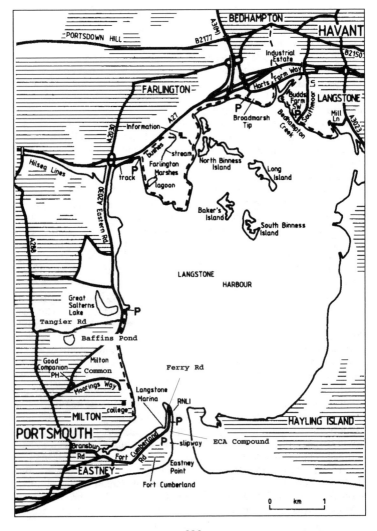

Landbird migrants are most likely to be found early in the morning when fall conditions prevail.

Access

Farlington Marshes and the north shore of Langstone Harbour are best approached from A27 between Portsmouth and Havant. Details of access to the east and west shores of the harbour are given in the sections on Hayling Island and Chichester Harbour (Site 64) and Other Sites Worthy of Attention – Site 69 Eastney Point and Site 70 Milton Common and Great Salterns Lake.

Farlington Marshes are reached from the A27/A2030 (Eastern Road) roundabout, by taking the rough road (immediately before Portsmouth exit) east along the harbour shore to the reserve entrance car park. A footpath follows the seawall around the marshes and returns to the car park across the north end of the reserve. The marshes can also be approached along the Solent Way footpath west from Broadmarsh Tip car park, which lies off Harts Farm Way just to the southeast of the A27/A3(M) junction.

Reserve Visit Arrangements: when visiting Farlington Marshes, organised groups must book well in advance with the Hampshire Wildlife Trust – see Useful Addresses. *Please note*: there is no access to the restricted areas of Farlington Marshes and Langstone Harbour.

Bedhampton Creek and Langstone Harbour is best reached by leaving the westbound carriageway of the A27 at the complex A3(M) junction, taking Harts Farm Way east through the industrial estate to a mini roundabout and then turning south along Southmoor Lane past Budds Farm Sewage Works to the shore car park. There are footpaths along the shore (i) west to Bedhampton Creek and returning northeast along the stream to Harts Farm Way; and (ii) east to Mill Lane at Langstone. There is also a car park overlooking Langstone Harbour at Broadmarsh Tip, which lies off Harts Farm Way just to the southeast of the A27/A3(M) junction.

Calendar

All Year: Cormorant, Little Egret, Grey Heron, Shelduck, Oystercatcher, Ringed Plover, Redshank, Reed Bunting.

Winter (mid-November–mid-March): occasional divers; Little, Great Crested, Slavonian, Black-necked and occasional Red-necked Grebes; wildfowl including Brent Goose, Wigeon, Teal, Pintail, Shoveler, Long-tailed Duck, Goldeneye, Red-breasted Merganser, occasional Gadwall, Eider, Common and Velvet Scoters, in cold weather occasional Bewick's Swan, grey geese (usually White-fronted), Pochard, Tufted Duck and Scaup, possible Smew and Goosander; Merlin, Peregrine and occasional Hen Harrier; Water Rail; waders including Knot, Jack Snipe, both godwits, occasional Ruff, Spotted Redshank, Greenshank, Green and Common Sandpipers; gulls including Mediterranean, occasional Little and Kittiwake, possible Iceland and Glaucous; occasional auks; Short-eared and occasional Long-eared Owls; Kingfisher, Rock Pipit, Chiffchaff, frequent Bearded Tit, occasional Black Redstart, Firecrest and Snow Bunting, possible Lapland Bunting.

Most likely oddity: rare wildfowl.

Spring (mid-March–mid-May): Garganey; migrant raptors including Hobby, near annual Marsh Harrier and occasional Osprey; migrant waders including Little Ringed Plover, Ruff, both godwits, Whimbrel, Spotted Redshank, Greenshank, Green and Common Sandpipers, occasional Avocet, Little Stint, Curlew and Wood Sandpipers; Little and occasional Mediterranean Gulls; terns including Black; Short-eared Owl; landbird migrants including Yellow Wagtail, Wheatear, occasional Black Redstart, Ring Ouzel, Firecrest and Pied Flycatcher.

Most likely oddities: Spoonbill, Temminck's Stint and other rare waders, landbird subrarity.

Summer (mid-May–mid-July): non-breeding waders; Sandwich, Common and Little Terns; Yellow Wagtail, Sedge and Reed Warblers.

Most likely oddity: rare wader.

Autumn (mid-July–mid-November): occasional Garganey; migrant raptors including Merlin, Hobby, near annual Marsh Harrier and Osprey; occasional Spotted Crake; migrant waders including Little Ringed Plover, Little Stint, Curlew Sandpiper, Ruff, both godwits, Whimbrel, Spotted Redshank, Greenshank, Green, Wood and Common Sandpipers, near annual Grey Phalarope; occasional Arctic Skua; Little and occasional Mediterranean Gulls; terns including Black; Short-eared Owl; landbird migrants including Yellow Wagtail, Whinchat, Wheatear, *Acrocephalus* warblers, occasional Black Redstart, Ring Ouzel, Firecrest and Pied Flycatcher.

Most likely oddities: Temminck's Stint and rare American waders, landbird subrarity.

64 HAYLING ISLAND AND CHICHESTER HARBOUR

OS Map 197
SZ69/79 & SU70

Habitat

Hayling is a large low-lying island situated between Langstone Harbour to the west and Chichester Harbour to the east. Apart from the built-up area of South Hayling, much of the Island is rural in character and given over to farmland. As a result, many sections of the shoreline retain considerable importance for birdlife. The west, north and east shores overlook the extensive mudflats and *Spartina* saltmarshes of the harbours. The southern shore, which faces the open sea, mostly consists of shingle beaches backed in places by sand dunes; whilst at low tide, long sandy strands are exposed offshore. Landward habitats of ornithological interest are comparatively few. Those that do exist, however, are found in the west, southwest and southeast of Hayling, namely the Hayling Billy Coastal Path, Sinah Common and Tourner Bury. Other features of note are the Oysterbeds, which are situated in the northwest of the Island, and the flooded gravel pit on Sinah Common.

Most of Chichester Harbour lies within the county of West Sussex. A significant portion of the harbour, however, abuts the east shore of Hayling Island and the mainland coast between the Langstone Bridge and Emsworth.

Species

For many years Hayling Island and the neighbouring harbours of Langstone and Chichester have been well known for their winter birds. During the early 1980s, however, the enthusiastic efforts of a group of local birdwatchers showed that Hayling is also the best area in Hampshire for landbird migrants and that Sandy Point on the southeast corner of the Island is a good site for spring seawatching.

During the winter the harbour areas support vast numbers of wildfowl, including the ubiquitous Brent Goose and waders, including Knot and both species of godwit. Chichester Harbour and the sandy strands of Hayling Bay, notably East Winner, and are amongst the best localities in the region for winter Sanderling. Sinah Gravel Pit is the main wintering site locally for Pochard, Tufted Duck and a variety of dabbling ducks. Divers, grebes – notably Slavonian, Shag, sea-duck and auks favour the offshore waters of Hayling Bay. The more sheltered waters of the harbours attract reasonable numbers of Little, Great Crested, Slavonian and Black-necked Grebes, Goldeneye and Red-breasted Mergansers together with a few Eider and Long-tailed Duck and occasionally divers, Red-necked Grebe, Common and Velvet Scoters and auks. There is obviously a considerable interchange of birds between Hayling Bay and the harbours. Gulls are very much a feature of Hayling Island during the winter. A few Mediterranean Gulls have regularly been seen in recent years; whilst Kittiwakes and odd Little Gulls sometimes occur in Hayling Bay and around the harbour entrances after winter gales. There are also several reports of Iceland and Glaucous Gulls. Of the winter raptors, the Peregrine is the most likely species to be seen; Hen Harrier, Merlin and Short-eared Owl being occasional visitors. In mild winters, the gardens, scrub and woodland areas usually hold a few Blackcaps, Chiffchaffs and sometimes Firecrests; whilst Black Redstarts and Snow Buntings are occasionally found along the shore.

Recent observations suggest that Sandy Point is one of the best vantage points along the Hampshire coast for spring seawatching. By comparison, seabird passage in the autumn is rather poor and mainly involves a few Common Scoter and terns. Severe gales, however, may produce storm-blown oddities such as Grey Phalarope, skuas, Sabine's Gull and Little Auk.

Although most of the waders that commonly winter in the harbours remain well into the spring, migrant species are rather scarce. Whimbrel and a few Common Sandpipers regularly occur; whilst the odd Greenshank may also be seen. Migrant waders are commoner in the autumn, but only Whimbrel, Greenshank and Common Sandpiper appear with any regularity; more unusual species such as Little Stint, Curlew Sandpiper, Ruff, Spotted Redshank and Green Sandpiper being scarce visitors. Sandwich, Common and Little Terns are present in the harbours and along Hayling Bay from spring through to autumn when post-breeding flocks congregate around the harbour entrances. Landbird migrants are also prominent at times of passage. Although smaller numbers of birds pass through in spring, a wide variety of species can be expected. These include near annual sightings of Black Redstart, Ring Ouzel,

Firecrest and Pied Flycatcher. Passage is stronger in the autumn when scarcer species like Black Redstart, Firecrest and Pied Flycatcher regularly occur in small numbers and Ring Ouzels are noted most years. A wide selection of subrarities and rarities have been seen on Hayling which confirms the area's potential for attracting unusual birds.

Since the late 1980s, the Little Egret has become an important feature of the area. Indeed one of the largest roosts for the species in Britain is located just outside the region on Thorney Island (West Sussex) where counts have exceeded 100 in recent autumns. A substantial proportion of these birds feed in the Hampshire part of Chichester Harbour, favouring the East Hayling shore, and in nearby Langstone Harbour. Although peak counts occur during the autumn, birds can now be seen throughout the year.

Timing

The ideal conditions for watching wildfowl and waders in the harbours and on the sandy strands of Hayling Bay are one to two hours before and after high-water when birds feed close to the shore. At high tide there are wader roosts at Black Point, the Kench, the Oysterbeds and sometimes in the fields behind West Hayling shore. High tide is also the best time to look for divers, grebes, sea-duck and auks in the harbours and Hayling Bay. As the tide ebbs, Sanderling fly out through Chichester Harbour entrance to their feeding grounds in Hayling Bay and at Ryde Sands off the Isle of Wight, returning to roost on the rising tide. Peak numbers of gulls feed off Eastney Outfall one hour after high-water, after which they tend to drift off to loaf and wash on Sinah Gravel Pit.

Spring seawatching from Sandy Point is most rewarding early in the morning, between mid-April and mid-May, when winds are from the SE. Good movements have been witnessed, however, with winds between S and NE in direction. Autumn seawatching is only worth contemplating during and after severe gales.

Landbird migrants should be searched for early in the morning when the weather is likely to induce fall conditions.

Access

The only access to Hayling Island is by the A3023 (Havant Road) south from the A27 roundabout in Havant.

Recommended Sites

64A WEST HAYLING SHORE (HCC)
AND THE OYSTERBEDS

Map p. 231, SZ79, SU70

Habitat and Species

Immediately behind the shore of West Hayling, which overlooks the mudflats and saltmarshes of Langstone Harbour, there is a scrub-lined track that follows the route of the disused Hayling Billy railway. This track also passes close to three small woods, Havant Road Copse in the north and Saltmarsh and Station Yard Copses in the south. The Oysterbeds, an impounded area of shallow lagoons that drain with the tide, are situated at the north end of this shoreline.

In winter a wide selection of wildfowl, notably Brent Geese, waders and gulls can be seen along the shore. The embankment around the

Oysterbeds is an excellent vantage point to observe the Black-necked Grebe flock as well as any divers, other grebes, sea-duck, Goldeneye and Red-breasted Mergansers that may be present in the Langstone Channel. The Oysterbeds themselves are an important site for feeding waders including the occasional wintering Greenshank; whilst roosting waders gather on the embankments at high-water. These shallow lagoons also support small numbers of wildfowl including Teal, Goldeneye, Red-breasted Merganser and sometimes Shoveler. One or two Goosander have also wintered here in recent years. A few Rock Pipits and the occasional Kingfisher also occur around the Oysterbeds in winter, when finches and buntings frequent the rough ground immediately to the south. At high tide, the fields behind the shore hold Brent Geese and roosting waders including Knot and Black-tailed Godwit. In mild winters, Blackcaps, Chiffchaffs and sometimes Firecrests can be found in the scrub and small copses along the disused railway. Recent winter oddities involve sightings of Long-tailed Skua and Shorelark.

The Oysterbeds are attractive to migrant waders, particularly in the autumn when Greenshank and Common Sandpiper are usually present along with the occasional scarcer species such as Little Stint and Curlew Sandpiper. The terns that breed locally in Langstone Harbour also favour this area. There is a now a good chance of seeing Little Egrets, mainly during the autumn and winter. The scrub and small woods along the disused railway are good sites to find landbird migrants, notably in autumn. Firecrest and Pied Flycatcher are the most likely species to be encountered, but there are reports of Black Redstart, mainly around the Oyster-

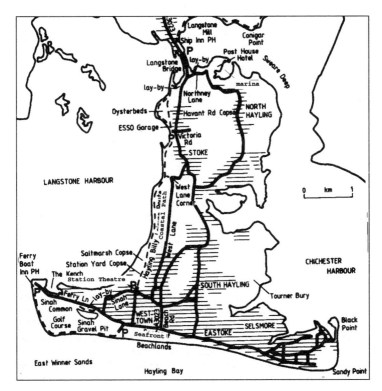

beds, and Ring Ouzel. There are also sightings of Hoopoe, Wryneck, Golden Oriole and Subalpine Warbler. The area supports such interesting breeding birds as Turtle Dove, Little Owl and Lesser Whitethroat.

Access

The Hayling Billy Coastal Path (HCC) along the disused railway can be accessed (i) from the lay-by to the west of the A3023 immediately south of Langstone Bridge; (ii) from foreshore car parks, which are reached west along a rough track from the A3023 in Stoke – just south of the shop next to the Esso Garage and opposite Victoria Road; (iii) west along a footpath from West Lane Corner 0.3 miles (0.5 km) southwest of the A3023 in Stoke – car parking very limited here; and (iv) north from the car park by the Station Theatre off Sinah Lane, West Town. Although there is access to the Oysterbeds, visitors are warned that they enter at their own risk.

64B SINAH COMMON AND HAYLING BAY

Map p. 231, SZ69/79

Habitat and Species

Sinah Common, which lies in the southwest corner of Hayling Island, offers a wide range of habitats centred around a flooded gravel pit. These include well-wooded gardens, thickets of sessile oak and willow, gorse scrub and a large golf course. Sinah Common extends west across the narrow entrance to Langstone Harbour. On the north shore, there is a small bay of mudflats and *Spartina* saltmarshes known as the Kench. The west and south shores, which overlook the harbour entrance and Hayling Bay respectively, comprise sandy beaches backed by shingle banks and sand dunes; whilst offshore the extensive sandy strand of East Winner is exposed at low tide.

The gravel pit is a favoured site for winter wildfowl, notably Pochard and Tufted Duck; whilst Gadwall, Teal and Shoveler are sometimes present in small numbers. The rarer winter grebes, Long-tailed Duck, Goldeneye, Red-breasted Merganser and cold weather birds such as Scaup and Smew are occasional visitors. When the pit freezes over during periods of severe cold, the diving ducks move to the harbour entrance. A few Mediterranean Gulls are frequently seen amongst the Black-headed and Common Gulls that gather on the gravel pit, usually after feeding off Eastney Outfall in the harbour entrance. The Kingfisher is also a regular inhabitant of the pit in winter.

The Kench provides feeding and roosting sites for a variety of wildfowl and waders including Brent Geese and Black-tailed Godwit. It is also a likely place to see Little Egrets. Hayling Bay is generally a good area for divers – most likely Great Northern, grebes – mainly Great Crested and Slavonian, Shag, sea-duck – notably Eider and Common Scoter, and auks. The number of these birds, however, varies considerably from one winter to the next. Sanderling and Bar-tailed Godwit often feed along the sandy beaches and offshore strands. Winter gales sometimes bring Kittiwakes and perhaps Little Gulls to seek the shelter of the harbour entrance where Grey Phalarope and Little Auk have also occurred. Sinah Common and the nearby gardens often hold Blackcaps, Chiffchaffs and sometimes Firecrests in mild winters; whilst Black Redstarts occasionally appear around the harbour entrance. There are several winter sightings of Snow Buntings from this area.

Sanderlings

Sinah Common is undoubtedly one of the best sites on Hayling Island for landbird migrants. In autumn these usually include a few Firecrests and Pied Flycatchers as well as the occasional Black Redstart and Ring Ouzel. There are also records of Hoopoe and Wryneck in spring and Long-eared Owl, Wryneck, Tawny Pipit, Melodious and Yellow-browed Warblers and Red-breasted Flycatcher in autumn. Sandwich, Common and Little Terns can be seen from spring through to the autumn when there is a post-breeding roost of terns at the Kench. Black Terns sometimes appear around the harbour entrance in autumn, when severe gales may produce occasional storm-blown oddities such as Grey Phalarope, skuas, Sabine's Gull and Little Auk. Migrant waders are not particularly obvious, but regularly include Whimbrel and Common Sandpiper in both seasons and Greenshank in the autumn. There is also a recent autumn record of a Buff-breasted Sandpiper on the golf course. Notable breeding birds include Little Grebe, Canada Goose and Tufted Duck on Sinah Gravel Pit with Ringed Plover, Sedge and Reed Warblers, Lesser Whitethroat and Reed Bunting present in the surrounding area.

Access

Sinah Common is best approached from the A3023 roundabout by the Beachlands Amusement Park in South Hayling. From here, take Sea Front and Ferry Lane west to the beach car park by the Ferry Boat Inn, which overlooks the entrance to Langstone Harbour. Ferry Lane can also be reached from West Town west and south along Sinah Lane. There is also limited parking just off Ferry Lane by the green overlooking Sinah Gravel Pit. General access to the foreshore areas and along Ferry Lane provides views over such private sites as the golf course and flooded gravel pit.

64C BLACK AND SANDY POINTS

Maps p. 231 and p. 235, SZ79

Habitat and Species

Black and Sandy Points are situated in the extreme southeast corner of Hayling Island. Black Point is a low short peninsula of shingle and sand which overlooks the broad entrance to Chichester Harbour to the east and, at low tide, the extensive sandbanks, mudflats and *Spartina* salt-marshes of the harbour to the north and west. Sandy Point lies to the south and basically provides a seafront vantage point suitable for sea-watching. The well wooded grounds of Sandy Point Hospital are situated between Black and Sandy Points.

Black Point is the most accessible site on Hayling Island to observe the wealth of wildfowl, waders, gulls and other waterbirds that inhabit Chichester Harbour in winter. Large flocks of Brent Geese are always on view; whilst amongst the more notable waders, Knot, Sanderling, Black-tailed and Bar-tailed Godwits are usually present. The East Hayling shore is a favoured feeding area for Little Egrets which are best looked for during the autumn and winter months. The waters of the harbour support good numbers of Great Crested Grebes, Goldeneye and Red-breasted Mergansers along with a few Slavonian Grebes. In some winters divers and Eiders are frequently seen, but in others they are scarce or absent; whilst the other rarer winter grebes and sea-duck along with the auks are occasional visitors. The local gulls are well worth checking through for the more unusual species; Mediterranean, Iceland and Glaucous have all been seen in the area. Small birds of interest include a few Rock Pipits along the shore; whilst Stonechat, Chiffchaff and Firecrest sometimes winter in the grounds of Sandy Point Hospital. There are several winter records of Black Redstart and Snow Bunting from Black Point.

Sandy Point is the best site for spring seawatching along the South Hayling Shore. This offshore passage mainly involves Common Scoter, waders including Bar-tailed Godwit and terns. Fulmar, Gannet, other sea-duck, Arctic Skua, Little Gull, Kittiwake and Black Tern can also be expected in small numbers. Both Pomarine and Great Skuas have occurred almost annually in recent springs; whilst there are several reports of Manx Shearwaters and at least one of Long-tailed Skua. These easterly movements apparently involve birds that pass through the Solent together with those that go around the Isle of Wight. When winds are strong and onshore in direction, the latter are forced into Hayling Bay before they can move out to sea again and pass Selsey Bill. Autumn passage is less productive, but gales may bring such storm-blown oddities as Grey Phalarope, skuas, Sabine's Gull and Little Auk close inshore. Sandwich, Common and Little Terns are present in the area from spring to autumn when flocks of post-breeding terns gather in the harbour entrance. These tern flocks are occasionally joined by passage Little Gulls and Black Terns. Amongst the migrant waders, Whimbrel and Common Sandpiper regularly appear in spring and autumn, but Greenshank can only be expected during the latter season. The grounds of Sandy Point Hospital can be a rewarding spot for landbird migrants, particularly in autumn when Pied Flycatchers occur fairly regularly and Black Redstart, Ring Ouzel and Firecrest are sometimes recorded. There are also autumn sightings of Wryneck, Icterine Warbler and Ortolan Bunting from this site.

Access

Black and Sandy Points can be reached from Eastoke by taking Southwood Road (off Rails Road) east to the seafront car park by the Millers PH. For Sandy Point, continue east along Southwood Road to the junction with Bosmere Road and then take the footpath south to the seafront. Please note that parking is very difficult here and it may be best to walk along the seafront from the car park by the Millers PH. For Black Point, turn north along Creek Road, take the second right (by Kittiwake PH and signposted to Lifeboat Station) along Sandy Point Road east to Sandy Point Hospital, turn left into Brackelsham Road, continue east to the junction with Wittering Road and then take the footpath east to the shore. Please note that parking is very difficult here. Although the road to Black Point is private, there does appear to be limited permissive parking along the foreshore. Alternatively there is a car park off Wheatlands Avenue (first right off Creek Road). It is also possible to walk along the shore from Sandy Point to Black Point and view the grounds of Sandy Point Hospital from the perimeter fence.

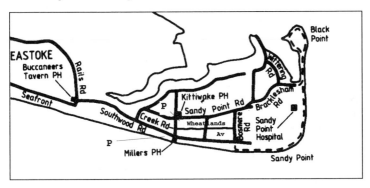

64D NORTH HAYLING AND CHICHESTER HARBOUR

Map p. 231, SU70

Habitat and Species

Sweare Deep, which is the channel draining the mudflats and *Spartina* saltmarshes in the northwest corner of Chichester Harbour, can be viewed from the shorelines of North Hayling and the mainland opposite. Noteworthy features along the mainland shore between the Langstone Bridge and Emsworth include a small reed-fringed lake at Langstone Mill and a small freshwater marsh at Conigar Point.

In winter a variety of estuarine wildfowl and waders including Brent Goose, Shelduck, Teal, Black-tailed and Bar-tailed Godwits can be seen feeding on the mudflats and saltmarshes; whilst at high tide Goldeneye and Red-breasted Mergansers along with the occasional grebe and sea-duck – most likely Long-tailed Duck, fish in Sweare Deep. A Red-breasted Goose wintered amongst the Brent Geese here in 1975/6. Like the other parts of Chichester Harbour, Little Egrets can be expected, particularly during the autumn and winter. Small numbers of waders including migrant Whimbrel and Greenshank occur in spring and autumn and Sandwich, Common and Little Terns are present throughout the summer. Autumn sightings of Wrynecks near Northney Marina suggests that it is worthwhile checking the shoreline areas for landbird migrants. The habitats immediately behind the mainland shore support breeding Lesser Spotted Woodpecker, Cetti's and Reed Warblers. Mandarin have also been seen on Langstone Mill Pond.

Access

North Hayling is reached by turning east into Northney Lane from the A3023 immediately after crossing Langstone Bridge. Sweare Deep can be viewed from a small lay-by; there is also access along the foreshore east towards the Post House Hotel and Northney Marina. The main access to the mainland shore is by means of the Solent Way footpath between the car park by the Ship Inn at Langstone Bridge and Emsworth. The footpath passes Langstone Mill; whilst at low tide it is possible to follow the shore east to Conigar Point and beyond to Emsworth.

Calendar

All Year: Little Grebe, Cormorant, Little Egret, Grey Heron, Shelduck, Tufted Duck, Oystercatcher, Ringed Plover, Redshank, Little Owl, Lesser Spotted Woodpecker, Cetti's Warbler, Reed Bunting.

Winter (mid-November–mid-March): divers; Great Crested, Slavonian, Black-necked and occasional Red-necked Grebes; Shag; wildfowl including Brent Goose, Wigeon, Gadwall, Teal, Pintail, Shoveler, Pochard, Eider, Common Scoter, Goldeneye, Red-breasted Merganser, frequent Long-tailed Duck, occasional Velvet Scoter and Goosander, in cold weather Scaup and occasional Smew; frequent Peregrine, occasional Hen Harrier and Merlin; Water Rail; waders including Golden Plover, Knot, Sanderling, both godwits, occasional Greenshank; gulls including Mediterranean, occasional Little, Iceland, Glaucous and Kittiwake; occasional auks; occasional Short-eared Owl; Kingfisher, Rock Pipit, Blackcap, Chiffchaff, frequent Firecrest, occasional Black Redstart and Snow Bunting.

Spring (mid-March–mid-May): sea passage best mid-April to mid-May – including divers; Fulmar; possible Manx Shearwater; Gannet; Common Scoter and other sea-duck; waders including Bar-tailed Godwit and Whimbrel; skuas including near annual Pomarine and Great; Little Gull and Kittiwake; terns including Black; occasional auks.

Migrant waders including Bar-tailed Godwit, Whimbrel, Greenshank, Common Sandpiper and occasional scarcer species; Sandwich, Common and Little Terns; landbird migrants including occasional Black Redstart, Ring Ouzel, Wood Warbler, Firecrest and Pied Flycatcher.

Most likely oddity: landbird subrarity.

Summer (mid-May–mid-July): Sandwich, Common and Little Terns, Turtle Dove, Sedge and Reed Warblers, Lesser Whitethroat.

Autumn (mid-July–mid-November): slight sea passage involving Common Scoter, Arctic Skua and terns; during/after severe gales occasional storm-blown seabirds such as Grey Phalarope, Pomarine Skua, Sabine's Gull and Little Auk.

Migrant waders including Whimbrel, Greenshank, Common Sandpiper and occasional scarcer species; occasional Little Gull; Sandwich, Common, Little and occasional Black Terns; landbird migrants including Firecrest, Pied Flycatcher, near annual Black Redstart and Ring Ouzel.

Most likely oddity: landbird subrarity.

SOUTHEAST HAMPSHIRE –
OTHER SITES WORTHY
OF ATTENTION

Part 1 – Portsmouth Area Including
Portsea Island

65 GILKICKER POINT AND STOKES BAY
(GOSPORT BOROUGH COUNCIL)

Map p. 221, SZ59/69

Gilkicker Point is a low headland overlooking the coastal waters of Spithead. The immediate hinterland consists of a golf course, some small areas of scrub and woodland and some freshwater pools. This is primarily a site for observing the passage of seabirds through the Solent in spring and autumn. Although waders and terns are the main groups involved in these movements, other birds such as Fulmar, Gannet, various sea-duck, skuas, Little Gull and Kittiwake are occasionally reported. The area also attracts a scattering of landbird migrants including the occasional Black Redstart, Ring Ouzel, Firecrest and Pied Flycatcher. There are also sightings of such rare and unusual birds as Bonaparte's Gull, Alpine Swift, Hoopoe, Richard's and Tawny Pipits. Gilkicker Point is best approached along Stokes Bay Road in Gosport. There is access from various car parks off Stokes Bay Road, notably Eastern Car Park at SZ600980 which is reached south from the roundabout at the junction with Anglesey Road and Fort Road.

66 PORTSDOWN HILL (PORTSMOUTH CITY COUNCIL)

Map p. 221, SU60

This prominent chalk ridge dominates the local landscape and provides superb views over Portsmouth and Langstone Harbours. Extensive scrub covers much of the steep southern slopes; whilst the more gently rolling northern slopes consist mainly of farmland. A wide variety of landbird migrants, which occasionally include Black Redstart, Ring Ouzel, Firecrest and Pied Flycatcher, occur on passage. Visual movements of landbirds, notably Skylarks, hirundines, Meadow Pipits, winter thrushes and finches, can be prominent particularly during the autumn. The potential of the site for attracting rare and unusual migrants is shown by sightings of White Stork, Red-backed and Lesser Grey Shrikes. Blackcap, Chiffchaff and Firecrest sometimes overwinter in the areas of scrub and neighbouring gardens. Immediately to the north, the fields of the Southwick Estate regularly hold a large flock of Whimbrel in spring and smaller numbers of Curlew in winter. Local breeding birds include Little Owl, Stonechat, Lesser Whitethroat and Corn Bunting. Portsdown Hill is best approached from Bedhampton Hill at SU700066 by taking Portsdown Hill Road (B2177 to Wickham) west along the ridge to the roundabout at SU648066 (between Fort Widley and Fort Southwick). From here continue west along the ridge on the minor road (Down End Road) to the A27 between Porchester and Fareham at SU595061. There are a number of car parks, notably Candy's Pit Trail at SU663064 (near Fort Widley), by the roundabout at SU648066 and Fort Nelson at SU608069.

67 HILSEA LINES RAMPARTS (PORTSMOUTH CITY COUNCIL)

Map p. 226, SU60

Hilsea Lines comprises an area of fields, scrub, woodland and freshwater pools bordering Portsea Creek which is the narrow channel linking Langstone and Portsmouth Harbours. In winter the creek is a favoured site for Little Grebes and Kingfishers. Various wildfowl, including Brent Goose and Goldeneye, common waders and gulls can also be expected; whilst hard-weather duck such as Scaup have been seen here. The fields, scrub and woodland occasionally attract Black Redstart and Firecrest both in winter and at migration times. Wintering Blackcap and Chiffchaff are sometimes present; whilst the occasional Pied Flycatcher may be found amongst the scattering of landbird migrants that occur in spring and autumn. The area is best approached along various footpaths from either the car park at SU655045 off the southbound carriageway immediately south of the A27/A3 roundabout; or the footbridge at SU659043 at the end of Peronne Road, which is reached north from Copnor Road (A288) in Hilsea (signposted to TA Centres Hilsea 1 & 2 and Highbury College).

68 SOUTHSEA CASTLE

Map p. 221, SZ69

Southsea Castle is situated on a low headland overlooking the coastal waters of Spithead. Behind the shore, the municipal gardens of Southsea Common extends northwestwards towards Clarence Pier and Old Portsmouth. To the east, Southsea Canoe Lake lies within the confines of a small park. This is the most reliable site in Hampshire for wintering Purple Sandpiper, albeit in small numbers. The species is best looked for either around the rocky shore of Southsea Castle as the tide falls or on the tank blocks just to the east of South Parade Pier at low spring tides. Good numbers of Sanderling and Turnstone also occur along the shoreline. A few Shag, which is a scarce bird in Hampshire, are usually present offshore; whilst divers, grebes, sea-duck and auks are occasionally noted. One or two Mediterranean Gulls are frequent visitors to nearby Southsea Canoe Lake. In spring and autumn passing seabirds may include the occasional Fulmar, Gannet, skua and Kittiwake. Both Southsea Castle and nearby Old Portsmouth are good areas to look for Black Redstarts in autumn and winter. Access is easy and straightforward along Clarence and Southsea Esplanades.

69 EASTNEY POINT

Map p. 226, SZ69 & SU60

Eastney Point provides an ideal vantage point to observe the entrance of Langstone Harbour and the nearby sewage outfall. In winter it is possible to see a good selection of the waterfowl, waders and gulls inhabiting

Langstone Harbour and the offshore waters of Hayling Bay. Local specialities include Shag and Sanderling; whilst Mediterranean Gulls are frequently found amongst the large numbers of gulls feeding off the sewage outfall where freshwater diving duck often gather during periods of severe cold. Nearby Fort Cumberland is a good site for wintering and migrant Black Redstarts. In autumn and winter, storm-blown seabirds sometimes seek the shelter of the harbour entrance. These movements have produced sightings of such notable birds as Grey Phalarope, Sabine's Gull and Little Auk. Eastney Point is best reached from Eastney Road (A288) in Milton, by taking Bransbury Road (opposite the Fort Cumberland Arms PH and signposted to Southsea Marina), Fort Cumberland Road (also signposted to Southsea Marina) and Ferry Road east to the Eastney Cruising Association (ECA) compound. There is general access to the foreshore areas from car parks by Eastney Public Slipway at SZ685994 (just before the ECA compound) and near Portsmouth Lifeboat Station at SZ685999 (just beyond the ECA compound).

70 MILTON COMMON AND GREAT SALTERNS LAKE (PORTSMOUTH CITY COUNCIL)

Map p. 226, SU60

This area of rough ground, scrub and freshwater pools, which borders the west side of Langstone Harbour, has developed on a disused landfill site. At present it is managed for its wildlife by Portsmouth City Council. Nearby there is a large reed-fringed lake (Great Salterns) surrounded by playing fields. A little further afield lies Baffins Pond. Like nearby Eastney Point, it is possible to see many of the waterfowl, waders and gulls frequenting Langstone Harbour from the seawall by Milton Common. In winter it is a good site to view Knot in the harbour; whilst the reclamation pools are favoured by waterfowl including Little Grebe, Tufted Duck and sometimes Shoveler. Flocks of Brent Geese feed on the nearby playing fields. Bearded Tits have occasionally visited the reeds bordering Great Salterns Lake, which also attracts small numbers of waterfowl including Little Grebe and Tufted Duck in winter. It is well worth checking the area for landbird migrants in spring and autumn. Amongst some of the more interesting birds seen here, there are reports of Red-crested Pochard, Red-necked and Grey Phalaropes and Wryneck. Nearby Baffins Pond supports a feral population of Canada and Barnacle Geese as well as winter wildfowl, notably Shoveler and Tufted Duck. Milton Common can be reached along the Solent Way footpath either south from the car park off Eastern Road (A2030) at SU677018, which lies opposite Great Salterns Lake; or north from the end of Moorings Way at SU676004, which lies off Eastern Road (A2030) by the Good Companion PH. Baffins Pond is situated off Tangier Road at SU665013.

Part 2 – Elsewhere in Southeast Hampshire

71 SOUTHAMPTON COMMON

SU41

This is an area of parkland, woods and small ponds situated in the middle of Southampton. A variety of the commoner woodland birds breed here; whilst the occasional Firecrest and Pied Flycatcher occur on migration. An Icterine Warbler was trapped here in October 1994. General access from the Avenue and Hill Lane in Southampton.

72 WESTON SHORE AND WESTWOOD WOODLAND PARK (HCC)

SU40/41

Weston Shore overlooks the upper reaches of Southampton Water. A foreshore of muddy shingle is exposed at low tide. Behind the shore there is an area of woodland (Westwood Woodland Park). In winter the offshore waters of Southampton Water support small numbers of Great Crested Grebes, Goldeneye and Red-breasted Mergansers; whilst divers, the rarer grebes – most likely Slavonian, sea-duck and auks are occasionally present. A good selection of the commoner waders, notably Oystercatcher, Ringed and Grey Plovers, Dunlin and Turnstone, feed along the foreshore at low tide. Mediterranean Gulls are seen with some frequency and there is one recent report of a Ring-billed Gull. The area appears to have some potential for attracting landbird migrants including the occasional Black Redstart, Firecrest and Pied Flycatcher; whilst in 1993 Honey Buzzard, Marsh and Montagu's Harriers and Osprey were all reported on passage. Weston Shore is best approached along Weston Lane between Weston and Netley. There are car parks either side of the road at SU446095, which provide access to both the foreshore and Westwood Woodland Park.

73 WEST WALK (FC)

SU51/61

This superb area of broadleaved woodland and forestry is a remnant of the once extensive Royal Forest of Bere. These woods and forests support a variety of interesting breeding birds including Woodcock, Turtle Dove, Nightjar, Tree Pipit, Nightingale, occasionally Wood Warbler and possibly Willow Tit. West Walk is best approached along minor roads between the B2177 and Newtown and between the A32 and Soberton Heath. Footpaths and forest walks from car parks at SU597123 (West Walk), SU592135 (Woodend) and SU590135 (Upperford Copse) give access to much of the area.

74 HAVANT THICKET (FC)

SU71

Havant Thicket is an area of broadleaved woodland and forestry situated between Rowland Castle and Horndean. Breeding birds include such notable species as Woodcock, Turtle Dove, Nightjar, Garden Warbler and Willow Tit. During the spring flocks of Whimbrel often feed in nearby fields. The best access point is from Staunton car park at SU724101, which lies off the B2149 in Red Hill, Rowland Castle. Please note that there is no access to The Holt section of Havant Thicket.

NORTHEAST HAMPSHIRE

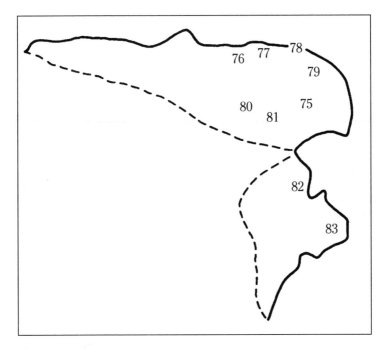

75 FLEET POND LNR
76 Stratfield Saye and Wellington
   Country Park
77 Warren Heath and Bramshill
   Plantation
78 Eversley and Yateley Gravel Pits
79 Yateley Common Country Park

80 Greywell and Warnborough
   Green
81 Dogmersfield Lake and
   Tundry Pond
82 Alice Holt Forest
83 Ludshott Common and
   Waggoner's Wells

General Introduction

This area of Hampshire covers those parts of the country that lie mainly to the north and east of the chalk downs, extending from Highclere in the northwest to Petersfield in the southeast. In some respects, Northeast Hampshire has more in common with the neighbouring counties of Berkshire, Surrey and West Sussex than with other areas within the region. Geologically the north of Hampshire belongs to the London Basin with its Tertiary sands, clays and gravels; whilst the eastern corner of the county consists of Wealden clays and greensands. These two geologically distinct areas are separated by a narrow ridge of chalk which extends eastwards from Hampshire to form the Hog's Back in Surrey.

Despite being one of the more densely populated and built-up areas of the region, Northeast Hampshire still retains many sites of ornithological interest. These can be broadly divided into those that are associated with heathland, woodland and forestry habitats and those that are essentially concerned with water-bodies.

The heathlands develop naturally on both the Tertiary sands and gravels of the London Basin and the greensands of the Weald. Like so many other areas of heathland in the region, there has been a considerable decline in this unique habitat over the past 150 years or so. This has been mainly due to afforestation, reclamation for farming and building development. The continuing presence of the Ministry of Defence, notably in the Aldershot and Bordon areas, is of particular significance since it controls a substantial proportion of the heathlands for training purposes. As such, these areas will enjoy a certain degree of protection for the foreseeable future.

The water bodies can be divided into two groups. First, there are the mature ornamental lakes that form an integral part of many large parks and country estates. The second group involves more recently developed pits which are associated with the extraction of gravel, particularly along the Blackwater Valley.

Ornithologically, Northeast Hampshire has been rather overlooked in the past. This state of affairs was not properly rectified until the early 1970s when the activities of an enthusiastic group of local birdwatchers resulted in the publication of the Hants/Surrey Border Bird Report. These reports, which have subsequently appeared annually, form the basis of J.M. Clark's excellent book – *Birds of the Hants/Surrey Border* – a must for anyone who has an interest in the area's birds.

Species

The heaths and forests of Northeast Hampshire support important breeding populations of many specialities closely associated with these habitats.

Little Ringed Plover

These include Hobby, Nightjar, Woodlark, Tree Pipit, Stonechat and Dartford Warbler; whilst Firecrest, Siskin and Crossbill have all bred sporadically in recent years. A rich assemblage of birds, including Woodcock, Lesser Spotted Woodpecker, Nightingale, Redstart, Wood Warbler, Willow Tit and Redpoll inhabit the broadleaved woodlands. The areas of heath and forestry are also very important for other forms of wildlife, notably dragonflies and rare reptiles – the smooth snake and sand lizard.

The Little Ringed Plover breeds more widely in Northeast Hampshire than anywhere else in the region. This species is very much associated with the flooded gravel pits along the Blackwater Valley. In addition, these pits and the more established lakes hold breeding waterfowl such as Little and Great Crested Grebes, Canada Goose and Tufted Duck.

The flooded gravel pits and lakes also provide haunts for a wide variety of wintering wildfowl including a regular flock of Goosander. They also attract small numbers of migrant waders and terns in spring and autumn. The potential of the area for interesting birdwatching is shown by the number of unusual species and rarities that have appeared in recent years, notably at Fleet Pond.

75 FLEET POND LNR (HART DISTRICT COUNCIL)

OS Map 186
SY85

Habitat

Fleet Pond is a large lake fringed by extensive reedbeds and patches of willow scrub. Birch and oak woodland, gardens and Fleet Station car park border the east, west and north shores respectively. There are also some small areas of dry heath and birch scrub present in the immediate environs of the lake. In recognition of its value to local wildlife, Fleet Pond has been designated a Local Nature Reserve by Hart District Council.

Species

Although this is an important site for breeding and wintering birds, Fleet Pond is perhaps best known for the rare and unusual species that have been seen here, mainly at times of passage. This is well exemplified by sightings of Little Egret, Blue-winged Teal, Black Kite, Collared Pratincole, Hoopoe, a superb male Citrine Wagtail and no fewer than three Great Reed Warblers in spring; Hoopoe and Golden Oriole in summer; Little Bittern, Little Egret, Ferruginous Duck, Spotted Crake, Grey Phalarope, Long-tailed Skua, Sabine's Gull, White-winged Black Tern, Yellow-browed Warbler and Serin in autumn; and Ring-necked Duck in winter. There are several reports of migrant Honey Buzzards (mainly autumn), Marsh Harriers (mainly spring) and Ospreys. Garganey are uncommon migrants, but they have been observed here more often than anywhere else in Northeast Hampshire. Although the Common Sandpiper is the only wader regularly seen on passage, a wide variety of other species have been recorded. Little Ringed and Ringed Plovers,

White-winged Black Terns

Dunlin, Whimbrel, Curlew, Greenshank and Green Sandpiper are the most likely species to occur. Common and Black Terns appear most years and noteworthy movements of both species have been witnessed. Little Gull, Kittiwake, Sandwich, Arctic and Little Terns are infrequent visitors; whilst there are several reports of overflying Arctic Skuas in autumn. The main feature of landbird migration is the visual passage of hirundines, pipits and finches – mainly during September and October. Amongst the finches, there is often a strong movement of Siskins and Redpolls; whilst smaller numbers of Bramblings regularly occur. A small visual passage of presumably local-bred Woodlarks also takes place, mainly during October. There is a scattering of other, predominantly nocturnal landbird migrants in spring and autumn, which includes the occasional scarcer species such as Ring Ouzel, Firecrest and Pied Flycatcher.

During the breeding season Fleet Pond supports a variety of waterfowl including Great Crested Grebe, Canada Goose, Mandarin, Pochard and Tufted Duck. The extensive reedbeds hold such typical species as Water Rail, Sedge and Reed Warblers and Reed Bunting; whilst both Kingfisher and Grey Wagtail breed locally and may visit the lake from the time to time. The adjacent areas of heath and woodland are inhabited by Woodcock, Lesser Spotted Woodpecker, Tree Pipit and possibly Redpoll. There are also sporadic reports of Wood Warblers and Crossbills during the breeding season. The Hobby is a frequent visitor during the summer and autumn. Both Cormorants and Grey Herons can be seen throughout the year.

The winter speciality of the site is the Bittern. Although elusive and never easy to see, one or two birds are recorded most years and sometimes over-winter. Small numbers of Bearded Tits used to occur regularly in the late autumn and winter, but recently they have become much scarcer.

Although Fleet Pond attracts a greater variety of waterfowl during the winter, only Great Crested Grebe, Cormorant, Canada Goose, Mandarin, Gadwall, Teal, Shoveler, Pochard and Tufted Duck can be expected. Most of the other likely species of wildfowl are sporadic in occurrence. Some like Shelduck and Pintail have been recorded here more frequently than at other waters in the area; whilst visits by Wigeon, Goldeneye, Smew and Goosander are usually associated with periods of cold weather. The numbers of Water Rails skulking in the reedbeds increase in winter. Snipe and perhaps the occasional Jack Snipe inhabit the marshy areas and gulls, mostly Black-headed and Common, gather on the lake during the afternoon. Large flocks of Siskins and Redpolls are a major feature of the nearby woodlands with counts well in excess of 100 regularly reported; whilst there is a substantial reedbed roost of Reed Buntings.

Timing

Although timing is not critical, Fleet Pond is popular with local walkers so early morning visits may be advisable. Cold winter weather often brings interesting birds to the lake, particularly if the water remains unfrozen.

Access

The most convenient access points to the footpaths around Fleet Pond are from the long-stay car park* at Fleet Station and the ends of Chestnut Grove and Westover Road. These roads are situated to the north of Avondale Road which can be reached from the B3013 0.3 miles (0.5 km) south of Fleet Station. Westover Road can also be approached north from Kings Road which lies between the A323 and B3013 roads in Fleet. The best viewing points are Fleet Station car park, the promontory at the end of Chestnut Grove and Sandy Bay.

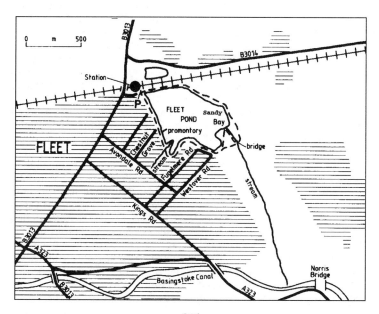

Calendar

All Year: Great Crested Grebe, Cormorant, Grey Heron, Canada Goose, Mandarin, Pochard, Tufted Duck, Water Rail, Woodcock, Kingfisher, Lesser Spotted Woodpecker, Grey Wagtail, Redpoll, Reed Bunting, common resident woodland birds.

Winter (mid-November–mid-March): near annual Bittern; wildfowl including Gadwall, Teal, Shoveler and occasional other species including cold-weather Wigeon, Goldeneye, Smew and Goosander; Snipe and occasional Jack Snipe; gulls; occasional Bearded Tit; Siskin.

Summer (mid-May–mid-July): Hobby, Tree Pipit, Sedge and Reed Warblers, occasional Wood Warbler and Crossbill.

Spring (mid-March–mid-May) *and Autumn* (mid-July–mid-November): occasional Garganey; migrant waders including Common Sandpiper and occasional other species; occasional Little Gull and Kittiwake; terns including Common, Black, occasional Sandwich and Little; landbird migrants including visual passage of hirundines, pipits and finches in autumn, occasional scarcer species like Woodlark, Firecrest and Pied Flycatcher.

Most likely oddities: rare wildfowl, Marsh Harrier, Osprey, storm-blown seabird.

76 STRATFIELD SAYE PARK AND WELLINGTON COUNTRY PARK

OS Map 186
SU66/76

Habitat and Species

Stratfield Saye Park is a large estate consisting mainly of parkland and woods which is situated about midway between Basingstoke and Reading. The River Loddon flows through the park and feeds a number of lakes and ponds, the most notable being located by the northern boundary. The main feature of nearby Wellington Country Park is a large flooded gravel pit set in landscaped grounds; whilst the remainder of the park supports an attractive mixture of broadleaved woodland and forestry.

Although most of the waterfowl generally favour Stratfield Saye Park, there is a regular interchange of birds between the two sites. The main attraction used to be the wintering flock of Goosander, but since the late 1980s this population has transferred to nearby Eversley and Yateley Gravel Pits. The species is now only an occasional visitor. Nevertheless a good selection of waterfowl including Great Crested Grebe, Cormorant, Wigeon, Gadwall, Teal, Shoveler, Pochard and Tufted Duck can be seen in winter. Periods of cold weather may produce more unusual wildfowl such as White-fronted Goose, Pintail and Smew. In winter Snipe and occasionally other species of wader may be found in suitable areas; whilst flocks of Black-headed and Common Gulls gather at Wellington Country Park during the afternoons. Flocks of Siskins and Redpolls often inhabit the birch and alder woods.

Stratfield Saye Park supports large feral populations of Greylag, Snow, Canada and Barnacle Geese; whilst Egyptian Geese sometimes appear, presumably wanderers from a small population nearby in Berkshire. The area also holds breeding Little and Great Crested Grebes and Tufted Duck. Unfortunately Mandarin have now virtually disappeared, possibly due to a drop in water level on the preferred lake in Stratfield Saye Park following damage to a weir during the Great Storm of October 1987. A few Shelduck are recorded most springs with breeding taking place in 1991. Sedge Warblers and Reed Buntings breed in patches of reed-swamp; whilst Kingfishers and Grey Wagtails nest beside the River Loddon. The woodlands support a wide range of breeding birds including Woodcock and Lesser Spotted Woodpecker. Singing Wood Warblers have also been noted at Wellington Country Park in summer. Migrant waders and terns occasionally pass through in spring and autumn. Amongst the more unusual birds seen at these sites, there are sightings of Bean Goose, Green-winged Teal, Garganey, Osprey, Peregrine, Mediterranean and Little Gulls and Yellow-browed Warbler.

Access

These sites are best approached from either the A33 Basingstoke to Reading road or the B3349 Hook to Riseley road.

The public entrance to Stratfield Saye Park* lies off the minor road to the west of the park at SU693619. The house and riverside area are open 11.30 am–4.00 pm daily (except Fridays) between 1 May and the last Sunday in September. In winter, the lake by the northern boundary can be partially viewed at SU705629 on the minor road signposted to Beech Hill 0.7 miles (1.1 km) west of the A33 roundabout. The River Loddon, fishing ponds and parkland fields (good for grazing geese) can also be seen from the roadbridge at SU692611 and the footpath south at SU693610 (by the entrance to Broadford Fly Fishers) on the minor road between the A33 by the Wellington Arms Hotel and Stratfield Saye.

The entrance to Wellington Country Park lies off the B3349 roundabout just south of Riseley at SU724628. The Country Park is open daily March to October from 10.00 am–5.30 pm, but weekends only November to February from 10.00 am–3.30 pm.

77 WARREN HEATH AND BRAMSHILL PLANTATION (FC) OS Map 186 SU75/76

Habitat and Species

Warren Heath and Bramshill Plantation form a huge area of mainly coniferous forestry which extends from the A30 road near Hartfordbridge northwest to Bramshill and beyond to the Blackwater River. Gravel extraction is a major feature of these plantations. This has left series of shallow pools and ponds set in large clearings within the forest. Although there are still small areas of bare gravel, notably where extraction is still proceeding, most of the forest clearings have been replanted with conifer seedlings and colonised by invasive birch scrub.

These habitats support a wide range of breeding birds; the main speciality being the Woodlark. This species favours the large forest clearings and young forestry plantations which also hold Nightjar, Tree Pipit, Stonechat and perhaps the odd pair of Dartford Warbler; whilst the Reed Bunting can be found in the damper areas. Turtle Dove, Garden Warbler and a few pairs of Redpoll frequent the more extensive birch thickets. The few patches of more open mature mixed woodland support a small population of Redstarts with birds often singing from horse chestnut trees. Siskins are now well established in the forest areas where Crossbills occur from time to time, usually during and immediately after their periodic invasions. Woodcock are a regular sight as they display over the clearings and neighbouring forest during spring and summer evenings. The forest pools and ponds attract a few waterfowl which may include Canada Goose, Mandarin and Tufted Duck; whilst the Grey Heron is a frequent visitor. Lapwings and perhaps Little Ringed Plovers may still attempt to nest on any remaining areas of bare gravel. It is worth looking out for the occasional Buzzard and Hobby flying overhead.

In winter the pools and ponds hold small numbers of wildfowl; mainly Teal, Pochard and Tufted Duck, but occasionally other species including Wigeon, Shoveler and Goosander. A few Snipe inhabit the damper areas; whilst there is always an outside chance of flushing a Jack Snipe from the young forestry plantations. Flocks of Siskins and Redpolls occur in suitable habitat throughout the forest and there are at least two reports of Great Grey Shrikes from the area.

In spring and autumn the shallow pools and ponds attract a few passage waders; Green and Common Sandpipers being the most likely species to be seen. There is also a trickle of landbird migrants which regularly include small numbers of Wheatear. There is also a recent spring report of Ring Ouzel from Bramshill Plantation.

Access

This area is best approached from the small car park at SU760613, which is next to St Neot's Playing Fields and opposite Bramshill Tip, on the minor road between the B3011 at Heckfield Place (SU732608) and the A327 at Eversley Centre (SU782616).

There is access to Warren Heath southeast along the footpath between Bramshill Tip at SU760613 and the entrance to Bramshill Quarry (Hall Aggregates) at SU785596 on the road between Eversley and the B3016.

To gain access to Bramshill Plantation (also known as Bramshill Forest and Bramshill Common Wood) take the footpath from the small car park at SU760613 and follow the line of the pylons north. This footpath eventually meets another footpath that runs from New Mill, Lower Common at SU762628 southwest into Bramshill Plantation. At the junction of these two footpaths (SU761626), follow the new footpath southwest and various tracks to the west give access across the plantation. Alternatively, access can be gained from the minor road (Ford Lane) along the west side of Bramshill Plantation, by following the footpath opposite Yew Tree Cottage at SU745617. Please note that the Forestry Commission signs for

Bramshill Forest and Bramshill Common Wood refer to 'Reserved Rights' and ask visitors 'Please Keep to the Rights of Way'.

78 EVERSLEY AND YATELEY GRAVEL PITS

OS Map 186
SU86

Habitat and Species

These are a series of flooded gravel pits of varying ages and maturity which extend along either side of the Blackwater River from Eversley Cross in the west to Darby Green in the east. Although some of the Yateley Pits are over 50 years old, excavation of the Eversley Pits commenced in the 1970s with work still continuing at one pit. All but the most recently excavated lakes are bordered wholly or in part by secondary deciduous woodland and scrub, notably willow, alder and silver birch. Within some of the lakes, there are gravel-capped islands, gravel beaches and muddy margins. Other habitats in the general vicinity include large areas of scrub and bramble, wildflower meadows, a number of mature trees – mainly oak, alder and elm, stretches of hedgerow and arable farmland. In 1993 Hall Aggregates (South East) Limited formed a local group to monitor and manage an area of 90 acres (36 ha) to the north of the river as a nature reserve. This area is known as Moor Green Lakes.

The site is best known for its wintering population of Goosander which is the only regular flock within the region covered by this book. As the pits have matured since the late 1970s, so the numbers of Goosander have increased. Prior to 1988, the site was mainly used as a daytime feeding area with most birds returning to Wellington Country Park or Stratfield Saye at dusk to roost. Since then Eversley Gravel Pits have become the main roost site for the Northeast Hampshire flock. During the winter of 1993/94, there was a dramatic rise in the number of birds coming to roost, although the numbers of the daytime population only showed a modest increase. The maximum roost count was 79 in February 1994.

The lake complex also holds a large population of Gadwall; whilst numbers of Wigeon have risen sharply in recent years. A wide variety of other waterfowl including Little and Great Crested Grebes, Cormorant, feral Snow, Canada and Barnacle Geese, Teal, Shoveler, Pochard, Tufted Duck and Goldeneye regularly frequent these lakes in winter. Other species of wildfowl including Smew and Ruddy Duck occasionally appear, notably during periods of cold weather. Snipe and perhaps the odd Jack Snipe, which favour areas of flooded *Juncus*, can also be seen; whilst large numbers of gulls gather on the pits during the afternoons. The alder thickets attract wandering flocks of Siskins and Redpolls.

The more recently excavated pits provide nesting sites for such notable species as Little Ringed and Ringed Plovers, Redshank and Common Tern. The lake complex as a whole supports a good selection of breeding

Great Crested Grebe and young

waterfowl including Little and Great Crested Grebes, feral Snow, Canada and Barnacle Geese, Tufted Duck and perhaps Mandarin; whilst Gadwall usually remain well into the spring and early summer. Sedge and Reed Warblers and Reed Buntings inhabit patches of marshy vegetation beside the lakes and Blackwater River, which is also the haunt of Kingfishers and Grey Wagtails. The large population of dragonflies regularly attracts feeding Hobbies, particularly in the late summer. Lesser Spotted Woodpecker, Lesser Whitethroat and Garden Warbler may be found amongst the commoner inhabitants of the scrub and woodland areas.

Spring and autumn produces a small passage of waders. Green and Common Sandpipers are regularly seen in both seasons; whilst there are frequent sightings of Dunlin, Whimbrel and Greenshank, particularly in spring. There have also been reports of Oystercatcher, Grey Plover, Knot, Sanderling, Little Stint, Ruff, both godwits, Curlew, Spotted Redshank, Wood Sandpiper and Turnstone. In addition to the local breeding birds, small numbers of Common Tern occur on passage along with a few Black Terns and the occasional Little Gull and Arctic Tern. There is a scattering of the commoner landbird migrants including Yellow Wagtail, Whinchat and Wheatear. It is not surprising that a number of rarer birds have been recorded at this site, mainly but not exclusively at times of passage. The most notable of these oddities are Ferruginous Duck, Honey Buzzard, Osprey, Avocet, Kentish Plover, Temminck's Stint, Glaucous and Sabine's Gulls, Hoopoe, Bluethroat, Golden Oriole and Great Grey Shrike.

Access

The more recently excavated of the Eversley Gravel Pits, including Moor Green Lakes NR, are best approached from Lower Sandhurst Road which lies east off the B3016 in Finchampstead. From the well signposted car park at SU805628 take the footpath south towards the hide and beyond to the Blackwater River at SU807622. From here footpaths run along the north bank of the river to Mill Lane at SU819619; and across the river south to Moulsham Copse Lane at SU807615, which lies north off the A327 in Yateley Green. Most of the pits can be viewed from these footpaths. There is also public access to the hide. For more information on the Moor Green Lakes Nature Reserve contact the Moor Green Lakes Group, Blackwater Valley Visitor Centre (tel: 01276 686615).

The older and less interesting Yateley Pits can be reached along Sandhurst and Yateley Roads between Yateley and Sandhurst; the best access points being Trilakes Water Park* at SU825615 and the footpath southwest from SU825613.

79 YATELEY COMMON COUNTRY PARK (HCC)

Habitat and Species

Yateley Common is the largest area (450 acres) of common land extant in this northeast corner of Hampshire and offers an interesting mixture of habitats including heathland, birch and oak woodland and several small ponds. The common is bisected by the main A30 road; the northern part being managed as a Country Park by Hampshire County Council and the southern part remaining under the control of the MOD. Much of the area enjoys protection as an SSSI.

This is a good site for breeding birds including such heathland specialities as Nightjar, Tree Pipit, Stonechat and Dartford Warbler. The habitat also looks suitable for Woodlarks. Reed Buntings frequent in the damper areas; whilst the birch thickets are favoured by Redpolls. The more mature woodlands support a wide range of species including Woodcock, Lesser Spotted Woodpecker and Redstart. There is always the chance of seeing a Hobby passing overhead during the summer; whilst winter may bring flocks of Siskins and Redpolls to feed in the birches.

Access

Yateley Common Country Park can be reached from the A30/B3013 roundabout either north along Cricket Hill Road towards Yateley or east along the A30 towards Blackwater. There are car parks at Wyndhams Pond – off Cricket Hill Road at SU821598 (obscure entrance by the telephone box), and at Strouds Pond and Gravel Pit – both off the eastbound carriageway of the A30 at SU833592 and SU839594 respectively.

The southern part of Yateley Common is best approached from the A30/A327 roundabout in Blackwater by taking the minor road south towards a new housing estate at Woodside. At the small roundabout take the MOD road for 0.2 miles (0.3 km) southwest to a parking area just before the MOD red signs at SU844593.

Numerous tracks and footpaths give easy access to both parts of Yateley Common.

80 GREYWELL AND WARNBOROUGH GREEN

Habitat and Species

There are a number of interesting sites, namely the Basingstoke Canal, Greywell Moors, Warnborough Green, Bartley Heath and Butter Wood in the general vicinity of Greywell and Warnborough Green. These sites offer a variety of habitats including the canal and associated marginal vegetation, wooded fen bordering the reed-fringed spring source of the River Whitewater, unimproved flower-rich meadows, birch scrub and woodland.

Although these sites are perhaps better known for their flora and insect (notably butterflies and dragonflies) fauna, a good selection of birds can be expected. An abundance of breeding waterfowl including Little Grebe, Tufted Duck, Moorhen and Coot frequent the Basingstoke Canal and River Whitewater. The Little Grebes are particularly confiding and provide excellent views of what can often be a rather secretive species. Both Kingfisher and Grey Wagtail can be found along the canal and river; whilst the adjacent reedswamps hold Water Rail, Sedge and Reed Warblers and Reed Bunting. Snipe used to breed in the area and attempts are being made to attract the species back. The birch scrub and mature woodland support a wide range of birds including Woodcock, Turtle Dove, Lesser Spotted Woodpecker, Tree Pipit, Garden Warbler, Willow Tit and Redpoll. Winter may bring a few extra wildfowl including Gadwall and Teal to the quiet reed-fringed waters of the River Whitewater. There is an increase in the numbers of Water Rails frequenting the reedswamps; whilst Snipe inhabit the marshy areas. The nearby alders attract flocks of foraging Siskins and there is a large winter roost of Reed Buntings.

Access

Generally the area is best approached from the village of Greywell where there is limited car parking along Deptford Lane at SU722512 (just to the east of the bridge over the River Whitewater and opposite the waterworks).

The best access points to the various sites are:

Greywell Moors: follow the footpath from the car parking area south through the nature reserve to the style at SU717502. Just beyond the stile follow the footpath north through the wood and along the east bank of the River Whitewater to the old mill. The footpath continues northeast along the river, through the churchyard and field beyond, before turning east and crossing the river again to meet the original footpath not far from the reserve entrance.

Basingstoke Canal: take the footpath from Deptford Lane at SU719514 (obscure entrance on the right just before the T-junction) to the canal towpath and continue northeast to Odiham Castle and beyond.

Warnborough Green: follow the footpath from the nature reserve entrance at SU728519 (just south of the ford) east through the meadow to the B3349.

Butter Wood: from the minor road between the A287 and Greywell, follow the footpaths either west at SU724525 (limited car parking on the old road) or northwest at SU719517.

Bartley Heath: from the end of the 'no-through' road in Bartley Heath at SU730527, follow the footpath northwest and then northeast through the woods to the motorway footbridge at SU733532. From here continue across the footbridge into the northern section of Bartley Heath.

81 DOGMERSFIELD LAKE AND TUNDRY POND

Habitat and Species

These two lakes lie in close proximity to each other in the grounds of Dogmersfield Great Park. Attractive woodland surrounds much of Dogmersfield Lake; whilst Tundry Pond is set in open parkland with scattered trees.

In winter these waters support a variety of waterfowl including Great Crested Grebe, Teal, Pochard and Tufted Duck. Cormorant, Gadwall and Shoveler are also usually present, but other species such as Wigeon, Goldeneye and Goosander are occasional visitors. The local population of Canada Geese are sometimes joined by feral Greylag, Snow and Barnacle Geese. A few Snipe skulk along the marshy fringes of the lakes. Breeding waterfowl include Little and Great Crested Grebes, Canada Goose and Tufted Duck. The odd pair of Reed Buntings nest around the lakes and both Kingfishers and Grey Wagtails can be seen along the nearby Basingstoke Canal. The woods hold a wide selection of breeding birds including Woodcock, Lesser Spotted Woodpecker, Garden Warbler and Willow Tit; whilst Hobbies can sometimes be seen hunting over the lakes for dragonflies. The occasional wader and tern may appear on migration; the most likely species being Common Sandpiper and Common Tern. Oddities seen in recent years include Black-necked Grebe, Little Egret, Red-crested Pochard, Ring-necked and Ferruginous Ducks.

Access

Both sites are best approached from the large lay-by at SU757512 on the A287 0.3 miles (0.5 km) east of the Odiham roundabout. From the lay-by walk west a short distance to North Lodge at SU756512 and follow the footpath northeast to view Dogmersfield Lake at SU761515. For Tundry Pond continue northeast on the track and, approximately 500 yards beyond the obvious black barn, follow the footpath across the field towards the bridge at the west end of the lake at SU772525. From here the footpath runs along the south shore of Tundry Pond and eventually reaches the footbridge over the Basingstoke Canal at SU776523. Tundry Pond can also be reached along the Basingstoke Canal towpath at SU777523. Although the closest access point to the towpath is the road-bridge at SU778520 on Chalky Lane (between the A287 and Dogmersfield Village), car parking is very difficult here. It is best to park either at Winchfield Hurst (SU778538) and follow the towpath south or park at Crookham Wharf (SU792518) and follow the towpath west.

82 ALICE HOLT FOREST (FC)

OS Map 186
SU73/74/83/84

Habitat and Species

Alice Holt Forest offers an attractive mixture of broadleaved woodland and forestry. The area is managed by the Forestry Commission, who have a major research station at Alice Holt Lodge. In addition to the birds, butterflies are well represented in this area, Straits Inclosure being particularly favoured.

A wide range of breeding birds including Woodcock, Turtle Dove, Nightjar, Lesser Spotted Woodpecker, Tree Pipit, Garden and Wood Warblers, Willow Tit, Siskin and Redpoll inhabit these woodlands and forests. Mandarin and Firecrest have also been recorded during the breeding season; whilst Crossbills are occasionally seen in the forestry areas. The Grey Heron is a frequent visitor to the woodland pools and streams.

Winter is generally a quiet season for birds, but flocks of Siskins and Redpolls may be encountered wandering through the woodlands.

Access

Alice Holt Forest is bisected by the A325 Petersfield to Farnham road. The Visitor Centre at Alice Holt Woodland Park can be reached from Bucks Horn Oak, by taking the minor road southeast for 0.2 miles (0.3 km) and then turning east into the access road leading to the car park at SU811415. There are also car parks at Abbots Wood Inclosure at SU811411, Goose Green Inclosure at SU804416 and Lodge Inclosure at SU803434. Well marked forest walks and footpaths give access to all the main woodland inclosures. For security reasons the car parks are closed from dusk to 8 am.

83 LUDSHOTT COMMON AND WAGGONER'S WELLS (NT)

OS Map 186
SU83

Habitat and Species

Although recovering from the effects of a devastating fire in 1980, Ludshott Common still offers some of the finest heathland habitat to be found in east Hampshire. Nearby, in a steep-sided valley, lies Waggoner's Wells. The main feature of this site is a series of small ponds which were constructed in the 17th century either as part of an iron foundry or to keep fish. These ponds are drained by the headwaters of the River Wey and surrounded by superb woodlands of mainly oak, beech and Scots pine.

Ludshott Common is an important site for breeding heathland birds including Nightjar, Woodlark, Tree Pipit, Stonechat and Dartford Warbler. Redpolls frequent the birch thickets; whilst Reed Buntings inhabit the wetter areas of the common. Hobbies are sometimes seen overhead during the summer. Both Hen Harrier and Great Grey Shrike have appeared here in winter when flocks of Siskins and Redpolls occur widely in the birch woodlands.

Redstart

Waggoner's Wells supports a wide range of woodland birds including Woodcock, Green and Great Spotted Woodpeckers, Marsh Tit, Nuthatch and Treecreeper. Small numbers of Redstarts and Wood Warblers also breed in these woods. Kingfishers and Grey Wagtails occur beside the River Wey; whilst Mandarin nest or attempt to do so most years and Tufted Duck often summer on the ponds.

Access

Ludshott Common can be reached along footpaths either northwest from Waggoner's Wells (see below); or from various points along the B3002 (Headley Road) between Grayshott and Headley Down notably (i) west from the junction with Waggoner's Wells Lane at SU862353, (ii) southwest from the National Trust car park at SU856358 and (iii) south by the 'Headley Down' sign at SU847361.

Waggoner's Wells is well signposted along Waggoner's Wells Lane south from the B3002 (Headley Road) at SU862353.

THE ISLE OF WIGHT

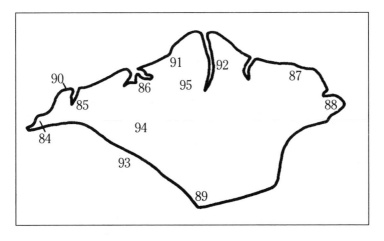

84 THE NEEDLES HEADLAND, ALUM
    BAY AND HEADON WARREN
85 YAR ESTUARY
86 NEWTOWN ESTUARY NNR
87 THE RYDE AREA
88 THE BEMBRIDGE AREA
89 ST CATHERINE'S POINT

90 Fort Victoria
91 Thorness Bay
92 River Medina
93 Brighstone, Atherfield and
    the Military Road
94 Brighstone Forest
95 Parkhurst Forest

General Introduction

In many respects the Isle of Wight offers a microcosm of the habitats that exist on the nearby mainland. A long ridge of chalk downland forms the backbone of the Island. Where this ridge meets the sea, some of the finest and most spectacular coastal scenery in the region can be found. Estuarine and wetland habitats are provided by the Western Yar, Newtown Estuary, River Medina, Wootton Creek, Eastern Yar, Brading Marsh and Bembridge Harbour. There are several large areas of woodland and forestry, mostly in the north and east of the Island. Perhaps the main differences from the mainland are the scarcity of heathland and the absence of large lakes. The most important features of the Island's varied birdlife are the breeding colonies of seabirds; seabird passage and landbird migration; and wintering waterfowl, waders and gulls.

84 THE NEEDLES HEADLAND, ALUM BAY AND HEADON WARREN (NT)

OS Maps 196 &
Isle of Wight
SZ28/38

Habitat

The Needles Headland (including Tennyson and West High Downs), Alum Bay and Headon Warren are prominent features of the landscape at the western tip of the Isle of Wight. A varied geology and topography has produced a diversity of habitats. To the south the high ridge of the Tennyson and West High Downs dominates the scene with spectacular chalk cliffs extending along the seaward side from Freshwater Bay west to the Needles. Although most of the ridge is covered by downland sward, extensive thickets of chalk scrub cloak the landward slope of Tennyson Down. To the north the high ground of Headon Warren offers a very different geology of Tertiary rocks. The flat top of the hill supports heathland and gorse; whilst the seaward slopes, which due to landslips present an irregular relief, are densely vegetated by scrub and damp thickets of willow. The narrow beaches of the northern coastline are backed by crumbling cliffs. These are highest at Alum Bay where they form the famous multicoloured sand cliffs. Behind Alum Bay, a valley consisting mainly of farmland extends inland between the ridges of high land.

A number of other habitats, which can be very attractive to landbird migrants, are present in this area. The most notable of these are the sycamore wood that lies either side of Alum Bay Chine, the trees and scrub immediately behind Alum Bay Tea Rooms and the wood around the Clock Museum. Further interest is provided by the gardens behind Alum Bay and near the junction of the B3322 and Alum Bay Old Road.

The outstanding natural beauty of the area enjoys the protection of the National Trust. In addition to the birds, this area also supports a rich flora and insect fauna; chalk flowers and butterflies being well represented.

Species

This area's commanding position, overlooking the western approaches to the Solent, gives it great potential for attracting migrant birds. Furthermore, the high chalk cliffs still support some colonies of breeding seabirds.

In spring a good selection of landbird migrants including Tree Pipit, Yellow Wagtail, Redstart, Whinchat, Wheatear, the commoner warblers and Spotted Flycatcher, pass through. The area is a favoured site for such scarce species as Black Redstart and Ring Ouzel which regularly appear in very small numbers – usually from mid-March through to early May. Other scarce migrants such as Wood Warbler and Pied Flycatcher occur most years from mid-April onwards, but the Firecrest is only occasionally reported during this season. The Hoopoe is the most likely subrarity to be encountered with several reports from this area; whilst Wryneck, Red-backed Shrike and Ortolan Bunting have also been seen. There are also spring sightings of such rarities as Black Kite, Alpine Swift, Red-rumped Swallow and most notably Alpine Accentor.

Due to the height of the cliffs, there are no suitable vantage points for seawatching, which is better undertaken from either Fort Victoria on the Solent shore or St Catherine's Point to the south. There is, however, always the chance of observing the occasional seabird passing the Needles.

Fulmar

In spring and summer the chalk cliffs provide nesting sites for small numbers of seabirds including Fulmar, Cormorant, Shag, Herring and Great Black-backed Gulls and Guillemot. Unfortunately Kittiwake, Razorbill and Puffin no longer breed along these cliffs. On the credit side, however, both Peregrine and Raven are now well-established in the area. Rock Pipits nest along the cliff-tops and at least one pair of Wheatears have held territory in most recent years; whilst the scrubby areas now support a few pairs of breeding Stonechats and Dartford Warblers. Summer fishing flocks of Gannets sometimes gather off the Needles.

The autumn passage of landbirds is more pronounced than during the spring and involves the same variety of commoner species. Several scarcer migrants also regularly appear in small numbers. These include Pied Flycatchers which mainly pass through in August and September, Ring Ouzels and Firecrests which occur from mid-September through to early November and Black Redstarts which usually arrive from early October onwards. Like the spring, the area is particularly favoured by passage Ring Ouzels which in some autumns may reach daily counts of ten to 20 birds. Visual migration is often conspicuous. Huge movements of hirundines have been witnessed during September; whilst the late autumn sees the overhead passage of Skylarks, Meadow Pipits and finches. The latter sometimes includes such species as Brambling, Siskin and Redpoll. An impressive variety of landbird subrarities have been seen in this area. The Yellow-browed Warbler is now virtually an annual visitor in October and November; whilst there are records of Wryneck, Tawny Pipit, Bluethroat, Icterine, Melodious, Barred and Pallas's Warblers, Golden Oriole, Red-backed and Great Grey Shrikes, Lapland and Ortolan Buntings. A Baird's Sandpiper took up residence on the Needles Headland for a few days in September 1988.

Migrant raptors include the occasional Hen Harrier, Merlin, Hobby and Short-eared Owl; whilst there are autumn reports of Honey Buzzard, Marsh Harrier and Osprey. West High Down is a favoured site for migrant

Dotterel which may occur more often than records suggest. Although autumn seawatching is generally rather poor, tern flocks and accompanying skuas can be observed off the Needles in strong southwesterlies. Severe gales in autumn and winter may also force seabirds to seek shelter in Freshwater Bay. These may include the occasional Grey Phalarope; whilst such noteworthy species as Leach's Petrel, Sabine's Gull and Little Auk have also been recorded from here during such conditions.

Relatively little is known about the winter birds of this area. Black Redstarts are occasionally seen, often in the vicinity of Freshwater Bay; whilst in mild winters there is always the chance of the odd Blackcap, Chiffchaff and possibly Firecrest. Since the late 1980s the Purple Sandpiper flock appears to have deserted its regular site in Freshwater Bay with very few reports in recent years. The occasional diver, grebe and sea-duck may be seen offshore.

Timing

Landbird migrants are best looked for when fall conditions prevail. Early morning visits are also recommended to avoid disturbance from holidaymakers, particularly in August and September.

Strong southwesterlies in autumn may induce some offshore movements of seabirds. It is also well worth checking Freshwater Bay for storm-blown seabirds during and after severe westerly gales in late autumn and winter.

Access

This area is reached by taking the B3322 southwest from the junction of the A3054 and A3055 roads in Freshwater. There is a large car park* at Alum Bay.

West High and Tennyson Downs: access to this high ridge of downland can be gained from a number of footpaths, notably (i) from Alum Bay – south and west along the Needles Old Battery road to the Coastguard Cottages, and then climb up the slope to West High Down; (ii) from the B3322 just to east of the Clock Museum and by the sign to Warren Farm – south past the gardens to the base of the ridge and then climb east up the slope to Tennyson Down; (iii) from the Old Beacon at the west end of Tennyson Down – east along the bottom of the ridge to Nodewell Pits, which can also be reached south from Alum Bay Old Road at the High Down Inn, and then either continue east to Freshwater Bay or climb up the steep slope to Tennyson's Monument; and (iv) from Freshwater Bay – follow the main coastal path southwest to Fort Redoubt and then west along the entire length of the ridge to Tennyson's Monument, West High Down and then the Needles.

Warning: great caution should be exercised near the unfenced edges of the cliff-top.

Alum Bay: the Tea Rooms (Headon Hall) are well signposted along the minor road northwest from the B3322 just before reaching Alum Bay proper. From this access road, there is a footpath west through the sycamore wood down into Alum Bay Chine. Alum Bay itself can be explored from the main car park.

Headon Warren can be reached by several footpaths, notably northwest from the access road to Alum Bay Tea Rooms and northeast from the B3322 just west of the Clock Museum.

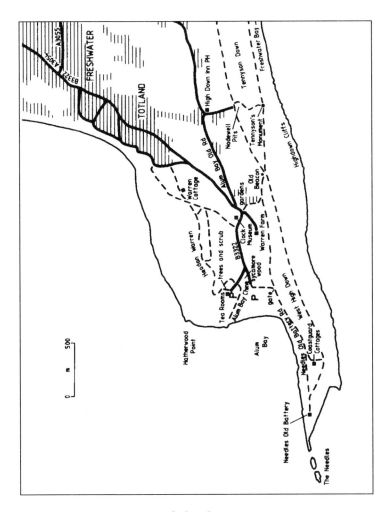

Calendar

All Year: Fulmar and occasional Gannet; Cormorant, Shag, Peregrine, Rock Pipit, Stonechat, Dartford Warbler, Raven.

Spring (mid-March–mid-May): possible offshore sea passage; breeding seabirds from mid-March – see Summer for species; landbird migrants including annual Black Redstart and Ring Ouzel, near annual Wood Warbler and Pied Flycatcher, and occasional Firecrest.
  Most likely oddities: Hoopoe and other landbird subrarity.

Summer (mid-May–mid-July): breeding seabirds including Great Black-backed Gull and Guillemot; occasional Wheatear.

Autumn (mid-July–mid-November): occasional offshore sea passage mainly involving skuas and terns; during/after gales – occasional storm-blown seabirds such as Leach's Petrel, Grey Phalarope, Sabine's Gull and Little Auk.

Migrant raptors including occasional Hen Harrier, Merlin and Hobby; occasional Short-eared Owl; landbird migrants including from early August Pied Flycatcher, from mid-September Ring Ouzel and Firecrest and from mid-October Black Redstart.

Most likely oddities: Dotterel, landbird subrarity.

Winter (mid-November–mid-March): occasional divers, grebes and sea-duck offshore; occasional Purple Sandpiper; occasional Black Redstart, Blackcap and Chiffchaff.

85 YAR ESTUARY

OS Map 196 &
Isle of Wight
SZ38

Habitat

The Western Yar forms one of the most attractive estuaries in the region, extending from the Freshwater Causeway north to the Solent shore at Yarmouth. *Spartina* saltmarshes interspersed by muddy creeks border the main channel; whilst reedbeds fringe the landward margins of the estuary. In the northeast corner of the area the Thorley Brook drains some low-lying marshy fields, which are prone to winter flooding, before flowing into the estuary by Yarmouth Mill. Upstream of some hatches by the Old Station, the Thorley Brook is ponded and bordered by some fine reedbeds. A little further south, another stream flows west through a small freshwater marsh to join the Yar Estuary. Damp woodland and scrub along both shores add further variety to the habitat.

The Western Yar rises very close to the southern shore of the Island near Freshwater Bay. The river then flows north through Afton Marsh, an area of willow swamp and reedbed, and eventually drains into the southern end of the Yar Estuary by the Freshwater Causeway.

Species

During the winter the Yar Estuary attracts a wide variety of waterfowl, waders and gulls. Flocks of Brent Geese and Wigeon are a familiar sight, frequenting the muddy creeks of the *Spartina* saltmarshes and the marshy fields bordering the estuary. Shelduck, Teal and small numbers of Shoveler can also be expected, but Gadwall and Pintail are scarce and erratic visitors. Wintering Little Grebes favour the more open waters of the Western Yar, which sometimes attract a few Goldeneye and Red-breasted Mergansers along with the occasional Great Crested and rarer winter grebe. Hard weather may bring Pochard, Tufted Duck and perhaps the likes of Scaup, Smew and Goosander to the area. At low tide most of the commoner waders including Grey Plover and Black-tailed Godwit can be found feeding on the exposed mud. Spotted Redshank frequently occur in winter, favouring the freshwater pools and marshes where Snipe are also found; whilst Bar-tailed Godwit, Greenshank and Green Sandpiper occasionally appear during this season. At high-water, Oystercatcher, Turnstone and sometimes Ringed Plover and Dunlin roost on the harbour breakwater and adjacent shingle beaches. Good

Wigeon

numbers of Black-headed and Herring Gulls are present along with a few Great Black-backed Gulls. Although the other species of gull are rather scarce, there have been several reports of Mediterranean Gulls in recent years. Cormorants and Grey Herons are non-breeding residents; whilst a few Little Egrets are usually present from early autumn through to spring. The local Peregrines along with the occasional Hen Harrier and Merlin visit the estuary in search of prey. Amongst the smaller birds of interest, Kingfishers regularly fish the waters of the estuary and nearby streams. Rock Pipits and Reed Buntings forage along the tideline; whilst the fresh-water pools, notably those near the Old Station, have attracted a few Water Pipits in recent winters.

Spring brings a general exodus of winter birds from the estuary. The departing waders are replaced by migrants which usually include a few Whimbrel, Spotted Redshank, Greenshank and Common Sandpiper. The Little Ringed Plover has been seen almost annually in recent years; whilst there are occasional sightings of other migrant waders such as Knot, Ruff and Green Sandpiper. Common and occasionally Little Terns visit the estuary throughout the spring and summer and there are a couple of recent reports of the delightful Garganey in spring. A scattering of landbird migrants, which usually include Nightingale, Redstart and Whinchat, frequent the scrub and woodland bordering the disused railway; whilst Yellow Wagtail, which sometimes occur in large numbers, and Wheatear prefer the more open areas. There is also an outside chance of finding a scarcer species such as Black Redstart, Ring Ouzel, Firecrest and Pied Flycatcher. Sedge and Reed Warblers sing from the reedbeds where they remain to nest alongside the resident Reed Buntings. Common and Lesser Whitethroats hold territory along the disused railway; whilst the woodlands support a good selection of the common-er birds including Green and Great Spotted Woodpeckers, Garden Warbler, Blackcap, Treecreeper and Jay. The estuary itself supports small breeding populations of Shelduck, Oystercatcher and Redshank; whilst Little Grebes have nested on Yarmouth Mill Pond and Afton Marsh. By July both passage and wintering waders have started to return to the estuary. During the next couple of months all of the commoner species occur together with small numbers of such migrants as Whimbrel, Greenshank and Common Sandpiper. Other passage waders including Ruff, Spotted Redshank and Green Sandpiper are infrequent visitors;

whilst there are recent autumn reports of Knot, Little Stint, Curlew and Wood Sandpipers. Landbird migrants including Yellow Wagtail, Redstart, Whinchat, Wheatear, the commoner warblers and Spotted Flycatcher also pass through in small numbers. Scarcer species such as Black Redstart, Firecrest and Pied Flycatcher are occasionally reported; whilst there have been three sightings of Bearded Tits in recent years.

The Yar Estuary area is not renowned for attracting scarce and rare species of bird. There is, however, a 1949 record of Black-winged Stilts; whilst more recently White Stork, Spoonbill, Red-crested Pochard, Marsh Harrier, Osprey, Grey Phalarope, Wryneck and Yellow-browed Warbler have been reported.

Timing

The estuary is best visited at low tide when the exposed mud attracts good numbers of feeding wildfowl, waders and gulls.

Early mornings are recommended to avoid any disturbance caused by walkers using the footpath along the disused railway.

Access

The Yar Estuary is the most accessible birdwatching site on the Isle of Wight to pedestrian visitors from the mainland.

The Yar Estuary can be reached from Yarmouth Harbour (the ferry), by following the A3054 (River Road) south and east past the car park*, and then taking Mill Road southeast to Yarmouth Mill. From here, continue on the footpath south along the seawall and disused railway to the Freshwater Causeway. This footpath provides excellent views over the estuary and marshes and passes through areas of scrub and woodland.

Thorley Brook: there is a footpath east from Yarmouth Mill along the disused railway to Thorley Bridge. This gives views over the reed-fringed ponded section of the stream and nearby fields.

Afton Marsh and Freshwater Bay are well signposted along footpaths west and south from the Freshwater Causeway.

Calendar

All Year: Cormorant, Little Egret, Grey Heron, Shelduck, Peregrine, Oystercatcher, Redshank, Reed Bunting, common resident woodland birds.

Winter (mid-November–mid-March): Little and occasional Great Crested and rarer winter grebes; wildfowl including Brent Goose, Wigeon, Teal, Shoveler, Goldeneye, Red-breasted Merganser, occasional Gadwall and Pintail, in cold weather occasional Pochard and Tufted Duck, possible Scaup, Smew and Goosander; occasional Hen Harrier and Merlin; waders including Grey Plover, Black-tailed Godwit and frequent Spotted Redshank; gulls including possible Mediterranean; Kingfisher, Rock and Water Pipits.

Spring (mid-March–mid-May): possible Garganey; migrant waders including Whimbrel, Spotted Redshank, Greenshank and Common Sandpiper; Common and occasional Little Terns; landbird migrants including Nightingale and occasional scarcer species.

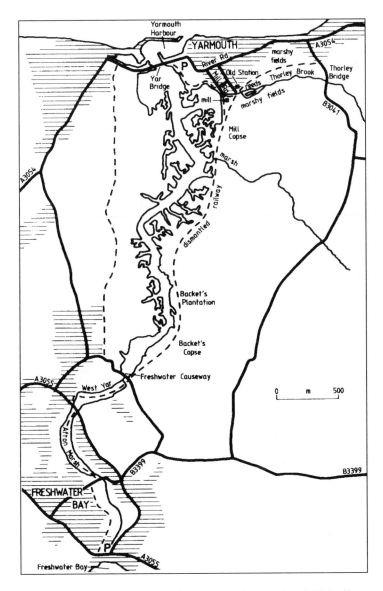

Summer (mid-May–mid-July): Common and occasional Little Terns; Sedge, Reed and Garden Warblers, Lesser Whitethroat.

Autumn (mid-July–mid-November): migrant waders including Whimbrel, Greenshank, Common Sandpiper and occasional other species; Common and occasional Little Terns; landbird migrants including occasional scarcer species.

Most likely oddities: Osprey, Grey Phalarope.

Habitat

This is undoubtedly the most important area of estuarine and saltmarsh habitat that exists on the Isle of Wight. The site owes much of its present character to the flooding of the Main (central) Marsh, which occurred after the seawall was breached by a combination of storm and high-water in November 1954. Subsequently the flooded grazing land has gradually converted to estuarine mudflats and *Spartina* saltmarshes. Since the Main Marsh is higher than the surrounding areas of the estuary, it remains exposed longer to the obvious advantage of the feeding wild-fowl and waders. In 1980 a scrape with four islands was constructed to provide additional feeding and nesting sites for birds. The Main Marsh remains partially protected by a low seawall.

The remainder of the estuary consists of long muddy channels bordered by *Spartina* saltmarshes. These are associated with the drainage of two main watercourses. The Newtown River in the west and the Clamerkin Lake in the east. These main channels merge just before the narrow entrance of the estuary which leads out to the Solent beyond. On the west side of the entrance there is a sand and shingle spit known as the Hamstead Duver. The estuary is set in a picturesque landscape of farmland and woods. The most attractive of these local woodlands are Town and Walter's Copses which are situated immediately to the east of Newtown village.

The Newtown Estuary was established as a local nature reserve in 1966. It is now managed as a national nature reserve by the National Trust. In addition to the birds, the reserve is important for other forms of wildlife. A number of interesting saltmarsh plants occur here; whilst Town and Walter's Copses support a good butterfly fauna and a small population of red squirrels.

Species

The Newtown Estuary provides a haven for a wealth of wintering and passage waterfowl, waders and gulls.

During the winter large flocks of Brent Geese feed in the estuary and surrounding fields. As at other sites along the Solent, this species has increased in recent years with peak counts now in excess of 1,500 birds. Shelduck, Wigeon and Teal are also commonly found here along with smaller numbers of Pintail and Shoveler; but Gadwall, Pochard and Tufted Duck are rare visitors. The waters of the Newtown River and Clamerkin Lake attract small parties of Little Grebes, Goldeneye and Red-breasted Mergansers as well as the occasional diver, Great Crested and rarer winter grebe and sea-duck. Small flocks of wild swans, mainly Whooper in recent years, and White-fronted Geese frequently appear during periods of hard weather. Such conditions may also produce such classic cold-weather species as Scaup, Smew and Goosander. From time to time, the local flock of Canada Geese are joined by feral Greylag and Barnacle Geese.

The mudflats, saltmarshes and nearby fields are important feeding and roosting areas for a wide selection of waders. These include good numbers of Golden Plover, Knot and Black-tailed Godwit together with a few Bar-tailed Godwit, Spotted Redshank and Greenshank. The Jack Snipe is reported most years and it seems likely that this elusive species may regularly winter in the area. There are also several sightings of the attractive Avocet at this season.

The Black-headed is the commonest of the gulls inhabiting the estuary during the winter. Herring and Great Black-backed Gulls occur in much smaller numbers; whilst Common and Lesser Black-backed Gulls are scarce visitors. Both Cormorants and Grey Herons are present in the area throughout the year. Like coastal sites on the mainland side of the Solent, the Little Egret is now a familiar sight with peak counts of 15–20 birds, sometimes more, during the autumn. This species can be seen throughout the winter and into the spring. Merlins and Peregrines are regular visitors in winter, the latter species often preying on waders in the Brickfields area; whilst Hen Harriers and Short-eared Owls are occasionally reported. Amongst the smaller birds, Rock Pipits and Reed Buntings feed along the fringes of the saltmarshes and one or two Kingfishers spend the autumn and winter months darting along the estuary's ditches and channels in search of fish.

Spotted Redshank

Waders continue to be a feature of the spring. In addition to the commoner species, Golden Plover and Black-tailed Godwit are present in moderate numbers along with a few Knot, Bar-tailed Godwit, Spotted Redshank, Greenshank and Common Sandpiper. There is also a regular off-passage flock of Whimbrel that often feeds in fields near Locks Green and roosts in the Brickfields area of Newtown. In some springs, this Whimbrel flock has reached peak counts of around 100 birds. Sanderling, Ruff and Green Sandpiper are occasionally seen; whilst there is always the chance that something more unusual will turn up – there are recent spring records of Avocet, Little Ringed Plover, Little Stint, Curlew and Wood Sandpipers. The first Sandwich Terns are seen in late March or early April to be followed within a couple of weeks by small numbers of Common and Little Terns. Spring sometimes produces such scarce visitors as Garganey, Hobby, Mediterranean and Little Gulls and Black

Tern or even something rarer like an Osprey. Otherwise there is a scattering of the commoner landbird migrants including Yellow Wagtail and Wheatear.

Spring and summer echo to the cries of Black-headed Gulls which nest in large numbers on the scrape and an island off Newtown Quay. Other regular breeding birds associated with the estuary and marshes include Canada Goose, Shelduck, Oystercatcher, Redshank, Common Tern, Reed Bunting and perhaps Ringed Plover, which attempts to nest most years. Great Black-backed Gull, Sandwich and Little Terns have occasionally bred in the area. Small numbers of non-breeding waders, such as Grey Plover and Black-tailed Godwit, and non-breeding Sandwich and Little Terns are usually present throughout the summer. Away from the estuary, the nearby woodlands hold an interesting selection of breeding birds including Nightingale.

The autumn passage of waders is well under way by July. Golden Plover and Black-tailed Godwit return to winter in the area; whilst more obvious migrant species such as Knot, Bar-tailed Godwit, Whimbrel, Spotted Redshank, Greenshank and Common Sandpiper regularly appear in small numbers. A few Little Stint, Curlew Sandpiper, Ruff and Green Sandpiper are seen most years, but Little Ringed Plover, Sanderling and Wood Sandpiper are infrequent visitors. There are also autumn sightings of Kentish Plover, Red-necked and Grey Phalaropes. Little Gulls and Black Terns may occasionally mingle with the commoner gulls and terns; whilst the autumn gull roost now regularly attracts Yellow-legged Herring Gulls from July to October. Peregrines regularly hunt over the area in autumn, and migrant Merlins, Hobbies and Short-eared Owls are seen from time to time. There are also several reports of Ospreys which often frequent the Solent area in autumn. There is a small passage of landbird migrants including Yellow Wagtail, Redstart, Whinchat, Wheatear and Spotted Flycatcher together with the occasional Black Redstart, Ring Ouzel, Firecrest, Pied Flycatcher and subrarity such as Wryneck. Autumn is the most likely season to find rarities with records of Great White Egret, Common Crane and Sociable Plover.

Timing

The state of the tide is important when visiting the site. At low-water the wildfowl and waders can feed throughout the estuary, but as the tide rises they move on to the mudflats of the elevated Main Marsh. As high-water approaches, these birds become increasingly concentrated in the southeast corner of this marsh, nearest to the East Hide, before they are eventually forced to leave for their roosting areas. There are more birds on the scrape at high tide, especially in the autumn.

Access

Newtown Estuary NNR is best approached from the Shell Garage on the A3054 just east of Shalfleet, by taking the minor road north towards Porchfield for 0.7 miles (1.1 km) and then turning north again on another minor road signposted to Newtown Old Town Hall. On reaching Newtown, take the first road on the left and continue past the Reserve Visitor Centre to the parking area at the west end of the village. From here, follow the well signposted footpath north across the field, through the gate and over the footbridge to Newtown Quay. Unfortunately further access along the seawall is difficult due to the lack of repair works. The main entrance to the restricted part of the reserve and the

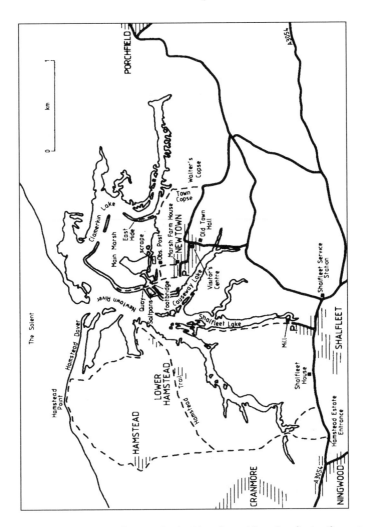

Observation Post can be reached either by taking the footpath east immediately after passing through the gate and before reaching the footbridge or directly from Newtown Village north on the footpath from Marsh Farm House.

The other main access point to the estuary starts from where the minor road bends sharply to the right 0.4 miles (0.6 km) to the east of the village. From here, follow the footpath north through Town and Walter's Copses to Clamerkin Marsh and then walk north along the embankment to the new hide. In addition, there are a number of other footpaths giving access to the west side of the estuary, notably from Shalfleet Mill car park north along the west side of the Shalfleet Lake; and from the entrance to the Hamstead Estate on the A3054, 0.6 miles (1 km) west of Shalfleet, north along the Coastal Path and Hamstead Trail.

Reserve Visit Arrangements: access to the restricted part of the reserve is by permit; whilst entry to the Observation Hide is by key. These should be booked in advance from the Warden, Reserve Visitor Centre, Newtown, Isle of Wight PO30 4PA (tel: Calbourne 341).

Calendar

All Year. Cormorant, Little Egret, Grey Heron, Canada and occasional feral Greylag and Barnacle Geese, Shelduck, Peregrine, Oystercatcher, Ringed Plover, Redshank, Reed Bunting, common resident woodland birds.

Winter (mid-November–mid-March): occasional divers; Little and occasional other grebes; wildfowl including Brent Goose, Wigeon, Teal, Pintail, Shoveler, Goldeneye, Red-breasted Merganser, occasional Gadwall, Pochard, Tufted Duck and sea-duck, in cold weather occasional wild swans (usually Whooper) and grey geese (usually White-fronted), possible Scaup, Smew and Goosander; Merlin and occasional Hen Harrier; waders including Golden Plover, Knot, both godwits, Spotted Redshank, Greenshank, near annual Jack Snipe, possible Avocet; common gulls; occasional Short-eared Owl; Kingfisher, Rock Pipit.

Spring (mid-March–mid-May): possible Garganey; possible Hobby; migrant waders including Golden Plover, Knot, both godwits, Whimbrel, Spotted Redshank, Greenshank, Common Sandpiper, occasional Sanderling, Ruff and Green Sandpiper, possible scarcer species; occasional Mediterranean and possible Little Gulls; Sandwich, Common, Little and possible Black Terns; common landbird migrants.
Most likely oddity: rare raptor.

Summer (mid-May–mid-July): non-breeding waders including Grey Plover and Black-tailed Godwit; Sandwich, Common and Little Terns; Nightingale.

Autumn (mid-July–mid-November): migrant raptors including occasional Merlin and Hobby; migrant waders including Golden Plover, Knot, Little Stint, Curlew Sandpiper, Ruff, both godwits, Whimbrel, Spotted Redshank, Greenshank, Green and Common Sandpipers, occasional Little Ringed Plover, Sanderling and Wood Sandpiper; Yellow-legged and occasional Little Gulls; Sandwich, Common, Little and occasional Black Terns; occasional Short-eared Owl; Kingfisher; landbird migrants including Yellow Wagtail, Redstart, Whinchat, Wheatear, occasional Black Redstart, Ring Ouzel, Firecrest and Pied Flycatcher.
Most likely oddities: Osprey, Grey Phalarope and other rare waders.

OS Map 196 &
Isle of Wight
SZ59/69

87 THE RYDE AREA

Habitat

The northeast coast of the Island between Woodside and Seaview overlooks the sheltered waters of the Eastern Solent. Low tide reveals extensive strands of sand off Ryde and Puckpool with a narrower muddy shore further west off Quarr and Woodside. The coastline is interrupted by a relatively short muddy estuary at Wootton Creek. Other features of ornithological interest are the woodlands at Woodside and Quarr, Ryde Canoe Lake and a small freshwater marsh with pools known as the Seaview Duver.

Species

This is very much an area for winter birds. The offshore waters are the best around the Island for divers, grebes and sea-duck. Good numbers of Great Crested Grebes and Red-breasted Mergansers can be expected along with a few Shags, Slavonian Grebes and Eider. Divers can be scarce in some years but small numbers are usually present; the most likely species to be encountered being Red-throated and Black-throated. Although Red-necked Grebes, Common and Velvet Scoters are more infrequent in occurrence, these species are reported most years and sometimes over-winter. Long-tailed Duck, Guillemot and Razorbill are occasionally seen; whilst the diminutive Little Auk is a rare visitor in late autumn and winter.

At low tide the foreshore areas and Wootton Creek attract flocks of Brent Geese along with smaller numbers of Shelduck and sometimes Wigeon. In addition, a few Teal can usually be found in Wootton Creek. There are large feral flocks of Canada and Barnacle Geese at Seaview Duver where the freshwater pools also support small numbers of Little Grebes, Pochard, Tufted Duck and sometimes Shoveler and Goldeneye. Ryde Canoe Lake is another regular site for diving duck, mainly Tufteds but also one or two Pochard and occasionally Scaup which has also been reported from the Seaview Duver.

Ryde Sands are the best site in the region for wintering Sanderling with peak counts usually in excess of 250 birds. It is also a good feeding area for Bar-tailed Godwits, but numbers have declined in recent years. Most of the commoner waders can be found along this coastline, favouring Wootton Creek and the foreshores off Quarr and Woodside. Both Greenshank and Common Sandpiper have wintered in Wootton Creek, but the most famous overwintering wader was the Spotted Sandpiper at Seaview Duver in 1987/88.

During the winter small numbers of Mediterranean Gulls mingle with the commoner gulls that frequent the shore areas between Ryde and Seaview. Since January 1990 an adult Ring-billed Gull has regularly wintered at Ryde, generally favouring the Canoe Lake area. In early 1996 no fewer than four different Ring-billed Gulls were reported from this site. Of the smaller birds of interest, a few Water Pipits often inhabit the field next to the Battery Inn in Puckpool.

From spring through to the autumn Common Terns regularly frequent Ryde Sands where counts usually build up to a peak in August and September. Smaller numbers of Sandwich and Arctic Terns are also present, particularly in the spring; whilst Black Terns are occasionally seen at times of passage. Seabird movements are rarely witnessed, but there have been sightings of Fulmar, Manx Shearwater, Gannet, skuas and Kittiwake. There is also a recent summer record of a Cory's Shearwater. Although migrant waders are not a particular feature of the area; Greenshank and Common Sandpiper are regular visitors, particularly to Wootton Creek and the Seaview Duver. Landbird migrants are most likely to be seen in the woods at Woodside and Quarr. Of the scarcer species, there are autumn sightings of Pied Flycatcher from Quarr and Black Redstart from Ryde. More notable reports of spring Golden Orioles at Quarr and an autumn Yellow-browed Warbler at Seaview are eclipsed by a Dark-eyed Junco at Wootton in April 1989.

Timing

High-water is required for observing divers, grebes and sea-duck offshore. In Wootton Creek and along the foreshore areas off Woodside and Quarr, wildfowl, waders and gulls are best observed at low-water. Due to the extensive nature of Ryde Sands, these are best visited two to three hours either side of high tide when birds are forced to feed closer inshore.

Access

All sites are within easy reach of Wootton Bridge and Ryde.

Wootton Creek and Woodside: from Wootton Bridge take New Road north and view Wootton Creek from the roadside. Alternatively view Wootton Creek from the A3054 roadbridge. For Woodside continue along New Road to the junction with Upper and Lower Woodside Roads. There are two footpaths leading to the shore – northeast from the

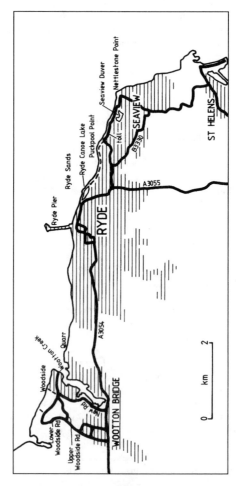

junction itself, and northeast by the caravan park 0.8 miles (1. 3 km) northwest along Lower Woodside Road.

Quarr: from the end of the B3325 road in Fishbourne, follow the Coastal Path (Quarr Road) east to Binstead.

Ryde to Seaview: from Ryde Pier there is easy access along seafront east to the Canoe Lake. From here continue on the Coastal Path east to Puckpool, Spring Vale and Seaview. For vehicles there is a toll road between Spring Vale and Seaview.

Seaview Duver: the marsh and pools can be viewed from the coastal toll road.

Calendar

All Year: Cormorant, Grey Heron, Canada and feral Barnacle Geese, common resident woodland birds.

Winter (mid-November–mid-March): divers – most likely Red-throated and Black-throated; Little, Great Crested, Slavonian and near annual Red-necked Grebes; Shag; wildfowl including Brent Goose, Shelduck, Wigeon, Teal, Shoveler, Pochard, Tufted Duck, Eider, Red-breasted Merganser, near annual Common and Velvet Scoters, occasional other wildfowl including Scaup, Long-tailed Duck and Goldeneye; waders including Sanderling, Bar-tailed Godwit, occasional Greenshank and Common Sandpiper; gulls including Mediterranean and recent annual Ring-billed; occasional auks; Rock and Water Pipits.
   Most likely oddity: rare gull.

Spring to Autumn (mid-March–mid-November): very occasional sea passage offshore – most likely species Fulmar, Gannet, skuas, Little Gull, Kittiwake, auks.
   Migrant waders including Greenshank, Common Sandpiper and occasional scarcer species; Sandwich, Common, Arctic and occasional other tern species; common landbird migrants, occasional Black Redstart, Pied Flycatcher and other scarce species.
   Most likely oddities: rare gull, landbird subrarity.

88 THE BEMBRIDGE AREA (NT)

OS Map 196 & Isle of Wight
SZ68

Habitat

St Helens, Bembridge Harbour, Brading Marsh, the Foreland and Culver Down are all sites of ornithological interest located at the eastern end of the Isle of Wight. Together these sites offer a wide range of habitats mostly centred around Bembridge Harbour. Here low-water exposes mud-flats and sandbanks; whilst behind a seawall in the northwest corner of the harbour, there is an area of *Spartina* saltmarsh and muddy creeks known as the Old Mill Ponds. The northern part of Bembridge Harbour is partially enclosed by the Duver, a low-lying spit of sand dunes colonised by coastal scrub and short grass. The seaward shore of the Duver consists of muddy shingle; whilst on the opposite side of the harbour entrance low tide reveals the vast expanse of Bembridge Sands which extend offshore from the beaches to the east of Bembridge Point. Immediately on the landward side of the road that borders the southern edge of Bembridge Harbour, there are some patches of remnant salt-marsh and brackish pools – Bembridge Pools, and a large freshwater lake fringed by reedbeds – Bembridge Pond. Further inland lies Brading Marsh, an extensive area of low-lying rough pasture intersected by various small streams and ditches. These drain into the Eastern Yar which in turn flows into Bembridge Harbour. There are small reedbeds and freshwater ponds scattered throughout Brading Marsh; whilst Bembridge Windmill, Bembridge Airfield and the woods around Centurion's Hill are additional features of note.

The Foreland is a low headland overlooking the eastern approaches to the Solent. Offshore, flat rocky ledges extend along the coast southwest to Whitecliff Bay which is backed by scrub-covered crumbling cliffs. Further south the high chalk ridge of Culver Down and its spectacular cliffs dominates the scene.

The St Helen's Duver and Culver Down belong to the National Trust; whilst Brading Marsh is privately owned. This entire area of the Isle of Wight is of interest to the general naturalist.

Species
With such a diversity of habitats, the Bembridge area supports the greatest variety of birds to be found on the Isle of Wight.

Most of the commoner waders can be seen in winter, but Bembridge Sands no longer appears to attract Sanderling and Bar-tailed Godwit in any numbers. Although a few individuals of both species may still occur

Purple Sandpipers

from time to time, Ryde Sands to the north is now the preferred area for these waders in East Wight. On a more positive note, Black Rock Ledge just to the south of the Foreland is still the main locality on the Island for wintering Purple Sandpiper with 10 to 20 birds recorded most years; whilst a single Whimbrel continued to overwinter at this site well into the early 1990s. One or two Greenshank are usually present, favouring the Old Mill Ponds and Bembridge Pools where Snipe and sometimes the odd Jack Snipe can be found. Spotted Redshank and Green Sandpiper are occasionally seen in winter, but other waders such as Golden Plover, Knot and Black-tailed Godwit are uncommon visitors.

Shelduck

Bembridge Pond is still one of the best sites on the Isle of Wight for wintering Pochard and Tufted Duck; whilst there are more reports of Gadwall from the Bembridge area than from anywhere else on the Island. Shelduck and Teal together with a few Shoveler can be found in suitable habitat throughout the area. Flocks of Brent Geese feed in Bembridge Harbour and along the foreshore areas including the rocky ledges off the Foreland, which is also a favoured site for Wigeon. Parties of Bewick's Swans and White-fronted Geese occasionally appear, mainly during periods of cold weather which may also bring Scaup, Smew, Goosander and even Whooper Swans to the area. The large population of Canada Geese sometimes attracts a few feral Greylag Geese. The offshore waters can be good for divers, grebes and sea-duck; Great Crested Grebe, Eider and Red-breasted Merganser being the most likely species to be seen. Small numbers of Little Grebes frequent Bembridge Harbour and Bembridge Pond. Cormorants, Shags and Grey Herons are residents, the former species roosting on St Helen's Fort in the Solent. Water Rails skulk in the reedbeds of Bembridge Pond which is also the best spot on the Island to find a Bittern during spells of severe cold. Although the Little Egret does not occur as regularly as at some other sites on the Island, it seems likely that this species will appear with increasing frequency.

Perhaps the most striking change to the local avifauna in recent years has been the dramatic increase in the numbers of Mediterranean Gulls recorded, particularly during the autumn and winter months. Although birds frequent Bembridge Harbour and the nearby foreshores, the Foreland is the favoured area where counts reached an impressive 72 in March 1996. Bembridge is now challenging Copt Point in Kent as Britain's premier site for this species. There is also a large roost of Black-headed and Common Gulls off the entrance to Bembridge Harbour. Although Ring-billed Gulls have been located amongst this roost, most recent reports of this species come from nearby Ryde.

Peregrines frequently hunt over the area; whilst Merlins and Short-eared Owls are recorded most years, the latter occasionally wintering on Brading Marsh. The Hen Harrier is rather an uncommon visitor, but like the previous species individuals occasionally overwinter in the area. Amongst the smaller birds of interest, Kingfisher, Rock Pipit, Stonechat and Reed Bunting can be expected; whilst Chiffchaffs are regularly seen in mild winters, notably around Brading Sewage Works, and both Black Redstarts and Firecrests occasionally overwinter in the area. There have also been three recent reports of Bearded Tits in late autumn and winter.

There is little published evidence of seabird movements off the Foreland. Since the mid-1980s, however, sightings of Manx Shearwater, Storm Petrel, Pomarine Skua and Black Tern suggest that this may be good site for seawatching in spring and summer.

Most of the waders that commonly winter in the area can be seen well into the spring. These are regularly joined by more obvious migrants such as Whimbrel, Greenshank and Common Sandpiper; whilst Little Ringed Plover, Knot, Sanderling, Ruff, Bar-tailed Godwit, Spotted Red-shank and Green Sandpiper occasionally appear on passage. A few Sandwich and Common Terns are usually present from mid-April on-wards, but Little and Black Terns are rare visitors. Although Bembridge Pond is one of the best sites on the Island for spring Garganey, the species does not appear every year. Of the rarer migrant raptors, Marsh Harriers are reported most springs. The area attracts a good selection of landbird migrants which occasionally includes Black Redstart, Ring Ouzel, Firecrest and Pied Flycatcher. A spring Hoopoe is also a distinct possibility; whilst the potential of the Bembridge area for attracting rare birds is clearly shown by spring sightings of Cattle Egret, Purple Heron, Bee-eater, Subalpine Warbler, Woodchat Shrike and Ortolan Bunting.

During the summer a number of interesting birds can be found in the area. Little Grebes regularly breed on Bembridge Pond where both Pochard and Tufted Duck also nest most years and there is a small heronry in nearby trees. Shelduck breed at various sites including Culver Down; whilst the Redshank still appears to be a regular breeding species, albeit in very small numbers. Sedge and Reed Warblers and Reed Bunting inhabit the reedbeds around Bembridge Pond and on Brading Marsh. At the latter site, the Cetti's Warbler regularly held territory in the late 1980s and early 1990s, but there were no reports in 1994. Further afield, Fulmars are present along the cliffs of Culver Down during the breeding season. These cliffs also hold a few pairs of nesting Shags, Great Black-backed Gulls and Rock Pipits; whilst both Peregrine and Raven are now local residents. Otherwise Sandwich and Common Terns can be frequently seen fishing the offshore waters of the Solent through-out the summer season.

Most of the commoner waders return during July. Of the more obvious migrants, Whimbrel, Greenshank, Green and Common Sandpipers regu-larly appear in small numbers, but other species such as Little Ringed Plover, Little Stint, Curlew Sandpiper, Ruff, Black-tailed Godwit, Spotted

Redshank and Wood Sandpiper are infrequent visitors. The now annual influx of Mediterranean Gulls into the area starts during July with birds remaining through to the early spring. Although Sandwich and Common Terns are regularly present and occasionally form large flocks off the Foreland, Little Gulls and other tern species are rarely seen. Seawatching from the Foreland may prove rewarding during or after gales. For example there are reports of Grey Phalaropes from this site in 1994 and 1990. As in the spring, the Marsh Harrier is the most likely of the rarer migrant raptors to occur.

During the autumn landbird migrants are very much a feature of the area; the most favoured sites being Culver Down, Whitecliff Bay, the Foreland and St Helen's Duver. Yellow Wagtail, Redstart, Whinchat, Wheatear, the commoner warblers and Spotted Flycatcher all occur in reasonable numbers; whilst a few Black Redstarts, Ring Ouzels, Firecrests and Pied Flycatchers are seen most years. The occasional sub-rarity is also a distinct possibility; there have been reports of Wryneck, Tawny Pipit, Yellow-browed Warbler, Golden Oriole, Red-backed Shrike, Lapland and Ortolan Buntings in recent years. Perhaps the most extraordinary records, however, concern two sightings of Desert Warblers – one on the old railway track at Bembridge in October 1988 and another well watched individual at Whitecliff Bay in October and November 1991. Other rarities of note seen in recent years involve a Night Heron and a Black Stork.

Timing

In Bembridge Harbour and along the nearby foreshore areas, including Black Rock Ledge, wildfowl and waders can be readily observed at low tide. Bembridge Sands, however, should be visited on a rising tide when birds are forced closer inshore. High tide brings wildfowl and waders to roost on the Old Mill Ponds, Bembridge Pools and Brading Marsh. Late afternoon in winter is the best time to watch the gull roost off Bembridge Harbour entrance.

In spring and autumn searching for landbird migrants will be most rewarding early in the morning when fall conditions exist.

The most productive conditions for spring seawatching from the Foreland are likely to occur between mid-April and mid-May when the winds are onshore in direction.

Access

All sites are within easy reach of St Helens and Bembridge.

St Helen's Duver and Bembridge Harbour (north): from St Helens follow the B3330 (Eddington Road) east to a sharp left-hand bend, then take Duver Road east to either the shore by St Helen's Church or the Duver car park. There is general access to the shore, the harbour entrance and the Duver. There is also a footpath from the Duver to St Helen's Mill, which runs along the seawall separating the Old Mill Ponds from the main harbour.

Bembridge Harbour (south), Bembridge Pools and Bembridge Pond: from St Helens follow the B3395 (Station Road) south to the Yar roadbridge and continue along the south side of the harbour (Harbour Strand) towards the Royal Spithead Hotel. Bembridge Harbour and Bembridge Pools can be viewed from the roadside. There is also a rough

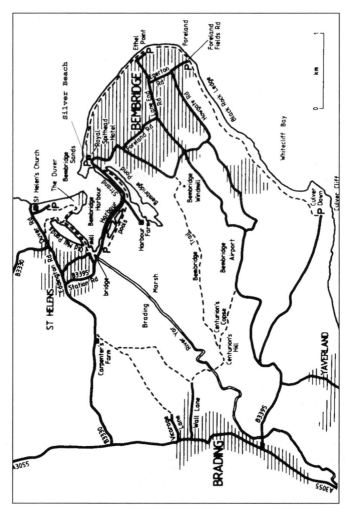

track that starts by a small car park just to the east of the Yar roadbridge. This footpath runs along the landward side of Bembridge Pools, then the harbour side of Bembridge Pond and finishes by some waste ground.

Bembridge Sands are reached by taking the rough track immediately to the east of the Royal Spithead Hotel north to the Silver Beach car park. There is general access along the shore.

Brading Marsh: access to this private area is by means of the following footpaths – (i) from Bembridge Windmill west along the Bembridge Trail past Bembridge Airport to Centurion's Hill and then northwest to Wall Lane in Brading; (ii) from the B3395 0.3 miles (0.5 km) west of Bembridge Airport, west to Centurion's Hill and the Bembridge Trail; (iii) & (iv) from the ends of either Wall Lane or Vicarage Lane in Brading, northeast across the fields to the B3330 just west of St Helens at Carpenters Farm.

The Foreland is reached by taking Lane End Road from the B3395 (Foreland Road) in Bembridge east to Ethel Point car park* by the Lifeboat Station. There is a footpath along the cliff-top northwest to Bembridge Point and south to the Foreland and Whitecliff Bay.

Black Rock Ledge and Whitecliff Bay can be reached either by the cliff-top footpath from Ethel Point – see above; or from Lane End Road in Bembridge by taking Egerton Road and Foreland Fields Road south to the cliff-top parking area. From here, there are steps leading down to the beach.

Culver Down is well signposted from the B3395 0.6 miles (1 km) east of Brading. There is a car park and general access to much of the area.

Calendar

All Year: Little Grebe, Fulmar, Cormorant, Shag, Grey Heron and occasional Little Egret, Canada Goose, Shelduck, Pochard, Tufted Duck, Peregrine, Redshank, Rock Pipit, Cetti's Warbler, Raven, Reed Bunting, common resident woodland birds.

Winter (mid-November–mid-March): occasional divers; Great Crested and occasional rarer winter grebes; possible Bittern in cold weather; wildfowl including Brent Goose, Wigeon, Teal, Shoveler, Red-breasted Merganser, occasional Bewick's Swan, Gadwall and sea-duck, in cold weather occasional grey geese (usually White-fronted), Scaup, Smew and Goosander; occasional Hen Harrier and Merlin; Water Rail; waders including Purple Sandpiper, Greenshank, frequent Sanderling and Bar-tailed Godwit, occasional other species; gulls including good numbers of Mediterranean; occasional Short-eared Owl; Kingfisher, Stonechat, occasional Black Redstart, Chiffchaff and Firecrest.
Most likely oddities: rare wildfowl and gulls.

Spring (mid-March–mid-May): probable sea passage off the Foreland – for likely species see Site 89 St Catherine's Point.
Occasional Garganey; possible Marsh Harrier; migrant waders including Whimbrel, Greenshank, Common Sandpiper, occasional scarcer species; Sandwich, Common, possible Little and Black Terns; landbird migrants including occasional Black Redstart, Ring Ouzel, Firecrest and Pied Flycatcher.
Most likely oddity: Hoopoe.

Summer (mid-May–mid-July): Sandwich and Common Terns, Sedge and Reed Warblers.

Autumn (mid-July–mid-November): during/after gales – probable sea passage off the Foreland – for likely species see Site 89 St Catherine's Point.
Possible Marsh Harrier; migrant waders including Whimbrel, Green-shank, Green and Common Sandpipers, occasional scarcer species; regular influx of Mediterranean Gulls in July, possible Little Gull; Sandwich, Common, possible Little and Black Terns; landbird migrants including near annual Black Redstart, Ring Ouzel, Firecrest and Pied Flycatcher.
Most likely oddity: landbird subrarity.

89 ST CATHERINE'S POINT (NT)

Habitat

St Catherine's Point lies at the southernmost tip of the Isle of Wight. Behind a rocky shoreline backed by low crumbling cliffs, the area immediately around St Catherine's Lighthouse and Knowles Farm consists of open grass and small stone-walled fields; whilst further inland, the upper slopes are covered by patches of dense scrub. To the northwest, Gore Cliff dominates the scene. Thick vegetation, including a small sycamore wood, cloaks the rocky slopes and gullies that extend from the base of these high cliffs down to the shore at Rocken End.

The National Trust owns much of the land to the north and west of Knowles Farm. The area supports an interesting flora and fauna with butterflies well represented.

Species

This is one of the main localities in the region for studying bird migration. Since the 1950s regular coverage has revealed that the pattern of bird movements is very similar to that recorded at other coastal sites like Portland Bill.

The arrival of Chiffchaffs and Wheatears in March heralds the start of spring passage. This is also a good time to look for such scarce migrants as Black Redstart, Ring Ouzel and Firecrest which mainly occur between mid-March and late April. The peak movement of landbirds, however, takes place in April and May when a wide variety of species including Turtle Dove, Tree Pipit, Yellow Wagtail, Redstart, Whinchat, Wheatear, the commoner warblers and Spotted Flycatcher together with a few Wood Warblers and Pied Flycatchers pass through. Amongst the rarer migrants, both Hoopoe and Serin have been recorded almost annually in recent years; whilst there are spring sightings of Alpine Swift, Bee-eater, Shorelark, Richard's and Tawny Pipits, Melodious Warbler, Red-breasted Flycatcher, Penduline Tit, Woodchat Shrike and a splendid Wallcreeper – the latter observed flying along the shore during a sea-watch. A few Hobbies are observed most springs along with the occasional Merlin; whilst a good selection of rarer raptors including Black and Red Kites, Marsh and Montagu's Harriers, Goshawk and Osprey have been reported on passage. Waders, including Common Sandpipers feeding along the rocky shore, may appear from time to time.

The bulk of sea passage occurs between mid-March and mid-May. The main birds involved in these predominantly upchannel movements are divers, Fulmar, Gannet, Common Scoter, Bar-tailed Godwit, Whimbrel, Arctic Skua, Kittiwake, Sandwich, Common and Arctic Terns and Guillemot. In addition, smaller numbers of Manx Shearwaters, Velvet Scoter and other sea-duck, Pomarine and Great Skuas, Little Gulls, Little and Black Terns, Razorbills and Puffins are regularly recorded. A number of rarities, including Cory's Shearwater, Surf Scoter and Gull-billed Tern, have been noted during these offshore movements; whilst Purple Heron, Black Stork and Spoonbill have also been observed flying in off the sea.

Gannets

Few birds of interest can be seen during the summer. Fulmars frequent Gore Cliff where a few pairs breed most years. Offshore, Manx Shearwaters, Storm Petrels (also trapped at night), Gannets, Kittiwakes, terns and other seabirds may occasionally pass by. In recent years there have been some large movements of Manx Shearwaters during the summer and early autumn. These have also included small numbers of Mediterranean Shearwaters. Breeding landbirds may include the odd pair of Rock Pipit and Stonechat.

Late July brings the first trickle of landbird migrants to the area. The main passage months, however, are August and September when the same variety of commoner species that occur in spring can be expected. A few Pied Flycatchers also pass through at this time. The other scarce migrants tend to occur later in the autumn; Ring Ouzels and Firecrests appearing from late September onwards followed by Black Redstarts in October. As at other coastal stations, visual passage is dominated by hirundines through much of September with Meadow Pipits and finches taking over during the latter part of the month and October. There is always a good chance of finding a subrarity – Wryneck, Richard's and Tawny Pipits, Bluethroat, Icterine, Melodious, Barred, Pallas's and Yellow-browed Warblers, Red-breasted Flycatcher, Red-backed, Great Grey and Woodchat Shrikes and Ortolan Bunting have all been recorded; whilst there is also a recent report of a Radde's Warbler. Migrant raptors include the occasional Merlin, Hobby and Short-eared Owl; whilst there are recent autumn sightings of such rarer species as Honey Buzzard, Marsh Harrier and Osprey. As in the spring, the rocky shore sometimes attract passage waders including Common Sandpiper.

Noteworthy movements of seabirds in the late autumn are largely dependent on strong winds and gales and mainly involve Gannets and Kittiwakes along with a few skuas (mainly Arctic and Great) and terns. Such conditions may also produce a storm-blown oddity such as Sooty Shearwater, Pomarine and Long-tailed Skuas, Sabine's Gull and Little Auk.

Winter is generally a quiet season for birds. Most interest lies with the offshore movements of divers – mostly Red-throated, Gannets, Kittiwakes, auks and sometimes sea-duck – mainly Common Scoter, which are usually associated with either gales or the presence of sprat shoals moving upchannel. On the land, Chiffchaffs and Firecrests are occasionally present, particularly if the weather is mild; whilst there is always the possibility of a wintering Black Redstart.

Timing

In spring and autumn the best time to search for landbird migrants is early in the morning when fall conditions prevail. Seawatching is most reward-ing between mid-April and mid-May when the winds are greater than force 4 and onshore (S–E) in direction. Most movement usually takes place dur-ing the early morning, but passage may persist all day if conditions are par-ticularly good. Autumn seawatching is only worth contemplating during or immediately after strong southwesterly winds and gales.

Access

St Catherine's Point is reached from the A3055 (Undercliff Road) in Niton, by taking St Catherine's Road southwest to a sharp right-hand bend. From here continue southwest to the end of road and walk along the main track to the lighthouse and Knowles Farm. Alternatively follow the road north back towards Niton and after 100 yards (100 m) take Sandrock Road west to the small car park below Gore Cliff.

There is general access to the National Trust land with a number of small and sometimes obscure footpaths penetrating the thick scrub and sycamore wood between Gore Cliff and Rocken End. Generally these foot-paths are best approached from the car park at the end of Sandrock Road.

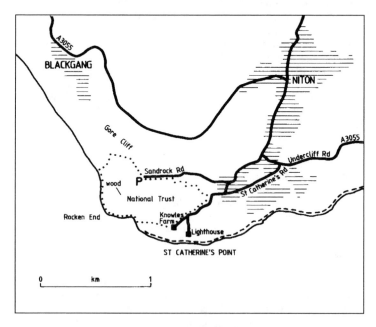

Calendar

All Year: Fulmar, Rock Pipit.

Spring (mid-March–mid-May): sea passage best mid-April to mid-May – involving divers, Fulmar, Manx Shearwater, Gannet, Common Scoter and other sea-duck; waders including Bar-tailed Godwit and Whimbrel;

skuas including Pomarine and Great; Little Gull; Kittiwake; terns including Black and occasional Little; auks including Puffin.

Migrant raptors including Hobby and occasional Merlin; migrant waders including Common Sandpiper and occasional other species; landbird migrants including from mid-March near annual Black Redstart, Ring Ouzel and Firecrest, from mid-April near annual Wood Warbler and Pied Flycatcher.

Most likely oddities: scarce/rare raptor, Hoopoe, Serin and other landbird subrarity.

Summer (mid-May–mid-July): occasional seabird movements including Mediterranean Shearwater and Storm Petrel; occasional Rock Pipit and Stonechat.

Autumn (mid-July–mid-November): sea passage most likely during/after gales – including occasional Manx and Mediterranean, and possible Sooty Shearwaters; Gannet; skuas including occasional Pomarine; Kittiwake, occasional Little and possible Sabine's Gulls; Sandwich, Common and Arctic Terns; auks including possible Little Auk.

Migrant raptors including occasional Merlin and Hobby; migrant waders including Common Sandpiper and occasional other species; occasional Short-eared Owl; landbird migrants including from early August Pied Flycatcher, from mid-September Ring Ouzel and Firecrest, from early October Black Redstart.

Most likely oddity: landbird subrarity.

Winter (mid-November–mid-March): occasional seabird movements involving divers, Gannet, Kittiwake and auks; occasional Black Redstart, Chiffchaff and Firecrest.

90 FORT VICTORIA (IOWCC)

SZ38

Fort Victoria overlooks the narrow western entrance to the Solent. This is a very underrated site for seawatching in spring (mid-April to mid-May) and autumn (mid-August to mid-September). Tern passage is particularly prominent in both seasons, mainly involving Sandwich and Common, but Little and occasionally Roseate and Black also occur. Other likely birds include Red-throated Diver, Fulmar, Gannet, various sea-duck and waders, skuas including occasional Pomarine, Little Gull, Kittiwake and auks. There are also reports of such storm-blown oddities as Storm Petrel, Leach's Petrel – notably in late December 1989, Sabine's Gull – *c* 50 after the Great Storm of October 1987, and Little Auk. The visual passage of landbirds can also be conspicuous; whilst the occasional rare migrant raptor such as Honey Buzzard and Marsh Harrier have been recorded. In winter divers, grebes and sea-duck are occasionally present offshore. Fort Victoria Country Park is well signposted from the A3054 in Norton at SZ345893.

91 THORNESS BAY

SZ49

Thorness Bay comprises a low shoreline overlooking the Solent which is backed by a small freshwater marsh with pools. In winter this is a good area for waterfowl including Great Crested Grebes and Red-breasted Mergansers offshore; Brent Geese, Shelduck, Teal and perhaps Shoveler along shoreline and on the marshes; and waders, notably Snipe and Turnstone. It is also a favoured site for Jack Snipe. Migrant waders and terns occur in spring and autumn. Both Oystercatchers and Ringed Plovers attempt to nest most years; whilst Sedge and Reed Warblers inhabit the reedbeds. Recent oddities include Marsh Harrier, Stone Curlew, Bearded Tit and Great Grey Shrike. Thorness Bay can be reached by footpaths north at SZ459926 and SZ465929 (near the lay-by and stream) on the minor road between the entrance to Thorness Bay Holiday Park and Hillis Corner near Gurnard.

92 RIVER MEDINA

SZ58/59

This long narrow estuary extends between Cowes and Newport. A small freshwater marsh at Dodnor is an additional feature of note. In winter the estuary and its immediate environs attract a good selection of waterfowl including Little Grebe, Brent Goose, Shelduck, Wigeon, Teal and Goldeneye; whilst Great Crested Grebe, Gadwall, Shoveler and Red-breasted Merganser are seen less frequently. This is one of the best areas on the Island for cold weather wildfowl such as Scaup and Smew. Divers, rarer winter grebes and sea-duck are rare visitors. Waders are well represented, the most likely species being Oystercatcher with the largest winter flock on the Island, Grey Plover, Dunlin, Black-tailed Godwit, Curlew, Redshank and Turnstone. It is the best Island site for Jack Snipe which favour the rough grass to the north of the old brick works near Werrar Farm; whilst there are also winter records of Greenshank and Common Sandpiper. Small birds of interest include Kingfisher, Rock Pipit and Reed Bunting. Whimbrel, Greenshank and Common Sandpiper are the most likely migrant waders to occur and there are occasional sightings of Knot and Curlew Sandpiper in autumn. The estuary can be reached by footpaths N29 and N30 from the Newport Industrial Estate at SZ500899 north to Dodnor Marsh, Werrar Farm and beyond to West Cowes at SZ498948; and from Newport Cemetery at SZ503895 north to the Folly Inn at SZ509929.

93 BRIGHSTONE, ATHERFIELD AND THE MILITARY ROAD

SZ38/48/47

The southwest coastline of the Island consists of low crumbling cliffs intersected by short, steep-sided scrub-covered valleys (chines) which overlook the waters of Brighstone Bay. The immediate hinterland offers a predominantly farming landscape. This is the Island stronghold for Grey Partridge and Corn Bunting – both scarce breeding residents which also form notable gatherings in winter when the area is also favoured by flocks of Golden Plover. The offshore waters of Brighstone Bay often attract divers, mostly Red-throated and sometimes in large numbers; whilst sea-duck, mostly Common Scoter, are occasionally reported. A small flock of Brent Geese usually inhabits the shoreline. There is some evidence of seabird movements through Brighstone Bay, mainly in spring and autumn with occasional reports of Fulmars, Gannets, sea-duck, waders, skuas and terns. Hanover Point is a regular site for autumn flocks of Sandwich Terns. Merlins and Short-eared Owls occasionally occur both as winter and passage birds; whilst there are occasional reports of rarer migrant raptors which include recent sightings of Honey Buzzard, Marsh and Montagu's Harriers and Osprey. Landbird migrants, particularly those preferring open country, e.g. Skylarks, pipits, Whinchat, Wheatear and finches, are also a feature of the migration periods. In addition, scarcer species such as Black Redstart, Ring Ouzel, Firecrest and Pied Flycatcher are occasionally found; whilst there are several recent reports of Wrynecks. The potential of the area for attracting subrarities and rarities is shown by recent occurrences of Great Spotted Cuckoo, Bee-eater, Hoopoe, Red-rumped Swallow, Richard's and Red-throated Pipits, Black-eared Wheatear, Red-backed Shrike, Serin and Lapland Bunting. There is a footpath (Coastal Path) along the entire stretch of coastline between Compton Down car park (SZ366854) and Cliff Farm, Chale (SZ481777). This footpath can be reached from various points off the Military Road, notably at Compton Chine (SZ370851), Hanover Point (SZ378841), Brook Bay (SZ385836), Chilton Chine (SZ410823), Grange Farm (SZ420820), Shepherd's Chine (SZ450800) and Whale Chine (SZ470785). Otherwise access to the hinterland is provided by a network of minor roads and footpaths.

94 BRIGHSTONE FOREST (FC)

SZ48

This is a large area of mixed woodlands and forestry which supports a good selection of breeding birds including Woodcock, Long-eared Owl and Nightjar; whilst Buzzards are a frequent sight and have also nested successfully in recent years. It is a good area to search for Crossbills in irruption years. In autumn a scattering of landbird migrants may include the occasional Pied Flycatcher. Access is by means of an extensive network of footpaths: the Forest Walk (west) and Nature Trail (east) start at SZ419849 on the minor road north of Brighstone. Nearby there is a small car park at Mottistone Down (SZ420845). There is a footpath to Rowborough Down west from Rowborough Farm at SZ462851 which lies on the B3323 road north from Shorwell.

95 PARKHURST FOREST (FC)

SZ48/49

Like the previous site, this is another large area of mixed woodlands and forestry which supports a good selection of breeding birds including Woodcock, Long-eared Owl, Nightjar and Marsh Tit; whilst Firecrest bred successfully in 1990 and occasionally appear in winter. It is a good area to search for Crossbills in irruption years. Parkhurst Forest is best approached from the car park at SZ482900 which lies off A3054 0.7 miles (1.1 km) west of the A3020 roundabout in Newport. Well marked forest walks give access to much of the area.

LIST OF ORGANISATIONS WITH ABBREVIATIONS USED IN TEXT

National

FC   Forestry Commission.
Reorganised in April 1992. The Forest Authority carries out regulatory, research and grant-aiding functions; Forest Enterprise is the executive agency which manages the Commission's forest estate.
Dorset: Dorset Forest District Office, Cold Harbour, Wareham, Dorset BH20 7PA.
Hampshire: New Forest District Office, Queens House, Lyndhurst, Hampshire SO43 7NH.
West Downs Forest District Office, Bucks Horn Oak, Farnham, Surrey GU10 4LS.
South Downs Forest District Office, Buriton, Petersfield, Hampshire GU31 5SL.

EN   English Nature (formerly NCC Nature Conservancy Council), Northminster House, Peterborough PE1 1UA.
Dorset: Slepe Farm, Arne, Wareham, Dorset BH20 5BN.
Hampshire and Isle of Wight: 1 Southampton Road, Lyndhurst, Hampshire SO3 7BU.

NT   National Trust, 36 Queen Anne's Gate, London SW1H 9AS.
Chief Adviser on Nature Conservation, Adviser's Office, 33 Sheep Street, Cirencester, Glos. GL7 1QW.

RSPB   Royal Society for the Protection of Birds, The Lodge, Sandy, Beds SG19 2DL.
South West Regional Office: 10 Richmond Road, Exeter, Devon EX4 4JA.
South East Regional Office: 8 Church Street, Shoreham, West Sussex BN43 5DQ.

Dorset

CHOG   Christchurch Harbour Ornithological Group.
General Secretary: Paul Morrison, 33 Minterne Road, Christchurch, Dorset BH23 3LD.

DCC   County Planning Office, Dorset County Council, County Hall, Dorchester, Dorset DT1 1XJ.

DWT   Dorset Wildlife Trust (formerly DTNC Dorset Trust for Nature Conservation). Half Moon House, 15 North Square, Dorchester, Dorset DT1 1HY.

DBC   Dorset Bird Club (formerly NDBC New Dorset Bird Club).
Membership Secretary: Mrs Eileen Bowman, 53 Lonnen

Road, Colehill, Wimborne, Dorset BH21 7AT.
County Recorder: Shaun Robson, 5 Pine Road, Corfe Mullen, Wimborne, Dorset BH21 3DW.
Bird Report Sales: Miss W Adams, 16 Sherford Drive, Wareham, Dorset BH20 4EN.

PBO   Portland Bird Observatory and Field Centre.
Warden: Martin Cade, Old Lower Light, Portland Bill, Dorset DT5 2JT.

WW   Wessex Water, 2 Nuffield Rd, Poole, Dorset BH17 7RL.

Hampshire

HCC   Hampshire County Council. Countryside Service, North Hill Close, Andover Rd, Winchester, Hampshire SO22 6AQ.
Information Centre, Mottisfont Court, High Street, Winchester, Hampshire SO23 8ZB.

HWT   Hampshire Wildlife Trust (formerly H&IOWNT Hampshire and Isle of Wight Naturalist's Trust). 8 Romsey Road, Eastleigh, Hampshire SO50 9AL.

HOS   Hampshire Ornithological Society.
Secretary: N. Peace, 4 Wincanton Close, Alton, Hampshire GU34 2TQ.
County Recorder: J.M. Clark, 4 Cygnet Court, Old Cove Road, Fleet, Hampshire GU13 8AL.
Bird Report Sales: G. Rowland, 14 Dunmow Hill, Fleet, Hampshire GU13 9AN.

SW   Southern Water (Hampshire Division), Centre of Operation, Sparrowgrove, Otterbourne, Hampshire SO21 2SW.

Isle of Wight

IOWCC   Isle of Wight County Council, County Hall, Newport, Isle of Wight PO30 1UD.

IOWOG   Isle of Wight Ornithological Group.
Membership Secretary: D.J. Hunnybun, 40 Churchill Road, Cowes, Isle of Wight PO31 8HH.
County Recorder: D.B. Wooldridge, 2 Parkside, The Causeway, Freshwater Bay, Isle of Wight PO40 9TN.
Bird Report Sales: from County Recorder – see above.

GLOSSARY

Ornithological Terms

Auk
A seabird of the auk family – Guillemot, Razorbill, Puffin etc.

Chats
Collective term for Redstart, Whinchat, Stonechat, Wheatear etc.

Common resident woodland birds
Collective term for the commoner woodland birds including woodpeckers, tits, Nuthatch, Treecreeper etc.

Commoner gulls
Collective term for Black-headed, Common, Lesser Black-backed, Herring and Great Black-backed Gulls.

Crepuscular
Active in dim light, particularly at dawn and dusk.

Dabbling duck
Duck that feed by dabbling on the surface or up-ending; also known as surface-feeding duck.

Diving duck
Duck that feeds by swimming underwater.

Fall
A mass arrival of small migrant birds suddenly grounded by adverse weather conditions.

Fall Conditions
Often difficult to predict, usually a sudden change in the weather, e.g. arrival of cloud and rain, change in wind direction etc, particularly during the night; see also Fall.

Feral
Species either escaped or released from captivity and living in the wild state.

Grey geese
Collective term for Bean, Pink-footed, White-fronted, Lesser White-fronted and Greylag Geese.

Hirundine
A member of the swallow or martin family.

Irruption
A mass arrival, often at irregular intervals, of certain specialised feeders, which is usually associated with high populations and/or food shortages in their native regions.

Landbird
Mainly includes the passerines (perching birds) together with a few other groups including doves and pigeons, cuckoos, nightjars, swifts, kingfishers, Hoopoe and woodpeckers.

Larger gull species	Collective term for Lesser Black-backed, Herring, Iceland, Glaucous and Great Black-backed Gulls.
Off-passage	Period of rest during migration.
Overshooting	A migrant bird flying beyond its normal breeding range, usually applied to rare and unusual birds that arrive in Britain from southern and eastern Europe.
Prospect	Investigate potential nesting sites, often used in reference to Fulmars.
Raptor	Generally a diurnal bird of prey such as Sparrowhawk, Buzzard, Kestrel etc. Sometimes including nocturnal birds of prey such as owls.
Rarer winter grebes	Collective term for Red-necked, Slavonian and Black-necked Grebes.
Rarity	Generally denotes a bird that is rare enough to be referred to the *British Birds* Rare Birds Committee for vetting.
Roding	Territorial flight of Woodcock, usually at dusk and dawn.
Seabird	Refers to both the 'true' seabirds – species of the open sea that under normal circumstances only come close inshore to breed, e.g. shearwaters, Gannet, skuas, Kittiwake, auks etc.; and other non-landbirds that are usually involved in offshore sea passage, e.g. divers, wildfowl, waders, gulls, terns etc.
Sea-duck	Duck mostly confined to the sea, e.g. Eider, scoter etc.
Sea movements	*see* Sea passage.
Sea passage	The offshore movements of seabirds, usually associated with migration in spring and autumn.
Seawatching	Scanning the sea to observe passing seabirds.
Subrarity	A bird that is not quite rare enough to be referred to the *British Birds* Rare Birds Committee for vetting.
Upchannel movements	Refers to the spring passage of seabirds, which is predominantly easterly (hence upchannel) in direction.

Vagrant	A rare accidental visitor hundreds of miles off-course, mainly at migration times; see also Rarity.
Visual movements	see Visual passage.
Visual passage	The diurnal migration of birds.
Wader	Mud- or marsh-feeding sandpipers, plovers etc. Divided into 'fresh' or coastal species depending on whether they normally feed in freshwater or saltwater areas when on migration.
Warbler, *Acrocephalus*	A warbler normally associated with reedbeds and marshy vegetation, e.g. Sedge Warbler, Reed Warbler etc., of the genus *Acrocephalus*.
Warbler, *Phylloscopus*	A 'leaf-warbler', e.g. Chiffchaff, Willow Warbler etc., of the genus *Phylloscopus*.
Warbler, *Sylvia*	One of the scrub-haunting warblers, e.g. Whitethroat, Blackcap etc., of the genus *Sylvia*.
Waterbirds	see Waterfowl.
Waterfowl	Refers to wildfowl and other birds associated with water, e.g. divers, grebes, Cormorant, rails.
Wildfowl	Birds belonging to the family Anatidae – ducks, geese and swans.
Wild swans	Whooper and Bewick's Swans, rather than the introduced Mute Swan.
Winter thrushes	Collective term for Fieldfare and Redwing, which mainly visit Britain during the winter.
Wreck	An arrival of storm-blown seabirds on the coast or miles inland.

Other Terms

Carr	Woodland, usually willow or alder, growing in waterlogged conditions.
Carrier	A side channel of the main river, often man-made such as in the construction of water-meadow systems.
Cetacea	Members of the mammalian order containing dolphins, porpoises and whales.
Chine	A deep, narrow, coastal ravine; term used only in Hampshire and the Isle of Wight.

Coppice	Woodland where trees are cut at ground level to encourage growth of many new shoots.
Foreshore	The area of shore that lies between the mean low-water mark and the mean high-water mark.
Forest lawn	Close-cropped grass sward found in the New Forest.
Forestry	Woods and plantations of coniferous (softwood) trees grown mainly for commercial purposes.
Hanger	A wood, often beech, on a steep hill side.
Hard winter weather	Periods of severe cold and frost.
Inclosure	An area of woodland or forest fenced off to prevent the damaging grazing of livestock; in this region mainly associated with the New Forest.
Inlier	A mass of older rocks surrounded by newer rocks.
Inundation	Flooding.
Invasive scrub	The encroachment of scrub over other vegetation.
Ley	Land temporarily under grass.
LNR	Local Nature Reserve.
Neolithic	The later Stone Age.
NNR	National Nature Reserve.
Plateau Gravels	Recent deposits, derived by erosion from the underlying rock strata and re-deposited by rivers.
Riverine	Associated with a river or its banks.
Saltmarsh	Intertidal mudflats colonised by plants adapted to saline (salty) conditions.
Scrape	A shallow excavation made to attract waterbirds.
Spartina	Cord grass or rice grass that colonises mudflats in coastal areas.
SSSI	Site of Special Scientific Interest.
Strand	Extensive intertidal sandbanks.
Sward	Expanse covered by short grass producing a lawn-like effect, often as a result of intensive/cropping on chalk downlands.

Unimproved (wet) meadow — A meadow, often prone to winter flooding, that has not been ploughed and re-seeded and continues to be managed in a traditional manner.

Water-meadows — Riverside meadows that are regularly flooded, most often associated with chalk rivers.

Also note — Cretaceous, Jurassic, Lias, Tertiary, Wealden are names of geological periods or ages.

FURTHER READING LIST

The authors would like to acknowledge the following sources of information.

Books

Boys, J.V. *Check List of the Birds of Dorset* (Dorset Natural History and Archaeological Society, 1974).

Chesil Bank and Fleet Nature Reserve. *The Birds of Chesil Bank, The Fleet and Portland Harbour* (Chesil Bank and Fleet Nature Reserve).

Clark, J.M. *Birds of the Hants/Surrey Border* (Hobby Books, 1984).

Clarke, P. and Clarke, M. *Where to Watch Birds in East Anglia* (Christopher Helm, 1987).

Cohen, E. *Birds of Hampshire and the Isle of Wight* (Oliver and Boyd, 1963).

Cohen, E. and Taverner, J.A. *Revised List of Hampshire and Isle of Wight Birds* (Oxford Illustrated Press, 1973).

Duffen, B. *An Annotated Checklist of the Birds of Titchfield Haven* (Hampshire County Recreation Department).

Hall, K. and Govett, J. *Where to Watch Birds in Somerset, Avon, Gloucestershire and Wiltshire* (Christopher Helm, 1988).

Hampshire Ornithological Society. *Birds of Hampshire* (Hampshire Ornithological Society, 1993).

Norman, D. and Tucker, V. *Where to Watch Birds in Devon and Cornwall* (Croom Helm, 1984).

Parslow, J. (ed.) *Birdwatcher's Britain* (Pan/Ordnance Survey, 1983).

Prendergast, Col. E.D.V. and Boys, J.V. *The Birds of Dorset* (David and Charles, 1983).

Annual Reports

Birds of Christchurch Harbour 1985 and 1987 (Christchurch Harbour Ornithological Group).

Birds of Newtown Nature Reserve 1984 (Isle of Wight County Council).

Dorset Bird Reports (Dorset Natural History and Archaeological Society to 1985; Dorset Bird Club 1986 to 1994).

Hampshire Bird Reports (Hampshire Field Club to 1977; Hampshire Ornithological Society 1978 to 1994).

Hants/Surrey Border Bird Report 1985 (Ed. J.M. Clark).

Isle of Wight Bird Report (Isle of Wight Natural History and Archaeological Society to 1985; Isle of Wight Ornithological Group 1986 to 1994).

Portland Bill Observatory and Field Centre.

Titchfield Haven and Hook-with-Warsash Nature Reserves 1983-4 Report (Hampshire County Recreations Department).

Others

Avon and Stour Bird Survey (RSPB/Wessex Water Authority, 1979).

Dorset Naturalists' Trust Nature Reserve Guide (Dorset Naturalists' Trust – now Dorset Wildlife Trust, 1980).

Hayling Island Bird Reports for Winter 1983/4, Spring, Summer and

Autumn 1984, and Winter 1984/5 (compiled for the Hayling Group by J.M. Walters).

Ornithological Survey of Poole Harbour – First Stage Winter-Spring 1984/5 (RSPB/D.R. Collins).

Stour Ringing Group Reports for 1984 and 1985.

Information leaflets for various reserves, country parks etc.

CODE OF CONDUCT
FOR BIRDWATCHERS

Today's birdwatchers are a powerful force for nature conservation. The number of those of us interested in birds rises continually and it is vital that we take seriously our responsibility to avoid any harm to birds.

We must also present a responsible image to non-birdwatchers who may be affected by our activities and particularly those on whose sympathy and support the future of birds may rest.

There are 10 points to bear in mind:
1. The welfare of birds must come first.
2. Habitat must be protected.
3. Keep disturbance to birds and their habitat to a minimum.
4. When you find a rare bird think carefully about whom you should tell.
5. Do not harass rare migrants.
6. Abide by the bird protection laws at all times.
7. Respect the rights of landowners.
8. Respect the rights of other people in the countryside.
9. Make your records available to the local bird recorder.
10. Behave abroad as you would when birdwatching at home.

Welfare of birds must come first
Whether your particular interest is photography, ringing, sound recording, scientific study or just birdwatching, remember that the welfare of the bird must always come first.

Habitat protection
Its habitat is vital to a bird and therefore we must ensure that our activities do not cause damage.

Keep disturbance to a minimum
Birds' tolerance of disturbance varies between species and season. Therefore, it is safer to keep all disturbance to a minimum. No birds should be disturbed from the nest in case opportunities for predators to take eggs or young are increased. In very cold weather disturbance to birds may cause them to use vital energy at a time when food is difficult to find. Wildfowlers already impose bans during cold weather: birdwatchers should exercise similar discretion.

Rare breeding birds
If you discover a rare bird breeding and feel that protection is necessary, inform the appropriate RSPB Regional Office, or the Species Protection Department at the Lodge. Otherwise it is best in almost all circumstances to keep the record strictly secret in order to avoid disturbance by other birdwatchers and attacks by egg-collectors. Never visit known sites of rare breeding birds unless they are adequately protected. Even your presence may give away the site to others and cause so many other visitors that the birds may fail to breed successfully.

Disturbance at or near the nest of species listed on the First Schedule of the Wildlife and Countryside Act 1981 is a criminal offence.

Copies of Wild Birds and the Law are obtainable from the RSPB, The Lodge, Sandy, Beds, SG19 2DL (send two 2nd class stamps).

Rare migrants

Rare migrants or vagrants must not be harassed. If you discover one, consider the circumstances carefully before telling anyone. Will an influx of birdwatchers disturb the bird or others in the area? Will the habitat be damaged? Will problems be caused with the landowner?

The Law

The bird protection laws (now embodied in the Wildlife and Countryside Act 1981) are the result of hard campaigning by previous generations of birdwatchers. As birdwatchers we must abide by them at all times and not allow them to fall into disrepute.

Respect the rights of landowners

The wishes of landowners and occupiers of land must be respected. Do not enter land without permission. Comply with permit schemes. If you are leading a group, do give advance notice of the visit, even if a formal permit scheme is not in operation. Always obey the Country Code.

Respect the rights of other people

Have proper consideration for other birdwatchers. Try not to disrupt their activities or scare the birds they are watching. There are many other people who also use the countryside. Do not interfere with their activities and, if it seems that what they are doing is causing unnecessary disturbance to birds, do try to take a balanced view. Flushing gulls when walking a dog on a beach may do little harm, while the same dog might be a serious disturbance at a tern colony. When pointing this out to a non-birdwatcher be courteous, but firm. The non-birdwatchers' goodwill towards birds must not be destroyed by the attitudes of birdwatchers.

Keeping records

Much of today's knowledge about birds is the result of meticulous record keeping by our predecessors. Make sure you help to add to tomorrow's knowledge by sending records to your county bird recorder.

Birdwatching abroad

Behave abroad as you would at home. This code should be firmly adhered to when abroad (whatever the local laws). Well behaved birdwatchers can be important ambassadors for bird protection.

This code has been drafted after consultation between the British Ornithologists' Union, British Trust for Ornithology, the Royal Society for the Protection of Birds, the Scottish Ornithologists' Club, the Wildfowl Trust and the Editors of *British Birds*.

Further copies may be obtained from The Royal Society for the Protection of Birds, The Lodge, Sandy, Beds. SG19 2DL.

INDEX OF SPECIES BY SITE NUMBER